Studies on the Text of
Seneca's *De beneficiis*

Studies on the Text of Seneca's *De beneficiis*

ROBERT A. KASTER

OXFORD
UNIVERSITY PRESS

OXFORD
UNIVERSITY PRESS

Great Clarendon Street, Oxford, OX2 6DP,
United Kingdom

Oxford University Press is a department of the University of Oxford.
It furthers the University's objective of excellence in research, scholarship,
and education by publishing worldwide. Oxford is a registered trade mark of
Oxford University Press in the UK and in certain other countries

First Edition published in 2022

Impression: 1

Published in the United States of America by Oxford University Press
198 Madison Avenue, New York, NY 10016, United States of America

British Library Cataloguing in Publication Data
Data available

Library of Congress Control Number: 2021945540

ISBN 978-0-19-284501-6

Printed and bound in the UK by
TJ Books Limited

D. M.

M. C. Gertz

Preface

This book emerges from my work on a new edition of *De beneficiis* for the Oxford Classical Text series, to appear in a volume that will also include *De clementia* and *Apocolocyntosis*. Unlike the latter two works, *De beneficiis* has not benefited from sustained critical attention more recently than the editions published by Martin Gertz (1876), Carl Hosius (1900, 2nd edn 1914), and François Préchac (1926), a fact that provides the rationale for this fresh review. Because the survival of the tradition's archetype (Vatican, Palatinus latinus 1547 = **N**) eliminates the need for a detailed reconstruction of the text's history, the Introduction simply surveys the documentary resources on which my edition will be based. Seven chapters follow, one for each of the work's books: as in the companion volumes (*Studies on the Text of…*) that have been paired with my earlier editions, the primary aim is to explain and (I hope) justify many of the textual choices I have made; secondarily, the full critical apparatus that accompanies each discussion will often make it possible to provide in the edition the sort of *breuis adnotatio* characteristic of the OCT series while yet making the information available to other scholars.[1] There are also three appendixes: the first discusses the relation between **N** and a German manuscript of the twelfth century (**Q**) that has been a matter of controversy; the second catalogues many of the scribal lapses that are especially characteristic of **N**; the third lists a number of previously unreported manuscripts of *De beneficiis*.

As always, there is reason to give thanks, in the first instance to the institutions that provided the digitized copies of manuscripts that made these studies possible: the Balliol College Library (Oxford), Bayerische Staatsbibliothek (Munich), Biblioteca Apostolica Vaticana, Biblioteca del monastero di San Lorenzo (El Escorial), Biblioteca Medicea Laurenziana (Florence), Biblioteka uniwersytecka (Wrocław), Bibliothèque municipale (Cherbourg), Bibliothèque nationale de France (Paris), Bodleian Library (Oxford), Herzog–August Bibliothek (Wolfenbüttel), Institut de Recherche et d'Histoire des Text (Paris), Lambeth Palace Library (London), Stiftsbibliothek Admont, Trinity College (Cambridge), Universitätsbibliothek (Leihgabe Leipziger Stadtbibliothek, Leipzig). I am also grateful, once again, to the HathiTrust, Google Books, Internet Archive, Münchener Digitalisierungszentrum (Bayerische Staatsbibliothek, Munich), and of course the stacks, services, and personnel of Firestone Library, for the countless books, reviews, and articles that

---

[1] Discussions of the passages treated at the end of Book 7 (7. 19. 5–31. 2) have previously appeared in Kaster 2020.

now reside on my hard drive: the last-named, especially, was a blessing as this book was being completed in the shadow of pandemic.

Though I have been retired ('retired', my wife says) for over two years, Princeton University and its Department of Classics have continued their unstinting support of my scholarship. The latter, in particular, gave me the opportunity to teach a graduate seminar on the textual criticism of *De beneficiis* and *De clementia* in Spring 2019, for which special thanks are owed, as they are owed also to the seminar's members, who thought through many of these problems with me: Frances Bernstein, Nick Churik, Katie Dennis, Djair Dias Filho, Will Dingee, Stephanie Fan, River Granados, Sherry Lee, Cait Mongrain, and Kyle Oskvig. Other individuals who provided various forms of help include Andrew Dunning, Roy Gibson, Matthew Holford, Anne Laurent, Ermanno Malaspina, Claudia Minners-Knaup, John D. Morgan, Lucian Palmer, and Tim Parkin. I am grateful as always to Charlotte Loveridge at Oxford University Press and to her colleagues Karen Raith, Henry Clarke, and Lisa Eaton; Tim Beck once again did a splendid job of copy-editing. Finally, Francesca Romana Berno and Harry Hine provided exceptionally helpful reviews both when this monograph was initially proposed and when a draft was completed: the latter's detailed comments, in particular, were dead on in every case and helped to improve the work materially. I'm very grateful to both and gladly accept responsibility for the shortcomings that doubtless remain.

It is nearly 150 years since Martin Gertz published his edition of *De beneficiis*, which remains the best available, though in common use it has been eclipsed by others. Prompted by my warm admiration for his work, through which he made the greatest contributions to this text after Erasmus and Gruter, I dedicate this book to his memory.

Robert A. Kaster

Princeton, New Jersey
1 October 2020

Contents

Introduction: The Text's Documentary Basis   1

Notes to Book 1   15

Notes to Book 2   38

Notes to Book 3   65

Notes to Book 4   94

Notes to Book 5   121

Notes to Book 6   144

Notes to Book 7   161

Appendix 1. **N** and **Q**   181
Appendix 2. *Orthographica*   186
Appendix 3. A Supplement to Mazzoli 1982   204

Bibliography   207
Index of Manuscripts   211
Index of Passages   213
Index of Names   223

Introduction

The Text's Documentary Basis

What follows is not a complete history of the text of *De beneficiis* but an overview of the sources cited in the textual notes that constitute Chapters 1–7. The aim is simply to introduce readers to the persons, editions, and manuscripts that they will see cited many times once the real work of the monograph begins.

THE ARCHETYPE AND THE APOGRAPH

The treatises *De beneficiis* and *De clementia* share two distinctions: among Seneca's *philosophica* they emerged earliest in the passage from antiquity to the Middle Ages; and they emerged together in a manuscript that still survives. Vatican, Palatinus latinus 1547, is the extant archetype of the tradition: copied in northern Italy *c.*800, it received two early sets of corrections, one by the original scribe, presumably catching his own slips as he wrote, and one by a careful contemporary who perhaps still had access to the book's exemplar.[1] Within a generation the book was taken to Lorsch, where it spent the rest of the Middle Ages in the Church of St. Nazarius, which gave it the name, *Nazarianus*, by which it is commonly known and the *siglum*, **N**, by which it has been designated in *apparatus critici* since the middle of the nineteenth century. Within another generation a copy of **N** was made, incorporating the early corrections to its text.[2] That copy, or a copy of it, is also extant: Vatican, Reginensis latinus 1529 (**R**)— written in the second quarter of the ninth century, probably in France, where it spent the Middle Ages in Fluery or Auxerre—is the source of all later copies of the two works.[3]

---

[1] There were at least two later correcting hands; Reinhard Kekulé, who produced the collation used by Martin Gertz (n. 19), thought that he discerned three later hands, the earliest of which he dated to the thirteenth or fourteenth century (Gertz 1876, iv–v), cf. Chapter 4 n. 24. On the possibility that **N** had a capital manuscript of *De beneficiis* in its proximate ancestry, see Appendix 2 n. 2.

[2] Corrections in **N** not reflected in **R**'s text are predominantly the work of the later correctors, though it appears that the odd suspension stroke or expunction point added by an early corrector was here and there missed: in my critical apparatus **Npc*** denotes a correction not found in **R**, with '(*man. post.*)' added in those cases that I feel confident in attributing to a later hand.

[3] Gertz first recognized **N**'s unique value, and Buck 1908, 1–38, first analyzed the relationship between **N** and **R**, which has again been meticulously studied by Busonero 2000; the shape of the tradition was further elaborated by Préchac 1921, vi–xlii, 1926, 1:xlii–liv, and esp. Mazzoli 1982;

An editor of *De beneficiis* or *De clementia*, then, is in much the same position as an editor of Tacitus' *Histories* and *Annals*, and that is a very different position from an editor of, say, Suetonius' *Lives of the Caesars*. The latter must try to reconstruct the transmission of the text in the extant manuscripts with the aim either of reconstructing the lost archetype (as can be done in the case of Suetonius) or of determining that no archetype be reconstructed (as in the case of the *Aeneid*). For the editor of the Senecan texts, the later manuscripts—close to three hundred are known, including excerpts and epitomes[4]—come into play only so far as they provide readings that are helpful when the archetype's text is possibly or certainly faulty. How specific manuscripts, or groups of manuscripts, came to have specific readings is, at most, of secondary importance.

MANUSCRIPTS OF THE TWELFTH CENTURY

That said, any worker in this field owes a very large debt of gratitude to Giancarlo Mazzoli, whose immense labours made the later tradition navigable. By surveying and sampling most of the extant manuscripts, he demonstrated that they descend from **R** in two main branches, φ and ψ, and that the latter, in turn, generated two sub-families, π and γ; representatives of φ are least numerous and most sincere, of γ, most common and least reliable; it is also likely that an intermediary, ρ, stood between **R** and φψ.[5] None of the witnesses to these branches antedates the twelfth century; apart from excerpts and epitomes, which I have generally ignored as

---

Brugnoli 1998, 79–81, rapidly surveys *Ben.*'s ancient and medieval *fortuna*. Bischoff thought it possible that **R** originated in Italy (1975, 81, cf. Mazzoli 1982, 170–1); Pellegrin 1978, 252 (Auxerre or Fleury), and Mostert 1989, 283 (Fleury?), regard it as French. The question whether **R** took its text directly from **N** or from an intermediary—though of methodological and historical interest—is in my view unanswerable on the basis of the evidence the two books provide: Malaspina 2016, xiii–xviii, compactly reviews the question, with references to earlier discussions. Whatever the answer, it has no practical bearing on the job of an editor: cf. Mazzoli 1982, 172, 'A noi tuttavia il contatto testuale tra i due mss. appare talmente stretto da non ammettere intermediario di sorta: a meno d'immaginare questo cosi simile al modello N da rendere pleonastica la sua funzione testuale.'

[4] See Mazzoli 1982 (a list is on pp. 216–23), with supplements in Malaspina 2001a, 50–1, and Appendix 3 of this volume; for the manuscripts down to the end of the twelfth century, the survey of Munk Olsen (1985, 365–473) is indispensable.

[5] That φψ are derived not directly from **R** but from a copy of **R** most economically explains the innovations they share relative to **NR**: see, e.g., 1. 3. 10 nomenclatori Npc* (nomen clatori CMGWU, nomendatori Nac Qψ : clatori R), 3. 3. 1 intentis NR : -ti CQψ, 3. 22. 4 acceperis CQMψ : acciperis NacR, acciperes Npc*, 4. 28. 6 ad quae CQψ : atqui N, atque R, 5. 22. 4 aberrantem CQψ : -te NR, 5. 20. 2 doleat NQ (by contamination, see Appendix 1) : dole R, dolere Cψ, 7. 6. 2 sint CQψ : sunt NR, with Malaspina 2001a, 78–9, 2001b, 150–6, 2016, xix–xx. I can add two notes: instances of ρ vs. **NR** seem to be relatively more common in *Clem.* than in *Ben.*; and where ρ corrects **NR**, the improvements generally involve minor adjustments of the sort found where **R** corrects **N**. It is the ubiquity of such agreements that points more probably to a common source than to coincidence or contamination. For the sake of formal precision I include ρ in the stemma presented on p. 5 but for simplicity's sake I refer to **R** in the discussions in Chapters 1–7, since that has been the convention familiar for over a century.

unreliable,[6] there are eighteen manuscripts datable to the twelfth century (in several cases, late twelfth or early thirteenth century) that preserve—or once preserved—complete texts, of which I have used seventeen.[7] I have not collated these manuscripts thoroughly, but I have examined all of them in each of the many places where I or one of my predecessors had reason to doubt **N**. These are:[8]

φ

　C PARIS, Bibliothèque nationale lat. 15085, s. XII², France? (Paris, St. Victor ex libris s. XIII or XIV). *De beneficiis* is on f. 86ʳ–136ᵛ (f. 136ᵛ–146ᵛ = *Clem.*).

The most faithful reflection of **R** among these manuscripts, **C** offers no singular innovation that is also an improvement.

ψ

　π

　　H CHERBOURG, Bibliothèque municipale 21, s. XII², northern France. *De beneficiis* is on f. 1ʳ–77ʳ (f. 77ʳ–90ᵛ = *Clem.*).
　　T FLORENCE, Biblioteca Medicea Laurenziana Plut. 45. 25, s. XII², France. *De beneficiis* begins on f. 73ʳa with 2. 20. 2 *ut regis nomen* and continues to the end of Book 3 on f. 82ᵛb; it has only excerpts (of the type σ¹: see below) thereafter, to f. 92ʳb (f. 92ʳb–ᵛb = a γ-class text of *Clem.*, to 1. 1. 7 *exprimitur esse*).
　　D LONDON, Lambeth Palace Library MS 232, s. XII, uncertain origin, probably France. *De beneficiis* is on f. 1ᵛ–87ᵛ (f. 88ʳ–103ᵛ = *Clem.*).
　　P PARIS, Bibliothèque nationale lat. 6382, s. XII², France (Normandy?). *De beneficiis* is on f. 1ʳ–93ᵛ (f. 93ᵛ–112ᵛ = *Clem.*).
　　E PARIS, Bibliothèque nationale lat. 6383, s. XIIᵉˣ·, France (Normandy?). *De beneficiis* is on f. 1ʳ–58ᵛ, with a lacuna (6. 23. 3 *habuerunt. Itaque*–7. 1. 7 *posuit. Si*) between f. 49ᵛ and f. 50ʳ (f. 58ᵛ–70ᵛ = *Clem.*).
　　O PARIS, Bibliothèque nationale lat. 6626, s. XIIᵉˣ·, France (Normandy: Mont-St-Michel). *De beneficiis* is on f. 13ʳ–83ᵛ (f. 1ʳ–12ᵛ = *Clem.*).

This is a very homogenous group, in time, place, and type of text; the three copies from Normandy are exceptionally uniform, and only **H** shows much inclination to innovate productively.[9]

---

[6] As Janus Gruter recognized at the end of the sixteenth century, the excerpts tend to engage in arbitrary omissions and, worse, lapse into paraphrase: see, e.g. Gruter 1594, 522 (on 1. 11. 5), 526 (on 2. 6. 2), 562 (on 6. 30. 3: 'male sit illis, si diis placet, Florilegis, qui criticorum oculis glaucoma obiiciunt').
[7] I have not used Leipzig, Universitätsbibliothek 1607, which has only *Ben.* 5. 21. 1 *omni lege ualentior*…5. 25. 1 *exercitus dispo-* on a single folium (*bis* f. 9ʳa–ᵛb).
[8] Here and following I adopt the dating of Munk Olsen (n. 4) unless otherwise indicated.
[9] e.g., 2. 7. 3 Tiberius HJpc (ty- V) : liberius N, *cett.*; 2. 10. 1 ignorantis H : -ti N, *cett.*; 3. 24 intellegas Npc* (*man. post.*) HQpc : -gis Nac, *cett.*; 3. 37. 1 in infantia HJVpc, *Pinc.* : infantia N, *cett.* (-tiae Npc*, *man. post.*).

γ

G WOLFENBÜTTEL, Herzog–August Bibliothek 274 Gud. Lat. (4579), s. XII/XIII, Germany. *De beneficiis* is on f. 1ᵛ–153ᵛ (*Clem.* is lacking).

W PARIS, Bibliothèque nationale lat. 15425, s. XII, France? *De beneficiis* is on f. 68ʳa–105ᵛa (*Clem.* is lacking).

U ADMONT, Stiftsbibliothek 221, an. 1162 (f. 48ʳ 'Collatus et emendatus est anno Christi M. C. LXII'), Austria. *De beneficiis* is on f. 48ᵛ–122ᵛ (f. 123ʳ–136ᵛ = *Clem.*).

V CAMBRIDGE, Trinity College O. 3. 31 (1203), s. XII/XIII, northern France or England. *De beneficiis* is on f. 1ʳa–37ᵛa (f. 42ʳa–49ʳb = *Clem.*).

I FLORENCE, Biblioteca Medicea Laurenziana San Marco 286., s. XIIᵉˣ·, Italy? *De beneficiis* is on f. 1ʳ–57ᵛ (f. 58ʳ–69ᵛ = *Clem.*).

F FLORENCE, Biblioteca Medicea Laurenziana Plut. 76. 36, s. XIIᵐᵉᵈ·, France? *De beneficiis* is on f. 1ʳ–35ᵛ (f. 35ᵛ–42ʳ = *Clem.*).

K PARIS, Bibliothèque nationale lat. 8542 + lat. fonds Baluze 270, s. XII/XIII. *De beneficiis* to 7. 24. 2 *emissem* is on f. 123ʳa–147ᵛb of lat. 8542, with a lacuna (3. 19. 2 *et eo perducam seruum*–4. 28. 5 *Ius et furi dicitur*) between f. 131ᵛ and f. 132ʳ; the balance of *Ben.* 7 is on Baluze 270 f. 96ʳ⁻ᵛ (lat. 8542 f. 148ʳa–153ᵛb = *Clem.* 1. 5. 3 [*mor*]*talem etiam illum*–2. 6. 4 *et ad omnium*).

J PARIS, Bibliothèque nationale, lat. 6630, s. XII/XIII, northern France. *De beneficiis* is on f. 30ʳ–98ʳ (f. 16ᵛ–30ʳ = *Clem.*).

In this geographically diverse group of manuscripts **JV** have an exceptionally close relationship and share a number of good readings that mark an advance over **R**;[10] **UI**, usually accompanied by **K**, also share some valuable innovations, along with a larger number of errors indicative of a family relationship,[11] and a late correcting hand in **I** entered a number of good readings that clearly draw on a source similar to that of the *recentiores* that cluster around ς₂ (see below). **G**, known since Gronovius' work in the mid-seventeenth century, is also productive.

Then there are two books of German origin, grouped by Mazzoli under the *siglum* μ, that he took to represent a line of descent from **N** independent of **R**:

---

[10] e.g., 1. 3. 5 adstricti WJVM, *1529–1585* : adscripti N (R), >*1515, 1605*‡; 2. 35. 2 quidquam *post* negamus *collocaui* (*post* stulti GJV, *Vinc. Bell.*, *Spec. Hist. 5. 28*) : quidquam *om.* Nac (R), aliquid Npc* (*ss. man. post.*), negamus rem stulti esse HIpc‡; 4. 21. 2 atqui JV, *Pinc.*, *1557*‡ : atque N (R), >*1529*; 5. 24. 1 Iulium *Will. Polyhist. p. 142. 21*, HJVς₄ς₅ς₁₂‡ : filium N (R); note also 1. 14. 1 et in illum uix bene notum sibi et *om.* JV.

[11] e.g., 6. 3. 1 si cito UIK : scito N, cito QHDpcOpcGVa, 6. 23. 6 non coercuit UIK : coercuit N, 6. 36. 2 inritauerant UIK : intrauerant N, 7. 22. 1 dedit UIK : reddi Nac, reddit Npc, cf. 7. 14. 2 faciendi occasionem QUIK : non esse occasionem Npc (acca- Nac), 7. 31. 4 lenioris spiritus QUIK : leniore͞spū N. Errors, e.g., 4. 32. 2 referri gratia illi Npc (gratiam i- Nac) : referri illi gratia ψ, referre i- g- UIK, 5. 18 ius *Madvig* ; eius N, uero UIK, 6. 12. 2 an et sua N : an nostra et sua π, an et sua et nostra UIacK, 6. 30. 6 nutant N : mutant GWJV, mutantur UIK, 6. 42. 2 piget N : penitet UIacK, 6. 43. 2 alieno N : alieno tempore UIK, 7. 2. 5 qua uenerat N : inuenerat UIK, 7. 6. 2 conscientia UI : sapientia UI, 7. 13 denique *Gertz* : sed qui N, sunt qui UIK.

Q LEIPZIG, Universitätsbibliothek Rep. I 47–I (Leihgabe Leipziger Stadtbibliothek), s. XII¹ (Mazzoli), Germany. *De beneficiis* is on f. 2ʳ–32ᵛ (f. 33ᵛ–39ᵛ = *Clem*).

M MUNICH, Bayerische Staatsbibliothek Clm 2544, s. XIIᵉˣ·, Germany (Aldersbach). *De beneficiis* is on f. 113ʳ–155ʳ, to 4. 22. 2 *et tutior est uita* (*Clem*. is lacking).

As I show in Appendix 2, however, the evidence does not sustain Mazzoli's contention. Nonetheless, he was unquestionably correct in believing both that these two books are more closely related to each other than to any other extant witness, and that **Q**, in particular, uniquely shares with **N** about three dozen good readings that probably or certainly reached it, presumably via correction earlier in its lineage, from a source that had had access to the archetype. In locating these manuscripts on the stemma drawn below, I place them in the φ branch with a dotted line indicating contamination from an unknown source of readings drawn from **N**: this is the view for which Ermanno Malaspina argued with respect to *De clementia*.[12] Note that though the books are undeniably kin, **M**, which is a half-century younger, has a more contaminated text, a fact that sometimes disguises the relationship.

Finally, I occasionally have reason to cite two manuscripts containing excerpts only, each representing one of the two different sets of excerpts that Mazzoli identified, one a blend of φ and γ (σ¹), the other derived primarily from φ (σ²). Respectively, these are:

B PARIS, Bibliothèque nationale lat. 6331, s. XII², France (Normandy). Excerpts (σ¹) of *De beneficiis* on f. 94ʳ–123ᵛ (f. 124ʳ–137ʳ = a φ-class text of *Clem*.).

S PARIS, Bibliothèque nationale lat. 16592 s. XIIᵉˣ·: France? (Midi?). Excerpts (σ²) of *De beneficiis* on f. 94ᵛa–102ᵛa (f. 103ᵛa–105ᵛb = σ² excerpts of *Clem*.).

This basic stemma summarizes the foregoing survey in graphic form.

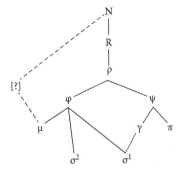

---

[12] Malaspina 2001a, 80–1 (stemma on p. 82), 2001b, 156–65 (stemma on p. 165), 2016, xxii–xxiii (stemma on p. xix).

RECENTIORES

Interest in Seneca and *De beneficiis* increased enormously in the fourteenth and fifteenth centuries, to which most of the extant copies date; beyond Mazzoli's survey, these books still constitute a vast *terra incognita*. I have used just over half of the thirty-odd complete copies, and one set of excerpts, that have been dated to the fourteenth century (in one case, the thirteenth century), primarily with the aim of tracing the earliest attestations of good readings that otherwise are known only from the early printed editions. Though Mazzoli, on the basis of his sampling survey, ascribed these books to one or another of the tradition's three families, contamination certainly accelerated in this period, and the group-identity of any given manuscript, while not completely effaced, is often blurred, so that a π-reading is apt to turn up in several γ-manuscripts, and vice versa; again, there are very few representatives of φ, among them ς_4 (mostly) and ς_{12} below:[13]

ς_1 = agreement of three or four of the following:

ς_2 VATICAN, Archivio Capitulare di San Pietro C. 121, s. XIV, northern Italy. *De beneficiis* is on f. 282^r–312^v (γ) (f. 111^r–116^v = *Clem.* [γ]).

ς_3 VATICAN, Vat. lat. 2212, s. XIV^2, northern Italy (?). *De beneficiis* is on f. 111^r–150^r (γ) (f. 150^r–157^r = *Clem.* [γ]).

ς_4 VATICAN, Vat. lat. 2216, s. XIV^1, France. *De beneficiis* is on f. 131^v–182^r (φ to 6. 13, thereafter γ) (f. 182^r–191^v = *Clem.* [γ]).

ς_5 WROCŁAW, Biblioteka Uniwersytecka IV. F. 39, an. 1375. *De beneficiis* is on f. 83^r–117^r (γ) (*Clem.* is lacking).

ς_6 = agreement of two or three of the following:

ς_7 PARIS, Bibliothèque nationale lat. 7698, s. XIV. *De beneficiis* is on f. 258^r–297^v (γ) (f. 231^v–239^r = *Clem.* [γ]).

ς_8 VATICAN, Vat. lat. 1769, s. $XIII^{ex.}$ (Mazzoli) / $XIV^{in.}$ (Buonocore 2000, 82), Italy. *De beneficiis* is on f. 121^v–143^r (γ) (f. 116^r–120^r = *Clem.* [φ]).

ς_9 VATICAN, Vat. lat. 2213, s. $XIV^{med.}$, Italy. *De beneficiis* is on f. 80^v–99^v (γ) (f. 100^v–102^r = *Clem.* [γ]).

ς_{10} OXFORD, Balliol College Library 129, s. XIV + s. XV. *De beneficiis* is on f. 167^r–252 (π to 6. 32. 1 [s. XIV], thereafter γ [s. XV]) (*Clem.* is lacking).

ς_{11} PARIS, Bibliothèque nationale lat. 6389, s. XIV. *De beneficiis* is on f. 17^r–60^r (γ) (f. 9^r–17^r = *Clem.* [γ]).

ς_{12} PARIS, Bibliothèque nationale lat. 8544, an. 1389. *De beneficiis* is on f. 86^r–117^r (φ) (f. 118^r–123^v = *Clem.* [φ]).

ς_{13} PARIS, Bibliothèque nationale lat. 8546, s. XIV. *De beneficiis* is on f. 79^v–129^v (π) (f. 135^r–144^v = *Clem.* [γ]).

---

[13] For Vatican manuscripts I adopt the dates assigned by Buonocore 2000; for Paris and Oxford, the dates assigned by the library catalogues.

ς_{14} PARIS, Bibliothèque nationale lat. 8717, s. XIV. *De beneficiis* is on f. 290^v–309^v (γ Books 1–2, thereafter σ^1 excerpts) (f. 283^v–290^v = *Clem.* [γ]).

ς_{15} PARIS, Bibliothèque nationale lat. 11855, s. XIV. *De beneficiis* is on f. 91^v–122^v (γ) (f. 122^v–128^r = *Clem.* [γ]).

ς_{16} VATICAN, Vat. lat. 2214, s. XIV^2, north-central Italy. *De beneficiis* is on f. 106^r–139 (γ) (f. 98^r–104^r = *Clem.* [γ]).

ς_{17} VATICAN, Vat. lat. 2215, s. XIV$^{in.}$, Italy. *De beneficiis* is on f. 211^r–254^v (γ) (f. 202^v–210^v = *Clem.* [γ]).

ς_{18} VATICAN, Vat. lat. 2220, s. XIII^1, France. *De beneficiis* is on f. 61^r–165^r (γ) (*Clem.* is lacking).

ς_{19} VATICAN, Pal. lat. 1540, s. XIV, northern Italy. *De beneficiis* is on f. 49^v–92^v (γ) (f. 39^v–47^r = *Clem.* [γ]).

ς_{20} VATICAN, Pal. lat. 1539, s. XIV, northern Italy. *De beneficiis* is on f. 78^v–106^v (γ) (f. 107^r–112^r = *Clem.* [γ]).

ς_{21} VATICAN, Pal. lat. 1538, s. XIV/XV, Italy. *De beneficiis* is on f. 91^r–103^r (σ^1) (f. 84r–91r = *Clem.* [σ^1]).

The last three items on this list are, respectively, the *Palatinus tertius, secundus*, and *primus* that were among the five manuscripts cited by Janus Gruter (a fourth was **N** itself) in his very influential commentary, about which more below. The most striking book noted here, however, is ς_2, the Vatican Library's Archivio Capitulare di San Pietro C. 121, which is often accompanied by the next three books listed: it offers a wild text that includes both a striking number of good innovations and at least an equal number of very bad innovations.[14] As luck would have it, it is also the manuscript that most closely resembles the source of the *editio princeps*, which launched the print tradition, to which we now turn, on a decidedly ill-omened course.

EDITIONS AND COMMENTARIES

The following editions, editors, and commentators are cited in the textual discussions of Chapters 1–7, as they will be in the critical apparatus of my edition:[15]

1475   *Incipit lucii annei Senecae cordubensis liber de moribus.* M. Morauus.
        Naples.

---

[14] e.g., 2. 24. 1 haereat] egeat ς_2, >*1503*, 2. 26. 2 nec dicit *ante* hoc mihi dedit *add.* ς_2, >*1515*, 3. 3. 1 in id quod deest, quod *Buck* : in id quod est quod N, non id quod est sed quod ς_2, >*1503*, 4. 28. 2 dignis dat] dignis dat. donatio imperatoris est ς_2, >*1515*, 4. 31. 3 consulem] heros ς_2, >*1515*, 4. 36. 3 *post* repetam *add.* errori fidem non esse praerandam [*sic*] ς_2, errori fidem non esse praestandum [*sic*] >*1503*.

[15] Kaster 2021 is a more detailed discussion of the early printed editions down to the mid-seventeenth century; I set aside here the negligible edition published by Dionysius Gothofredus in Basel in 1590.

1478   *Incipit lucii annei Senecae cordubensis liber de moribus.* Bernardus
              de Colonia. Treviso.

1490   *Seneca moralis.* Bernardinus de Cremona et Simon de Luero.
              Venice.

1492   *Senece opera omnia.* Bernardinus de Coris de Cremona. Venice.

1503   *Senece opera omnia.* Bertholomeus de Zanis de Portesio. Venice.

1515   *Lucii Annaei Senecae…philosophi lucubrationes omnes…Erasmi
              Roterodami cura.* Basel.

1529, Eras.   *L. Annae Senecae opera…per Des. Erasmum Roterod.* Basel. ('Eras.'
              refers to the notes printed at the end of each book; '*Eras p.*' refers to
              the critical appendix inserted after the *Epistulae Morales*, with further
              notes by Erasmus and the conjectures of Rodolphus Agricola =
              '*Agric. p.*')

Pinc.   *Fernandi Pinciani* [= Hernán Núñez de Toledo y Guzmán]…*In
              omnia L. Annaei Senecae philosophi scripta…castigationes utilissi-
              mae.* Venice 1536.

1557   *L. Annaei Senecae Philosophi…opera quae extant omnia, Coelii
              Secundi Curionis uigilantissima cura castigata.* Basel.

1585, Mur.   *L. Annaeus Seneca a M. Antonio Mureto correctus et notis illustratus.*
              Rome. ('*Mur.*' refers to the notes printed at the end of each book.)

Grut.   J. Gruter, *Iani Gruteri Animadversiones in L. Annaei Senecae opera,*
              in: *L. Annaeus Seneca a M. Antonio Mureto correctus et notis illustra-
              tus.* Heidelberg 1594, 517–1004.

1605, Lips.   *L. Annaei Senecae Philosophi opera, quae exstant, omnia: a Iusto
              Lipsio emendata, et scholiis illustrata.* Antwerp. ('*Lips.*' refers to the
              notes printed at the bottom of each page, where Lipsius typically
              signalled the innovations that he favoured.)

1628, Dale.   *L. Annaei Senecae Philosophi opera omnia quae extant…a
              I. Dalechampio castigata.* Geneva. ('*Dale.*' refers to readings
              recorded in marginal notes.)[16]

1649, Gron.   *L. Annaei Senecae Philosophi opera omnia, ex ult. I. Lipsii & I. F. Gronovii
              emendat.* Vol. 1. Leiden. ('*Gron.*' refers to the textual notes published in
              the same year and place under the title *Joh. Fred. Gronovii ad L. &
              M. Annaeos Senecas Notae*, where the observations on *Ben.* appear on
              pp. 112–78; an expanded edition was published under the same title in
              1658 in Amsterdam, with the observations on *Ben.* on pp. 133–206.)

Ruh.   *L. Annaei Senecae Philosophi opera omnia quae supersunt.*
              F. E. Ruhkopf. Vol. 4 (of 5). Leipzig 1808. (Ruhkopf's textual notes
              stand between the text and his more broadly explanatory notes.)

---

[16] Though this edition is generally negligible, two of Dalechamps' notes are worth citing, at 1. 12. 4
sibi and 5. 8. 2 *aliquis* ⟨*quod*⟩.

Vogel   *Lucii Annaei Senecae opera philosophica.* E. F. Vogel. Leipzig 1830. (Brief *Observationes criticae ad libros septem De beneficiis* are printed on pp. 492–503.)

Fick.   *L. Annaei Senecae Opera.* K. R. Fickert. Vol. 2 (of 3). Leipzig 1843. (References to manuscripts and earlier editions stand at the bottom of each page.)

Haase   *L. Annaei Senecae Opera quae supersunt.* Friedrich Haase. Vol. 2 (of 3). Leipzig 1852. (There are no notes or critical apparatus.)

Gertz p.   *L. Annaei Senecae Libri De beneficiis et De clementia.* M. C. Gertz. Berlin 1876. ('*p.*' refers to the *Adnotationes criticae* printed on pp. 191–283.)

Hos.   *L. Annaei Senecae De beneficiis libri VII: De clementia libri II.* Carl Hosius. 2nd edn Leipzig 1914. ('*Hos. 1*' and '*Hos. 2*' distinguish different readings adopted by Hosius in the 1st edn [Leipzig 1900] and the 2nd edn).

Pré.   *Sénèque: Des bienfaits.* F. Préchac. Budé. Paris 1926.

As I have already hinted, the edition of *De beneficiis* published in Naples in 1475 was a very poor product, even judged against the generally low standard set by incunabular editions of classical Latin texts. As the work of publishing—it cannot be called editing—moved north in the course of the next generation, the text was passed along virtually unchanged, and in the handful of places where the next four editions introduced a change—from Treviso 1478 to Venice 1503—it was a change for the worse almost as often as it was a change for the better. The real work of criticism did not begin until Erasmus undertook to edit Seneca, at the same time that he was producing enormous editions of St. Jerome and the New Testament. The edition of 1515 was produced while Erasmus was in England, from which he sent drafts and notes to Beatus Rhenanus, serving as proxy-editor in Basel, and the proofreader Wilhelm Nesen. Though the edition produced a much improved text of *De beneficiis* and the *philosophica* more generally, Erasmus became dissatisfied with it, in the belief that his notes and directions had been ignored or betrayed. He therefore began to work on a new edition in 1525, and its appearance four years later brought hundreds of further improvements to the text. While most of these were attributable to Erasmus' immense skill as a critic, a number of them mark the first impact of the archetype on the text's modern reception: for as he neared the end of *De beneficiis* 4 he began to refer in his annotations to a new source that he called the 'Lombard book' (*codex Longobardicus*), from its distinctive northern Italian script, and to introduce readings that clearly are derived from **N**.[17]

---

[17] The first such reference appears in the note on 4. 36. 2 (see Appendix 1 n. 5), and there are twenty-six more references of that sort down to the end of Book 7. Erasmus was able to bring **N** to bear on the earlier books only in the critical appendix that he inserted after the text of *De beneficiis*

The next major critical advances were made by two scholars who did not produce editions. In 1536 Hernán Núñez de Toledo y Guzmán—known as 'Pincianus' from the Latin name of Valladolid, his birthplace in north-west Spain—published *In omnia L. Annaei Senecae philosophi scripta…castigationes*, including many hundreds of comments on *De beneficiis* alone that acknowledged or recommended new readings relative to the edition of 1529, from which he largely drew his lemmata. The readings he promoted—some his own conjectures, others drawn (as he says in his prefatory letter) from 'exemplaria scripta et peruetusta quindecim'—are often clearly right and regularly worthy of reflection.[18] Accordingly, they powerfully influenced the next two editions that appeared: Curio enthusiastically incorporated many of Pincianus' suggestions in his edition of 1557, with selections from Erasmus' and Pincianus' notes inserted after each book, and Muretus appropriated much of Pincianus' work, without acknowledgement, while heaping unmerited scorn on Erasmus. (Muretus' knowledge of Latin was unsurpassed in his day, but his edition—which he produced while dying and did not live to see published in 1585—does not do justice to his talents.)

The still more voluminous *Animaduersiones* that Janus Gruter published in 1594 were even more influential, both because of his penetration as a critic and because his notes—in which the name 'Nazarianus' appears for the first time—publicized **N**'s readings far more copiously than Erasmus had been able to do, from one end of *De beneficiis* to the other. Gruter gained access to **N** because he was at the time professor of ancient history in Heidelberg, where his connections at the court of the Elector Palatine of the Rhine gave him access to its fabulous library, and to four of the five manuscripts that he regularly cites throughout his commentary (the fifth, from Cologne, cannot be identified today). The wealth of new knowledge that Gruter made available was readily seized upon by the two estimable critics whose editions followed, Gruter's former teacher Justus Lipsius and, several decades later, J. F. Gronovius, who now and again sounds very much like a nineteenth-century critic embracing the doctrine of the *codex optimus*: 'nihil lubrici, nulla titubatione opus, modo adhaereamus Naz(ariano)' (*Notae* p. 119).

For five generations, starting with Erasmus' work, improvements in the text (along with a much smaller number of new deformations) were passed along and augmented from one edition to the next, producing a vulgate text that, with the appearance of Gronovius' edition in 1649, contained more than two thousand readings—the vast majority of them improvements—that had not stood in the *editio princeps*: roughly one every twenty-two words. And then work on the text

and *Epistulae Morales* had already been printed (= 1529, 271–3, on *Ben.*): though there he does not use the epithet *Longobardicus*, at least some of the thirty-six notes on Books 1–4 that cite a *uetustus* or *uetustissimus codex* should rely on **N** (e.g., 1. 12. 3 *obseruet personas* Nac, *obseruet et personas* Npc (superscript *&* added): 'Vetustus [sc. codex] habebat *et personas*, sed ascripta super uersum coniunctione'; 4. 13. 1 *facere* Nac, *l farcire* Npc: 'in uetustissimo codice…pro *facere*, subnotatum erat *farcire*').

[18] On Pincianus, see Kiekebusch 1912, who demonstrated that the manuscripts he cited belonged to what we now call the ψ-branch.

essentially stopped for nearly two hundred years. Very few new editions were produced, and those that were—two Bipontine editions, of 1782 and 1809, F. R. Ruhkopf's edition of 1808, and E. F. Vogel's of 1830—differed only in very minor ways from the vulgate of 1649 or from each other. Something of a change was signalled by K. R. Fickert's edition of 1843—notable less for its criticism than for the immense labour devoted to reporting the text's documentary basis, as it was then known—and Friederich Hasse applied genuine critical attention to his Teubner of 1852. But a new level of excellence was achieved by M. C. Gertz, thanks both to his exceptional penetration as a critic and to his good fortune: for he was the first editor able to base his work on a complete collation of N, which Reinhard Kekulé produced for Moritz Haupt, who in turn made it available to Gertz.[19] His edition of 1876 is the best approximation to date of what Seneca wrote; the subsequent editions of Hosius (1900, 2nd edn 1914) and Préchac (1926), though more commonly used, fall short of the standard Gertz set.[20]

Beyond the *sigla* and other information provided above, the following abbreviations and symbols are also used in the discussions and *apparatus critici* of Chapters 1–7.

AE	*L'année épigraphique: Revue des publications épigraphiques relatives à l'antiquité romaine.* Paris 1888– .
Agric.	Rodolphus Agricola, critical notes on Seneca: in *L. Annae Senecae opera…per Des. Erasmum Roterod.* Basel 1529, 268–73.
Basore	J. W. Basore (trans.), *Seneca: Moral Essays*, vol. 3. Loeb Classical Library 310. Cambridge, MA, 1939.
CIL	*Corpus Inscriptionum Latinarum*, 17 vols. Berlin 1862– .
Flor. Mor.	*Florilegium morale Oxoniense* (*Ms. Bodl. 633*): *Secunda pars, Flores Auctorum*, ed. C. H. Talbot. Analecta Medievalia Namurcensia, 6. Louvain and Lille 1956.
Griffin and Inwood	M. Griffin and B. Inwood (trans.), *Seneca: 'On Benefits'.* Chicago 2011.
H.-S.	J. B. Hofmann, *Lateinische Syntax und Stilistik*, rev. A. Szantyr. Munich 1965.

---

[19] Gertz 1876, iii: 'Codicem Nazarianum…in Hauptii usum cum exemplari editionis Haasianae contulerat R. Kekulé' with p. vi, 'Praeter codicis Nazariani conlationem in his libris Senecae edendis nulla aliorum codicum subsidia adhibere potui' (he goes on to say that he very occasionally used the reports of other manuscripts found in Fickert's apparatus).

[20] Hosius lacked Gertz's penetration and independence of judgement, and because he refused to believe that N was the archetype, he cluttered his apparatus with irrelevant reports of later manuscripts. As a critic Préchac personified the dictum, 'When your only tool is a hammer, every problem looks like a nail', inserting in the text scores of his own emendations that are without exception mechanically paleographical in inspiration and almost as invariably implausible.

Iuret.	The notes of Franciscus Iuretus, incorporated in: *L. Annaei philosophi et M. Annaei Senecae rhetoris quae extant opera.* Paris 1607.
K.–S.	R. Kühner, *Ausführliche Grammatik der lateinischen Sprache*, vol. 2: *Satzlehre*, rev. C. Stegmann. Hannover 1976.
MRR	T. R. S. Broughton, *Magistrates of the Roman Republic*, vols 1–2. New York 1951; *Supplement*, vol. 3. Atlanta, GA, 1986.
NLS	E. C. Woodcock, *A New Latin Syntax*. Cambridge, MA, 1959.
OLD	P. G. W. Glare (ed.), *The Oxford Latin Dictionary*. Oxford 1968–82.
PIR²	W. Eck, E. Groag, et al. (eds), *Prosopographia Imperii Romani saec. I. II. III*, 2nd edn. Berlin 1933–2015.
SRPF³	O. Ribbeck (ed.), *Scaenicae Romanorum Poesis Fragmenta*, 3rd edn, 2 vols. Leipzig 1897–8.
TLL	*Thesaurus Linguae Latinae. Munich 1900–* .
Vinc. Bell.	Vincentius Bellovacensis = Vincent of Beauvais (1184–1264), author of the *Speculum Historiale* (*Spec. Hist.*) and *Speculum Doctrinale* (*Spec. Doct.*), two parts of the *Speculum Maius*, in which he included excerpts of Seneca: ed. Graz, 4 vols. 1964–5 (reproducing the edition of 1624).
Will. Polyhist.	William of Malmesbury *Polyhistor*, a collection of stories excerpted from classical Latin literature, with excerpts of *De beneficiis* near the end of Book 3: see 'Bibliography' s.v. Ouellette, H. T.
(1°), (2°), etc.	denotes the first (second, etc.) time that a given word appears in a section of text.
***	denotes the presence of a lacuna.
{ }	denotes a deletion made by the editor where some inauthentic text is judged to have been interpolated.
⟨ ⟩	denotes a supplement introduced by the editor where some authentic text is judged to have been lost in transmission.
#	denotes a space left by a corrector's erasure (one symbol for each letter).
[#?]	denotes a letter rendered illegible by erasure (one symbol for each letter).
>	preceding the publication date of the edition cited (e.g., *>1503*), the symbol indicates that all earlier editions also have the reading in question.
‡	denotes that the reading in question (typically, non-archetypal) became the vulgate text, transmitted by all (or virtually all) printed editions down to 1830; affixed to an edition's publication date (e.g., *1515‡*), the symbol denotes that the reading first appeared in that edition.

|	denotes the end of a line of text in **N**.
||	denotes the end of a page of text in **N**.
ac	*ante correctionem*: affixed to a manuscript's *siglum* to indicate that the reading reported was the reading written by the scribe; used in conjunction with '*pc*'.
add.	*addidit*: denotes a supplement introduced into the text, typically used in the critical apparatus when the symbols ⟨ ⟩ appear in the text.
adn.	*adnotat, adnotationuncula* (etc.).
agnosc.	*agnoscit*: indicates that a commentator acknowledges the existence of (but does not expressly approve) a given reading.
ap.	*apud* (e.g., *Madvig ap. Gertz*): denotes a conjecture suggested by a scholar to an editor who judged it worth printing in the text or mentioning in the apparatus.
coll.	*collata* (etc.), denoting citation of a parallel passage for comparison (e.g., *coll. Tac. Ann. 2. 48*); or *collocat* (etc.), denoting the placement of a word, phrase, or clause in the text (e.g., *post* §17. 1 deberet *coll. Niemeyer 1899, 441–2*).
def.	*defendit*: denotes a scholar's defense of a given reading.
del.	*delevit*: indicates that the editor placed between brackets—{ }— one or more words regarded as an interpolation.
dist.	*distinxit*: denotes a punctuation introduced into the text, typically one that changes the text's meaning.
dub.	*dubitanter*.
edd.	*editiones*: indicates that a given reading appears in all (or virtually all) printed editions.
fort.	*fortasse*.
in app.	*in apparatu* (e.g., *Hos. in app.*): denotes an editor's conjecture mentioned in the critical apparatus but not printed in the text.
in ras.	*in rasura*.
lac. stat. / *deneg.*	*lacunam statuit / denegavit*: indicates that an editor posited (or denied) the existence of a lacuna in the text.
man. post.	*manu posteriore* (*manus posterior*): denotes an alteration made in the text by a hand significantly later than that of the original scribe.
mg., mg. inf.	*in margine, in margine inferiore*, denoting the placement of a notation in a manuscript or early printed edition.
n. l.	*non liquet*: indicates that the text of a given manuscript was altered in such a way as to obscure the original reading.
Npc*	denotes a correction in **N** not reflected in the text of **R**, typically because it was the work of one of **N**'s late correctors.

obel.   *obelat*: indicates that an editor placed the symbol † at a point of corruption in the text where no acceptable correction had been proposed.

om.   *omisit*.

pc   *post correctionem*: affixed to a manuscript's *siglum* to indicate that the reading reported was entered after the text was copied by the original scribe; used in conjunction with '*ac*'; *pc1* and *pc2* indicate that the text was altered more than once.

pr. man.   *prima manu* (*prima manus*): denotes an alteration that seems to have been made in the text by original scribal hand.

prob.   *probat* (*probante*): indicates that a commentator regarded a given reading as authentic.

recc.   *recentiores*: denotes a reading found in many or most of the fourteenth-century manuscripts surveyed in the preparation of this work.

recip.   *recipit*: denotes the named editor's acceptance of the reading as authentic.

resp.   *respuit*: denotes a scholar's rejection of a predecessor's argument or conjecture.

ss.   *suprascriptum* (etc.): an intended alteration (or a variant reading preceded by *ł* = *uel*) entered above the original text.

susp. habet   *suspectum habet*: indicates that a scholar regards the reading as possibly inauthentic.

v.   *vide*.

Notes to Book 1

In this and the following chapters, the text of the passages discussed is that of Carl Hosius' Teubner (2nd edn 1914), the edition that is now the standard in the field. For the *sigla*, abbreviations, and symbols used in the *apparatus criticus*, see the tables at the end of the Introduction; 'S.' = 'Seneca' throughout, and all citations refer to the works of S. unless otherwise indicated.

1. 1. 1 Inter multos ac uarios errores temere inconsulteque uiuentium nihil propemodum, uir optime Liberalis, dixerim, *** **quod** beneficia nec dare scimus nec accipere.

ante quod *lac. stat.* Gertz ('equidem locum interfectum pronuntio' *Grut. p. 517*), *lac. deneg.* Buck 1908, 42–3, Alexander 1950–2, 6
    nihil propemodum...⟨quam⟩ quod MGpc
    n- p-...⟨peius⟩ d- ⟨quam⟩ q- ς₄ς₁₂ (n- p-...d- ⟨peius quam⟩ q- ς₁₀pc)
    n- p-...d- ⟨nocentius quam⟩ q- *1515–1605*
    n- p-...d- ⟨turpius quam⟩ q- *Agric. p. 271*
    n- p- ⟨indignius⟩...d- ⟨quam⟩ q- ς₃ς₂₀, *1649‡*
    n- p-...⟨foedius⟩ 'alii' *teste Lips.*
    n- p-...d- ⟨quod magis societatem humanam turbet, quam⟩ quod *Gertz (p. 192)*
    ineptum p-...d- quod *Feldman 1887, 17–18*
    '*mallem prope tam odiosum*' *Hos. 1 in app.*
    n- p-...d- ⟨uolgarius quam⟩ q- *Brakman 1909, 34*
    n- p- ⟨diffusius⟩...d- ⟨quam⟩ q- *Bourgery 1913, 108*
    n- p-...⟨discerni haec duo⟩ d- quod *Pré.*
    nihil propius odium...d- ⟨quam⟩ q- *Georgii 1929, 111*
    n- p- ⟨mirandum⟩...d- quod *Mazzoli 1974, 55–6*

The archetype's text poses an insoluble problem barely a dozen words into the treatise; the denials of Buck and Alexander are futile:[1]

> I...subscribe to the view of J. Buck, viz., that there is no lacuna in the text and that *nihil propemodum dixerim* means 'ich möchte es als etwas nicht der Rede Wertes bezeichnen dass usw.' Certainly, as compared with a great many of the mistakes made by people living recklessly and unreflectively, failure to know how to bestow a benefit or how to receive it is *nihil propemodum*, a gaucherie rather than an error, regarded mostly with an amused eye by the world in general—

[1] Alexander 1950–2, 6.

as though S. were launching himself on a discourse that will consume seven books in order to address a mere 'gaucherie', not a corruption of one of the most important components of social stability (so correctly Gertz, though his solution is implausible). The position is refuted almost immediately by the reference to *plurima maximaque uitia* at the start of 1. 1. 2.

The comparably structured opening of Book 4—*Ex omnibus quae tractauimus, Aebuti Liberalis, potest uideri nihil tam necessarium aut magis, ut ait Sallustius, cum cura dicendum quam quod in manibus est*—shows that *quam* should stand before *quod* (pace Feldman, Préchac, and Mazzoli): it is more economical to assume that a comparative adjective has been lost than a *tam…quam* expression, and to assume that it stood immediately before *quam*, the two being lost together; placing a comparative adjective (or *tam* + adj.) after *nihil propemodum* (or before *dixerim*) and *quam* before *quod* implies two independent errors. Approaches that avoid a comparative form seem to me strained (Préchac) or inadequate in sense (Feldman, Mazzoli).

To provide a plausible stop-gap, I will print *nihil propemodum, uir optime Liberalis, dixerim ⟨turpius quam⟩ quod…* and assume a *saut du même au même* (-m…-m); cf. 2. 14. 5 *Quid autem turpius quam quod euenit frequentissime, ut nihil intersit inter odium et beneficium?*, and similarly 4. 1. 2 *Quid enim est turpius quam aliquem conputare quanti uir bonus sit, cum uirtus nec lucro inuitet nec absterreat damno*). *peius quam* implies a slightly shorter leap of the scribe's eye, and *nocentius quam* is thematically well suited.[2]

1. 1. 1 Sequitur enim, ut male conlocata male debeantur; de quibus non redditis sero querimur; **ista** enim perierunt, cum darentur.

ista N : iam tum *Mur.* (*prob. Stephanus 1586b, 36*), statim *Grut. p. 517*

I doubt Muretus' haughty fault-finding—'Qui Latini sermonis periti intelligentesque sunt, quos quotidie pauciores esse quam credideram animaduerto, facile sentiunt, uocem *Ista* huic loco non conuenire'—for if we take *ista* to have pejorative force, that force could reasonably be aimed at *male conlocata*. Yet Gruter's *statim*, answering *sero*, is really very attractive, and certainly worth mentioning in the apparatus: compare 4. 39. 2, distinguishing an ill-placed loan from an ill-judged *beneficium* on the ground that the law is of some avail in the former case, but in the latter, 'beneficium et totum perit et statim'.

1. 1. 6 quis non…in angusto uero **conprensus** aut distulit—id est timide negauit—aut promisit sed difficulter, sed subductis superciliis, sed malignis et uix exeuntibus uerbis?

conprensus *Fick.*, conprehensus MCpcK‡ : conpressos Nac, -pressus Npc

---

[2] The latter is adopted by Griffin and Inwood in their translation (incorrectly ascribed to Lipsius).

The subject is a reluctant benefactor who finds himself cornered after his evasive tactics have failed him. The reading *conprensus* was introduced by Fickert, apparently as his own conjecture, and was taken over by his successors; all previous editions had *conprehensus*, first attested in a few manuscripts of the twelfth century. But the archetype read *conpressos*, changed by the scribe or an early corrector to *conpressus*, and the same verb elsewhere provides S. with the means of saying 'hem(med) in, besiege(d),' *vel sim.*: note especially *EM* 66. 13— *Magnus Scipio, qui Numantiam cludit et comprimit....* (cited at *OLD* s.v. *comprimo* 1b, 'to hem or shut in')—and compare 6. 34. 4 *si animaduerteris obsessos ingenti frequentia uicos et conmeantium in utramque partem cateruis itinera conpressa,* where *conpressa* corresponds to *obsessos.* That these examples involve a place or space, while the present case involves a person, does not seem to me to make a material difference: at *EM* 66. 13 S. could as easily have written *Magnus Scipio, qui Numantinos cludit et comprimit....*

1. 1. 8 Eodem animo beneficium debetur quo datur, et ideo non est neglegenter dandum, sibi enim quisque debet quod a nesciente accepit; **ne** tarde quidem, quia, cum **omni in officio** magni aestimetur dantis uoluntas, qui tarde fecit diu noluit.

ne N : nec *1475‡*
omni in officio JV, *Gertz* : omni & officio Nac (RCacQ), in omni officio Npc*K (*recc. plerique ex* γ *deriuati*), *1515‡,* o- o- BCpcMψ (*recc. plerique ex* π *deriuati*) >*1503*

For the reason why **N**'s *ne* should be retained here, see the discussion of 5. 12. 3. In what follows, the archetype's original reading, *omni et officio*, cannot be correct. A reader expunged *&* and added a superscript *in* before *omni* too late for the change to be reflected in **R**, but *in omni officio* subsequently appears in a manuscript of the twelfth or thirteenth century and thereafter in a number of the *recentiores*, before becoming the print vulgate starting with the Basel edition of 1515. Previously, the most common reading was *omni officio*, both in the manuscripts after **R** and in the earliest printed editions. *omni in officio* was proposed and printed by Gertz,[3] who argued that 'abesse illa [sc. praepositio]...non potest sed in conrupto "&" latere uidetur; nam haec duo uerba 'et' et 'in' non raro inter se permutata esse ostendit Haasius...(= Haase 1853, 10, citing examples in *Marc.*); cfr. mea...(= Gertz 1874, 154, on *Brev.* 9. 3)'. That the preposition is needed is certainly true; but however common the interchange of '&' and 'in' might be in the manuscripts of the *Dialogi*, it is unexampled in **N**. Perhaps more to the point, there is very good reason to doubt that S. wrote *omni in genere* here: for in the twenty-five other places where he used *omnis* to modify a noun in the ablative

---

[3] It is already attested in a pair of closely related twelfth-century books, but that is neither here nor there.

with *in*, we find *in omni* every time. I cannot explain the origin of '&' (by contrast, haplography easily accounts for the loss of *in* after *cum*); but I have little doubt that *in omni officio* is what S. wrote.

1. 1. 9 ne deos quidem inmortales ab hac tam effusa **nec cess⟨ante benign⟩itate** sacrilegi neglegentesque eorum deterrent. utuntur natura sua et cuncta interque illa ipsos munerum suorum malos interpretes iuuant.

effusa nec cess⟨ante benign⟩itate *Lips.* : effusa necessitate N >*1529, 1649‡ (def. Grut. pp. 517–18, Gronovius 1639, 99–100* ['hoc est, a prolixa illa & necessaria ipsis insitaque mente uniuersae mortalitati prouidendi'], *Buck 1908, 43–4*), effusa liberalitate *Agric. p. 271, 1557,* effusa benignitate *Mur.,* 1605, e- n- cess⟨ante com⟩itate *Feldman 1887, 18,* effusa nec umquam intermissa benignitate *Häberlin 1890, 39–42*

The idea is one that S. emphasizes more than once: being benefactors by their very nature, the gods bestow their benefactions on humankind irrespective of the recipients' merits (cf., e.g., 4. 28. 1ff.). It is plain that the paradosis can be defended only if one imports ideas that S. neglected to include: e.g., Gronovius' gloss, 'hoc est, a prolixa illa & necessaria ipsis insitaque mente uniuersae mortalitati prouidendi'; Buck's explanation wanders still farther afield from *effusa necessitate,* which he fairly conspicuously does not try to translate. Of the remedies that have been suggested, Lipsius' *nec cess⟨ante benign⟩itate* is by some distance the most satisfying, not just paleographically but also substantively, for it very economically stresses not just the extent (*tam effusa*) but the unbounded duration (*nec cessante*) of divine kindness. At best, it recaptures S.'s *ipsissima uerba*; at worst, it is an adequate stop-gap. I certainly cannot think of anything better.

1. 2. 1 nullius rei—minime beneficiorum—honesta largitio est, quibus si detraxeris iudicium, **desinunt** esse beneficia, in aliud quodlibet **incident** nomen.

desinunt N : desinent ς₁₀ (*sic et cod. Guelf. Gud. 186 ap. Fick.,* desinet ς₉) | incident N >*1503* : incidunt *1515‡*

Because the text transmitted from antiquity presents a shift in the apodosis from present indicative to future indicative, we find attempts to harmonize the tenses: *desinunt* becomes *desinent* in a small handful of late witnesses, including a fourteenth-century book preserved in Balliol College and a Wolfenbüttel manuscript cited by Fickert; more consequentially, *incidunt* was substituted for *incident* in the Basel edition of 1515, after which it remained the vulgate text for more than three centuries, until it was evicted by Fickert. The first change was the more expectable (I am somewhat surprised that it does not appear in the manuscripts more frequently), since future does normally follow in the apodosis when future or (as here) future perfect stands in the protasis, typically when it describes a specific response to some specific action or circumstance: e.g.—from among the

dozens of examples in *Ben.*—4. 6. 1 *Si pecuniam tibi aliquis donauerit..., beneficium uocabis*, 4. 34. 3 *Si promiseris...te daturum beneficium et postea ingratum
esse scieris, dabis an non?*, 5. 19. 5 *si filius meus pecuniam mutuam sumpserit,
creditori numerabo*, 6. 5. 5 *si quis apud me pecuniam deposuerit, idem postea furtum mihi fecerit, et ego cum illo furti agam et ille mecum depositi.* But the present is
sometimes used when the condition offers an observation of a less specific or cir-
cumstantial kind—about the sorts of things that tend to happen—and the apodosis expresses a kind of generalization or gnomic truth: e.g., 3. 1. 4 *aliquando ad
referendam gratiam conuerti...* [sc. *ingrati*] *possunt, si illos pudor admonuerit.*[4]
That is what I take *desinunt* to be doing here; and I take *incident* simply to express
the consequences that *will* in fact follow when 'benefits cease to be benefits'.

1. 2. 3 Beneficiorum simplex ratio est: tantum erogatur; si **reddet aliquid**,
lucrum est, si non **reddet**, damnum non est.

reddet...reddet N (*def. Mazzoli 1974, 56–7*) : redit...redit *Eras.* (*prob. Grut. p. 518*), reddit...reddit Vac *Gertz* (*qui et aliquis recip., v. seq.*), reddet...reddet Vpcς₁₁ς₁₈, reddit...red-
det ς₁₉ | aliquid N : aliquis GIJV, *Fick.*

There are two questions: which tense or tenses are appropriate in the two conditions? and what is the correct verb in the protases, *reddere* or *redire*? To take the
latter first: Erasmus' change to a form of *redire* was plainly prompted by the
desire to give the verb an express subject, *aliquid*—'something comes back [sc. to
the person who gave the *beneficium*]'—and about this two points need to be
made. First, an express subject is not necessary, since S. commonly leaves it to
the reader to understand an implied subject when it can readily be inferred from
the context, as here the implied subject can be understood from the equally implied
beneficiary in the preceding clause, *tantum erogatur.* (Gertz's substitution of
aliquis, found in some γ-manuscripts, for *aliquid* is equally mistaken: in fact, if a
form of *aliquis* were to be used anywhere, it should have appeared as *tantum
⟨alicui⟩ erogatur.*) Second, *redire* is not the verb that is wanted. Hundreds of times
in *Ben.* S. speaks of the expression of *gratia* as a matter of 'making a return', and in
so doing he all but exclusively uses *reddere* or *referre.* The closest parallel I can
find to a notional use of *redit* here is 5. 8. 5—*Rerum natura nihil dicitur perdere,
quia quidquid illi auellitur ad illam redit*—which has nothing to do with *gratia*: it
refers to the impersonal fact that all matter 'returns' to nature, not to the action of
some agent making a return, which is the essence of the virtue. As for tense, Gertz
read *reddit* to bring the protasis into line with *est* in the apodosis; but as in the
preceding case the use of different tenses can stand, since *lucrum est* and *damnum
non est* have a generalizing—or perhaps better, clarifying or definitional—force: if

---

[4] Cf. Pinkster 2015, 397–8, on the 'timeless' present.

at some point after the act of *erogari* the recipient will make some return, we can call that *lucrum*; if not, it's not a case of *damnum*.[5]

1. 2. 5 Ingratus est aduersus unum beneficium? Aduersus alterum non erit. Duorum oblitus est? **Tertium etiam in eorum quae exciderunt memoriam reducet.**

in eorum N : eorum VK >*1515*
exciderunt R : excitetur N, exciderint S
memoriam BGK‡ : memoria N
reducet K (*recc. plerique ex* γ *deriuati*) : reducetur N, tertio…reducetur *Gertz*, tertio etiam eorum…memoria reducetur *Feldmann 1887, 19*

N's text—*tertium etiam in eorum quae excitetur memoria reducetur*—is a tangled mess: the relative clause should refer to *eorum* but obviously cannot as it stands, while *memoria* makes no sense as an ablative with *in* but leaves both *tertium* and *in* without a function if it is construed as the nominative subject of *reducetur*. No sword can cut the tangle with a single stroke; any solution requires multiple interventions. That being the case, the first step must be **R**'s *exciderunt*, to solve the conundrum of the relative clause; and **R** should be given credit in passing for a far bolder and more imaginative move here than the easy corrections of obvious errors that constitute the manuscript's most characteristic contributions.

With *in eorum quae exciderunt* in place, four solutions have been adopted or proposed, each of them requiring at least two further alterations of the archetype's text:

- *tertium etiam in eorum quae exciderunt memoriam reducet*: the version above, printed by Hosius, which returns to the text that stood in the earliest printed editions down to Basel 1515, with *memoriam* for *memoria* and *reducet* (with subject *tertium* and implied object) for *reducetur*;
- *tertium etiam eorum quae exciderunt memoriam reducet*: the version first attested in a manuscript of the twelfth or thirteenth century (**K**), which became the vulgate after it was printed by Erasmus, with a third modification—deletion of *in*—added to the previous two;

---

[5] Beyond referring to S.'s 'impiego estremamente elastico' of tenses in conditions, Mazzoli based his defense of the archetype's text on the fact that the value of *beneficia* is not to be understood in consequentialist terms: 'la fruttuosità dei beneficii…non è il presupposto del loro valore; questo è gia tutto presente ed espresso nell'atto benefico per sé preso…e perciò non può essere affatto modificato dagli eventuali futuri effetti reddizi dell'atto.' This view is certainly correct as a matter of Stoic doctrine, but it does not quite line up with the way S. has framed the matter here, which is more commonsensical than doctrinaire: if orthodoxy were his concern, the first condition would better read, *si reddet aliquid, non est lucrum*; for if any true 'gain' is realized in the transaction, it consists entirely in the knowledge that one has behaved virtuously in extending the *beneficium* (for *lucrum* used to denote non-material 'gains', cf. 2. 3. 3 *magnum hodies lucrum feci; malo quod illum talem* [sc. *uirum bonum*] *inueni, quam si multiplicatum hoc* [sc. *beneficium*] *ad me…alia uia peruenisset*, and *OLD* s.v. 1b). Thus S.'s more orthodox formulation immediately following: *ego illud dedi ut darem*.

- *tertio etiam in eorum quae exciderunt memoriam reducetur:* the version printed by Gertz, retaining N's *reducetur* (and with it the subject of the preceding verbs, *est... erit... oblitus est*) but modifying both *memoria* and *tertium*;
- *tertio etiam eorum quae exciderunt memoria reducetur:* the version proposed by Feldman, retaining the archetype's *memoria* and *reducetur*, but accepting both Gertz's *tertio* and the older vulgate's deletion of *in.*

Of these—and I confess that I cannot see a more plausible but as yet undiscovered alternative—I find the last to be the most elegant and satisfying: retaining *reducetur*—while allowing *memoria* to vary the subject at the sequence's end—respects a notable trait of N, which nowhere introduces an unwanted passive ending in *-tur* (observed by Gertz p. 193); the corruption of *tertio* to *tertium*—no doubt encouraged by the fact that each of the three previous counting words (*unum... alterum... duorum*) ends in *-um*—is not difficult; and the introduction of an unwanted *in*, by dittography after *etiam*, is easier still.

1. 3. 3 Alii quidem **uideri** uolunt unam [sc. Gratiam] esse quae det beneficium, alteram quae accipiat, tertiam quae reddat; alii tria beneficorum esse genera, promerentium, reddentium, simul accipientium reddentiumque. **(4)** Sed utrumlibet ex istis iudica uerum: quid ista nos scientia iuuat?

uideri *del. Häberlin 1890, 43,* diuidere *Busche 1917–18, 465–6*

The passage stands near the start of S.'s excursus on the allegory of the three *Gratiae*. At first sight, it seems difficult to disagree with Häberlin, who found *uideri* not simply otiose but actually obstructive; so too Busche, though he preferred to think that the infinitive represented an original *diuidere*, not a dittography after *quidem*. But *alii uideri uolunt* X *esse* Y, *alii* Z is a genuinely Senecan manner of comparing divergent speculative interpretations, especially those that S. thinks wrong or pointless: compare *Vit. beat.* 19. 1, on the suicide of the Epicurean philosopher Diodorus, who cut his own throat:

Alii dementiam uideri uolunt factum hoc eius, alii temeritatem. Ille interim beatus ac plenus cona conscientia reddidit sibi testimonium uita excedens laudauitque aetatis in portu et ad ancoram actae quietem....

Compare also the similar use of *uideri uolunt* to characterize interpretations or claims that are merely wrong-headed: *EM* 74. 15 *Adice quod multa quae bona uideri uolunt* [Graver and Long: 'would-be goods'] *animalibus quam homini pleniora contingent,* 82. 19 *Nostri quidem uideri uolunt interrogationem ueram esse, fallacem autem alteram... quae illi opponitur* (S. disagrees with the Stoic framing of the comparison).

Continuing, then, from *quid ista nos scientia iuuat?*...:

1. 3. 4–5 Quid ille consertis manibus in se redeuntium chorus? Ob hoc, quia ordo beneficii per manus transeuntis nihilo minus ad dantem reuertitur et totius speciem perdit si usquam interruptus est, pulcherrimus si cohaeret et uices seruat. **In eo est aliqua tamen maioris dignatio, sicut promerentium. (5) Vultus hilari sunt**, quales solent esse, qui dant uel accipiunt beneficia; iuuenes, quia non debet beneficiorum memoria senescere; uirgines, quia incorrupta sunt et sincera et omnibus sancta.

in eo *Madvig 1871–84, 2:407* : ideo N >*1503*
est aliqua tamen maioris dignatio, sicut N >*1503* (dignatio. sicut *dist. N edd.*) : ridentes quia ς₈pcς₁₇, *1515‡*
post promerentium *dist.* ς₄ς₇, *Gertz, post* dignatio N, *post* sunt ς₃ς₈ς₁₀ς₁₅‡, *post* uultus ς₅ς₁₈ς₁₉
uultus N : uultu *Bentley (Hedicke 1899, 6)* | hilari N (RacC) : hilares Rpcρ, *Valmaggi 1905–6*, hilaris Sac *Gertz p. 194*

Though the final sentence of §3. 4 is correctly punctuated in some *recentiores*, Gertz was the first editor to recognize the structure of the thought, which requires a period after *promerentium*: *In eo* [sc. *choro*] *est aliqua... maioris* [sc. *sororis*] *dignatio, sicut promerentium. Vultus hilaris sunt, quales solent esse, qui...* ('In that dance the elder enjoys some distinction, as do those who confer benefits. They have a joyful expression, as do those who..': on the reading *uultus hilaris*, see the following discussion). The punctuation in **N** and most manuscripts, taken up in the printed editions down to 1503, placed the sentence-break after *dignatio*, joining *sicut promerentium* with what follows and making *quales... beneficia* largely otiose: it was ultimately condemned as an intrusive gloss by Gronovius (1649, 115) and secluded in several later editions, including those of Gertz's immediate predecessors, Fickert and Haase. Beginning with Erasmus' first edition and continuing through Gronovius' own, editors printed a version found in some *recentiores*, which simply replaced *in eo est aliqua... maioris dignatio* with *ideo ridentes* (*Ideo ridentes, quia promerentium uultus hilares sunt, quales solent esse...*).

S. next addresses one of the questions concerning the three Graces noted at 1. 3. 3: *Quare tres Gratiae et quare sorores sint et quare manibus implexis et quare ridentes ⟨et iuuenes⟩ et uirgines solutaque ac perlucida ueste*; the opening phrase here resumes *ridentes*.[6] **N**'s *uultus hilari* (so also **R** before correction and its

---

[6] S. seems not to explain why they are sisters: Gertz's proposed supplement in 1. 3. 4, *Quid ille consertis manibus in se redeuntium chorus ⟨sororum⟩?*, still leaves the question unanswered (if a supplement were wanted, a more paleographically plausible choice would be *In eo est aliqua tamen mai⟨oris sor⟩oris dignatio, sicut promerentium*, at the end of the same section, cf. the following n.). But S. addresses the other questions, in the order in which they were raised. Beginning in the late twelfth century, manuscripts began to supply the category *iuuenes* that **N** omitted, resulting in at least nine different attested solutions, which inserted *iuuenes* at varying points in the sequence, with varying combinations of *et* and *quare*. Of these the most straightforward is the one given here, found in ς₃

descendant **C**) is unacceptable, as either genitive singular or nominative plural, because S. uses only third declension forms of the adjective (more than twenty times, e.g., 3. 17. 4 *laeetus, hilaris, occasionem referendae gratiae expectans, Ira* 2. 33. 1 *potentiorum iniuriae hilari uultu...ferendae sunt, Marc.* 1. 2 *gemitus...non...hilari fronte texisti*); the nominative plural phrase *uultus hilares*, **R**'s corrected reading that was passed on to the rest of its descendants, is unacceptable because *quales solent esse qui dant* shows that the subject of *sunt* must the Graces themselves, not their *uultus*. We are left to choose between two conjectural restorations, each involving the change of one letter: the ablative of description *uultu hilari*, conjectured by Bentley and found already in ς_4, and genitive of description *uultus hilaris*, the original reading of **S**, a collection of excerpts dating to the end of the twelfth century. Gertz was on the point of printing the former (cf. p. 194) but was persuaded by his colleague Oskar Siesbye—like Gertz, a student of J. N. Madvig—to favour the latter, and for S. that was the right choice (cf. *EM* 67. 11 *sunt quaedam tristis uultus bona, Helv.* 13. 7 *neminem...puri oris*):

> Originally the genitival noun phrase was used for denoting permanent and inherent properties, and the nouns involved denoted type, price, or measure.... However, there is an increase in the use of the genitive for denoting temporary and external properties to the detriment of the ablative, which was originally used for that purpose.... This development is especially prominent from Livy onwards.[7]

hilaris became *hilari* by haplography before *sunt*.

1. 3. 8 Chrysippus quoque,... qui rei agendae causa loquitur et uerbis non ultra quam ad intellectum satis est utitur, totum librum suum his ineptiis replet, ita ut **de ipso officio** dandi, accipiendi, reddendi beneficii pauca admodum dicat, nec his fabulas sed haec fabulis inserit.

ipso officio *Gertz et Madvig* : ipso beneficio N, ratione $\varsigma_1\varsigma_{14}$‡, ipso beneficio ⟨et commercio⟩ *Pré.,* i- b- ⟨et uinclo⟩ *Alexander 1950–2, 6*

N's text—*de ipso beneficio dandi, accipiendi, reddendi beneficii*—is intolerably redundant. Préchac and Alexander took *beneficio* to be authentic and devised paleographically based solutions (omission of a second noun through *saut du même au même*): respectively, 'Chrysippus says very little about benefit in and of itself and the exchange entailed in giving, receiving, returning a benefit', or 'Chrysippus says very little about benefit in and of itself and the bond of giving, receiving, returning a benefit'. To my eye neither does much to mitigate the repetition; in any case, it is rather beside the point to stress that 'Chrysippus says very

---

and apparently conjectured independently by Gertz; the printed editions through the end of the sixteenth century have *quare ridentes, quare iuuenes et quare uirgines* (found earlier in ς_2), which was supplanted as the vulgate reading by the version chosen by Lipsius, *quare ridentes, iuuenes, et uirgines* (it also appears as a correction in ς_8).

[7] Pinkster 2015, 1002, with refs; cf. ibid. 1025 (on the ablative noun phrase).

little about benefit in and of itself', since Chrysippus' topic was not 'benefit' but χάρις.

A different course occurred independently to Gertz and Madvig (p. 194), who took *beneficio* to be an error of anticipation, produced when an *oscitans librarius* (Gertz's phrase) glimpsed *beneficii* four words farther on;[8] and the print vulgate's *ratione*, attested earlier in several *recentiores* ($\varsigma_1 \varsigma_{14}$, a common constellation), similarly presupposes an error of substitution. If the word S. wrote is lost, then, we should either bracket *beneficio* or—my preference—replace it with a plausible stop-gap, which must be a masculine or neuter noun: for though *beneficio* is probably not authentic, there is no reason to doubt the authenticity of *ipso*. In view of all that, *officio* is in fact the best candidate, appropriate in sense and with the same root as the word that replaced it.

It happens that a very similar error occurred, in a very similar way, in the next section of the text, concerning the mother of the Graces, Eurynome (< εὐρύς / 'wide' + νωμᾶν / 'distribute'):

1. 3. 9 tres Chrysippus Gratias ait Iouis et Eurynomes filias esse.... Matris quoque nomen ad rem iudicat pertinere, Eurynomen enim dictam **quia late patentis patrimonii** (Erasmus : **matrimonii N**) **sit beneficia diuidere** ('because distributing benefits is characteristic of an inheritance that spreads far and wide')—tamquam matri post filias soleat nomen imponi...!

Here *patri-* was supplanted by *matri* when a scribe's eye, having just passed *matris*, caught *matri* five words farther on.[9]

1. 5. 1 Sed quemadmodum superuacua transcurram, ita exponam necesse est hoc primum nobis esse discendum, quid accepto beneficio debeamus. **Debere enim se ⟨ait⟩ alius pecuniam**, quam accepit, alius consulatum, alius sacerdotium, alius prouinciam.

se ⟨ait⟩ *Madvig ap. Gertz* : se N (.s. [= scilicet] meminit *ss. ad* alius 2°, *man. post.*), *de aliis testibus, v. inf.*

---

[8] At 4. 3. 1 *ciues suos magno aestimarent, ab iis certaminibus remouerunt*, N's scribe wrote *suos certaminibus magno*, then repeated *certaminibus* four words farther on: in that case the scribe caught his slip—no doubt aided by the fact that the noun's second occurrence fell directly under the first—and placed expunction points around the error.

[9] The sixteenth-century editors who followed Erasmus accepted *patrimonii*, but near the century's end the great Janus Gruter—whose own contributions to the text of Seneca rival those of Erasmus—defended *matrimonii*, accepting the contention of the jurists Jacques Cujas and François Connan that *matrimonium* could denote an inheritance derived from one's mother, in a manner analogous *patrimonium* (pp. 519–20); but the word is unattested in that sense (the two texts Gruter cited from Connan, Val. Max. 7. 8. 2 and Suet. *Aug.* 40. 1, in fact have *patrimonium*). Persuaded by Gruter, Lipsius put *matrimonii* in the text; removed by Haase, it was restored by Hosius. Compare 3. 33. 1 *seruauit in proelio patrem*, where the last word was supplanted, weirdly, by *matrem* in all editions before Erasmus' second: in that case there is no form of *mater* in the vicinity to provide even a semblance of an explanation.

S. is coming to grips with one of the fundamental issues of the work: having received a *beneficium*, what exactly is one obliged to do in return? in that context, what exactly does *debere* mean? He begins to answer the question negatively, by showing a wrong way to come to grips with it. To make good the obvious deficiency of the text, Gertz (followed by Hosius) printed the simple *ait* that Madvig suggested to him, probably placed before *alius* (Gertz did not make the point explicit) to suggest that at some point AIT was lost before ALI. It was the latest in a long line of attempted emendations attested from the twelfth century on. The others are:

- ait *add.*
  Debere enim se alius pecuniam, quam accepit, alius consulatum, alius sacerdotium, alius prouinciam **ait** H
- dicit *add.*
  Debere enim **dicit** se alius pecuniam, quam accepit, alius consulatum, alius sacerdotium, alius prouinciam $\varsigma_2\varsigma_3\varsigma_{14}$‡
  Debere enim se **dicit** alius pecuniam, quam accepit, alius consulatum, alius sacerdotium, alius prouinciam ς_{17} (**dicit** enim se debere alius... B)
- putat *add.*
  Debere enim se alius pecuniam **putat** quam accepit, alius consulatum, alius sacerdotium, alius prouinciam G
  Debere enim se **putat** alius pecuniam, quam accepit, alius consulatum, alius sacerdotium, alius prouinciam $\varsigma_{16}\varsigma_{19}$
  Debere enim **putat** se alius pecuniam, quam accepit, alius consulatum, alius sacerdotium, alius prouinciam Q$\varsigma_5\varsigma_6$, *cod. Pinc.*, 'non improbauerim' *Grut. p. 520*
  Debere enim se alius pecuniam, quam accepit, alius consulatum, alius sacerdotium, alius prouinciam **putat** ς_{12}
- (a)estimat *add.*
  Debere enim se alius pecuniam **aestimat**, quam accepit, alius consulatum, alius sacerdotium, alius prouinciam WJV
- scit *add.*
  Debere enim se alius **scit** pecuniam, quam accepit, alius consulatum, alius sacerdotium, alius prouinciam ς_{13}

A few are obvious non-starters (e.g., the *ait* placed at the end of the sentence, the *scit* that ineptly injects the idea of 'knowledge'), most are roughly adequate, but Madvig's suggestion is the best of the lot and quite possibly correct. Yet there is room for doubt: are we certain that it is a verb of speaking that we want, to represent one person after another voicing a mistaken claim? Since S. is addressing a fundamental misunderstanding that people have of the concept represented by *debere*—supposing that it is one sort of thing when in fact it is quite another—it is perhaps more likely, all else being equal, that we want a verb denoting supposition: on the assumption that one *p*-word was lost before another, I will print—with appropriate indications of caution and uncertainty—*Debere enim se alius ⟨putat⟩ pecuniam quam accepit, alius consulatum, alius sacerdotium, alius prouinciam.*

1. 5. 2 Non potest beneficium manu **tangi: res** animo geritur. Multum interest inter materiam beneficii et beneficium; itaque nec aurum nec argentum nec quicquam eorum, quae **pro maximis** accipiuntur, beneficium est, sed ipsa tribuentis uoluntas. Imperiti autem id, quod oculis incurrit et quod traditur possideturque, solum notant, cum contra illud, quod in re carum atque pretiosum ⟨**est, parui pendunt**⟩.

tangi: res *Gron. p. 116‡* : tangiles Nac, tangi, sed Npc >*1557*, tangi: animo *Mur.* ('acute; nescio etiam an uere' *Grut. p. 520*), –*1649*

pro maximis *Grut. ibid.* : proximis Nac (Rac), a proximis Npc1 (Rpc‡), *dein* ximiis *expunct.* xeniis *ss.* (*et in mg.* sinist.) Npc2* (*man. post.*) *Modius 1584, 136*, pro summis *Lips.* ('uerum est' *Gron. pp. 116–17, qui et* pro eximiis), proximius *dub. Buck 1908, 46*

cum contra Nac : contra sit Npc* (*man. post.*), cum *del. Rossbach 1907, 1487*

pretiosum est BWJVK : pretiosum N (*Pré.*)

parui pendunt $\varsigma_1\varsigma_{14}$‡ : *om.* N (*Pré.*), negligant $\varsigma_5\varsigma_6$, pretiosum, ⟨praetereant⟩ *Hos. in app.*

Three interesting corruptions in the space of as many sentences, each offering a slightly different challenge. In the first, **N** itself was corrupt, and a corrector made a trivializing change that became the vulgate when it was transmitted by **R**: *beneficium* is joined with *gerere* neither by S. nor by any other writer of classical Latin. Knowing **N**'s text from Gruter's report, Gronovius made one of his happiest conjectures.

In the second case, **N**'s original text offers up a Latin word but no sense; the first correction, by an early hand (but not the scribe's), gives a construable phrase with no readily applicable sense; and the final correction, by a later hand, introduces a rather exquisite word with (to my eye) a weirdly specific sense (could S. really have been thinking of party-favours?). I am happy to join Gertz and Hosius in accepting Gruter's neat *pro maximis*.[10]

As for the third case, unless we are willing to join Préchac in following **N** off a cliff, we must either mark a lacuna or adopt a stop-gap that captures S.'s likely intended meaning, if not his actual words.[11] All editors since the *editio princeps* have chosen the second alternative, and I think they have been right to do so.[12]

---

[10] Lipsius' *pro summis* is comparable in sense but too far from the starting point provided by **N**.

[11] The loss stands near a page-break in **N** (between *atque* and *pretiosum*), but that does not seem relevant.

[12] They have also adopted the supplement of *est* after *pretiosum*, found in some γ-manuscripts, which I take to be uncontroversial.

I doubt, however, that they have all been right to choose the phrase *parui pend-unt*, first attested in the fourteenth century:[13] for apart from one use by Cicero (*Att.* 15. 3. 1), the idiom occurs only in Plautus and Terence (seven times, e.g., *Rud.* 650, *And.* 526) and Sallust (*BC* 12. 2, 52. 9), and then reappears in Apuleius (*Met.* 4. 25, 9. 36), a pattern that all but guarantees that the idiom was an archaism in S.'s day and not likely to be part of his active lexicon.[14] *neglegant*, found in some *recentiores*, and *praetereant*, suggested tentatively by Hosius, are common verbs (in S.'s usage and more generally) that provide appropriate sense and rhythm (spondee [-*ōsumst*] + cretic or spondee + choriamb, respectively), and there is not much point in generating further plausible stop-gaps just for the sake of doing so: I will print *neglegant*.

1. 7. 1 (against the premise that the magnitude of a *beneficium* is a measure of its worth) Id autem falsum est; non numquam enim magis nos obligat qui dedit parua magnifice, qui 'regum aequauit opes animo', qui exiguum tribuit sed libenter, qui paupertatis suae oblitus ⟨est⟩ dum meam respicit, qui non uolun-tatem tantum iuuandi habuit sed cupiditatem, qui accipere se putauit beneficium cum daret, **qui dedit tamquam ⟨non⟩ recepturus, recepit tamquam non dedis-set**, qui occasionem qua prodesset et occupauit et quaesiit.

tamquam non *Vinc. Bell., Spec. Hist. 8(9). 106, Spec. Doct. 5. 46,* ς₁₃pcς₁₆ς₁₇ς₁₉, *1515–1605* : tamquam N >*1503, prob. Grut. p. 521, Gron. p. 117, 1649‡, def. Kruczkiewicz 1877, 432*[15] (*prob. Buck 1908, 46–7*), tamquam ⟨numquam⟩ *Pré.* (*coll. 5. 20. 7 do tamquam numquam repetiturus nisi fuerit necesse*)

I confess that I can see no merit in the attempt to defend **N**. The structure of *dedit tamquam ⟨non⟩ recepturus, recepit tamquam non dedisset* could not be more care-fully worked out, with the verbs arranged chiastically while the negations occur at the same point in their clauses, and the thought could not be more apt: a man of proper understanding gives a *beneficium* without thought of a grateful return and receives a grateful return as though he had not bestowed a *beneficium*, regarding the expression of *gratia* as though it were a *beneficium* and so feeling obligated to make a return of his own. As for the choice of supplement, Préchac (as always) placed most weight on paleography and so favoured a solution that assumes an easy *saut du même au même*. But the parallel with *non dedisset* should be given equal weight, nor is *non* paleographically less probable: **N**'s script sometimes abbreviates the adverb, and in any case the *nota* 'n̄' was ancient and 'remained in

---

[13] I set aside the mood of *pendunt*: not impossible, though it would be easier if Rossbach's deletion of *cum* before *contra* were right.

[14] S. criticizes those who 'ex alieno saeculo petunt uerba' at *EM* 114. 13; cf. the discussion of 5. 12. 2 *creperi*.

[15] 'Der Zusatz *tamquam recepturus* bezeichnet trefflich die Bereitwilligkeit des Wohlthäters, *tam-quam non recepturus* ist matt und deutet eher auf die Zaghaftigkeit des Spendenden.'

constant use all over Europe except Spain'.[16] It would obviously have been vulnerable after *tamquam*.

1. 8. 1 Socrati cum multa pro suis **quisque facultatibus offerrent**, Aeschines, pauper auditor: 'Nihil' inquit 'dignum te, quod dare tibi possim, inuenio et hoc uno modo pauperem esse me sentio...'

quisque Nac : quique Npc | offerrent Npc : -rit Nac, offeret *Buck 1908, 47*

A corrector—not the scribe, but a hand probably not much later—changed N's impossible *offerrit* to *offerrent* and also (to judge from the colour of the ink) changed *quisque* to *quique*. Buck wanted to retain *quisque* and read *offerret*, and in that he was as certainly correct as one can be in these matters. S. never uses *quique* as the plural of *quisque*;[17] in contrast, he writes *quisque* over eighty times, never with a plural verb; and in N the third-person singular endings *-it* and *-et* are confused and interchanged so often—literally hundreds of times—that the soundness of any given instance can hardly be taken for granted.

1. 9. 1–2 Ingeniosus adulescens inuenit, quemadmodum Socraten sibi daret. Non quanta quaeque sint, sed **a quali profecta, prospiciendum**. *** (2) **callidus** non difficilem aditum praebuit inmodica cupientibus spesque improbas nihil re adiuturus uerbis fouit; at peior opinio, si lingua asper, uultu grauis cum inuidia fortunam suam explicuit.

a quali profecta, prospiciendum *Hos.* : a quali proficiend(um) ‖ callidus Nac, ł p(ro)fecta Npc* (*ss. man. post.*)
   a quali proficiscenda M
   a quali ⟨uoluntate⟩ prospiciendum ς₅
   a quali pro⟨ficiscantur animo resp⟩iciendum *Gertz in app.*
   a quali profitendum *Gundermann ap. Buck 1908, 47*
   {a}qualia prouidendum *Buck ibid.*
   a quali prof⟨ecta uoluntate prosp⟩iciendum *Albertini 1923, 158–9*
   profecta, scire proficit *Pré.*
   a quali prospiciendum *Alexander 1950–2, 6–7*
   a quali ⟨perspiciendum uoluntate. itaque ad⟩ proficiendum callidus...*Mazzoli 1974, 57–60*
ante callidus lac. stat. Lips. (sic et hic dee(st) Rmg.), ante non quanta Agric. p. 271 (prob. Grut. p. 521), ⟨bene audit homo diues si⟩ callidus Gertz in app. (at peior opinio...prospiciens), ⟨en dominus⟩ Pré

In demonstrating that it is the benefactor's character and intention that matter, not the magnitude of the benefaction, S. is making a transition from the positive

---

[16] Lindsay 1915, 143 (*POxy.* 1027 is cited on p. 145).

[17] *quique* appears in the corpus only a handful times—more often in the tragedies (twelve times) than in the prose works (five times)—and only when *qui* is a relative pronoun joined by enclitic *-que*.

exemplum of the *ingeniosus adulescens* to a negative case, a crafty rich man: Lipsius was the first editor to 'sniff out a loss' (*defectum odoror*) before *callidus*, which follows a page-break in **N** (a marginal note in **R**, *hic dee(st)*, pointed the same way). Editors agree, and assume that the loss was not large; there is less agreement about what to do about **N**'s unsatisfactory text, *non quanta quaeque sint, sed a quali profi-ciendum*: I will take my cue from Gertz and print *sed a quali profici⟨scantur respici⟩endum*, which builds on what **N** provides and supplies a verb, parallel with *sint*, that matches up well with *a quali*. I do take a more minimalist approach in one respect, since I do not think it necessary to supply a noun for *quali* to modify: the candidates that have been put forward are plausible enough—*uoluntate* (ς₅, reprised by Albertini and Mazzoli), Gertz's *animo* (cf. *EM* 81. 6 *nec quantum sit sed a quali uoluntate perpenditur*)—but the addition is superfluous in this context, given that S. is talking about sorts of persons and that *a quali* by itself adequately conveys that idea (*a quali proficiscantur* = 'from what sort of person they originate / are derived'): cf. 1. 15. 4 *cogitantem magis a quo quam quid accep-eris*, *EM* 19. 12 *magis ad rem existimes pertinere quis quam quid acceperit*.

1. 9. 3 Rusticus, inhumanus ac mali moris et inter matronas **abominandus conuicio** est, si quis coniugem suam in sella prostare uetuit et uulgo admissis inspectoribus uehi perspicuam undique.

inhumanus N >*1605* : inurbanus *Pinc.* (*prob. Grut. p. 521, Gron. pp. 117–18*), *1649‡*
abominandus conuicio *Haupt 1875–6, 3:456* : abominanda conditio (abho- -tio Nac) *1649‡*
(*def. Grut. p. 988, Gron. pp. 118–19, 1662, 62–3, Mayor 1907, Buck 1908, 48, recip. Pré.*),
abominandae condicionis Npc >*1605*

Whoever (*si quis* = *quisquis*) does not allow his wife to prostitute herself is... what? For starters, 'a subhuman bumpkin': a comma should not stand after *rusticus*.[18] *mali moris*, next, is unproblematic, but what to do about the third predicate expression? The archetype's nominative phrase, *abhominanda conditio*, soon became a genitive of description, *abominandae condicionis*, the reading taken over by **R** and passed on to later copies.[19] When Moritz Haupt found both nominative and genitive unacceptable, he proposed *abominandus conuicio*, 'in the view of proper ladies, to be detested and abused', which was accepted by Gertz and Hosius.[20] But as J. E. B. Mayor pointed out, Gronovius had adequately defended *abominanda condicio*, citing among other things a passage from the

[18] Pincianus' *inurbanus*, though approved by Gruter and Gronovius, was in any case redundant.
[19] It seems that both corrections of **N**'s original text—*abho- -tio > abo- -cio* and *-da -cio > -dae -cionis*—were made by the same hand, the former via erasure, the latter via superscript addition of *e* and *nis*: for while the corrector mainly converted *-tio* to *-cio* by erasing the loop on the left half of *t*'s crossbar, as he converted *abho-* to *abo-* by erasing *h*, he also added a small downward curving stroke to the remnant of *t*'s crossbar, in ink the same colour and shade as the added superscript letters.
[20] Lit. 'worthy of being abominated by means of abuse'; *inter* 'indicat[es] a group in which a common attitude, opinion...exists' (*OLD* s.v. 4a), cf. *matronae...uocant* immediately following.

lesser declamations of Quintilian (*DMin.* 257. 12 *coepi bona esse condicio*), where *condicio* = 'a (prospective) marriage partner, match' (*OLD* s.v. 2b, *TLL* 4. 130. 36–8), a sense very much at home here: 'an awful marriage prospect.'

Two sentences immediately follow in the same sarcastic vein.

1. 9. 4 Si quis nulla se amica fecit insignem nec alienae uxori annuum praestat, hunc matronae humilem et sordidae libidinis et ancillariolum uocant. **Inde decentissimum** sponsaliorum genus est adulterium et **in consensu uidui caelibatus, quoniam** nemo uxorem duxit, nisi qui abduxit.

Inde decentissimum *Pinc.* (*prob. Grut. p. 521, recip. Gertz*) : indecertissimum Nac, inde-centissimum Npc *>1529*, decentissimum *Agric.* (*p. 271*: 'recte notarat, legendum: loquitur enim, non de re, sed de peruersa hominum opinione' *Eras. ibid.*), hinc decentissimum *Pinc. 1557‡*, inde certissimum *Pré.*
uidui caelibatus quoniam ς₁₇ (q̅m̅), *Kienzle 1906, 49 n. 4* (*prob. Buck 1908, 48, recip. Hos. 2*) : uiduicae libatus quem Nac, uidui caelibatus quam Npc*, uidui caelibatus ς₂ς₁₄ς₁₉‡, uiduitas caelibatusque *Gertz (Hos. 1)*

At the start of the second sentence, **N**'s original text is very much at home when properly articulated—*inde certissimum*—as Préchac saw: in the topsy-turvy moral world S. describes, 'adultery is the most stable sort of betrothal'. What follows is much more difficult. **N**'s text was word salad, which a corrector formed into actual Latin words, though not construable Latin words. *uidui caelibatus* originated in some *recentiores* and became the print vulgate until Gertz introduced *uiduitas caelibatusque* (retained in Hosius' first edition) and Kienzle conjectured *uidui caelibatus quoniam*, a reading found already in ς₁₇. Neither of these is wholly satisfying. The latter, accepted by Hosius in his second edition, was translated by Basore in the Loeb edition as 'the bachelor is in accord with the widower, since...', which points to the conjecture's weaknesses: Kienzle's text speaks not of 'bachelor' and 'widower' but of 'bachelorhood' and 'widower', abstract noun paired awkwardly with human person;[21] further, when *consensus* is construed with a genitive, the genitive should be either subjective, denoting the parties to the agreement (*consensus omnium ciuium*), or objective, denoting the thing on which the parties agree, as in Cicero's definition of a *populus*: *Rep.* 1. 39 *coetus multitudinis iuris consensu... sociatus*: I know of no instance in which *aliquis est in consensu alicuius* = 'Entity A agrees with entity B.' And even if the words could have that sense, it would remain unclear exactly what the two parties agree on and how that agreement is related substantively to the thought that precedes or logically to the one that follows (Kienzle's *quoniam* merely gestures at

---

[21] In defending the emendation, Buck sidesteps this objection by taking *uidui* to be dependent on *caelibatus* ('*Vidui caelibatus* bedeutet Ehelosigkeit, die eigentlich Witwenstand ist') but does not explain how that idea is related to *in consensu*, which goes unmentioned.

such a relation). As for Gertz's *in consensu uiduitas caelibatusque*, the most obvious understanding of the words—'widowhood and celibacy (are) in agreement'—is vulnerable to much the same objection, and I doubt that *in consensu* can be pushed so far as to mean '(are) in accord / harmony' = 'amount to the same thing.' But *consensus* can also denote 'a general practice, custom' (*OLD* s.v. 2b), hence the line taken by Griffin and Inwood in their translation, 'both widowhood and bachelorhood have become a general practice'. The sense suits S.'s theme—the institution of marriage has fallen into disrespect and desuetude—and I am prepared to follow the same line, but only *faute de mieux* and not without misgivings: for that meaning of *consensus* is not common, and I cannot find another case in which *in consensu esse* = 'to be customary' / 'a matter of general practice.'[22]

1. 9. 5 Iam rapta spargere, sparsa **fera et acri** auaritia recolligere certant, nihil pensi habere, paupertatem alienam contemnere, suam ⟨**magis**⟩ **quam** ullum aliud uereri malum, pacem iniuriis perturbare, inbecilliores ui ac metu premere.

iam rapta spargere N (*agnosc. Eras. p. 271*) 1557mg., 1605‡ : iam raptam. agros spargere ς₂ς₃ς₁₄ >1557, iam…certant *om.* 1585[23]
sparsa fera et acri auaritia recolligere Hos. : sparsa erat agri auaritia recolligere Npc1 (-legere Nac), *obel. Gertz*
    rapaci uł acri Npc2* (*ss. man. post.*)
    sparsa rapaci auaricia recolligere *agnosc. Eras. p. 271, Lips.,* 1649‡ (sparsa acri
    au- re- *Fick.*)
    auaritiam recolligere ς₂ς₅ς₁₄ (a- -lige ς₃) >1557
    sparsa erant, pari auaritia recolligere *dub. Pinc.*
    sparsa recolligere pari auaritia *1557mg.*
    sparsa pari auaritia recolligere *Modius 1584, 137–8, 1605*
    sparsa aegra et acri a- *Gertz in app.*
    sparsa sera et acri a- *Pré.*
    sparsa aspera et acri a- *Walter 1930, 255*
suam magis quam ullum aliud *Gertz* (*recip. Hos. 1*) : suam quam ullum aliud N (*def. Buck 1908, 48, recip. Hos. 2 Pré.*)

I would prefer Hosius' *fera et acri* to *aegra et* or *sera et* or *aspera et* if I could persuade myself that in the swift and clipped pairing of *rapta spargere, sparsa… recolligere*, S. thought it worth spending two adjectives on *auaritia*, or (to put it another way) if I could persuade myself that there was any motivation for the first epithet beyond the paleographical. At the same time, though I believe *rapaci* is

---

[22] *TLL* (4. 391. 67–8) gives no help in all of this, since it quotes the passage as *decentissimum sponsaliorum genus est adulterium et in consensu*, construing the phrase with what precedes and leaving all else obscure.
[23] The omission seems accidental, since Muretus quotes Ov. *F.* 1. 213–14 next to the lemma *iam rapta spargere* in his note ad loc.

the only other suggestion worth considering, I cannot quite see how it accounts for *erat agri*. I think *acri* is sufficiently plausible to print, but for the rest I will follow the example set by Pincianus ('hunc locum…in medium relinquimus, ut ingeniosus lector…aut emendet aut in meliore statu reponat'), Gruter ('laudo ingenuitatem [sc. Pinciani] imitorque'), and Gertz, and surround *erat* with the daggers of despair.

A few words farther along, Hosius again adopted Gertz's text in his first edition but reversed himself in his second edition, persuaded by Buck.[24] He was probably on firmer ground in this instance. Commenting on *Annals* 1. 4. 4 (*ne iis quidem annis quibus… exulem egerit aliud quam iram… meditatum*), Goodyear wrote:

> [T]he ellipsis of *potius* or *magis*, much favored by T., occurs only when a contrast or opposition of notions is clearly expressed. So with nouns (e.g. 3. 17. 3 *miseratio quam inuidia*), with adjectives (e.g. 4. 61 *claris maioribus quam uetustis*) or the equivalent (e.g. 5. 6. 3 *per maerorem quam laeti*), and with infinitives (at 5. 15. 3 *condere quam cremare*).[25]

We have a clearly expressed contrast of a similar sort here, where the phrase *suam* (sc. *paupertatem*) exerts its adversative force in both directions, the adjective looking back to *alienam*, the noun ahead to *aliud malum*. In a passage where S. is writing with a pointedness and compression worthy of Tacitus, we can take it that he probably gave himself the same liberty.[26]

1. 10. 4 Erunt homicidae, tyranni, fures, adulteri, raptores, sacrilegi, proditores; infra omnia ista ingratus est, nisi quod omnia ista ab ingrato sunt, sine quo uix ullum magnum facinus adcreuit. Hoc tu caue tamquam maximum crimen ne admittas, ignosce tamquam leuissimo, si admissum est. Haec est enim iniuriae **summa: beneficium** perdidisti. Saluum **est enim** tibi ex illo, quod est optimum: dedisti.

summa: beneficium N : summa: ⟨beneficii materiam, non⟩ beneficium *Gertz* | enim (2°) N : *om.* ς₁₆ς₁₇, *1529‡, autem* Shackleton Bailey 1970, 361

S. is playing with a series of somewhat paradoxical contrasts: compared with the worst kinds of crime, ingratitude is rather trivial—and yet ingratitude is the source of virtually every great crime; accordingly, guard against being *ingratus* as though it were the greatest crime—and yet, if someone is *ingratus* toward you, treat the offense as inconsequential; for the worst of it is that you have wasted a benefaction (sc. in receiving no return)—and yet the best of it—the fact that you

---

[24] Buck wrote that 'Gertz und Hosius lesen *suam magis quam* obgleich Gertz selbst sagt *magis* könne fehlen', but that is not quite right: '*magis* addidi, cum Haasius "plus" addidisset, quod parum rectum uidebatur; sed aduerbium hoc abesse posse ne ego quidem credo, et exempla, quae ad hunc usum defendendum adferuntur, nimis incerta sunt' (p. 197).

[25] Goodyear 1972, 123–4, citing also Timpanaro 1970.

[26] On the construction see H.–S. 593 (citing this passage, among others), and Timpanaro 1970 (citing exx. from Velleius and Valerius Maximus, p. 469, and this passage, p. 470).

gave the benefaction—remains unspoiled. Gertz's supplement was intended to restore Stoic orthodoxy (cf. 1. 5. 2 *multum interest inter materiam beneficii et beneficium*), but that rather spoils the series of contrasts, and in any case this is another instance where S. is speaking in commonsensical rather than doctrinaire terms (cf. the discussion of 1. 2. 3, with the n. there ad fin.). There is, however, an awkwardness, in the repetition of *enim* after *saluum est*: we should expect the contrast to be marked, either by a particle like Shackleton Bailey's *autem* or by the simple juxtaposition of antithetical clauses, as in the first two members of the sequence (*Erunt homicidae...*; *infra omnes...*, *Hoc tu caue...*, *ignosce tamquam...*) and the text of some *recentiores* and the printed editions from Erasmus to Haase, in which *enim* is absent (cf. Griffin and Inwood's translation: 'For the sum total of the injustice is that you have lost the benefit you gave; you have preserved what is best about it, the fact that you gave it'). I am fairly confident that there is an error of perseveration here, as the memory of *haec est enim* caused a scribe either to write *enim* where he saw *autem* or to add *enim* after *est* where he saw nothing at all: the choice is not obvious, but I take the latter to be somewhat more likely, especially given the juxtaposed clauses earlier in the sequence, and will seclude *enim* in my text.

1. 11. 1 Sequitur, ut dicamus, quae beneficia danda sint et quemadmodum. **Prima** demus necessaria, deinde utilia, deinde iocunda, utique mansura.

prima N (*def. Buck 1908, 49, recip. Hos. 2, Pré.*) : primum BUK (*Hos. 1*), primo M

Another change of mind on Hosius' part, following the argument of Buck:

> Richtig is *prima*; es ist prädikativ zu dem substantivierten *necessaria* zu fassen. *Primo* und *primum* sind Vermutungen, veranlasst durch die Häufigkeit dieser formen und die folgenden *deinde*. Ebenso gut könnte folgen *secunda ... tertia.*

The point looks plausible but is certainly mistaken relative to S.'s actual usage, in which an adjectival form of *primus* is all but unknown to play a comparable role in such a sequence,[27] against sixty-odd times when *primum ... deinde ... (deinde...)* occur. Here *primum* had the bad luck to be nestled in the midst of six neuter plural nominative / accusative forms in -*a*, which proved to be too many for at least one scribe to resist.

1. 12. 1 Si arbitrium dandi penes nos est, praecipue mansura quaeremus, ut quam minime mortale munus sit. Pauci enim sunt tam grati, ut, quid acceperint, etiam si non uident, cogitent. **Ingratos** quoque memoria cum ipso munere incurrit, ubi ante oculos est et obliuisci sui non sinit, sed auctorem suum ingerit et inculcat.

ingratos N : ingrato ς₁₁, ingratis ς₁ς₁₄‡, ⟨in⟩ ingratos Gertz

---

[27] I believe the only instance is *EM* 95. 50 *Primus est deorum cultus deos credere, deinde reddere illis maiestatem suam.*

Gertz did not explain his emendation in his *Adnotationes*, perhaps because he thought the rationale obvious: S. uses *incurrere* over three dozen times in the prose works, never transitively with a direct object, a usage that is quite uncommon in Latin more generally. Apart from instances where it occurs absolutely in S.'s writings, it is very occasionally accompanied by a dative—to evoke the collision of stars (6. 22. 1 *sidera sideribus incurrant*, sim. *Marc.* 26. 6) or something that 'strikes' the eye (1. 5. 2 *imperiti...id quod oculis incurrit...solum notant*)—and most commonly by *in* + accusative, especially in the sense—'occurs', 'presents itself'—relevant here: e.g., *Const.* 5. 4 *iniuria deminutio eius est in quem incurrit*, *Tranq.* 11. 10 *quidquid in ullum incurrit posse in te quoque incurrere*, *EM* 37. 5 *fortuna in nos incurrit*. Given the pattern of S.'s usage and the ease with which *in* could be lost before *ingratos*, Gertz's correction is more likely right than the dative of the *recentiores* and earlier printed editions; either would be better than *ingratos*, which Fickert (followed by Haase) put in the text.

1. 12. 3 Sit in beneficio sensus communis; tempus, locum obseruet, personas, quia **momentis quaedam grata et ingrata sunt**.

quia momentis quaedam grata et ingrata N : quia momentis quaedam grata ⟨quaedam⟩ ingrata S, quibus momentis quae dam⟨us⟩ grata et ingrata *Gertz*, quia momentis ⟨quibusdam⟩ quaedam grata aut ingrata *Hos. in app.*, quia momentis quae dam⟨us⟩ grata aut ingrata *Alexander 1950–2, 7–8*

The key word here is pretty clearly *momentis*, which has motivated the various emendations that have been suggested.[28] But I believe the sentence can be correctly understood without altering the text if we take the meaning of *momentis* to fall in the same semantic field as the definition given at *OLD* s.v. 6: 'a decisive stage in a course of events, *change of a situation*' (emphasis added): 'let (the benefactor) carefully attend to time, place, and persons, since according to / because of changes [sc. in respect of these factors] certain things are welcome and unwelcome.'[29] In most of the passages cited in the *OLD* entry, *momentum* is accompanied by a noun in the genitive specifying the events or circumstances to which the 'stages' or 'changes' refer (e.g., *Ira* 3. 21. 1 *bellum, cuius maxima momenta in occasionibus sunt*). Here that frame of reference is supplied by the preceding *tempus, locum,...personas*, after which *momentis* sc. *horum* is implied: so similarly Cic. *Fam.* 6. 10b. 2 (also cited in the *OLD* entry) *quae quoniam in temporum inclinationibus saepe paruis posita sunt, omnia momenta obseruabimus*.

---

[28] Gertz, Hosius, and the person responsible for the second *quaedam* in **S** all seem to have taken it to mean 'moments'; Alexander took his proposed text to mean '...because it is *by attention to such small considerations* that the things we give are welcome or unwelcome' (emphasis added), which would be a great deal to get out *momentis* even if it could mean 'small consideration'.

[29] Only 'certain things', because *beneficia* that belong to the category of *necessaria* surveyed in 1. 11. 1–4 are welcome absolutely.

In their translation—'... since for certain things minor circumstances determine whether they are appreciated or not'—Griffin and Inwood were presumably following *OLD* s.v. 4d ('a minute amount or degree'), where this passage is cited: but since in all of the passages assembled there *momentum* is accompanied by an adjective (*paruo momento, aliquo momento*, or the like), we would probably need to supply a comparable adjective here (e.g., *paruis momentis*), though even then the idea of 'change' or 'variation', which seems to me crucial, would be lacking.

1. 14. 1 Beneficium ⟨si⟩ qui quibuslibet dat, nulli gratum est; nemo se stabularii aut cauponis hospitem iudicat nec conuiuam dantis epulum, ubi dici potest: 'Quid enim in me contulit? Nempe hoc, quod et in illum uix bene notum sibi et in illum etiam inimicum ac turpissimum hominem. Numquid enim me dignum iudicauit? morbo suo morem gessit.' **Quod uoles gratum esse, rarum effice: quis patitur sibi imputari ⟨uulgaria⟩?**

⟨si⟩ qui...dat *Hos.* : qui...dat N (*def. Sjögren 1919–20, 168–9, recip. Pré.*), quod...datur M‡ (qui...datur K), {qui}...datum *Skutsch ap. Hos.*
gratum est N *prob. Grut. p. 523* (*def. Buck 1908, 49, et dist. post* est; *recip. Hos. 2*) : datum *cod. Pinc.*, dat *Flor. Mor. p. 137. 5* (*post* qui...dat), gratum dat *Gertz* (*Hos. 1*), gratum praestat *J. Müller 1892, 2*
effice: quis patitur sibi imputari ⟨uulgaria⟩ *1557‡* : effice. quis patitur sibi inputari? N *>1529*
    effice. quis patitur sibi inputari ⟨communia⟩? *Agric. p. 271*
    effice. quis patitur ⟨uilia⟩ imputari? *Grut. p. 523* ('sed potius est ut credamus multa praecessisse has uoces')
    effice ⟨quod⟩ quis patitur sibi imputari *Haase*
    effice: quis patitur sibi inputari ⟨nimia⟩ *Mazzoli 1974, 62*
    effice: qui⟨uis⟩ patitur sibi imputari *Pré.*
    effice: quis ⟨non⟩ patitur sibi imputari *Alexander 1937, 55*

The point that S. makes here is perfectly plain, but the precise words he used cannot be reclaimed with certainty. Regarding the first sentence, Sjögren defended N's text on the ground that in Latin before the mid-first century BCE *qui* could function by itself as *si qui* or *si quis*. But it does not function that way in the Latin of S.'s day or in S.'s own Latin: *beneficium qui quibuslibet dat* demands that the person denoted by *qui* have a role somewhere in the main clause, typically as subject when the relative clause is fronted as it is here. That being the case, it is impossible to judge independently the issues raised by *qui* and *gratum est*. Retain N's *qui...dat*, and *est* cannot stand, hence Gertz's *dat* and Müller's *praestat*;[30] but as Buck rightly remarked, it is quite difficult to see how either *dat* or *praestat* became *est*. Retain *est* and something fairly invasive must be done in the relative clause: delete *qui* (as dittography before *quibuslibet*) and read *datum* for *dat*, with

---

[30] The *datum* that Pincianus found in one of his manuscripts is worse still.

Skutsch; read *quod* for *qui* and *datur* for *dat* (a medieval fix found in **M**, subsequently the print vulgate); or read ⟨*si*⟩ *qui* with Hosius. The last is least acceptable, since *si qui* (for *si quis*) is vanishingly rare in S.[31] Both of the other options imply a two-stage corruption, and I cannot see that either is obviously more likely than the other: both imply an error of anticipation before *quibuslibet*, and once that error was made, the second change—from *datur* or *datum* to *dat*—would quickly follow. I will print *beneficium {qui} quibuslibet datum nulli gratum est.*

As for the second problem, not even **N**'s foremost champions, Buck and Préchac, thought its text could be construed as satisfactory Latin; solutions have followed two main lines. Préchac (*quiuis patitur sibi imputari*) and Alexander (*quis non patitur sibi imputari*) take the subject of *imputari* to be understood from *quod uoles gratum esse, rarum effice*: but if the last clause is bound so tightly to what precedes—the equivalent in thought of *si quid gratum esse uoles, rarum efficies*—present indicative *patitur* is not what should follow. Alternatively, an express subject has been supplied for the infinitive *imputari*, in the form either of *quod* (Haase)—producing a sentence with relative clauses at its beginning and end, separated only by *rarum effice*—or a neuter plural adjective used substantively— *communia* (Agricola) or *uulgaria* (the print vulgate after Curio's edition of 1557) or *nimia* (Mazzoli). The first two are appropriately antithetical to *rarum*;[32] after *imput̲a̲r̲i̲, uul̲g̲aria* is the more promising candidate for omission. That being the case, and since here again there is nothing to be gained by multiplying candidates for the role of stop-gap, *uulgaria* is what I will print.

1. 14. 2 Licet ita largiri, ut unusquisque, etiam si cum multis accepit, in populo **se esse** non putet.

se esse Npc : esse Nac, esse se *Gertz*

The location of the correction in **N** cannot be assumed to be authoritative. It was made early enough to stand in the text taken over by **R**, but since the hand is not that of the scribe, it was not certainly derived from **N**'s exemplar; the lack is obvious and the remedy would not require a manuscript source.[33] Gertz preferred *esse se*, presumably on paleographical grounds: after *esse* the pronoun could be

---

[31] Only at Apoc. 7. 4 *si qui a me notorem petisset, te fui nominaturus, qui me optime nosti*, against more than one hundred instances of *si quis*. *si qui* has also been introduced by conjecture at *EM* 109. 8 '⟨Vt⟩ in summum' inquit 'perducto calorem calefieri superuacuum est, et in summum perducto bonum superuacuum est ⟨si⟩ qui prosit' (Bücheleer's proposal, accepted by Reynolds), where Schweighäuser's *superuacuus* (for the second *superuacuum*) would perhaps be a better choice.

[32] Of *nimia* Mazzoli wrote, 'il supplemento soddisfa pienamente il senso, creando più d'ogni altro precedente emendamento il dovuto contrasto con *rarum effice*'; but *nimium* is not an antonym of *rarum*, and the word seems to have been chosen for purely paleographical reasons, before *nemo*.

[33] Contrast, e.g., 3. 20. 1 *mens* [sc. *serui*]...*adeo libera...est ut ne ab hoc quidem carcere cui inclusa est teneri queat...*, where *cui*, initially omitted, was added above the line in the hand of the scribe.

lost through haplography as easily as it is elsewhere added through dittography.[34] S.'s practice gives no definitive guidance: when *se* is juxtaposed with *esse* as the subject, it immediately follows the infinitive seven times and immediately precedes it six times. If, therefore, the call could go either way, *esse se* is the better choice, both paleographically and because it produces a preferable rhythm (double cretic vs. trochee + cretic).

[34] e.g., *Pol.* 2. 1 *Eriperes illi amicos? Sciebas tam amabilem esse {se} ut facile in locum amissorum posset alios substituere?*

Notes to Book 2

2. 1. 1 Inspiciamus, Liberalis uirorum optime, id quod **ex priori** parte adhuc superest, quemadmodum dandum sit beneficium; cuius rei expeditissimam uideor monstraturus uiam: sic demus, quomodo uellemus accipere.

ex priori ψ : experiore Nac, ex priore Npc‡ (*def. Buck 1908, 49*)

R reproduced **N**'s corrected text, then transmitted it to the better medieval manuscripts (φ) and, ultimately, to the printed editions down to Vogel's text of 1830; *ex priori* originated in the more interpolated medieval branch of the paradosis and was put in the text by Fickert. That he did so is confounding, since it is otherwise clear that for S. *priori* is only the dative form (4. 37. 3, *EM* 81. 2, *Med.* 604), *priore* only the ablative (a dozen times, including 1. 1. 2 *in priore uersu*); it is equally confounding that *priori* was retained by Haase, Gertz, and Hosius.

2. 1. 2 Nam cum in beneficio iucundissima sit tribuentis uoluntas, quia nolentem se tribuisse ipsa cunctatione testatus est, non dedit sed aduersus ducentem male retinuit. Multi autem sunt, quos **liberales** facit **frontis** infirmitas

liberales ς₁ς₇ς₁₂ς₁₄ς₁₆ς₁₇‡ : liberalis N (liu- Nac; Liberalis *uocatiuum habet Buck 1908, 50, acc. pl. secundum cett.*), ante quod in add. ss. man. post.
frontis 1515‡ : fortes N (*def. Buck 1908, 50*), fortis ς₁ς₆ς₁₀ς₁₆ς₁₇ >1503, fors et *Radermacher 1891* (*in 'sententiis controuersis' ad fin.*), ⟨in⟩ fortes *Alexander 1937, 56* ('toward the persistent'), ⟨et⟩ ⟨uel ⟨ut⟩⟩ fortes facit *Mazzoli 1974, 62–3*

Critics have made heavy weather of this passage, including Buck's attempt to defend **N**'s text.[1] But S.'s point has been clear since the Basel edition of 1515 introduced *frontis* in place of *fortis* (so the earlier editions and some *recentiores*): a ready willingness (*uoluntas*) to grant a *beneficium* is the most important trait of a benefactor; 'however, there are many whom a sense of shame makes generous.' *frons* here denotes 'a person's brow regarded as expressing modesty or shyness or the lack of these' (*OLD* s.v. 3), and as the phrase *os durum* or *os ferreum* describes a shameless person—one incapable of blushing—*infirmitas frontis* is a trait of someone whose proper sense of shame makes him inclined to blush: compare,

---

[1] Reading *liberalis* as a vocative and taking the rest to mean 'there are many…whom weakness makes bold'. Griffin and Inwood, though generally very sensible in their approach to the text, accept Alexander's suggestion: 'In fact, many people become generous only because they are feeble in the face of determined requests' (⟨*in*⟩ *fortes*).

e.g., *Tranq.* 6. 2 *parum idonea est uerecundia rebus ciuilibus, quae firmam frontem desiderant*, Plin. *Ep.* 6. 29. 6 *nec uero Isocrati quo minus haberetur summus orator offecit quod… mollitia frontis ne in public diceret impediebatur*, Juv. 8. 189 *populi frons durior huius,* | *qui sedet et spectat triscurria patriciorum.*[2]

2. 2. 1 Molestum uerbum est, onerosum, demisso uultu dicendum, 'rogo'. Huius facienda est gratia amico **et quemcumque amicum** sis promerendo facturus; properet licet, sero beneficium dedit, qui roganti dedit.

et quemcumque *Siesbye ap. Gertz* : et cuicumque | quem N, et cui⟨uis⟩cumque quem *Pré.*, ei, utcumque, quem *Mazzoli 1977, 71–2*

Before Gertz accepted Siesbye's suggestion N's reading was the vulgate, even though no collocation like it (*quicumque quem, quocumque quem, cuiuscumque quem*) appears in classical Latin, because *quicumque* is itself a subordinating word. Préchac ('to anyone at all you wish') and Mazzoli ('in whatever circumstances') try hard, but S. uses no pronouns of the kind represented by *quiuis* + *-cumque*, and he uses *utcumque* almost exclusively as a subordinating conjunction, never as a quasi-parenthetical expression. N's text presumably arose when *quemcumque* was attracted into the dative after *amico*, with *quem* resulting from a botched superscript correction or just the insertion of the accusative that was obviously needed.

2. 4. 1 At plerique sunt qui beneficia asperitate uerborum et supercilio in odium adducunt, eo sermone usi, ea superbia, ut impetrasse paeniteat. Aliae deinde post rem promissam secuntur morae; nihil autem est acerbius quam **ubi quoque ⟨quod⟩** impetrasti rogandum est.

The variations that occur here are so numerous that they need to be presented in tabular form to be perspicuous:

quam <u>ubi quoque quod</u> impetrasti ς_{14} >*1503, prob. Grut. p. 525, 1649‡, Gron. p. 125* : quam <u>ubi quoque</u> impetrasti N

   quam <u>ubi</u> impetrasti QMpc
   quam <u>ubi quoque postquam</u> impetrasti JV
   quam <u>ubicumque quod</u> impetrasti ς_2
   quam <u>ubi quod</u> impetrasti $\varsigma_5\varsigma_7\varsigma_{17}\varsigma_{19}$, *1529–1585*
   quam <u>ubi qu(a)e</u> impetrasti $\varsigma_8\varsigma_{15}$
   quam <u>ubi quid</u> impetrasti $\varsigma_9\varsigma_{16}$, *cod. Pinc.*[3]

---

[2] Cf. 7. 28. 3 (on the way to treat an imperfectly *gratus* person) *Meliorem illum facies ferendo, utique peiorem exprobrando: non est quod frontem eius indures; sine si quid est pudoris residui seruet* (with the discussion of the passage in Chapter 7; further examples are gathered at Kaster 2005, 162 n. 18); with *frontis infirmitas* here compare the *tenera frons* said to be characteristic of *iuuenes* at *EM* 11. 3.

[3] This is presumably what was intended in *1515*, but a typographical error produced *quamque ubi quid impetrasti*.

quam <u>ubi quidquid</u> impetrasti ς_{12}, *Buck 1908, 50*
quam <u>ubi quoque cum</u> impetrasti *1605*
quam <u>ubi id quoque quod</u> impetrasti $\varsigma_3$pc, *Madvig 1871–84, 2:408, Gertz*
quom <u>ubi quoque</u> impetrasti *Festa 1900, 431*
quam <u>ubi quamquam</u> impetrasti *Gundermann ap. Buck 1908, 50*
quam <u>ubi quoque</u> impetrasti, rogandum esse *Pré.* (*resp. Alexander 1950–2, 8*)

We can begin by eliminating every version in which *ubi quoque* appears: when
S. uses the adverb *quoque* ('even', 'also' / 'too')—more than 650 times—it invariably
(and unsurprisingly) throws its force on the word that precedes, and that word
is never one with a subordinating function; in fact (and again unsurprisingly),
the collocation *ubi quoque* occurs nowhere in classical Latin. In the versions
that remain,

quam <u>ubi</u> impetrasti QMpc
quam <u>ubicumque quod</u> impetrasti ς_2
quam <u>ubi quod</u> impetrasti $\varsigma_5\varsigma_7\varsigma_{17}\varsigma_{19}$, *1529–1585*
quam <u>ubi qu(a)e</u> impetrasti $\varsigma_8\varsigma_{15}$
quam <u>ubi quid</u> impetrasti $\varsigma_9\varsigma_{16}$, *cod. Pinc.*
quam <u>ubi quidquid</u> impetrasti ς_{12}, *Buck 1908, 50*
quam <u>ubi id quoque quod</u> impetrasti $\varsigma_3$pc, *Madvig 1871–84, 2:408, Gertz*
quam <u>ubi quamquam</u> impetrasti *Gundermann ap. Buck 1908, 50,*

the most common unifying element is the replacement of *quoque* with a direct
object for *impetrasti*—*quod* or *quae* or *quid* or *quidquid*—and though S. does
use the verb absolutely at the end of the preceding sentence (cf. *OLD* s.v. 1c),
such a replacement is more likely than not correct.[4] But *quid* or *quae* is impossible and *quidquid* far-removed from the *ductus literarum*;[5] that being the
case, it is most economical to suppose that *quod* became *quoque* and accept
the version found in several *recentiores* and first printed by Erasmus. That is
what I too will print, though I will also note *quodcumque* as a possibility in the
apparatus.

2. 5. 2 Quare uerissimum existima quod ille comicus dixit:

Quid? tu non intellegis
tantum te gratiae demere quantum morae adicis?

---

[4] With intransitive *impetrasti*, the best choice would be Gundermann's *quamquam*, since the
ancient abbreviation for *quoque* (*qq* with abbreviation stroke above) was sometimes also used for
quamquam, and confusion was probably not uncommon: Lindsay 1915, 269. It is impossible to judge
how likely it is that S. also used *rogandum* intransitively ('a / the request must be made'), since the
neuter singular gerundive occurs only here in his corpus.

[5] *quid* is impossible, not because S. unfailingly uses the subjunctive in indirect questions (he does not),
but because *ubi quid impetrasti rogandum est* would mean, 'When you must ask, "What have you gained?"'

Inde illae uoces quas ingenuus dolor exprimit, 'Fac, si quid facis' et 'Nihil tanti est, malo mihi iam neges'.

tantum te gratiae demere N : demere tantum te gratiae *Gertz*

Lipsius was the first editor to present the words of the *comicus* as verse, leaving the printed line blank after *intelligis* (c.5–6 letter-spaces) and printing *tantum…adicis* together at the start of the next line; and in that arrangement he has been followed, incorrectly, by every editor save Gertz. The problem is this: whereas the first four words can be read as either the last three and a half feet of an iambic senarius (*Quid?* | *tu non* | *intel*|*legis*) or the last four feet of a trochaic septenarius (*quid? tu* | *non in*|*telle*|*gis*), the remaining words, as transmitted, conform to neither pattern. Friedrich Leo made them iambic by replacing *demere* with *adimere* and transposing the infinitive to precede *gratiae*:[6]

…tantum | te adi|mere gra|tiae | quantum | morae
adicis?

Otto Ribbeck (*SRPF*[3] 2:149 fr. 71) created a different iambic version by inserting a supplemental *beneficiis* and transposing both *te* and *gratiae*:

…⟨benefici|is⟩ tan|tum gra|tiae | te de|mere
adicis?,

and he suggested a trochaic version in his apparatus by again transposing *te* and *gratiae* and transferring *adicis* to the middle of the line:

…tantum | grati|ae te | demere |ad(i)i|cis quan|tum mo|rae?

Gertz's solution, requiring only the transposition of *demere*, is both more economical than any of these and elegantly juxtaposes the contrasting verbs at the start of successive lines:

Quid? | tu non | intel|legis
demere | tantum | te gra|tiae | quantum | morae
adicis.

That is the version I will print.

2. 5. 3 Vbi in taedium adductus animus incipit beneficium odisse, dum expectat, potest ob id **gratus esse?** Quemadmodum acerbissima crudelitas est, quae trahit poenam, et misericordiae genus est cito occidere quia tormentum ultimum finem sui secum adfert, quod antecedit tempus, maxima uenturi supplicii pars est, ita

---

[6] Leo 1895, 327 n. 1.

maior est muneris gratia, quo minus diu pependit. **Est enim etiam bonarum rerum sollicita expectatio,** et cum plurima beneficia remedium alicuius rei adferant, qui aut diutius torqueri patitur, quem protinus potest liberare, aut tardius gaudere, beneficio suo manus adfert.

gratus esse Npc* (esse *ss. man. post.*), γ >*1503* : gratuse|uaest Nac (gratus eua e(st) C, -tu seua est RQac)

> gratus ei iam esse π (ei gratus iam esse Qpc)
> ei grauissimum esse M
> ingratus esse *1515, 1529* (*post* potes ob id), *1585, 1605* (*post* potest ob id, *cf. Mur., Lips.*), 'hic musso' *Grut. p. 525*
> gratus esse? ⟨ita est:⟩ *Gertz*
> gratus re uera esse *Hos. in app.* (*Pré.*)
> gratus quaeri *Gundermann ap. Buck 1908, 50*
> gratus euadere *dub. Buck ibid.*
> gratus etiam esse *Shackleton Bailey 1970, 361*
> gratum seruare se? *Mazzoli 1974, 64–5*

etiam bonarum N : bonarum >*1515*, et bonarum ς5, bonarum etiam *1529*‡

sollicita Npc* (ł a *ss. man. post.*) : sollicitis Nac (*def. Pasoli 1953, 270–1*), sollicitis expectatio ⟨grauis⟩ *Pinc.*, sollici⟨ta quid salu⟩tis *Pré.*, sollicitis⟨sima⟩ *Alexander 1937, 56*, ⟨sollicita animis⟩ sollicitis *Mazzoli 1974, 65–6*

S.'s theme in 2. 5 is the importance of promptness in responding to requests for *beneficia*: in the first sentence here, he stresses that long delay causes the favour to be despised and makes it impossible for the recipient to feel gratitude. That much is clear, but N's scribe created something of a mess in passing the thought along, writing *gratuse* at the end of one line, *uaest* at the beginning of the next: the stray *-e* at line-end was erased, and *e* was added at the start of the next (*gratus | euaest*), though it is unclear what the person who made the addition thought he was accomplishing. Be that as it may, what **R** took away from the scene was *obidgratu seuaest*, which is roughly replicated in two later manuscripts that generally have less interpolated texts, **C** and **Q**. The two manuscript families with more interpolated texts reflect attempts to dispose of the nonsense that is *euaest*, one (γ) simply by replacing those characters with *esse* (also written above *euaest* by a late correcting hand in **N**), the other (π) by adding to *esse* the superfluous *ei iam* (presumably, *eua > eiia*).[7] *gratus esse*, which certainly makes sense, became the text of the first printed editions. But if that is what S. wrote, how do we explain *gratuseuaest*?

Gertz's *gratus esse?* ⟨*ita est*⟩ was the first serious attempt to answer that question, and I believe it remains preferable to the suggestions—by Hosius, Gundermann, Buck, Shackleton Bailey, and Mazzoli—that have since been

---

[7] **M**, which generally keeps company with **Q**, here reflects a more elaborate effort: *potest ob id ei grauissimum esse.*

made.[8] First, the origin of Gertz's reading can be better understood if it is written as *gratus e⟨sse⟩? ita est*. The last two words represent a characteristically Senecan gesture: thus,

2. 29. 6 Ita est: carissimos nos habuerunt di inmortales habentque, et, qui maximus tribui honos potuit, ab ipsis proximos conlocauerunt;

Marc. 23. 5 Ita est: indicium imminentis exitii nimia maturitas est;

Brev. 10. 1. 4 Ita est: non accipimus breuem uitam sed facimus nec inopes eius sed prodigi sumus;

Pol. 1. 1 Ita est: nihil perpetuum, pauca diuturna sunt; aliud alio modo fragile est, rerum exitus uariantur, ceterum quidquid coepit et desinet;

EM 5. 7 Ita est, mi Lucili: cum uideantur dissidere, coniuncta sunt,

and eleven other instances. *ita est* became *uaest* after the omission or obliteration of t's crossbar left two adjacent minims (it > u).[9]

As for *gratus e⟨sse⟩*, I take it that the scribe began to write *esse* after *gratus* at the end of the line (*gratuse*) and neglected to complete it at the start of the next: if that seems improbable, consider *Clem.* 1. 24. 2 *generosi ac nobiles equi melius facili freno reguntur*, where **N**'s scribe wrote *generosi ac no* at the end of one line and continued with *equi melius* at the start of the next (*nobiles* is one of the very few non-trivial corrections of **N**'s text that we owe to **R**). At the very least, *Vbi in taedium adductus animus incipit beneficium odisse, dum expectat, potest ob id gratus e⟨sse⟩? Ita est: quemadmodum acerbissima crudelitas est…*provides a very satisfying stop-gap where the train of thought is uncontroversial.

In the final sentence, the late correction in **N**, *sollicita*, provides appropriate sense ('Anticipation even of even favourable circumstances causes anxiety'), though it is unclear how or why *sollicitis* came to be. Critical responses have taken two paths. Pasoli defended *sollicitis*, on the ground that it could be construed either with *bonarum rerum* (on the model of *Marc.* 19. 6 *non sollicitus futuri pendet*: the deceased 'does not hang suspended, anxious over what is to come') or absolutely: but neither of these alternatives—respectively, 'Those anxious over even favourable circumstances experience anticipation' and 'Anxious people experience anticipation even of favourable circumstances'—produces a thought with the emphasis falling where it should. Other responses acknowledge that *sollicitis* cannot be sound as it stands but attempt to salvage it by positing textual loss of one sort or another. The proposals of Préchac—*Est enim etiam bonarum rerum sollici⟨ta, quid salu⟩tis expectatio*—and Alexander—*Est enim etiam bonarum rerum sollicitis⟨sima⟩ expectatio*—do not produce appropriate sense: I do not see how the former derives the translation he provides—'En effet, l'attente, même d'un bien (à plus fort raison de notre salut), ne va pas sans un vif émoi'—from the

---

[8] All but Shackleton Bailey's stray too far from the traces in **N**; as for *gratus etiam esse, etiam* is regularly prospective in S. (*etiam gratus* esse), who never writes *etiam esse*.

[9] Cf. 3. 38. 2 and 6. 1 *ingenii* Npc, initially *ingenti*, 5. 11. 4 *aliquis ut* Npc, initially *aliquisui*; cf. also 2. 11. 1 *fortune* Npc (i.e., -*nae*), initially *fortuite*.

Latin he proposes, while the statement that 'the anticipation of even favourable circumstances is extremely anxiety-provoking' is just odd as an assertion about human psychology. Mazzoli's supplement—*Est enim etiam bonarum rerum* ⟨*sollicita animis*⟩ *sollicitis expectatio* (better represented as *sollici*⟨*ta animis sollici*⟩*tis*)—produces a kind of sense—'Anticipation even of favourable circumstances is anxiety-producing for anxious souls'—but is pointlessly redundant. Only Pincianus' suggestion—*Est enim etiam bonarum rerum sollicitis expectatio gravis* ('Anticipation even of favourable circumstances is grievous for the anxious')—is worthy of consideration; but then it is no more evident why *gravis* would be omitted in this context than why *sollicita* would become *sollicitis*. That being the case I will print *sollicita*, because it involves the smaller alteration, and—more important—because in the context of 2. 5 S.'s observation must concern the way human beings in general—not just 'the anxious'—experience anticipation.

2. 10. 1 Interdum etiam ipse, qui iuuatur, fallendus est, ut habeat nec, a quo acceperit, **sciat. Arcesilan aiunt** amico pauperi et paupertatem suam dissimulanti, aegro autem et ne hoc quidem confitenti deesse sibi in sumptum ad necessarios **usus, clam succurrendum iudicasse**; puluino eius **ignorantis** sacculum subiecit, ut homo inutiliter uerecundus, quod desiderabat, inueniret potius quam acciperet.

sciat Npc : *om.* Nac (*Pré.*)
Arcesilan Npc (-lam Nac arche- Npc) *Gertz* : Arc(h)esilaus ut aiunt *Vinc. Bell., Spec. Doct.* 4. 50 ς₁ς₁₄‡, Archesilaus aiunt ς₆
usus, clam N : usus cum clam ψ, *Vinc. Bell.*
iudicasse QpcHM : iudicassit Nac, iudicasset Npc1‡, iudicauit et Npc2*
ignorantis H *Vinc. Bell., Pinc., 1557*‡ : -ti N >*1529*

Arcesilan aiunt...iudicasse is the centre of interest, though it is worth noting that the passage also includes two necessary post-archetypal corrections. *sciat* was inserted in **N** by a hand later than the scribe's but early enough for it to have been captured by **R**, and among editors only Préchac has doubted that S. must have written, if not *sciat*, then some verb very much like it. Near the end of the passage, *ignorantis* lost its *-s* before *sacculum*: we find the loss first made good in one of the twelfth-century manuscripts and in the influential version of the passage quoted (or paraphrased) in Vincent of Beauvais's *Speculum Doctrinale*, to which we can now turn.

In the crux that is the passage's centrepiece, it is plain that the archetype's text, which originally read *iudicassit*, cannot stand, and that all other decisions depend on what one decides to do about that verb. If you examine **N** now, you see that *ss* has been erased, *it* has been converted to *et* in the usual way (a tiny loop added at the top of the *i*), and superscript *auit* stands in the space above the erasure: *iudicauit et*. But we can be sure that that correction was not made all at one go—that the mechanical 'correction' of *iudicassit* to *iudicasset* preceded the change to *iudicauit et*—because *iudicasset* is the reading that **R** took over and passed to the later manuscripts, causing it to become the starting point of the version first attested by Vincent of Beauvais—*Arcesilaus, ut aiunt,...cum...iudicasset*—which in turn became the text of all editions before Gertz's. It is a very unattractive form of words, because the injection of *cum* causes *amico pauperi* and *succurrendum* to occupy different levels of syntax, when they should stand in the same clause.[10] It is also a form of words that is achieved by very uneconomical means, since acceptance of *iudicasset* demands three changes in the archetype's text (*Arcesilan* > *-las, aiunt* > *ut aiunt, clam* > *cum clam*; *iudicauit et* requires the first two). In contrast, *Arcesilan aiunt...iudicasse* implies merely that the infinitive gained an unwanted *t* (*iudicasset*), which in the archetype's version became *iudicassit* through one of **N**'s countless confusions of *e* and *i*. The opening phrase, *Arcesilan aiunt*, also represents one of S.'s favourite ways of introducing a historical *exemplum*: cf. 6. 37. 1 *Callistratum aiunt...*, Ira 2. 2. 6 *Alexandrum aiunt...*, 2. 5. 4 *Hannibalem aiunt...*, 2. 10. 5 *Democritum contra aiunt...*, 2. 25. 2 *Mindyriden aiunt...*, 3. 11. 2 *Socraten aiunt...*(*EM* 10. 1 *Crates ut aiunt...*is unique). As Gertz remarked, the sudden change from indirect (*Arcesilan...iudicasse*) to direct speech (*subiecit*) is common in S. (p. 202, with examples).

2. 10. 2 Contentus eris te teste, **alioqui non** bene facere delectat sed uideri bene fecisse.

alioqui non *Gertz* : alioquin Nac, -quin non Npc

Anonymous benefaction is still the theme, and only a small textual point is at issue. The *non* originally missing from **N**'s text is plainly needed, and Gertz was probably correct to prefer *alioqui non* to *alioquin non*, the corrected text in **N** (superscript *ñ*) that had previously been the vulgate. According to **N**, S. wrote *alioqui* eight other times in *De beneficiis* and twice more in *De clementia*, against three occurrences of *alioquin*. It would be wrong to suppose arbitrarily that S. never varied his practice; on the other hand, the fact that in two of those three occurrences *alioquin* is followed by *nullum* (2. 12. 1) and *nobis* (4. 13. 2) is unlikely to be a matter of sheer coincidence.[11] I will print *alioqui* here and in those three other places, encouraged by the fact that the record of the other *philosophica* at least suggests that the line of reasoning followed here is not obviously wrong: in *Dial.* and *EM* Reynolds generally printed *alioqui* whenever the manuscripts

---

[10] One might suspect that this inconcinnity inspired the correction *iudicauit et*, save that the person who produced that reading in **N** evidently did not notice the problem posed by *Arcesilan aiunt*. That *amico* must be construed with *succurrendum*, and cannot depend on *subiecit*, is made obvious by *puluino eius* before the latter.

[11] The third occurrence is 4. 35. 2 *alioquin quidquid*. At 5. 10. 1 Gruter, who took more thorough account of **N**'s text than any critic before Gertz, was certainly correct to prefer *alioqui* to *aliqui*, **N**'s nonsensical reading before correction, and to *aliquid*, the merely specious corrected reading.

presented it, nine times in the former (*alioquin* once) and sixteen times in the latter (*alioquin* eleven times); but in eleven of the sixteen places where the earliest manuscripts of *EM* (esp. pVP, s. IX) read *alioqui, alioquin* either was introduced by correction in the earliest manuscripts or is the reading of the later manuscripts, or both, whereas the opposite change never occurs;[12] and this seemingly marked tendency to normalize in the direction of *alioquin* appears to be confirmed by the primary witnesses to the text of *NQ*, none of which is older than the twelfth century, and all of which read only *alioquin* (six times).[13]

2. 11. 2 Ne aliis quidem narrare debemus; qui dedit beneficium, taceat, narret, qui accepit. Dicetur enim, quod **illi** ubique iactanti beneficium suum: 'Non nega-bis' inquit 'te recepisse'; et cum respondisset: 'Quando?' 'Saepe quidem' inquit 'et multis locis, id est, quotiens et ubicumque narrasti.'

illi Npc : ille Nac

Do we want *illi*, pointing ahead two words to *iactanti*, or *ille*, pointing to 'that fellow', the anonymous figure whose *mot* is about to be quoted (*inquit*). Gertz chose the latter, Hosius reverted to *illi*, the vulgate text before Gertz, and Préchac—who embraced **N**'s original text whenever possible (and often when it was not)—chose *ille*. Gertz was almost certainly right: insofar as the demonstrative serves as a spotlight, the spotlight belongs not on the boastful benefactor but on the speaker who reproves him. The pattern is the same as that found a few sentences earlier, 2. 11. 1: <u>*Libet exclamare quod ille*</u> *triumuirali proscriptione seruatus a quodam Caesaris amico* <u>*exclamauit*</u> *cum superbiam eius ferre non posset:* '*Redde me Caesari!*'; *illi* was introduced by a reader who did not see the pattern but allowed himself to be seduced by *iactanti*. S. often uses what might be called the '*ille* of the anonymous other' when he finds it useful to introduce such a figure to make a point: e.g., 1. 14. 3 *'Accepi idem quod ille, sed ultro. Accepi quod ille, sed ego intra breue tempus, cum ille diu meruisset'*, 6. 9. 1 *Nempe, ut gratus sim, uelle debeo idem facere quod ille, ut beneficium daret, debuit.*

2. 11. 5 Numquid ulla maiora possunt esse quam quae in liberos patres con-ferunt? haec tamen inrita **sunt**, si in infantia **deserantur**, nisi longa pietas munus suum nutrit.

sunt N : sint *Madvig 1871–84, 2:409* | deserantur N : -runtur Gertz

---

[12]   See Reynolds's *apparatus* at *EM* 22. 8, 49. 3, 66. 23, 68. 4, 71. 14, 24, 36, 77. 7, 82. 19, 84. 7, 85. 34. At 19. 11, where most manuscripts have the *alioquin* printed by Reynolds, he might have done better to print the *alioqui* that is the original reading of p (s. IX$^{3/4}$), 'a remarkable manuscript with a very primitive text, sometimes right where all the other witnesses are wrong' (Reynolds 1983, 370).

[13]   Strictly, at *NQ* 4a. 2. 28 the most reliable manuscript, **Z**, reads *alioquim*, against the *aliquando* of **PR**, which became the vulgate; Madvig conjectured *alioquin*, which was also entered as a correction in **W** by a reader who drew on a source cognate with **Z** (it later appears in the humanist manuscripts **UW**).

I can see no rationale for maintaining a mixed condition, much less for accepting subjunctive in the *si*-clause and indicative in the *nisi*-clause, when the two parallel protases modify the main clause independently: remove either, and the condition remains intact. I will print Gertz's *deseruntur*, which implies only a trivial confusion; and as Gertz remarked (p. 203), 'coniunctiuum in uno uerbo mutare mallem quam indicatiuum in duobus'.

2. 12. 1 C. Caesar dedit uitam Pompeio **Penno**, si dat qui non aufert; deinde absoluto et agenti gratias porrexit osculandum sinistrum pedem.

Penno *Lipsius 1585, 68, 1585‡* : poeno N, *1492–1557*, paeno MGF, peno Bψ *>1490*

A distinguished man (*consularis*, according to S.: see the next passage discussed), this Pompeius is usually identified with the Pompeius also mentioned (without cognomen) in connection with Caligula at *Tranq.* 11. 10 (cf. *PIR*[2] P. 636): the latter passage refers to his imprisonment in the imperial palace, where he is ultimately starved to death; in the present episode he is on trial for his life (§12. 2 *de capite consularis uiri soccatus audiebat* [sc. *Gaius*]). In the archetype his cognomen is *Poenus*; Lipsius' conjecture, *Pennus*, has been the vulgate since Muretus' edition. Both names are quite rare: the latter is *prima facie* more likely, since it is attested as a cognomen of members of the socio-political elite of the early and middle Republic (respectively, T. Quinctius Pennus Cincinnatus cos. 431, T. Quinctius Pennus Capitolinus Crispinus cos. 354; M. Iunius Pennus pr. 201, M. Iunius Pennus cos. 167, M. Iunius Pennus tr. pl. 126, aed. [?] 119); the former appears only on scattered provincial inscriptions (e.g., *CIL* 2. 2242 [Corduba], 5. 7108 [Augusta Taurinorum], 7797 [Pamparato]). It is also clear that *Pennus* was exceptionally liable to corruption: when the cognomen of the consular Quinctii appears in the manuscripts of Livy and the consular *fasti* (and thence in *MRR* 1), it is given as *Poenus*, an error that Broughton corrected in his supplement (*MRR* 3:178); the praetor of 201 is *Penus* in all the manuscripts of Livy 29. 11. 12 and in one of them at 30. 40. 5; and the tribune of 126 appears as *P. Enni* in the codex Farnesianus of Festus (362. 35 L.). Only in the manuscripts of Cicero (*Brut.* 109, *Off.* 3. 47) does the name appear to escape entirely unscathed.[14]

2. 12. 2 Homo [sc. C. Caesar] natus in hoc, ut mores liberae ciuitatis Persica seruitute mutaret, parum iudicauit si senator [sc. Pompeius Pennus], senex, summis usus honoribus in conspectu principum supplex sibi eo more iacuisset quo hostes uicti hostibus iacuere: inuenit aliquid infra genua quo libertatem detruderet.…Parum enim foede furioseque insolens fuerat qui de capite consularis uiri soccatus audiebat, nisi in os senatoris ingessisset imperator **epigros** suos.

---

[14] I owe thanks to John D. Morgan for invaluable help as I was writing this note.

epigros *Scaliger ap. Gron. p. 128* : pigros N, *obel. Gertz*, pictos soccos *Pinc.*, 'expecto *crepidas*' *Hos. in app.*, epiuros *Weise 1882, 640*

The story of Pompeius ends as it began, with the emperor sticking his foot in the man's face to be kissed, though the idea is expressed much more clearly at the beginning (*porrexit osculandum sinistrum pedem*) than it is here, where **N**'s *in os...ingessisset...pigros suos* is unintelligible. The correction that has found most favour since the mid-seventeenth century is Scaliger's *epigros*, an unattested Greek word taken to be formed from ἐπίουρος ('wooden peg'), as ἀνιγρός is formed from ἀνιαρός, 'troublesome' (so Gronovius' argument); if wooden pegs were what is wanted, however, one might as well read *epiuros* (as Weise argued), which is tolerably close to *pigros* and actually attested in later Latin (Pallad. 12. 7. 15, August. *CD* 15. 27. 3, Isid. *Or.* 19. 19. 7, cf. *TLL* 5. 694. 77–695. 20). But are wooden pegs what we are looking for? S. emphasizes more than once that Caligula's footwear was part of the scene's indecency, for he was *soccatus*, dressed in the soft slippers (*socci*) worn by comic actors, though in Caligula's case they were gilded and decorated with pearls (2. 12. 1 *socculum auratum, immo aureum, margaritis distinctum*). It is difficult to see how wooden pegs would complete the ensemble; and given the stress S. lays on the *socci*, it is hardly plausible or coherent to suppose that S. alludes to the hobnailed military footwear from which Caligula's nickname was derived.[15] I join Gertz in throwing up my hands and obelizing *pigros*.

2. 13. 1 O superbia, magnae fortunae stultissimum malum, ut a te nihil accipere iuuat! ut omne beneficium in iniuriam **conuertis! ut te omnia nimia delectant! ut te omnia dedecent!** quoque altius te subleuasti, hoc depressior es **ostendisque tibi non ⟨datum⟩ adgnoscere ista bona**, quibus tantum inflaris; quidquid das, corrumpis.

conuertis, ut te omnia nimia delectant, ut te omnia dedecent ς₃ς₅‡ (*Hos. 2* 'dub. addidi ex **V** [= ς₅]'; *resp. Buck 1908, 51, Georgii 1929, 112*) : conuertis! ut te omnia dedecent N

    conuertis, ut te omnia nimia delectant ς₄

    conuertis, ut te omnia nimia conuertant, ut te omnia dedecent ς₂

    uertis quod te omnia dedecent ς₈pcς₁₅ (decent ς₈ac)

    uertis ut te omnia dedecent ς₇

    conuertis te omnia decent ς₉

tibi non datum agnoscere *Haase* (*post quod* tibi non datum dignoscere *Madvig ap. Gertz p. 204*): tibi non adagnoscere Nac (*Pré.*)

    tibi non agnoscere Npc >*1503*

    quo tibi non agnoscere ς₄

    te non agnoscere ς₅ς₆ς₁₁ς₁₇, *1515*‡

    haeret *Grut. p. 527* ('mihi hic non favet cortina Apollinis'), tibi non adaugescere *Gertz p. 204*

---

[15] So apparently Préchac ('les clous de sa semelle'), expressly Griffin and Inwood 194, Griffin 2013, 193.

tibi non adesse agn- *Kruczkiewicz 1877, 433*
te non ⟨satis⟩ agnoscere *Hos. 1 in app.*
tibi non adeo ignoscere *Gundermann ap. Buck 1908, 52*
tibi non ad⟨apertum⟩ ['revealed'] agnoscere *Alexander 1937, 56*
te ibi non adcognoscere *Mazzoli 1974, 66-7*

At the first *locus* a virtual blizzard of innovations arose in the *recentiores*, none of them worthy of consideration, though one of them did prove to be consequential: in the version found in ς₄, *dedecent* was displaced by *delectant*, prompting the addition of *nimia* to improve the sense; this version in turn was blended with the transmitted text to produce *ut te omnia nimia delectant, ut te omnia dedecent*, found in ς₃ and ς₅ and thereafter in all the printed editions down through Haase's.[16] The interpolated clause was ejected by Gertz, the first editor with full knowledge of **N**:[17] Hosius followed him in his own first edition but unaccountably reintroduced the clause in his second.

The more serious difficulty here lies in the second *locus*. Gertz obelized **N**'s *adagnoscere*, but that form seems merely to be a stutter for *agnoscere* or *adgno-*;[18] *tibi* is another matter. Apart from the earliest printed editions and Préchac's, which simply retained **N**'s impossible text, and apart from Gruter, who despaired, editors and critics who would retain *tibi* must either introduce some supplement (Haase and Madvig, Kruczkiewicz, Alexander) or change the infinitive (Gertz, Gundermann): of these, Haase's solution is the cleanest, though like the other supplements it does not imply an obvious *ratio corruptelae*. But why retain *tibi*, instead of supposing that after *ostendis*, a verb that so often takes the dative, some daydreaming scribe wrote *tibi* instead of *te*? (Granted, reading a couple of words farther along would show that *tibi* cannot serve, but reading a couple of words farther along is exactly what daydreaming scribes do not do.) Mazzoli's *te ibi* is mechanical and unconvincing, and Hosius' proposed addition of *satis* is otiose: I will print *te non agnoscere*, the reading found among the *recentiores* that became the print vulgate until awareness of **N** introduced the problem of *tibi*.[19]

2. 13. 2 Iucunda sunt quae humana fronte, certe leni placidaque tribuuntur, quae cum daret mihi superior non exultauit supra me sed quam potuit benignissimus

---

[16] ς₂ shares the text of ς₃ and ς₅ but with an error of perseveration that caused *delectant* to become *conuertant*.

[17] The clause was previously suspected by Fickert, aware that it was lacking in several manuscripts he knew.

[18] **N** generally represents S. as using *agno-* (eight times elsewhere, *adgno-* at 3. 32. 5); Hosius imposed *adgno-* throughout, but I will allow the variation. On the forms cf. *TLL* 1. 1354. 31–47, remarking, 'in codd. saepius *agnosco* quam *adgnosco* (sed hoc frequenter in Vergili codd. vetustis)'.

[19] Or 'reintroduced': Gruter remarked **N**'s reading in his note ad loc. before registering his despair; from Gruter's comment Fickert reported **N**'s reading in his own note, adding, 'quid uitii hic lateat adhuc, non perspicio', which in turn prompted Haase to suggest *tibi non datum*.

fuit descenditque in aequum et detraxit muneri suo pompam, **si obseruauit** idoneum tempus ut in occasione potius quam in necessitate succurreret.

si obseruauit N >*1503* : obseruauit ς_{15} >*1515‡*, sed ob- ς_1 *Grut. p. 527*, sic ob- *Ruh.*

N's *si* is problematic: choosing a suitable moment for bestowing a benefit is not logically subordinate to avoiding a show of arrogance (or conversely, avoiding a show of arrogance is not conditioned on the choice of a suitable moment); they are rather distinct and co-equal dimensions of a tactful benefactor's behaviour. I think it likely that *f;* (= *sed*) was here miscopied as *ſi:*[20] *sed quam potuit benignissimus fuit…, sed oberuauit idoneum tempus* is the sort of asyndetic parallelism of which S. is very fond.

2. 14. 2 Vt frigidam aegris negamus et lugentibus ac sibi iratis ferrum, ut amentibus quidquid contra se usurus ardor petit, sic **omnium**, quae nocitura sunt, impense ac submisse, non numquam etiam miserabiliter rogantibus perseuerabimus non dare.

amentibus *Haupt 1875–6, 2:274* : amantibus N
usurus MU : usuros N >*1503*
omnium N >*1503* : omnia $\varsigma_4\varsigma_{10}\varsigma_{15}\varsigma_{19}$, ea ς_3, *1515‡*, omnino Gertz (*Pré.*), omnibus *Skutsch ap. Hos.*

To illustrate the principle that is this chapter's subject—2. 14. 1 *Sunt quaedam nocitura impetrantibus quae non dare sed negare beneficium est*—S. introduces three specific categories of persons to whom potentially harmful things should be denied: cold water, for the physically ill; a weapon, for 'people filled with grief and self-loathing' (Griffin and Inwood); and for the insane (accepting Haupt's *amentibus*), whatever their agitation might turn against them. He then concludes with a generalization introduced by some word with the root *omni-*; but the form supplied by **N**, *omnium*, is so lacking in construction—every bit as lacking as **N**'s *usuros* in the previous clause—that even Préchac abandoned it. Among the candidates for replacement, Gertz's *omnino* is attractive and the *omnia* of some *recentiores* is perhaps the most obvious, creating a parallel with the foregoing *quidquid*. But that parallel is a distraction, for anaphoric *ut…ut…* guarantees that *quidquid…petit* is the object of *negamus*, understood from the previous clause: *sic* prepares the way for a new predicate, *perseuerabimus non dare*, and the parallel that serves to tie the sentence together is provided by Skutsch's *omnibus*, looking back to *aegris…lugentibus ac sibi iratis…amentibus* and ahead to *rogantibus*: 'so to all who request…things that would be harmful we will persist in not giving (them).'

---

[20] For apparent instances of the reverse error, see the discussions of 5. 5. 4 and 7. 19. 8.

2. 14. 5 Siue illum ira quo non debebit impellet siue ambitionis calor abducet a tutis, **in nullum malum uires a ⟨me⟩ sumere ipsas patiar** nec committam ut possit quandoque dicere, 'Ille amando me occidit'.

in nullum malum uires a ⟨me⟩ sumere ipsas patiar *Hos.* : sin nullum malum uires a se|med (-met Npc1) ipsa patiar Nac[21]

si nullo modo potero ad se ipsum reuocare, patiar Npc2* (*ss. man. post.*)
si nullum malum uires a semet ipsa patiar $\varsigma_{15}\varsigma_{16}$ac(ipso pc)$\varsigma_{19}$
sin nullum malum a semet ipso uires sibi conferri patiar ς_5
non a semet ipso uires sibi inferri patiatur $\varsigma_1\varsigma_{14}$ >*1503*[22]
om. 1515–1605 ('quid de his sentiam tunc aperibo, cum apparuerit mihi in somnis diuinus ille Apollo' *Grut. p. 528*)
in ullum malum uirus a semet ipso pati patiar $\varsigma_{11}\varsigma_{18}$
non a semet ipso uim sibi inferri patiar *cod. Pinc.*, *1649‡*
in nullum malum uires nisi a semet ipso ⟨peti⟩ patiar *Madvig 1871–84, 2:409–10*
in nullum malum uires adsumet nisi a semet ipso *Gertz* (*prob. Alexander 1950–2, 10*)
in nullum malum uires a me ⟨peti⟩ patiar *Kronenberg 1923, 46*
in nullum malum uires ⟨asserere sibi nisi⟩ a semet ipso patiar *Pré.*
in nullum malum uires ⟨a me esse, sed⟩ a semet ipsas patiar *Mazzoli 1974, 67–8*

This is among the most troubled passages in the work; in the small sea of variations it has inspired, perhaps the most eloquent is the one first found in Basel 1515, where the text leaps gracefully from *a tutis* to *non committam*. One sympathizes with the impulse, but the nettle must be grasped.

A quick triage can be performed by eliminating versions that I believe have no chance of being correct: beyond the bold omission of the clause, these include versions that begin with *si* or *sin* (after *siue…siue* another protasis is not wanted, and *nec committam* shows that the preceding clause was part of the apodosis; **N**'s *sin* resulted from dittography after *tutis*) and those that omit *in nullum malum uires*, words that are wholly in line with the thought being developed and that offer no reason for doubt. That leaves:

in nullum malum uires a ⟨me⟩ sumere ipsas patiar *Hos.*
in nullum malum uires nisi a semet ipso ⟨peti⟩ patiar *Madvig 1871–84, 2:409–10*
in nullum malum uires adsumet nisi a semet ipso *Gertz* (*prob. Alexander 1950–2, 10*)
in nullum malum uires a me ⟨peti⟩ patiar *Kronenberg 1923, 46*
in nullum malum uires ⟨asserere sibi nisi⟩ a semet ipso patiar *Pré.*
in nullum malum uires ⟨a me esse, sed⟩ a semet ipsas patiar *Mazzoli 1974, 67–8*

---

[21] **R** took over this version, with correction of *-med* to *-met*, and it is the version found in the manuscripts down to the end beginning of the thirteenth century. Innovation seems not to have begun before the fourteenth-century *recentiores*.

[22] The words *in nullum malum uires* were omitted by editors before Fickert, who construed them with *abducet a tutis*.

Among these candidates, I very much doubt the version introduced by Madvig, and still more the elaborations of Préchac and Mazzoli, which represent the speaker as expressing indifference to the self-harm the other party might incur: in effect, 'I'll be fine with the thought (*patiar*) of your hurting yourself, just don't expect any help from me'. This approach to the text obviously follows from the desire to salvage **N**'s *a semed ipsa*, which is—along with the absence of an infinitive complementing *patiar*—the chief problem posed by the archetype's text.[23] But such indifference to another's harm is fundamentally at odds with the tenor of 2. 14 as a whole (to say nothing of Stoic ethics more generally), where the lesson has been focused entirely on preventing damage to the other, to the point of implicitly adopting the paternalistic stance of looking out for the other's good from a position of superior understanding.[24]

The remaining proposals—in chronological order, those of Gertz, Hosius, and Kronenberg—dealt with these issues in fairly radical ways. Gertz salvaged *a semed ipsa* (with *a semet ipso*) but avoided the appearance of indifference by suppressing *patiar* and introducing *adsumet*.[25] Hosius took over that verb, replacing *a semed* with *a me sumerem* but left *ipsas* at an awkward remove from the word it ostensibly stresses. Kronenberg replaced *a semed ipsa* with *a me peti*, which provides the expected sense but leaves unexplained how the latter series of letters morphed into the former, beyond suggesting that *ipsa* (i.e., *ip̄a*) was produced by dittography before *patiar*.[26] Given that *semet* is very uncommon in S.'s prose works, I do not feel very acutely the need to salvage it.[27] But neither do I find any of these three options attractive enough to place it in the text as a plausible stop-gap; nor can I devise a better solution of my own. I will obelize *a semed ipsa*, consoling myself with thought that the passage defeated even Janus Gruter, and cite Gertz, Hosius, and Kronenberg in the apparatus, to suggest the thrust of S.'s thought.

[23] In **N**, *a se* was written at the end of one line, *medipsa* at the beginning of the next, but this fact seems to have no bearing on the problem.

[24] In this regard, the version that became the vulgate after Gronovius' edition, first reported by Pincianus from one of his *codices*—*non a semet ipso uim sibi inferri patiar*—is much more in the spirit of S.'s argument, though regrettably far from the transmitted text. The problem inspired Kronenberg's own attempt, below.

[25] That avoidance was not quite his intention, however. Rather, he thought that *patiar* had no authority but stood in **N** only as a superscript variant entered by a late correcting hand: thus his apparatus ad loc., 'sin nullum malum uires a semed ipsa nec committam **N**[1] corrupte; *si nullo modo potuero ad se ipsum reuocare* **N**[2](?), quibus *patiar* adscr. **N**[3], ut uidetur'; cf. p. 205, on Madvig's conjecture, 'eo minus ueri similem esse quod uerbi '*patiar*' nullam auctoritatem esse nunc constat.' But *patiar* stands squarely in **N**'s original text (the freewheeling superscript version, *si nullo modo…patiar*, was written all at one go by the same late hand, with a comma between *reuocare* and *patiar*). The error must be attributable to Kekulé's collation of **N**, on which Gertz relied: see Introduction n. 19; for a similar oversight apparently attributable to Kekulé, see the discussion of 6. 2. 1–2.

[26] Presumably, then, *peti* had already been lost by haplography before *patiar*, but Kronenberg does not elaborate.

[27] Only at *Vit. beat.* 22. 5 *mihi diuitiae si effluxerint, nihil auferent nisi semet ipsas*, *NQ* 1. 2. 8 [sc. *coronae*] *dilapsae sunt aequaliter et in semet ipsae euanuerunt*, and twice more at *NQ* 2. 8. 1 (where *semet* is not directly followed by a form of *ipse*).

2. 16. 2 Liceat istud sane tibi et te in tantum fortuna sustulerit ut congiaria tua urbes sint…: est tamen aliquis **minor quam in sinu eius condenda sit ciuitas**.

quam N : quam ut *1515‡*

In his first edition, Hosius printed *quam ut*, with the supplement that editors had regularly incorporated since it first appeared in Basel 1515; he removed it in his second edition, evidently convinced by the arguments (which he cites) of Baehrens (1912, 375) and Bourgery (1913, 103), who contended that the conjunction was dispensable. As a general matter, this is true when *quam* is preceded by a comparative adjective or adverb, as here; S.'s practice, however, strongly suggests that he regarded *quam ut* as the proper idiom. In the forty-odd places where he writes *minor quam* (or the like) + subjunctive, *ut* follows *quam* in the manuscripts everywhere but here and *Otio* 3. 3 (*res publica corruptior quam adiuuari possit*), where it was again supplied in the edition of 1515, I think correctly in both cases.[28] The construction—comparative adjective / adverb + *quam ut*—expresses a kind of result (*NLS* §166): here, literally, 'someone is smaller than that he should have a city…', 'someone is too small to have a city…', or more freely, 'there are some people who just aren't grand enough to have a city put in their pocket' (Griffin and Inwood).

2. 17. 4 Si cum exercitato et docto negotium est, audacius pilam mittemus: utcumque enim uenerit, manus illam expedita et agilis repercutiet. Si cum tirone et indocto, non tam rigide nec tam excusse sed languidius et in ipsam eius derigentes manum **remisse** occurremus.

remisse N : ⟨mittemus⟩, remisse *Gertz*, remissae *Alexander 1937, 56* (*post* languidius *dist.* : *cf. Alexander 1950–2, 10–11*)

In 2. 17. 3, to illustrate how a benefactor must judge the character of the recipient and adjust his own behaviour accordingly, S. borrows Chrysippus' analogy with ball-playing: to play the game as it should be played, by keeping the ball going back and forth, one must judge the skill of the other party involved. The two parallel sentences considered here concern the return of the ball, in a game that involves batting it back and forth (thus *repercutiet*) rather than throwing and catching: like volleyball, but with the aim of hitting the ball to, not past, the other. The first sentence concerns a skilled partner, to whom you can send the ball more spiritedly (*audacius*); in the second, where the other is a tiro, Gertz correctly saw that *remisse* is problematic (p. 207). The two parallel phrases—*non tam rigide nec*

---

[28] For the constructions of the sort *minor quam* + subjunctive without *ut* K.–S. 2:301 cites this passage and *Otio* 3. 3 in Seneca, two passages in Plautus (*Men.* 831–2, *Rud.* 328, *melius quam*…in both) and one passage each in Cicero (*Phil.* 9. 9 *gravior quam*…), Livy (39. 16. 3 *maius est quam*…, where Walsh reads *quam ut* in his OCT), and Velleius (2. 52. 3[4] *antiquius…quam*…, where Hellegouarc'h reads *quam ut* in his Budé).

tam excusse (where *rigide* describes the degree of tension in the hand and arm
as the ball is struck), *sed languidius et in ipsam eius derigentes manum* (with a
participial phrase replacing the second adverb)—together do a thorough job of
modifying the action (*occurremus*), leaving *remisse* isolated and without a function. Gertz's solution, supplying *mittemus* after *manum* (*non tam rigide…sed
languidius…⟨mittemus⟩, remisse occurremus*), is ungainly and redundant. But
Alexander's suggestion, taking *remisse* to represent *remissae* (sc. *pilae*), is simplicity itself and gives excellent sense: 'we will meet the ball, when it has been
returned, not so stiffly nor so forcefully, but in a more relaxed manner, guiding
it into his very hand.' I will print *remissae* but not punctuate after *languidius*, as
Alexander suggested, which I think misses the structure.

2. 18. 3 A quibus ergo accipiemus? Vt breuiter tibi respondeam: ab his quibus
dedissemus. **Videamus num etiam maiore dilectu quaerendus est** cui debeamus, quam cui praestemus. Nam ut non sequantur ulla incommoda (secuntur
autem plurima), graue tamen tormentum est debere, cui nolis; contra iucundissi-
mum ab eo accepisse beneficium, quem amare etiam post iniuriam possis, ubi
amicitiam alioqui iucundam causa fecit et iustam.

dedissemus. uideamus Nac : ł debuissemus Npc* (*man. post.*), dedisse uideamur ψ >1557
(*Grut. pp. 528-9*), dedisse uellemus *Mur.‡* (*resp. Stephanus 1586a, 209*), dedisse uoueamus
vel gaudeamus *Lips.*
num N *1605‡* : non Dς₂ς₁₁ς₁₇ >1503, nam Upcς₄ς₁₂, 1515–1585 (*Haase 1878, xxv*), nunc
ς₁₇ς₁₉ (*Grut. p. 529*), nimirum *Weidner 1864, 5*, num non *Pré.*
quaerendus est N (*def. Buck 1908, 52*) : q- sit *Madvig 1871–84, 2:410*, quaerendum est >1585

In line with a familiar pattern, Hosius followed Gertz in printing Madvig's *sit* in
his first edition but was persuaded by Buck's defence of **N** and put *est* in his second edition. **N**'s *num* consists only awkwardly with *quaerendus est*: the indicative
could most readily be defended if the question were felt to be independent of
uideamus, which is in fact the justification Buck found for retaining it ('Offenbar
ist *Videamus* der Frage vorausgeschikt und zwar so, dass es ausser deren
Konstrucktion fällt: "*Videamus! Num…est?* = Lasst uns enimal sehen! Ist etwa…"
Dann ist der Indikativ ganz am Platz').[29] But only when it introduces an indirect
question can *num* = 'whether by any chance…'. If the question really does stand
on its own two feet, the meaning—'It's not the case, is it, that we must more care-
fully choose the person we owe than the person we benefit?'—directly contradicts
S.'s point: we certainly must choose our benefactors more carefully than our bene-
ficiaries, because if the latter disappoint, it is no loss—the giving of a *beneficium* is

---

[29] On indirect questions with subjunctive and indicative in S. more generally, see Axelson
1933, 13–14.

its own reward—whereas (as S. says immediately following) *graue tamen tormen-tum est debere cui nolis.* That is probably why *nam* and *nunc* replaced *num* in some *recentiores,* and certainly why Weidner and Préchac, respectively, preferred *nimirum* and *num non* (the latter non-existent in S. and very rare elsewhere). None of these alternatives is terribly attractive; in any case, *num* in **N** is more often subsequently corrupted to *non* or *nunc* or *nam* than *num* itsef can plausibly be regarded as corrupt.[30] I will print *quaerendus sit.*

2. 18. 6 'Non semper' inquit 'mihi licet dicere "nolo", aliquando beneficium accipiendum est et inuito. Dat tyrannus crudelis et iracundus, qui munus suum fastidire te iniuriam iudicaturus est: non accipiam? eodem loco latronem pone, piratam, regem animum latronis ac piratae habentem. Quid faciam? **parum dignus est cui debeam?'**

A small point. Hosius was the first editor to punctuate with a question-mark after *debeam,* evidently because he took the whole of *quid faciam… debeam* to be par-allel with *non accipiam?* But the thought, admittedly compressed, is different. *quid faciam?* looks to the dilemma the speaker faces: on the one hand, turning down the offer obviously means death; on the other, the person making the offer is not the sort to whom one wishes to be indebted. The first horn of the dilemma, being obvious, is left unstated; the second—*parum dignus est cui debeam*—is addressed in the sentences discussed immediately following, where S. argues that when coercion is applied, debt, properly understood, cannot be incurred:

2. 18. 7 Cum eligendum dico cui debeas, uim maiorem et metum excipio, quibus adhibitis electio perit. Si liberum est tibi, si arbitrii tui est utrum uelis an non, id apud te ipse perpendes; si necessitas tollit arbitrium, scies te non accipere sed parere. Nemo **id** accipiendo obligatur quod illi repudiare non licuit: si uis scire an uelim, effice ut possim nolle.

id *1585‡* : in id N *>1529,* enim id *Agric. p. 272, 1557, prob. Grut. p. 529*

After **N**'s pointless *in id* was taken over by **R**, it remained in the later manuscripts and held its place in the printed editions until Muretus deleted *in,* after which *id* became the vulgate. But Rodolphus Agricola (d. 1485) had previously jotted *enim id* in his copy of Treviso 1748: when that book reached Erasmus—after *De bene-ficiis* and much of the *Epistulae Morales* were already typeset—he endorsed the reading in the critical appendix he inserted after the *Epistulae.* S.'s style allows the logical sequence to be marked explicitly or left implied; but a connective word is

---

[30] *Num* is corrupted in the later manuscripts at 2. 19. 1, 3. 28. 1, 4. 23. 1, 6. 9. 1, 7. 24. 1; *num* appears to have replaced *non* twice in **N** (2. 31. 5, 3. 32. 6), each time before *quid* or *quis.*

more common, and it seems to me more likely that *in* is a remnant of *enim* than the product of dittography before *id*.

2. 23. 2 Quidam furtiue gratias agunt et in angulo et ad aurem. non est ista uere-cundia sed infitiandi genus: ingratus est qui remotis arbitris agit gratias. quidam nolunt nomina secum fieri nec interponi pararios nec signatores aduocari ⟨**uix**⟩ chirographum dare; idem faciunt qui dant operam ut beneficium in ipsos conla-tum quam ignotissimum sit.

nolunt N : uolunt *Pinc.*
uix *Havet 1898, 526 (Hos.)* : *om.* N *(Pré.)*, nec ς₁ς₁₄, sed *Madvig ap. Gertz*, tantum *(post chirographum) Gertz*, uolunt *Rossbach 1888, 147*

In speaking of those who prefer not to express thanks before witnesses, S. draws an analogy with people engaged in a financial transaction who do not want it to be entered in a ledger (*nomina fieri*), do not want intermediaries to be involved (*interponi pararii*), do not want witnesses to be summoned to sign (*signatores aduocari*): then comes the last item, giving a signed bond, *chirographum dare*, which simply follows *signatores aduocari* in **N**. Those who have suggested *uix* or *sed* or *tantum* or *uolunt* as a supplement were misled by *remotis arbitris* in the preceding sentence into supposing that a distinction is to be drawn between (unwanted) persons—*pararii, signatores*—and a (more or less acceptable) docu-ment (*chirographum*). But the first item in the sequence here, *nomina...fieri*, shows that S.'s thought has shifted slightly from the previous sentence: he is now imagining someone who would prefer that the transaction not be attested in any form, human or documentary. I will print the *recentiores'* *nec*, which is preferable to supposing that S. suddenly lapsed into asyndeton at the end of the sequence.

2. 24. 2–3 Nec delicate accipiendum est nec submisse et humiliter, nam qui negle-gens est in accipiendo, cum omne beneficium recens **pateat**, quid faciat cum prima eius uoluptas **refrixit**? alius accipit fastidiose, tamquam qui dicat, **(3)** 'Non quidem mihi opus est, sed quia tam ualde uis, faciam tibi mei potestatem', alius supine, ut dubium praestanti relinquat an senserit, alius uix labra diduxit et ingra-tior quam si tacuisset fuit

nec submisse et humiliter N : nec submisse et humiliter, ⟨nedum neglegenter⟩ *Alexander 1934, 54*
pateat N *>1503* : placeat *1515‡*
refrixit Npc, *1515–1557* : refrixet Nac, refrixerit Facς₅ς₆ς₁₆*mg.*ς₁₉, *1585‡*, restrinxit ς₂ς₁₄ *>1503*, restrinxerit ς₁₆

Alexander's conjecture mistakes the force of *neglegens* and the structure of §24 as a whole. *neglegens* broadly characterizes the behaviour of the ethically inattentive person who through lack of tact and circumspection fails to respond to the occasion as the occasion demands: the specific forms such failures take are then captured in the sequence *alius...fastidiose...alius supine...alius uix labra diduxit...*, which recapitulates *delicate*, *submisse*, and *humiliter*, in the same order.

Shunned by Gertz, the first editor who knew it to be **N**'s reading, *pateat* was printed by Hosius, though it is difficult to see why: 'every *beneficium* is evident when fresh' is insipid (Griffin and Inwood's 'when the whole thing is fresh in his mind' conspicuously ducks the verb), while *uoluptas* points to *placeat*. And though a corrector of **N** made the obvious move of changing *refrixet* to *refrixit*, *cum...placeat* (or *pateat*) points instead to *cum...refrixerit*.

2. 26. 2 Incipiamus a primo. Nemo non benignus est sui iudex: inde est ut omnia meruisse se existimet et in solutum accipiat nec satis suo pretio se aestimatum putet. 'Hoc mihi dedit, sed quam sero, sed post quot labores? quanto consequi plura potuissem, si illum aut illum **ita me colere** maluissem?'

ita me colere *Feldmann 1887, 20* : aut me colere N (*def. Buck 1908, 52, recip. Pré.*), me colere *Gertz*, a me coli *Madvig 1871–84, 2:410*, aeque colere *Hermes ap. Hos.*

In defending **N** and arguing against Hosius' adoption of Feldman's emendation, Buck contended that if *me* were the subject, not object, of *colere*, it would stand between *colere* and *maluissem*. I doubt that so strict a distinction can be so strongly asserted (he cites no evidence), and in any case that is not the main reason why *me* is probably not the subject of *colere*. Rather, beyond an alliterative comic oath like *perire me malis malim modis* (Pl. *Bacch.* 490), a first-person singular form of *malo* is coupled with *me* as the subject of the dependent infinitive only rarely (the cases I cite are the only ones I have found), and then only in a limited range of circumstances (in a few cases the categories overlap):

- when *me* is juxtaposed with *ego* or *ipse*, for emphasis: Liv. 29. 25. 3 *me ipse in re dubia poni malim*, Front. *Ad amic.* 1. 13. 1 *ego me neque Graecum neque Latin uocabulum...nosse mallem*;
- when *me* is contrasted with another person: Cic. *Div. Caec.* 16 *quemuis...hoc mallem...suscipere quam me, me...mallem quam neminem*, Planc. 13 *me... quam socios tua frui uirtute malebam*, Att. 1. 5. 4 *mallem Peducaeum tibi consilium...quam me dare*, Fam. 11. 12. 2 *hoc quam uim habeat te existimare malo quam me apertius scribere*, Front. *Ad Marc.* 3. 14. 5 *me carere...malim quam te...subire*;
- when *me* is the subject of a passive infinitive: Cic. *Rosc. Am.* 10 *opprimi me onere offici malo*, Lucull. 10 *uinci me mallem quam uincere*, Fam. 12. 13. 1 *malim me a te commendari*;
- or when *me* is the subject of *esse*: Cic. *Brut.* 257 *me Phidiam esse mallem quam optimum fabrum tignuarium*, Caesar in Cic. *Fam.* 9. 16. 2 *nihil enim malo quam et me mei similem esse et illos sui.*

The only clear instance of the usage in S. belongs to the last category: *EM* 81. 6 *alter ille remissior iudex, quem esse me malo.* If we keep **N**'s text, the disappointed man is saying, 'Quanto consequi plura potuissem, si illum aut illum aut me colere maluissem!': 'How much better off I'd have been had I preferred to devote myself to that fellow or to that fellow—or to myself!' With *me colere* Préchac well compares *Brev.* 2. 4 *ille illius cultor, hic illius, suus nemo est.*

2. 27. 1 Cn. Lentulus augur, diuitiarum maximum exemplum ante quam illum libertini pauperem facerent, hic qui quater miliens sestertium suum uidit (proprie dixi; nihil enim amplius quam uidit), **ingenii fuit sterilis, tam pusilli quam animi**. Cum esset auarissimus, nummos citius emittebat quam uerba: tanta illi inopia erat sermonis.

ingenii fuit Npc : ingeni fuit Nac, ingenii sui >*1503*
sterilis R : sterelis N, *del. Madvig 1871–84, 2:410–11*
tam pusilli quam animi Npc* QpcIpcJV, *1515, 1557* (*Haase, Gertz*)
    tempus|illi quam animi Nac
    et tam pusilli quam animi ς17, *Stephanus 1586a, 202, Lips.*
    tam pusilli oris quam animi G (*Fick.*)
    tam pusilli >*1503*
    tamquam animi *1529*
    tam sterilis quam pusilli animi *Pinc., 1649‡*
    tam sterilis quam pusilli *1585, 1605*
    'ego hic nihil pronuntio' *Grut. p. 530*
    tam pusilli quam ⟨contracti⟩ animi *Watt 1994, 226*

The archetype's unintelligible text—*ingeni* (*-ii* corr.) *fuit sterelis tempus illi quam animi*—was taken over by **R**, whence it was transmitted to most of the later medieval copies.[31] **N**'s text was later altered to the form printed by Hosius (following Haase and Gertz):[32] it requires *sterilis* and *pusilli* to modify *ingenii* independently (Lentulus was 'characterized by a sterile talent, (one) as stunted as his mind'), the second adjective coordinating, with *tam…quam*, a comparison between *ingenium* and *animus*. The number of subsequent variations upon that theme, listed above, shows that many readers and critics have been dissatisfied (e.g., W. S. Watt:

---

[31] Equally unintelligible was the text—*ingenii sui sterilis tam pusilli*—of the first five editions, down to Venice 1503. Note that the most glaring problem in **N**'s text—*tempus illi* for *tam pusilli*—was probably encouraged, if not actually caused, by the line-break that separates *tempus* from *illi*. **R**'s replacement of **N**'s *sterelis* with *sterilis* is the sort of minor tweak typical of **R**'s innovations relative to **N**.

[32] 'Later' because the change was presumably made after the uncorrected text passed to **R**; the correction of *tempus illi* is certainly in a much lighter ink than the (possibly scribal) change of *ingeni* to *ingenii*, but the intervention it required is so slight (*a* above *e*, a virgule separating *m* from *p*, and short strokes indicating that *pus* at line-end belongs with *illi*) that it is impossible to judge whether it represents one of the significantly later hands that left traces in the book. The alteration *tempus illi* > *tam pusilli*, also found in a few of the medieval manuscripts (as a correction or already in the base text) and in most of the *recentiores* I have examined, is the sort of correction that could occur independently to more than one reader.

'the last phrase can hardly be sound; it is too unbalanced'), and in that I believe they have been correct. Attempts at improvement have pursued several different lines of attack. Two conjectures fall under the heading 'supplement': **G**'s addition of *oris* after *pusilli*, anticipating the remark about Lentulus' *inopia...sermonis*, provides a noun to balance *animi*, while Watt's *contracti*—inspired by 2. 34. 4 *pusilli animi et contracti*—is meant to balance *pusilli*; but these strike me as merely formal improvements, since *inopia...sermonis* is already anticipated by the reference to Lentulus' *ingenii*, while *contracti* adds nothing to the thought.[33] Under the heading 'deletion' fall Erasmus' elimination of *pusilli* and Madvig's of *sterilis*: we will return to these suggestions. The remaining adjustments entail either relocation of more than one word—so Pincianus' *tam sterilis quam pusilli animi*, moving *tam* to precede *sterilis* and *pusilli* to follow *quam*—or a combination of relocation and deletion: so Muretus' *tam sterilis quam pusilli* also moves *tam* to precede *sterilis* and deletes *animi*. Other considerations aside (the deletion of *animi*, for example, is very undesirable), none of these suggestions should be preferred if a more economical solution can be found.

This brings us back to Erasmus, who justified his deletion in his note ad loc. (1529, 18): 'Pusilli non erat in manu descripto Codice, et sensui superesse uidetur. sterilis ingenii dicit, ob tarditatem, sterilis animi ob ingratitudinem.' We know he was incorrect to believe that *pusilli* lacked manuscipt authority.[34] But his judgement that there is a superfluous adjective on hand points in the right direction, which leads to Madvig's deletion of *sterilis*. He thought that *sterilis* was added 'cum corruptum iam esset *tam pusilli*'; I think it more likely that *sterilis* began as a gloss on *pusilli* that eventually made its way into the text: *ingenii fuit {sterilis} tam pusilli quam animi*—'his talent was as stunted as his spirit [= his moral capacity]'—gives excellent sense at very little cost.

2. 29. 1 Vide, quam iniqui **sunt** diuinorum munerum aestimatores et quidem professi sapientiam: queruntur, quod non magnitudine corporum aequemus elephantos, uelocitate ceruos, leuitate aues, impetu tauros, quod solida sit cutis beluis, decentior dammis, densior ursis, mollior fibris, quod sagacitate nos narium canes uincant, quod acie luminum aquilae, spatio aetatis corui, multa animalia nandi facilitate.

sunt N >*1557* (cf. *Buck 1908, 53, Baehrens 1912, 521, Bourgery 1922, 337*) : sint *1585‡*

After Muretus replaced *sunt* with *sint* it remained in the text through Hosius' first edition. He then restored *sunt* in his second edition, under the influence of Buck

---

[33] One other addition, Stephanus' *et* before *tam*, is still less of an improvement.

[34] The note was written before he saw **N**; it was his bad luck not to find *pusilli* in the other manuscripts he consulted, one of which we know was from England, another from Basel (1529, 29, on 3. 14, and 1529, 42, on 4. 18; the latter is now Basel, Öffentliche Bibliothek der Universität F. IV. 14, s. xv).

and Baehrens; Bourgery, too, soon cited the passage among his examples of 'l'indicatif dans l'interrogation indirecte'. I grant that the indicative could be defended, not as an example of the mood used in an indirect question, but on the ground that what we have here are two essentially independent exclamations: 'Look! How unfair are those who assign a value to the gods' gifts—even those who claim to be philosophers!' But parallel instances like 5. 17. 4 *Vide, quam ingrata sit iuuentus: quis non patris sui supremum diem... optat?* and 6. 40. 1 *Vide, quam sis aequus: horum optares nihil, si tibi beneficium non dedisset* (where, in sarcasm, *aequus = iniquus*) persuade me that in such settings S. reflexively used the subjunctive.

2. 31. 2–3 Quotiens quod proposuit, quisque consequitur, capit operis sui fructum. Qui beneficium dat, quid proponit? prodesse ei, cui dat, et uoluptati esse. Si, quod uoluit, effecit peruenitque ad me animus eius ac mutuo gaudio adfecit, tulit, quod petit. Non enim in uicem aliquid sibi reddi uoluit; aut non fuit beneficium, sed negotiatio. **(3)** Bene nauigauit, qui quem destinauit portum tenuit; teli iactus certae manus peregit officium, si petita percussit; beneficium qui dat, uult excipi grate: habet, quod uoluit, si bene acceptum est. **Sed sperauit emolumenti aliquid**: non fuit hoc beneficium, cuius proprium est nihil de reditu cogitare.

emolumenti Npc : & emolumenti Nac, emolumentum aliquod ς₂ς₅ς₁₄‡

Explicating a Stoic paradox central to the doctrine of benefits and gratitude—that the person who gladly receives a *beneficium* has *ipso facto* made a suitable return (2. 31. 1 *ex paradoxis Stoicae sectae minime mirabile... est: eum qui libenter accipit beneficium reddidisse*)—S. examines the matter from the perspective of the righteous benefactor, asking the question, what is his aim, what does he look for in making the grant? Accordingly, the verbs and other expressions that he uses—*proposuit . . . proponit . . . uoluit . . . petit . . . uoluit . . . destinauit . . . petita...uult...uoluit*—are all goal-oriented and forward-looking, ending with *sperauit*. One way of approaching the textual issue here, then, is to regard all the verbs as functionally equivalent to *uult* or *uoluit*; and if S. had written, *Beneficium qui dat, uult excipi grate: habet, quod uoluit, si bene acceptum est. Sed uoluit et emolumenti aliquid*, I doubt that one reader in a thousand would blink at *et emolumenti*. If that is so—if in the structure of the passage *sperauit* stands in for *uoluit* for the sake of *uariatio*—we probably should not blink at *sperauit et emolumenti*, either. Whatever the motive of the reader (or readers) of **N** who first cancelled *&* and then erased it, it was very likely a mistake.[35]

---

[35] The deletion was an early alteration, since *et* is lacking in **R** and the later manuscripts: it could be defended only on the supposition that it was made by the scribe himself, checking his work against his exemplar and seeing that *et* was not there, for then *et* would very likely lack the authority of a reading transmitted from antiquity. For another apparently erroneous erasure of *&*, see the discussion of 3. 2. 1–2. I take it to be obvious that *emolumentum aliquod*, the print vulgate derived from some *recentiores*, need not be considered.

2. 33. 2 Facit Phidias statuam.... Triplex illi fructus est operis sui: unus conscientiae, hunc absoluto opere percipit; alter famae; **tertius utilitatis, quem adlatura
est** aut gratia aut uenditio aut aliqua commoditas.

quem ψ : quam N (*def. Buck 1908, 53*)

Practical benefit (*utilitas*) is the third kind of reward (*fructus*) that Phidias could
derive from creating a statue: the textual question is, did *quem* displace *quam* under
the influence of *hunc* in the quasi-parenthetical expression *unus conscientiae* (*hunc
absoluto opere percipit*),[36] or was an original *quem*, referring to *fructus*, displaced by
quam because of the proximity of *utilitas*. In a different sort of tradition—say, that
of the *Aeneid*—in which we are often faced with two ancient variants that are *a priori* of equal authority, we would ask 'Is either one a *lectio difficilior*?' or the closely
related question, *utrum in alterum abiturum erat?*, and the answer to both would
clearly be *quem*. But in our tradition, the variants cannot be assumed to be of equal
authority: *quam* is possibly, even probably ancient (though not therefore necessarily
correct), while *quem* is certainly a medieval innovation—and not only that, it is an
innovation that appears uniquely in what is generally the less reliable branch of
the medieval tradition. Perhaps, then, the situation can be clarified by refining the
original question asked just above: not 'did *quem* arise to displace *quam* under
the influence of *hunc*?', but 'since we know that *quem* arose as an innovation to displace *quam* in this branch of the tradition, how did it arise?' Here it seems to me less
likely that *quem* is a mechanical error of perseveration, committed when *hunc* got
stuck in a scribe's mind eight words earlier in the text (more than a full line of
text separates *quam* from *hunc* in **N**), than a conscious attempt at a non-obvious
correction by an attentive reader who noticed an apparent discrepancy; which is
to say, I think it more likely that *quam* first displaced *quem* (either before or
during the copying of **N**) and that ψ here recaptures the original text.[37]

2. 34. 3 Fortitudo est ⟨uirtus⟩ pericula iusta contemnens aut scientia periculorum repellendorum, excipiendorum, prouocandorum; dicimus tamen et gladia-
torem fortem uirum et seruum nequam, quem in contemptum mortis temeritas
impulit. **(4)** Parsimonia est scientia uitandi sumptus superuacuos aut ars re familiari
moderate utendi....

---

[36] So Buck contended in defending **N**'s *quam*.

[37] If this is correct, *quem* is of a piece with a number of other singular readings of ψ that are certain
or probable corrections of an archetypal error: 3. 27. 3 *credet* (*credit* N), 4. 6. 1 *sola, aurum* (*solarum*
Nac, *uel solum* Npc*, *man. post.* (*sic* M), *solum* aurum QMpc, *sol aurum* C), 5. 6. 5 *libere mittet* (*liber
emittet* N, *liberemittet* R), 5. 8. 3 *dum accipit* (*accipit* N), 6. 5. 2 *numerauerimus* (*numerauimus* N),
6. 26. 1 *si sine* (*sine* N), 6. 27. 2 *rationem* (*ratione* N), 7. 19. 9 *sepositus* (*positus* N); at 6. 37. 3 *difficultatibus uult opprimi* (*difficultatibus uult* N) the infinitive is probably the wrong choice, but the diagnosis
was correct. One might think that most of these, even supplements like those found at 5. 8. 3 and
6. 26. 1, would be within the reach of any attentive reader, but no other medieval scribe or reader
whose work is on record grasped any of them.

uirtus G$\varsigma_5\varsigma_6\varsigma_{19}$, *cod. Pinc.* : *om.* N >*1529* (*def. Buck 1908, 53*)
    scientia ς_3
    mens *E. Thomas 1893, 288–90*
    et (*post* contemnens) *Hermes ap. Hos.*
    animus *Bourgery 1922, 416 n. 1 (Pré.)*
    peritia *Alexander 1934, 54*
    ars *Alexander 1950–2, 13–14*
iusta N (*def. Buck 1908, 54*) : iuste *Madvig ap. Gertz* (*resp. Buck 1908, 54, Alexander 1937, 57, sim. Alexander 1950–2, 13*)
    instantia *Kruczkiewicz 1877, 434*
    '*an* ui sua' *Hos. in app.*
    funesta *Busche 1917–18, 466–7*
    iustitia olim *Pré.*
    usque (*uel* inita, *quod mauult*) *Birt 1928, 50–1*
    iustā contemnens ⟨animus patientiā⟩ *Mazzoli 1977, 72–5*

I am surprised that Erasmus, at least, was not bothered by *fortitudo est pericula iusta contemnens*, but most readers have welcomed the medieval supplement *uirtus*, which entered the print tradition with Curio's edition of 1557 (drawn from Pincianus, as most of that edition's improvements were). I do not think that anyone has believed the defence offered by Buck, who claimed that *scientia* was to be construed ἀπὸ κοινοῦ with *contemnens* and *periculorum repellendorum*, which I doubt would be possible even if *scientia* stood before *aut* (one of the *recentiores* does supply a second *scientia* there). Any noun selected would be a plausible stop-gap at best,[38] and *uirtus* is better than anything else that has been proposed: *fortitudo*, like any virtue, is strictly the mind in a certain condition (see following), not the *mens* or *animus* itself, and *ars*, like *scientia*, would call for a genitive construction, as the following sentence on *parsimonia* shows (so too *peritia*, cf. Plin. *NH* 18. 32 *peritia castra metandi*, Gell. 15. 31. 1 *peritia disciplinaque faciendi*); if one wished to venture yet another guess, *ratio* would perhaps not be bad, cf. *ille fortis dicatur cum ratione fortuita despiciens* at the end of §34. 4.

As for *iusta*, a fair amount of critical churning followed Gertz's report that Madvig suggested *iuste*. But *pericula iusta*—'actual dangers', 'dangers properly so called' (cf. *OLD* s.v. 8)—is correct, as Alexander saw (1937, 57): the point is that *fortitudo*, again like any virtue, depends on the mind's correctly assenting to, or withholding assent from, the impressions presented to it, and *fortitudo* is properly *fortitudo* only when the mind correctly assents to the true impression that dangers actually are present, even though—as S. soon remarks (2. 34. 4)—in common usage the term *fortis* is stretched to cover *et hic sine ratione in pericula excurrens*.

---

[38] Gertz may well have been right in remarking, in his apparatus, 'sed uereor, ne sic locus [sc. uocabulo *uirtus* addito] non plane sanatus sit'.

2. 35. 2 A consuetudine quaedam, quae dicimus, abhorrent, deinde alia uia ad consuetudinem redeunt: negamus iniuriam accipere sapientem, tamen, qui illum pugno percusserit, iniuriarum damnabitur; **negamus stulti ⟨quidquam⟩ esse**, et tamen eum, qui rem aliquam stulto **subripuit**, furti condemnabimus; insanire omnes dicimus, **nec omnes curamus elleboro**; his ipsis, quos uocamus insanos, et suffragium et iuris dictionem committimus.

negamus stulti quidquam esse GJV, *Vinc. Bell.*, *Spec. Hist. 5. 28* : quidquam *om*. Nac, aliquid Npc* (*ss. man. post., mauult Grut. p. 532*), negamus rem stulti esse HIpc‡, negamus stulti furtum esse F, negamus stulti esse ⟨assem⟩ *Pré.*
subripuit N : -puerit ς₂ς₅‡
nec omnes N: nec tamen omnes ψ, *Vinc. Bell.*

Certain Stoic claims involving categories like the wise man and the fool sometimes depart from the common understanding of language (*consuetudo*), for example the denial that the wise man can receive an *iniuria*, or that the fool possesses anything, the mate of the claim that all things belong to the wise.[39] Clearly something has dropped out here in the statement about the fool: as a plausible stop-gap, *negamus quidquam stulti esse* most nearly provides the negative counterpart to *dicimus omnia sapientis esse*, and placing *quidquam* between *negamus* and *stulti* perhaps will make it easier to see how *quidquam* was lost though a *saut du même au même* after *negamus*.

In what follows, it requires excessive loyalty to **N** to retain *subripuit* after the preceding *percusserit*; but the impulse to insert a third *tamen* after *nec*, seen in the ψ-manuscripts and Vincent of Beauvais, should be resisted, since *nec* by itself commonly conveys the idea, 'and yet…not' (*OLD* s.v. *neque* 5).

2. 35. 3 Sic dicimus eum qui beneficium bono animo accipit gratiam rettulisse, nihilo minus illum in aere alieno relinquimus gratiam relaturum, etiam cum rettulit. Exhortatio est illa, **non infitiatio ⟨beneficii, ne ⟩beneficia timeamus, ne ut intolerabili** sarcina pressi deficiamus animo.

⟨beneficii, ne⟩ beneficia *Gertz* : beneficia Nac, beneficii Npc >*1557*, beneficii. ne *1585*‡
ne ut *Reinecke 1890, 9* : ne uel N, *Pré.*, ne uelut *Haase*, neue ut *Gertz*

Muretus' text—*Exhortatio est, non infitiatio beneficii. ne timeamus, ne…*—at least made better sense than the text previously printed, *Exhortatio est, non infitiatio beneficii. Timeamus, ne…* (quite an exhortation…). But *infitiatio* unquestionably requires a genitive, where **N** originally had *beneficia*, and Gertz's *infitiatio ⟨beneficii, ne⟩ beneficia timeamus, ne…*, is one of his best efforts, giving both *infitiatio* and *beneficia* fitting constructions, making satisfactory sense of *timeamus*, and

---

[39] e.g., the 'proof' at 7. 5. 7 that the *sapiens* must be a *leno*: '*Is*' inquit, '*cuius prostitutae sunt, leno est; omnia autem sapientis sunt; inter omnia et prostitutae sunt; ergo prostitutae sapientis sunt. Leno autem est, cuius prostitutae sunt; ergo sapiens leno est*'.

allowing the second *ne*-clause to elaborate the first in a very Senecan manner (see 2. 35. 4 discussed just below). I have only a corroborating detail to add, involving **N**'s *mise en page*, which Gertz did not know because he had not seen the manuscript. *Exhortatio* stands on the line immediately above *beneficia timeamus*, and the exceptionally large capital *E*'s lower crescent extends below the line and interferes with *beneficia*, causing an interruption after *benefi*, thus: *benefi   cia timeamus* (a line was subsequently drawn to connect the bits, *benefi___cia*). I suggest that the interruption was just the thing that caused the scribe's eye to commit a *saut du même au même*, so that the correction would best be represented as *benefi⟨cii, ne benefi⟩cia timeamus*.

As for what happened after the second *ne*: given the state of **N** (and given that its reading, *pace* Préchac, is not acceptable), Haase's *ne uelut* seems preferable to Gertz's *neue ut* or Reinecke's *ne ut*, cf. *EM* 83. 7 *hoc a me exige, ne uelut per tenebras aeuum ignobile emetiar.*

2. 35. 4 Nullas tibi proponam difficultates, ne despondeas **animum**, ne laborum ac longae seruitutis expectatione deficias; non differo te, de praesentibus fiat.

animum *1515–1585, Gertz* : animo N *>1503, 1605–Haase* ('nescio an recte' *Hos., recip. Pré.*)

An exceptionally nice example of the way that editorial fashion and judgement have shifted and swayed. *animo* was transmitted from **N** to all the later manuscripts, and so it inevitably became the early print vulgate. After Basel 1515, *animum* was in the text of all the sixteenth-century editions, until Lipsius reinserted *animo*. There it stood until Gertz returned to *animum*; Hosius followed Gertz in his text but flirted in his apparatus with **N**'s reading, which Préchac predictably accepted. That reading cannot be ruled out: *despondere* is used intransitively, in a different connection, by another writer whose *patria* was in Hispania Baetica, S.'s contemporary Columella (8. 10. 1 *caueis clausi* [sc. *turdi*] *plurimi despondent*). But Varro, for example, took it for granted that *despondere animum* was a familiar idiom (*LL* 6. 71 *sic despondisse animum quoque dicitur, ut despondisse filiam,* cf. *RR* 3. 5. 6, 16. 5), which occurs several times in Livy (3. 38. 2, 26. 7. 8, 31. 22. 5); *despondere animo* is first found in a second-century funerary inscription from Telesia in Samnium (*CIL* 9. 2220 *post dies XV fati eius* [sc. *filii*] *animo despondit* [*sic*] *mater*) and thereafter, e.g., in Servius' commentary on *Aen.* 1. 92 (Aeneas' lamentation during the storm at sea): *et ille intra se, ne exaudiant socii et timidiores despondeant animo, hic uero uociferatur.* It is the later usage that appears in **N**, possibly under the influence of the idiom *deficere animo* that occurs a few words earlier in 2. 35. 3.

Notes to Book 3

3. 1. 2 Nam quae recentia apud illos uiguerunt ea interiecto spatio obsolescunt; de quibus fuisse mihi tecum disputationem scio, cum tu illos non ingratos uocares sed oblitos, tamquam ea res ingratum excuset quae facit **aut, quia** hoc accidit alicui, non sit ingratus, cum hoc non accidat nisi ingrato.

aut quia N >*1503* : aut qui Fς₁₁ς₁₈, aut cui ς₁₅ς₁₆*mg.*, ς₁₉, aut cum ς₅ς₆, an quia *1515‡*, ut quia *Gron. p. 130, haeret Grut. p. 532*

The subject is ingrates, specifically the lapses of memory that cause ingratitude—or is it just the appearance of ingratitude?[1] S. and Liberalis have discussed the point, the latter taking the position that such people should be called 'forgetful', not 'ungrateful', and offering—in **N**'s text—two justifications for that view, coordinated by *aut*: *tamquam...excuset...aut...non sit ingratus*. It is clear, however, that *aut* proved to be something of a stumbling block, both among the *recentiores* and in the printed editions, where it was replaced in Basel 1515 by *an*, which remained in the text until Ruhkopf returned to *aut* in his edition of 1808. *aut* is perhaps not impossible, though it would be a good deal easier if *quia* could suggest 'just because' ('...or just because this happens to someone, he's not an ingrate, though this only happens to an ingrate'); but even then *aut* would not be acting disjunctively, to supply an alternative explanation or excuse. On the other hand, *an* actually is impossible, for nowhere in classical Latin does the sequence *tamquam...an...* coordinate alternative explanations. Gruter, who knew both *aut* and *an*, candidly confessed that he could not find a way out ('...ut ingenue fatear quod res est, non satis me hinc expedio'). Lipsius took S.'s point to be, 'Is the person who forgets excused for that reason, so that he is not an ingrate, though only an ingrate can forget?'[2] Gronovius then took the next step, proposing that *ut* be read for *aut*, a simple move that produces excellent sense, offering not an alternative explanation but a *reductio ad absurdum* very much in S.'s manner: 'you would call those people, not ingrates, but forgetful, as though the thing that makes him an ingrate lets him off the hook, with the upshot that because he forgets he's not an ingrate, though only an ingrate forgets.'[3]

---

[1] The first sentence is a variation on a theme already found at 2. 24. 2, discussed ad loc.: *qui neglegens est in accipiendo, cum omne beneficium recens placeat, quid faciat cum prima eius uoluptas refrixerit?*

[2] 1605, 290 *adn.*: 'Mihi hic lux est, & dicit: ideone qui oblitus est excusetur, ut non sit ingratus, cum nemo obliuisci possit, nisi ingratus?'

[3] For the error see, e.g., 4. 20. 3 *de hereditate aut* (Npc: *ut* Nac) *de legato*, and similarly 7. 24. 1 *at* recc. Erasmus : *aut* N.

3. 1. 5 Vitiosi oculi sunt qui lucem reformidant, caeci qui non uident, et parentes suos non amare impietas est, non agnoscere insania.

uitiosi oculi N : luscitiosi *Mur.*, uitiosis oculis *Grut. pp. 532–3*

Muretus made his conjecture because he knew a *liber uetus* in which *oculi* was absent, and because 'caecos…oculos nusquam alibi legi' (1585, 26). His first point carries much less weight than the second, both because we know that the archetype had *oculi*, and because in fact there is only one passage extant in classical Latin in which *caecus* certainly modifies *oculus*: Publilius Syrus C. 20 *caeci sunt oculi cum animus alias res agit*;[4] and this record tends to reinforce my sense that the subjects of the first three verbs here—especially *reformidant*—should be persons, not organs. There is little in favour of Muretus' suggestion, particularly since the defect S. has in mind seems not to entail nearsightedness.[5] Gruter's ablative of description is more attractive, but *uitiosi oculis* is slightly simpler: an epithet parallel with *caeci* and an ablative of specification that lost its terminal *s* by haplography before *sunt*.

3. 2. 1–2 Quis tam ingratus est quam qui quod in prima parte animi positum esse debuit et semper occurrere ita seposuit et abiecit ut in ignorantiam uerteret? adparet illum non saepe de reddendo cogitasse cui obrepsit obliuio. **(2)** Denique **ad reddendam gratiam** et uirtute opus est et tempore et facultate et adspirante fortuna; qui meminit **sine impendio** gratus est.

reddendam Npc : reddendum Nac
gratiam N : gratia *Gertz*
sine Npc (##sine) : & sine Nac (*ut uid.*) *Gertz*, sat sine *Pré.*

reddere is unsurprisingly one of the most common verbs in the work, and S. uses it both intransitively (= 'to make a return'), as in the first sentence here, and with an object. But as Gertz observed (p. 209), though S. once writes *gratiam…reddidit*,[6] he elsewhere says (*EM* 81. 9), *sic certe solemus loqui, 'ille illi gratiam rettulit.' Referre est ultro quod debeas adferre. Non dicimus 'gratiam reddidit'*; and that distinction is borne out by the scores and scores of places in the prose works where S. uses *gratiam referre* to denote an expression of gratitude. Given the great preponderance of the evidence, given the fact that S. speaks of *de reddendo* a few words earlier and that *ad reddendum* was **N**'s original reading, given the ease with which *gratia* could be attracted into the accusative after *-dum* (with *-dum* then altered to *-dam*) and the appropriateness with which *gratia* would head the list of factors that must converge for a return to

---

[4] The *iunctura* also is found in a very heavily restored passage of Festus: ⟨γλαυκ⟩ῶπις appellatur | ⟨*Minerva a Graecis, quod ea, ut noctua, ocu*⟩*lis est caecis* (178. 30–1 L.).

[5] Gell. 4. 2. 11 *De myope…qui 'luscitiosus' Latine appellatur.*

[6] 5. 16. 4 [sc. *Pompeius*] *hanc gratiam rei publicae reddidit.*

be made, I believe that Gertz was right to read *ad reddendum gratia et uirtute opus est et....*

S. goes on to draw a distinction between the act of making a return, with its enabling factors, and the state of being grateful, which requires only an attitude of the mind. Here too I think Gertz was right, in reading *et sine*, which I am fairly sure was N's original reading: Préchac thought that *sed* had been erased before *sine* (hence his *sat*), but the digital image that I have, courtesy of the Vatican Library, pretty clearly reveals the remains of *&*.[7] 'The person who remembers is grateful even without incurring expense' makes fine sense, and this would not be the only place where an erasure of *&* was ill-judged.[8]

3. 2. 3 quidquid frequens cogitatio exercet **ac** renouat, memoriae numquam subducitur, quae nihil perdit, nisi ad quod non saepe respexit.

ac Npc : *om.* Nac, et *Gertz* (Pré.)

exerc& stands at the end of a line in N, after which *ac* has been added, in smaller letters and a slightly lighter ink than the text. Since the correction was apparently not made by the scribe, with his exemplar still before him, it has no certain claim to authority; and this is true of all the non-scribal corrections in the manuscript, which in principle should be subject to the same scrutiny as modern conjectures. If *ac* and *et* are both judged as conjectures, it is evident that *et* is the better conjecture to make, since *et* would have been more readily lost after *exerc&*.

3. 3. 1–2 Praeter hanc causam aliae quoque sunt quae nobis merita non numquam maxima euellant. Prima omnium ac potentissima, quod nouis semper cupiditatibus occupati non quid habeamus sed quid petamus ⟨**spectamus**⟩: **in id, quod adpetitur, intentis**, quidquid est domi, uile est. (2) Sequitur autem ut ubi quod acceperis leue nouorum cupiditas fecit, auctor quoque **eorum** non sit in pretio.

spectamus *Madvig 1871-84, 2:411* : *om.* N, inspicimus Bς₁ς₁₉‡, intendimus ς₆, attendimus ς₁₂
in id quod adpetitur intentis *Grut. p. 989* (*Haase, Gertz*) : in id quod est quod adpetitur intentis NR (-peditur Nac), quicquid *ss. super* quod (1°) Npc* (*man. post.*)
    in id quod est quod adpetitur intenti Cψ
    in id quidem quod a(p)petitur intenti QMGK
    non id quod est sed quod appetitur intenti. ς₂ >*1503*
    non in id quod est sed quod appetitur intenti ς₁ (-petimus ς₄), *1515, 1529, 1605‡*
    in id quod appetitur intenti ς₁₅

---

[7] Because Gertz relied entirely on Kekulé's collation of N (Introduction n. 19), it is unclear whether the note in his apparatus, 'in ras. fort. fuit *&*', is a conjecture based on Kekulé's report of an erasure or Kekulé's suggestion of what the erasure concealed.

[8] Cf. the discussion of 2. 31. 2–3.

sed in id quod appetimus intenti B, *cod. Pinc., 1557, 1585*
non in id quod est quod adpetimus intentis *Grut. p. 533*[9]
ita non in quod est sed quod adpetitur intentis *Madvig 1871–84, 2:411*
in id quod deest, quod adpetitur intentis *dub. Buck 1908, 54 n. 4*
in id quod dest, quod adpetitur intentis *Pré.*
quidquid N : quidquid enim ς_2‡
eorum N : eius *Shackleton Bailey 1970, 361 (aut delendum)*

A verb is unquestionably wanted after *quid petamus*, for without one various forms of trouble must be visited on *in id...intentis* (see following). Of the stop-gaps previously proposed, both *intendimus* and the print vulgate's *inspicimus* can be quickly discarded: the former does not have anything like the needed sense in S.'s lexicon, and the sense of the latter is not much more appropriate (with an indirect question, 'inspect' or 'consider', e.g., 2. 1. 1 *inspiciamus...quemadmodum dandum sit beneficium). adtendimus*—'pay attention to'—is more nearly acceptable in its sense, and it produces an excellent clausula (*-tamus adtendimus* = double cretic). But 'more nearly acceptable' is not 'just right', for in S.'s usage *adtendere* = 'pay attention (sc. for the purpose of understanding)': *EM 22. 3 quam sententiam feram adtende, 58. 20 quid sit hoc idos adtendas oportet, 108. 4* and *118. 12 adtende quid dicam, Vit. beat. 24. 4 hoc primum adtendite.* Though it produces a slightly less desirable rhythm (*-mus spectamus* = double spondee), Madvig's suggestion, recruiting one of S.'s favourite verbs (nearly two hundred occurrences), gives better sense—'look to' / 'keep an eye on', as with a goal or target—and there is no reason to think he would have avoided the rhyming assonance of *-amus...-amus* (e.g., 4. 33. 2 *sic navigamus, sic militamus*, 6. 43. 3 *referamus reddamusque, Ira 3. 24. 4 prudentiori credamus, stultiori remittamus, NQ 7. 1. 4 spectamus interrogamus ostendimus*).

The crux that follows is harder, one of those in which **N**'s disastrous text caused variations to proliferate. Those that attempt to retain *in id quod est quod* usually introduce a contrast, *non* or *non...sed...*, often with a secondary change of *intentis* to *intenti* (parallel with *occupati*); that in turn requires either construing *in id quod...intenti* with the preceding clauses, ruining the structure of the passage, or introducing yet another change, *adpetimus* for *adpetitur*, and in either case leaving *quidquid est domi uile est* isolated.[10] Of those that distance themselves from *quod est quod*, the reading *in id quidem quod adpetitur* (found first in several twelfth-century manuscripts, with the unhappy *intenti*) is superior to Gruter's *in id quod adpetitur* (printed also by Gertz and Hosius, with antecedents in some *recentiores* and earlier editions), since *quidem* at least nods in the direction of *quod est*, whereas *in quod adpetitur* sweeps it under the rug.

---

[9] This is the version Gruter initially favoured, but in the appendix to his *Animaduersiones* (p. 989) he proposed the version later adopted (probably independently) by Haase, followed by Gertz.

[10] One of the *recentiores* provided a fig-leaf—*quidquid enim*—which became the print vulgate.

Against this backdrop the version suggested by Buck has a brilliance belied by the hesitation with which he advanced it, hiding its light, if not under a bushel, then in a footnote: *nouis semper cupiditatibus occupati non quid habeamus sed quid petamus ⟨spectamus⟩: in id quod deest, quod adpetitur intentis quidquid est domi uile est*, 'ever preoccupied by new desires, we look not to what we have but to what we seek: to those intent on what is lacking, what is desired, whatever is at hand is worthless.' On the one hand, *quod deest, quod* produces sense by adding two letters where they are most likely to have gone missing, respecting the fact that errors caused by a simple misreading of *scriptura continua* are even more frequent in **N** than the countless confusions of *e* and *i*.[11] On the other hand, the reading produces an excellent rhetorical structure that parallels the preceding clause while working variations on it: for example, *quod deest* gives *quid habeamus* a foil that it previously lacked; *intentis* remains, providing *variatio* in its syntactic contrast with the semantically parallel *occupati*; and the jabbing asyndeton of the antithetical relative clauses answers the explicit coordination that the antithetical indirect questions receive from *non…sed.*…I might say that if S. did not write this, he should have; but that is not a way of thinking an editor should entertain.

As for *eorum*, I see no way around Shackleton Bailey's objection:

> *eorum* can only refer to *nouorum*; but these new benefactions have no auctor since they exist only in the desire of the beneficiary. Either replace by *eius* (i.e. *quod acceperis*) or delete.

Griffin and Inwood tacitly opt for deletion—'But inevitably, when the desire for novelties makes what you have seem unimportant, the donor comes to be under-appreciated'[12]—but I think it slightly more likely that *eius* became *eorum* under the influence of *nouorum* than that the inept pronoun was generated *ex nihilo*.

3. 5. 1 Quemadmodum, mi Liberalis, quaedam res semel perceptae haerent, quaedam, ut scias, non est satis didicisse (intercidit enim eorum scientia, nisi **continuetur**)—geometriam dico et sublimium cursum et si qua alia propter suptilitatem lubrica sunt—ita beneficia quaedam magnitudo non patitur excidere, quaedam minora sed numero plurima et temporibus diuersa effluunt, quia, ut dixi, non subinde illa tractamus nec libenter, quid cuique debeamus, recognoscimus.

continuetur ς₁₃ς₁₆, *cod. Pinc., 1557‡* : continetur NacG (*def. Buck 1908, 54–5*), -neatur Npc >*1529, 1557mg.*, continuentur ς₁₇, continuent *Lips*.

coninuetur became a fixture in the text after Curio imported it from Pincianus and inserted it in his edition of 1557, replacing *contineatur*, the corrected reading

---

[11] N's text is, strictly, *inid quod estquod*. Préchac gilds the paleographical lily by suggesting *quod dest, quod*, which receives not much encouragement from *TLL* 5. 778. 50–4.

[12] Compare the illogic of Basore's translation: '…when the desire of new benefits has diminished the value of one that has already been received, the author of them[?] also is less esteemed.'

of **N** that **R** transmitted to the later manuscripts. But Buck was right to maintain that **N**'s original reading is blameless: in fact 'maintain'—'keep in place' / 'keep a firm hold on', 'to prevent from passing away' (cf. *OLD* s.v. 5)—is just the sense that is wanted here, in contrast with *intercidit* and (as Buck noted) *effluunt* a bit later in this long sentence; cf., e.g., 4. 6. 3 *sanguinem cuius cursu uitalis continetur calor*, 6. 33. 2 *illam* [sc. *felicitatem*] *multis et fidis manibus continentur, Brev.* 3. 1 *adstricti sunt in continendo patrimonio, simul ad iacturam temporis uentum est, profusissimi in eo cuius unius honesta auaritia est.*

3. 5. 2 Post exiguum tempus idem illi uerba priora quasi sordida et parum libera euitant, perueniunt deinde eo quo, ut ego existimo, pessimus quisque atque ingratissimus peruenit, ut obliuiscantur. Adeo enim ingratus est qui oblitus est **ut ingratus sit** cui beneficium in mentem uenit.

ut ingratus sit Nac (ut ingratus ς₂) : ut non ingratus sit Npc* (ñ *ss. man. post.*), ut gratus >*1515*, ut gratus sit *1529‡* (uti *1605, 1649*), ut ingratus sibi sit ς₁₁ς₁₈, ut is gratus *Alexander 1950–2, 14–15* (*resp. Mazzoli 1974, 72*)

The consecutive clause does not follow easily and clearly from the main clause whether one reads *ingratus* or *non ingratus / gratus*. To consider the latter alternative first: the meaning would be, 'One who has forgotten is so thoroughly ungrateful that one to whom thought of the *beneficium* (merely) occurs counts as grateful.' If that was S.'s intent, he might have expressed it more clearly by adding, say, *tantum* before *in mentem*. But even then I would sense that some slippage had occurred between *adeo* and the result, a sense that is only confirmed when I read Alexander's argument in favour of *gratus*:

> The idea is, that so generally and completely has 'remembering' or 'not forgetting' become treated as the equivalent of 'gratitude' in the field of benefits, that a man can qualify as 'grateful' who from time to time recalls a benefit done him,

where note that the force of *adeo*—'so generally and completely'—is directed to a different purpose entirely and an idea is summoned up—the equivalence of remembering and not forgetting in relation to gratitude—that has no clear counterpart in the Latin.

Furthermore—this is Mazzoli's objection—if S. is being consistent he should *not* grant that the man who thinks of a *beneficium* only now and then counts as *gratus*; for he had previously insisted that the *gratus* person is one who keeps awareness of the *beneficium* in the forefront of his mind, where it always recurs (3. 2. 1 *Quis tam ingratus est quam qui quod in prima parte animi positum esse debuit et semper occurrere ita seposuit et abiecit ut in ignorantiam uerteret?*). Yet S. is surely known to lapse from perfect consistency in the heat of the rhetorical moment; and if his point is what Mazzoli suggests, he could have expressed it more clearly by writing, say, *etiam cui beneficium in mentem uenit* (more clearly still by adding *interdum* before *in mentem*).

In short, I am not at all certain which alternative is correct but will bet on S.'s consistency and print **N**'s original text.

3. 6. 2 Nostri maiores, maximi scilicet uiri, ab hostibus tantum **res repetierunt**, beneficia magno animo dabant, magno perdebant; excepta Macedonum gente non est in ulla data aduersus ingratum actio. Magnumque hoc argumentum est dandam non fuisse, quia aduersus maleficium **omne** consensimus et homicidii, ueneficii, parricidii, uiolatarum religionum aliubi atque aliubi diuersa poena est sed ubique aliqua; hoc frequentissimum crimen nusquam punitur, ubique improbatur....

scilicet N > *1557, 1649‡* : illi *1585–1605,* maximi scilicet uiri *susp. habet Grut. p. 533*
res repetierunt *Mur.‡* (*Grut. p. 533*) : aes petierunt N, *Pinc., 1557* (*def. Buck 1908, 55*), expetierunt > *1529*
beneficia magno animo *dist.* N, *Pinc., 1557‡* : beneficia. magno animo > *1529*
omne N : omnes *Gertz*

Cf. Cic. *Off.* 1. 36 *Ac belli quidem aequitas sanctissime fetiali populi Romani iure perscripta est. Ex quo intellegi potest nullum bellum esse iustum, nisi quod aut rebus repetitis geratur aut denuntiatum ante sit et indictum.* Muretus' correction of **N**'s *aes petierunt* would be clearly correct, and Buck's defense would be clearly misguided, even if it were not the case that the expression *aes petere* occurs only at Pl. *Aul.* 526 and Gell. 9. 2. 2, in neither place in connection with warfare.

When used attributively, *omnis* vastly more often precedes the word it modifies; but 'vastly more often' is not 'always', and it is not terribly difficult to find exceptions demonstrating that *maleficium omne* is not impossible here (e.g., 7. 20. 1 *corrumpendo fas omne ut nihil in eum nefas esset effecerit*, Ira 1. 7. 4 *consilium omne et paenitentiam irruocabilis praecipitatio abscidit*, Marc. 22. 6 *ita iussit lumen omne praecludi*). But the placement of *omne* was not the basis of Gertz's emendation; rather, '"omnes" solum recte illi uerbo respondet, quod paulo post scribitur: "sed u b i q u e aliqua"'—and in that he was exactly right. When S. wrote *consensimus* he did not mean 'we' as in 'you and I', nor even as in 'you and I and all other Romans'; he meant 'we human beings', and we can be certain of that because he is talking about the kinds of malefaction that are recognized as such by the *ius gentium*, the 'law of nations' constituted by the broad consensus of humankind that doing certain things is just wrong, however differently the wrong might be requited by this *gens* or that.

3. 7. 3 Ita duas res quibus in uita humana nihil pulchrius est corrumpimus, gratum **hominem** et **beneficium**; quid enim aut in hoc magnificum est, si beneficium non dat, sed commodat, aut in illo, qui reddit, non quia uult, sed quia necesse est?

hominem N >*1557, prob. Lips. 1649‡* : animum *Mur., prob. Grut. p. 534, 1605 (Castiglioni 1920, 170)*

beneficium (1°) N : beneficum *Pinc. (resp. Grut. p. 534, prob. Lips.), 1649‡*

Muretus and Castiglioni independently conjectured *animum* for *hominem*, the latter expressly on the ground that S. refers to 'two things', *duas res*.[13] But *res* here = 'entities', and the man who wrote *homo sacra res homini* (*EM* 95. 33) would not balk at writing *hominem* after *res* here.

In a work about *beneficia* the nominative singular form of the masculine adjective, *beneficus*, would in a sense be protected, since it could not be confused with the noun (thus 4. 17. 2 *quis est qui non beneficus uideri uelit*). But the oblique forms of the masculine singular and all the plural forms were vulnerable: so at 3. 11. 1 '*Quaedam*' inquit '*priuilegia parentibus data sunt; quomodo horum extra ordinem habita ratio est, sic aliorum quoque beneficorum haberi debet*'—where *aliorum*, like *horum*, must refer to persons—the adjective conjectured by Koch (1874, 13) must be correct and the archetype's *beneficiorum*—despite Buck's defense (1908, 56)—must be wrong (see the discussion ad loc.). Similarly here: where *hoc* = 'the latter' and *illo* = 'the former', and both (as Lipsius saw) are presented as agents—*si beneficium non dat, sed commodat* and *qui reddit*—*hoc* must refer to a person just as *illo* does.

3. 7. 6 Ingrati actio non erat iudicem adligatura **sed regno liberrimo positura**. Quid sit enim beneficium non constat, deinde quantum sit; refert quam benigne illud interpretetur iudex. Quid sit ingratus nulla lex monstrat; saepe et qui reddidit quod accepit ingratus est et qui non reddidit gratus.

regno N (*def. Buck 1908, 55–6, recip. Hos. 2*) : in regno *Madvig et Wesenberg ap. Gertz (Hos. 1)*

S. argues that subjecting the exchange of *beneficia* to positive law and allowing a benefactor to bring a suit for ingratitude (*ingrati actio*) would open a large can of worms, because gratitude and ingratitude are concepts and attitudes too flexible and variable to make clear legal definition possible (*Quid sit ingratus nulla lex monstrat*). As a result, too much interpretive power would have to be vested in the judge: he would have to be given *regnum liberrimum* ('unrestricted authority' in Griffin and Inwood's version). Madvig and Wesenberg convinced Gertz that *in* was required before *regno*, presumably because S. nowhere uses *ponere* with the bare ablative, and the matter apparently seemed sufficiently self-evident that Gertz did not think it necessary to offer an explanation in his *Adnotationes*. Hosius adopted the emendation in his first edition but then removed it after Buck defended **N**'s text, granting that S. nowhere used *ponere* with the bare ablative but

---

[13] Alexander 1950–2, 15, accepted Castiglioni's point but thought that the 'error' should be attributed to S.

pointing to other authors who did: the authors he cites are Vergil—than whom no one used the ablative more freely—and three epic poets influenced by Vergil.[14] Madvig and Wesenberg were correct.

3. 9. 3 Haec quis aestimabit? quis dissimilibus beneficiis iubebit beneficia pensari? '**Donaui** tibi domum'; sed ego tuam supra te ruere praedixi. '**Dedi** tibi patrimonium'; sed ego naufrago tabulam. '**Pugnaui** pro te et uolnera **excepi**'; at ego uitam tibi silentio dedi. Cum aliter beneficium detur, aliter reddatur, paria facere difficile est.

donaui *Haase* : donauit N
dedi *Haase* : dedit N
pugnaui *Grut. p. 535* ('non spreuerim scribere'), *Haase* : pugnabi Nac, pugnauit Npc
excepi. at *Grut. p. 535, Haase* : excipiat Nac, excepit. at Npc

It was known since Gruter's report of **N** that the oldest manuscript offered a problematic text:[15] within the same rhetorical frame—an *ego* contrasting his own services to *tu* with those of a hypothetical other—two third-person singular verbs (*donauit, dedit*) are followed by a first-person singular verb (*pugnabi*) and a verb that is third-person singular but the wrong mood and tense (*excipiat*).[16] The corrections in **N** that turned *pugnabi* into *pugnauit* were certainly made by the same hand, and so probably were the corrections that turned *excipiat* into *excepit. at.* The hand was not the scribe's, but the corrections were made early enough for *pugnauit* and *excepit. at* to be picked up by **R**, and so the four third-person forms became the vulgate in the manuscripts and printed editions; Haase was the first editor to believe that was the wrong choice, and his text was accepted by Gertz, Hosius, and (to infer from his silence) Buck. I take it that Haase's implied premise is correct—all four verbs must have the same person—and that S.'s rhetorical habits make neither option *a priori* more likely than the other, since he is as apt to ventriloquize an imagined other speaking in the first person as he is to conjure up the action of an imagined other in the third person. In either case, more than one error must be assumed; the question *utrum in alterum abiturum erat?* perhaps allows us to choose the more economical scenario. If S. wrote *pugnaui* and *excepi. at*, the errors that produced *pugnabi* and *excipiat* are trivial,[17] and we must suppose that *donaui tibi* and *dedi tibi* became *donauit tibi* and *dedit tibi* through dittography, either simultaneously or (more likely) with one influencing the other. If S. wrote *donauit* and *dedit*, establishing the third-person singular for his

---

[14] *Aen.* 6. 507–8 *te...patria...ponere terra*, Ov. *Met.* 8. 685 *longo uestigia ponere cliuo*, Val. Flacc. *Arg.* 4. 378 *saxo posuit latus*, Sil. Pun. 6. 397–8 *patria uestigia...ponentem terra*.

[15] I say 'oldest manuscript' because **N** was not treated as the extant archetype before Gertz.

[16] Confusion of *u* and *b* is very common, even if not as ubiquitous as confusion of *e* and *i*: whatever other difficulties the passage poses, S. must have written -*ui* (or -*uit*) and *excep*-.

[17] *excepi. at* probably first became *excipiat* through a misreading of *scriptura continua*, after which *excipiat* was inevitable.

conceit, it seems to me somewhat more difficult to explain both why *pugnauit* became *pugnaui* and why, through a different mechanism, *excepit. at* became *excipiat*. The conundrum has no certain solution, but my reading of the probabilities gives the edge to Haase.

3. 10. 3 Quam deinde poenam ingratis constituimus? unam omnibus, cum disparia sint? inaequalem et pro cuiusque beneficio maiorem aut minorem? Age, intra pecuniam uersabitur taxatio: quid quod quaedam **uitae beneficia** sunt et maiora uita? His quae pronuntiabitur poena? minor beneficio? iniqua est: par et capitalis? quid inhumanius quam cruentos esse beneficiorum exitus?

uitae beneficia N: uitae ⟨paria⟩ beneficia *Badstübner 1888, 82,* uitae = *nom. pl. secundum Grundmann ap. Buck 1908, 56,* ⟨aequanda⟩ uitae beneficia *Walter 1927, 1567*

I will punctuate with a question mark after *taxatio*, to suit the spirit and movement of the passage; the issue worth discussing here is the soundness and meaning of *uitae beneficia*.[18] The *prima facie* meaning of *uitae* as a genitive—'What of the fact that some benefits of life are even greater than life'—is nonsense, and though Buck was satisfied with Gundermann's suggestion that *uitae* is nominative plural (*quaedam uitae = uitae quorundam*) and *beneficia* a predicate noun ('Some lives are benefits even greater than life'), that does not seem a large improvement. I was at one point tempted by the thought that *uitae* might be a genitive of value— an approach that Griffin and Inwood seem to take ('some benefits are worth a life')—but that hardly seems likely absent some word expressly denoting appraisal (e.g., *aliquem magni aestimare, aliquem ne assis quidem facere*), even if *uitae* could serve the purpose regularly served by *magni, assis, nihili,* and the like. It seems that either something is missing that should be present or something is present that is not wanted. Badstübner and Walter took the former view in suggesting supplements that first assert equivalence of value before *maiora uita* raises the stakes ('some benefits are equivalent to life and greater than life', i.e., '…as valuable as life, and more'), though the bald *et* then seems awkward, where 'and even' is wanted. I think it cleaner to assume that an unwanted *uitae* has crept in, anticipating *uita* just ahead:[19] 'Come now, will the assessment be limited to *money*? What about the fact that some benefits are even greater / more important than *life*?', with the emphatically antithetical terms, *pecuniam* and *uita*, placed at the beginning and end of the thought.

---

[18] Gertz's *uersabatur* was intended to resolve a conflict between *age…taxatio?* and *quid quod…uita?* that, so far as I can see, does not exist (pp. 210–11). As for *constituimus*, S.'s fluid use of tenses allows him to shift from present to the futures that follow, especially given the break caused by the two intervening questions: Matthias's *constituemus* is not wanted (1888, 179), still less the *constituamus* printed in editions before Fickert.

[19] If the *mise en page* of N's exemplar resembled that of N itself, *uita* stood directly under *quaedam*.

3. 11. 1 'Quaedam' inquit 'priuilegia parentibus data sunt; quomodo horum extra ordinem habita ratio est, sic aliorum quoque **beneficiorum** haberi debet.' Parentium condicionem sacrauimus, quia expediebat liberos tolli; sollicitandi ad hunc laborem erant incertam adituri fortunam. Non poterat illis dici, quod beneficia dantibus dicitur: 'Cui des, elige; ipse tecum, si deceptus es, querere; dignum adiuua.' In liberis tollendis nihil iudicio tollentium licet, tota res uoti est. Itaque ut aequiore animo adirent aleam, danda aliqua illis potestas fuit.

beneficiorum N (*def. Buck 1908, 56*) : beneficorum *Koch 1874, 13*

This passage was touched on in the discussion of 3. 7. 3, where the distinction between *beneficium* and *beneficus, -a, -um* also arises; here another of Hosius' shifts in judgement is involved. After Gertz accepted Koch's *beneficorum*, Hosius followed suit in his first edition, then reverted to *beneficiorum* after Buck defended N's text on the ground that *horum* refers to *priuilegia*, not *parentibus*. But this is pretty clearly mistaken. As often, the thought is presented as the objection or alternative viewpoint of an interlocutor, who is represented as saying, 'Certain privileges have been granted to parents: as special account has been taken of these [sc. parents, namely by granting them privileges], so should special account be taken of other benefactors', where *extra ordinem* and *ratio* are supplied with *haberi* from what precedes, *aliorum* is parallel with *horum*, and *beneficorum*, not *beneficiorum*, is needed. S. then proceeds to knock this viewpoint down by stressing the 'sacrosanct' position of parents and enumerating the factors that distinguish them from other *beneficia dantes* and justify their *priuilegia*.

3. 11. 2 Deinde alia condicio parentium est, qui beneficia, quibus dederunt, dant nihilo minus daturique sunt, nec est periculum, ne dedisse ipsos mentiantur; in ceteris quaeri debet, non tantum an receperint, sed an dederint, horum in confesso merita sunt, **et, quia utile est iuuentuti regi, imposuimus illi quasi domesticos magistratus sub quorum custodia contineretur**.

et quia... contineretur *post* merita sunt *coll.* N (*def. Alexander 1950–2, 15*), *post* 11. 1 potestas fuit *Gertz, del. Pré.*
sub ψM : sed N (*def. Buck 1908, 56*), et *Gertz*, s⟨cilic⟩et *Pré.* (*qui et* domesticos ⟨coss.⟩ *olim pensitauit*), eosdem *Mazzoli 1974, 73*

Gertz transposed *et, quia utile... custodia contineretur* to follow the allusion to the *uitae necisque potestas* at the end of 3. 11. 1 (above), where it would also be at home. But as Alexander observed, neither Gertz nor Préchac, who secluded the passage, could suggest how the words ended up where they are, and I am satisfied by the explanation Alexander gave for the transmitted order:

> The part of the sentence coming after the *et quia* is not actually an additional factor, but an explanation of the *horum merita* preceding. 'The services of these (= parents) are admitted openly, not only in the bringing up of their children as

a family matter, but in controlling them like domestic magistrates, because youth needs discipline and direction', would be a better sentence; but Seneca falls, as even the best authors in all ages have fallen, for the all too facile *et*, and simply tacks on a statement which should have been framed in some reasonable hypotactic arrangement.

As for **N**'s *magistratus sed*, Buck defended it on the ground that '*sed…cont.* gibt den Gegensatz zu *domesticos*', which I confess I do not understand: *quorum…contineretur* does not stand in contrast to *domesticos* but explains what is meant by *domesticos magistratus* and the purpose they serve. Of the other suggestions, the medieval correction *sub* and Gertz's *et* are more attractive than the paleographically inspired but very awkward suggestions of Préchac and Mazzoli. As for *et*, it is true that *magistratus et* could easily become *magistratus set*, then *magistratus sed*; but *domesticos…et quorum…contineretur* makes for an awkward and unbalanced pair of modifiers, and since *quorum…contineretur* is a relative final clause, the equivalent of *ut eorum…contineretur* ('…so that the youth would be held in check under their guardianship'), I would not expect it to be preceded by either *sed* or *et* unless it was being contrasted with (in the case of *sed*) or joined to (in the case of *et*) another expression of a similar type. *magistratus sub* > *magistratus sed* is not much more difficult than *magistratus et* > *magistratus sed*; as for Buck's claim that *continere sub* in the sense needed is 'nicht lateinisch' (the sort of thing he perhaps said too often), it is refuted by *EM* 25. 1 *quadrigenarium pupillum cogitas sub tutela tua continere?*, to look no farther.

3. 12. 2 Hic auxilia tribuit, ille ornamenta, ille solacia. Inuenies qui nihil putet esse iocundius, nihil maius quam habere in quo calamitas adquiescat; inuenies rursus qui dignitati suae quam securitati consuli malit; **est qui** plus ei debere se iudicet per quem tutior es quam ei per quem honestior. Proinde ista maiora aut minora erunt, prout fuerit iudex **aut huc aut illo** inclinatus animo.

inuenies rursus…consuli malit *post* et qui plus…honestior *coll.* G *Madvig 1871–84, 1:49–50*

est, qui *Haase* : et qui N (*def. Buck 1908, 56–7*)

aut huc aut illo *Hos.* (*pro* aut hoc aut illo) : aut haec[?] aut illa Nac
    aut in haec aut in illa Npc* (*man. post.*).
    aut ad haec aut ad illa BGIpcKEpc‡
    aut ad haec aut illa JV
    ad haec aut illa *Gertz* (*Pré.*)

Madvig's transposition of the clause concerning *auxilia* to follow the clause concerning *solacia* makes a certain sense, bringing together the private values of safety and comfort and allowing *inuenies rursus* to introduce the clearly contrasting category of those who prefer public honour. But again it is not clear how the dislocation would have arisen, and in any case the introductory sentence—listing *auxilia, ornamenta,* and *solacia* before the same categories are taken up in reverse order—suggests that no dislocation has occurred. If that is the case, then Haase's *est qui* for *et qui* is unwanted, since those who prefer *dignitas* to *securitas* and those who prefer being *tutior* to being *honestior* constitute contrasting sets suitably joined by *et*.

Near the end, correction has left **N**'s original text unclear, but the reading of **R** and most of the later medieval manuscripts suggest that it was *aut haec aut illa*: through a later correction in **N**, *h* and *a* were erased and replaced by *in*, a small superscript *h* was added before *e*, to which a *cauda* was added (*ę*), and a small superscript *in* was inserted before *illa*. The later tradition consists wholly of variations on *aut ad haec aut ad illa*, but as far as I have been able to discover the pairings *ad haec / ad illa* and *in haec / in illa* are not joined with *aut* in classical Latin to produce the sense desired here.[20] Turning his back on that approach, Hosius wrote *aut huc aut illo*: I think that was essentially correct, but if one is going to go that far, one might as well venture *aut hoc aut illo*, which is closer to something that we know S. actually wrote to express the idea 'this way or that': cf. 5. 6. 5 *ista sidera hoc et illo diducet uelocitas sua* (of a solar eclipse, where *huc* became the vulgate after Basel 1515 introduced it), *NQ* 2. 11. 2 *positiones hoc aut illo uersae*, 5. 1. 1 *nec hoc nec illo impetum capiat*. I conjecture that *illo* became *illa* and that *hoc* was altered to complete the pair.

3. 12. 3 Praeterea creditorem mihi ipse eligo, beneficium saepe ab eo accipio a quo nolo, et aliquando ignorans obligor: quid facies? ingratum uocabis eum cui beneficium inscio et, si scisset, non accepturo impositum est? **non uocabis eum qui utcumque acceptum non reddidit.**

impositum est? non uocabis…reddidit. N : i- est ⟨si⟩ utcumque acceptum non reddidit (*del.* non…qui) *Gertz p. 212*
　　impositum est, omnino vocabis…reddidit? *J. Müller 1892, 3–4*
　　impositum est? non uocabis…reddidit? *Pré. (prob. Alexander 1950–2, 16)*
　　impositum est: non uocabis…reddidit? *Alexander 1937, 57*

To the question 'Ingratum uocabis…impositum est?',[21] the righteous answer is 'No, I certainly will not: one is obliged to respond gratefully only when a benefit has been given by a willing benefactor to a willing recipient' (2. 18. 8 *Non refert quid sit quod datur nisi a uolente, nisi uolenti datur*). Gertz regarded *non uocabis eum qui* as an intrusion and replaced it with *si*. In refutation Alexander wrote:

> Gertz's complaints about the infelicity of the repeated *uocabis eum* are dissipated completely, it seems to me, by Préchac's simple device of writing the

---

[20] S. does write *in hoc aut in illud* at 4. 33. 3, but only there.
[21] **N** (and **R**) omitted *cui* after *eum*; the loss was made good in some of the later medieval manuscripts (**ψM**).

interrogation sign again at the end of the second *uocabis eum* sentence. Cf. for verb repetition, with a negative attached to the second verb, 3. 17. 2: *an tu infelicem uocas qui caruit acie…, non uocas miserum* etc.

But the example quoted only highlights one of the two problems that the transmitted text presents. A predicate expression—even if it is the same adjective—is wanted with the repeated *uocabis eum*, and the awkwardness of its absence is compounded by a second awkwardness, the presence of *non*: for the most natural way to express the question that Alexander desiderates—and at the same time the most effective way to give it the emphasis it deserves as a climactic *reductio ad absurdum*—is simply to repeat *ingratum uocabis eum*; to ask 'Won't you call ungrateful…?' is to put a different question, with the stress placed on entirely the wrong word.[22] Taken together, these two clumsy touches convince me that Gertz was correct to delete *non uocabis eum*. But rather than introduce *si* in place of *qui*, I will just allow the second relative clause to follow the first in asyndeton, as S. often does: 'Will you call ungrateful someone who did not know a benefit had been imposed and would have rejected it had he known, who failed to make a return no matter how the benefit reached him?' I take it that *non uocabis eum* entered the text either intentionally, as a misguided supplement, or accidentally, when *uocabis eum* on the preceding line caught a scribe's eye, with *non* then ineptly added by a reader who thought that an antithesis was intended by the repetition.

3. 14. 3 Aequissima uox est et ius gentium prae se ferens, 'Redde quod debes'; haec turpissima est in beneficio, 'Redde!' **Quid? reddet uitam, quam debet?** dignitatem? securitatem? sanitatem?

reddet ς₁ς₁₈, *1529‡, Grut. p. 535* : reddit N >*1515*, reddidit M, reddat ς₁₆ς₁₇
quid? reddet uitam quam debet? *dist. Grut* : quid reddet? uitam *dist. Eras.‡*, quid reddit uitam? quam debet? Nac, quid reddit? uitam quam debet? Npc, *1529‡ (prob. Buck 1908, 57)*, haec turpissima…quid reddit *om.* >*1515*
uitam quam debet N >*1503 (Grut. p. 535)*, *1649‡* : uitam, inquam, debet *1515–1605*, qui eam debet *Wesenberg ap. Gertz*

I take it to be uncontroversial that the future tense is wanted (N's *reddit* is just another instance of *i* swapped in for *e*) and that the *inquam* introduced by Erasmus' first edition is not. Gruter's punctuation, first adopted by Fickert, is possibly correct, but to my ear the retort is more forceful if *reddet* is included in the question immediately following the imperative: '"Give back!" What will he give back? The life that he owes?…' That is the punctuation of **N** as corrected,

---

[22] To ask the question that Préchac and Alexander suppose S. is putting, one would far better say, *num ingratum uocabis eum….*

which Erasmus introduced after discovering the words—omitted by the previous editions—in two manuscripts he had been given.[23]

3. 15. 3 O turpem **humani generis** {et} **fraudis ac** nequitiae publicae confessionem! Anulis nostris plus quam animis creditur. In quid isti ornati uiri adhibiti sunt, in quid imprimunt signa? Nempe ne ille neget accepisse se quod accepit.

humani generis fraudis ac Fpcς₁₃, *1529, 1557* : h- g- et f- ac N >*1515 (Pré.)*
    humano generi fraudis ac *1585‡*
    inhumani fenoris et f- ac *Klammer 1878, 65–7*
    h- generis istam f- ac *Schultess 1878, 512*
    h- generis ⟨degeneri⟩ et f- ac *Alexander 1950–2, 17*
    humani generis ⟨sceleris⟩ et f- ac *Mazzoli 1974, 73–4*

The theme: that people believe they must rely on written legal instruments sealed with the impress of a signet ring is merely an acknowledgement of our depravity. The text passed down from **N** has exercised critics, but the simplest solution is the deletion of *et*, found as a correction in **F** and in one of the *recentiores*, introduced (probably conjecturally) by Erasmus, and reintroduced by Haase after it had been superseded by Muretus' *humano generi*. It is also probably the correct solution: 'Alas, that the human race must shamefully admit to universal fraud and rascality!' Alexander thought otherwise:

> I think that the *et* after *generis* is too hard a core of MS rock to be lightly blasted out of the sentence; it is not ours to eject it, but rather to show how it came there.

But the reason it came to be there provides the reason it should be ejected: in a word, hyperbaton. Coming upon *humani generis*, a scribe or reader—overlooking the hint provided by *turpem* and too impatient to await the construction's confirmation in *confessionem*—decided that it must belong to the sequence of genitives that immediately follow. Muretus' conjecture, tying the phrase to *turpem*, is owed to a similar impatience, which is a frequent cause of stumbles: compare the remarkably similar error found at *Clem.* 2. 1. 3 *O uocem publica generis humani innocentia dignam…*, where the clearly correct reading, *publica*, was assimilated to *uocem* in N's text (*publicam*).[24]

3. 16. 3 Numquid iam ullus adulterii pudor est postquam eo uentum est ut nulla uirum habeat nisi ut adulterum inritet? Argumentum est deformitatis pudicitia.

---

[23] The break after *reddit* is marked in **R** (which punctuates with a comma after *debet*), and the question mark appears in most of the twelfth-century manuscripts. Erasmus found the words in manuscripts he received from England and Basel, cf. Chapter 2 n. 34.

[24] *Publica* first appears in the version of *De clementia* contained on f. 42ʳ–49ᵛ of Paris, BnF 8542 (= **T**); another version appears on f. 148ʳa–153ᵛb (1. 5. 3]*talem etiam illum…*–2. 6. 4 *et ad omnium*) of the same book (both versions date to the twelfth century). For another example, see Kaster 2016, 184–5, on an unwanted *quam* that worked its way into the text of Suet. *Claud.* 20. 1 for a similar reason.

Quam inuenies tam miseram, tam sordidam ut illi satis sit unum adulterorum par, nisi singulis diuisit horas? et non sufficit dies omnibus, nisi apud alium gestata est, apud alium mansit. Infrunita et antiqua est, quae nesciat matrimonium uocari unum adulterium.

Quam inuenies…adulterorum par, nisi singulis diuisit horas? et non sufficit…mansit. Infrunita et…adulterium. *dist. edd.* : Quam inuenies…adulterorum par, nisi…horas, et non sufficit dies omnibus? nisi…mansit, infrunita et…adulterium. *dist. Alexander 1950–2, 17*

Allowing suits to be brought for ingratitude would only reveal how many ingrates there are, which would in turn lessen the stigma and undermine the effectiveness of shame as a source of restraint (3. 16. 1): just look what has happened since adultery has become so common (3. 16. 2). So the line of thought that brings us to the present passage, in which (with the traditional punctuation) we pass from one question—how many adulterers are sufficient for one woman?—to another—how can she divide her time among them?—with an abruptness that seems to me impossible: the inconsequence is laid bare by the translation of Griffin and Inwood ('Where will you find a woman so wretched and squalid that she settles for just one pair of lovers?—without having a new lover for each hour of the day!'), in which the gap is not papered over even by importing an idea ('a new lover') that I cannot find in the Latin.

If there is not a lacuna before *nisi*—a possibility I would not entirely abandon—the problem can be addressed only by repunctuating. Alexander made the following suggestion:

I place a period after *omnibus*, begin a new sentence with *nisi apud alium*, and continue that sentence through to *adulterium*. My corresponding translation is as follows: 'What woman will you find so wretched, so unattractive, as to be satisfied with just one "pair" of paramours, without assigning each hour of the day [for an individual lover], and the day is too short for all of them [at that]. Unless she takes her afternoon drive with this one, and spends the night with that, she is a frump and out of date, because she doesn't know that to have only a single paramour is called "being married".'

To my eye, this does not solve the problem caused by the change of topic mid-sentence. At a minimum, a new sentence should begin with *nisi singulis*, and *et non…omnibus* should be treated as an aside:

Quam inuenies tam miseram, tam sordidam ut illi satis sit unum adulterorum par? Nisi singulis diuisit horas—et non sufficit dies omnibus—nisi apud alium gestata est, apud alium mansit, infrunita et antiqua est, quae nesciat matrimonium uocari unum adulterium.

This at least gathers in a single sentence the thoughts relevant to the time-management problem: 'What woman will you find so wretched, so repellent that one pair of lovers is enough for her? If she hasn't devoted an hour to each—and a day is not enough for all—if she hasn't gone for a jaunt with one and spent the night with another, she's an old-fashioned ass, unaware that "having a single affair" is another name for "marriage".'

3. 16. 4 Quemadmodum horum delictorum iam euanuit pudor, postquam res latius euagata est, ita ingratos **plures efficies et auctiores**, si numerare se coeperint.

auctiores Npc (-tores Nac) >*1557, Hos. 2, Pré.* : altiores BK, audaciores *1515mg., 1529mg., 1585‡*, auidiores *Haase (Hos. 1)*, tutiores *Gertz*

In his first edition Hosius printed Haase's *auidiores*, then reverted in his second to the reading of **N** as corrected, which had not stood in the text since the sixteenth century.[25] But *auctior*, used of persons, is barely attested before S. and has to do with public standing or authority when is does occur (Caes. *BG* 1. 43. 8 *socios et amicos…gratia, dignitate, honore auctiores*, Liv. 3. 68. 5 *re domum auctior rediit*, 4. 2. 4 *plebs gloriari posset ⟨se⟩ auctiorem amplioremque esse*): neither *auctior* nor *altior* nor *auidior* has much to do with the argument S. develops in 3. 16, which does not concern an increase in power, standing, or appetite but is all about the loss of *pudor* and the resultant increase in brazen behaviour. *audaciores*—perhaps a conjecture by Erasmus, first found in the margin of Basel 1515—suits the sense perfectly and is at least as close to the *ductus litterarum* as the other candidates.

3. 17. 1–2 'Quid ergo? impunitus erit ingratus?' Quid ergo, impunitus erit impius? quid malignus, quid auarus, quid impotens, quid crudelis? impunita tu credis esse quae inuisa sunt aut ullum supplicium grauius existimas publico odio? **(2)** Poena est quod non **audet** ab ullo beneficium accipere, quod non audet ulli dare, quod omnium designatur oculis aut designari se iudicat, quod intellectum rei optimae ac dulcissimae amisit.

audet (1º) N : sperat *Shackleton Bailey 1970, 362*, gaudet *Mazzoli 1974, 74–5 (sic et Watt 2001, 232)*

The impulse to emend the first *audet* is understandable, and *gaudet* would be easy enough; but I think the impulse misses the rhetoric of the paragraph, in which S. has veered away from the preceding jeremiad on the depravity and increasing shamelessness of the age to exploit quite a different idea. Like others who are dispositionally vicious—the impious, the malignant, the greedy, and so on—the ingrate is the object of 'universal hatred' (*publicum odium*) and so feels himself to be an outcast, a pariah (*omnium designatur oculis aut designari se iudicat*). Accordingly, he does not have the brass—or in Roman terms, the *os*

---

[25] This change cannot be attributed to the influence of Buck, who does not comment on the passage.

ferreum—that would allow him to participate in the everyday rituals of social life as though he were guiltless: he does not dare either to bestow or to receive a *beneficium*.

3. 18. 1–3 Quamquam quaeritur a quibusdam, sicut ab Hecatone, an beneficium dare seruus domino possit. Sunt enim, qui ita distinguant, quaedam beneficia esse, quaedam officia, quaedam ministeria: beneficium esse quod alienus det (alienus est qui potuit sine reprehensione cessare); officium esse filii, uxoris, earum personarum quas necessitudo suscitat et ferre opem iubet; ministerium esse serui, quem condicio sua eo loco posuit ut nihil eorum quae praestat imputet **superiori.** *** (**2**) **Praeterea** seruum qui negat dare aliquando domino beneficium, ignarus est iuris humani; refert enim, cuius animi sit, qui praestat, non cuius status. Nulli praeclusa uirtus est; omnibus patet, omnes admittit, omnes inuitat, et ingenuos et libertinos et seruos et reges et exules; non eligit domum nec censum, nudo homine contenta est. Quid enim erat tuti aduersus repentina, quid animus magnum promitteret sibi, si certam uirtutem fortuna amitteret? (**3**) Si non dat beneficium seruus domino, nec regi quisquam suo nec duci suo miles; quid enim interest, quali quis teneatur imperio, si summo tenetur? Nam si seruo, quo minus in nomen meriti perueniat, necessitas obstat et patiendi ultima timor, idem istuc obstabit et ei, qui regem habet, et ei, qui ducem, quoniam sub dispari titulo paria in illos licent. Atqui dant regibus suis, dant imperatoribus beneficia: ergo et dominis.

post superiori *lac. stat. Lips.* | praeterea N *>1557, prob. Grut. p. 536, Lips. 1649‡* : propterea *1585*

S. introduces the second major topic to which Book 3 is devoted: as 3. 6–17 considered the question whether the *ingratus* should be subject to an action at law and 3. 29–38 will consider the question whether children can give parents greater *beneficia* than they received through the gift of life, so 3. 18–28 considers the question whether a slave can bestow a *beneficium* on a master; and just as the topic is formally introduced by a sentence with the verb *quaeritur* in the other two *diuisiones* (3. 6. 1 *Hoc tam inuisum uitium an impunitum esse debeat quaeritur...*, 3. 29. 1 *Quaeritur enim...*), so it is here, with *quaeritur a quibusdam*. But soon trouble arises, as became evident once Lipsius pointed it out: the sentence beginning *praeterea* does not follow from what precedes (nor would it if Muretus' specious *propterea* were adopted). Accordingly, all editions since Lipsius', save one, have marked a lacuna after *superiori*, as mine will also.

The exception was Préchac, who sought to uphold the soundness of N's text by joining *praeterea* to *imputet superiori*. But that move is doubly unfortunate: first, *praeterea* rarely ends a sentence, and when it does it is in a context like Cic. *Att.* 6. 4. 1 *multa molesta, discessus noster, belli periculum, militum improbitas, sescenta praeterea* ('...and countless others besides'), clearly not relevant here; and like

Muretus' *propterea*, it does not address the main problem, which we will consider in a moment. In another attempt to sidestep a lacuna, Alexander suggested that 3. 18. 1 is nothing more than a parenthesis and should be marked as such 'by the appropriate punctuation', so that 3. 18. 2 could follow directly on 3. 17. 4 (1950–2, 17–18): but so far from being parenthetical, 3. 18. 1 plays a key structural role, as we have seen. Nor, finally, would it help to transpose 3. 18. 3 to precede 3. 18. 2, a radical move that has been attributed to Martin Sonntag;[26] but understanding why that transposition would be insufficient allows us to see what the fundamental problem is.

Besides stating the *quaestio* to be addressed, S. notes three categories, *beneficia*, *officia*, and *ministeria*, the last stereotypically the province of the slave. The question this section seeks to answer, however, is not, 'What does a slave normally provide?', but, 'Can a slave bestow a *beneficium* on a master?' In fact the text lacks what we find when S. takes up the *quaestiones* posed in the book's two other section: an express statement, suggesting an answer to the question posed, that S. can use as a foil to argue against—as at 3. 6. 1 *Quae uidetur aequa omnibus: 'Quidni? cum urbes quoque urbibus quae praestitere exprobrent et ⟨in⟩ maiores conlata a posteris exigant'*—or as a starting point for further development—as at 3. 29. 2 *Quod si constat* [sc. *multos filios maiores... extitisse quam parentes suos*], *potest fieri, ut meliora tribuerint, cum et fortuna illis maior esset et melior uoluntas*. But *praeterea seruum qui negat dare aliquando... beneficium* at the start of §2 and *Si non dat beneficium seruus domino* at the start of §3 both imply that such an answer, in the form of a denial, was given here as well; and *praeterea* at the start of §2 further implies that S. had already offered at least one reason to believe the denial was misconceived. The lacuna need not have been longer than a sentence— 'Quidam uero seruum domino ministeria tantum dare posse asserunt, beneficia omnino negant, sed errant quia...'—but the fact of the lacuna cannot itself be reasonably denied.[27]

3. 18. 4 Potest seruus iustus esse, potest fortis, potest magni animi: ergo et beneficium dare potest, nam et hoc uirtutis est. **Adeo quidem** dominis serui beneficia possunt dare ut ipsos saepe beneficii sui fecerint.

adeo quidem Q (*Fick.*) : adeo qui Nac, adeoque Npc*, Ppcγ‡ (*Buck 1908*, 57, *qui autem corr. in N non uidit*), adeo quia M

adeo quidem was brought into the text by Fickert, who knew it from one of his *recentiores*, and it is true that -*dem* could easily have been lost before *dom*-,

---

[26] Sonntag 1913 is an *explanatio* of De beneficiis (*L. Annaei Senecae De beneficiis libri explanantur*), that is, it provides a running paraphrase of its arguments: strictly, Sonntag did not say that the two sections should be transposed, he simply paraphrased 3. 18. 3 before he paraphrased 3. 18. 2 (p. 27).

[27] For other suggestions concerning the lacuna, see, e.g., Cooper and Procopé 1995, 255 n. 29, and Griffin 2013, 218, in both cases accepting the transposition of §3, which I think mistaken.

producing **N**'s original reading (*adeo quidominis*); but given **N**'s record in these matters, it is *prima facie* more likely that *i* replaced an original *e*. Equally to the point here, S. is not beginning a new thought, the context in which the only other pairing of *adeo* and *quidem* appears in the work (1. 1. 13 *Adeo quidem ista res fugare nos…non debet ut…*); he is continuing and extending the same thought, as the pairing *dare potest…possunt dare* shows and as *adeoque* elsewhere serves to do (1. 1. 10 *Et liberi et coniuges spem fefellerunt, tamen et educamus et ducimus, adeoque aduersus experimenta pertinaces sumus ut…*, similarly 3. 1. 1, 4. 1. 2, 15. 4, 17. 2): a slave is capable of displaying various virtues, 'therefore a slave is also capable of bestowing a benefit—for this too is an element of virtue—and slaves are so capable of benefiting their masters that….'[28]

3. 22. 3–4 Inter se contraria sunt beneficium et iniuria; potest dare beneficium domino, si a domino iniuriam accipere. Atqui de iniuriis dominorum in seruos qui audiat positus est, qui et saeuitiam et libidinem et in praebendis ad uictum necessariis auaritiam conpescat. Quid ergo? beneficium dominus a seruo accipit? immo homo ab homine. **(4)** Denique, quod in illius potestate fuit, fecit: beneficium domino dedit; **ne a seruo acceperis**, in tua potestate est.

Inter se contraria…iniuriam accipere. *dist. edd.* : 'Inter se contraria…iniuriam accipere?' (sc. *ut uerba interlocutoris*) *dist. Axelson 1939, 39–40 (prob. Alexander 1950–2, 18)* acceperis ρ‡ (*def. Alexander 1950–2, 18–19*) : acciperis Nac, -peres Npc* (*Pré.*)

The sequence of thought has been found puzzling: what does the opening statement about the complementarity of *beneficium* and *iniuria* (cf. 4. 15) have to do with the observation, introduced by *atqui*, about the official (the city prefect) 'appointed to hear cases concerning the wrongs done to slaves by masters'? Axelson suggested that the first sentence should be punctuated as a question raised by an imagined interlocutor, but I do not see how that helps matters. In fact to the extent that there is a problem, it is one of compression, for the conditional clause *si a domino iniuriam accipere* (sc. *seruus potest*) means a great deal more than its five words seem to say. If a slave can be wronged by a master, he is not merely an *instrumentum uocale*, in Varro's phrase (*RR* 1. 17. 1); he is also a human being with a right to be free from certain kinds of treatment. As Miriam Griffin says:

> If a master can be considered to have injured his own slave, then the master's power is not unlimited, and there is an area of freedom within which the slave can act from choice.[29]

---

[28] Buck, too, thought *adeoque* correct, though he also thought that N had only *adeo qui* ('von einer Korrektur *adeoque* konnte ich in N² nichts merken'). But the corrector canceled *ui* by drawing a line beneath the letters and added ; after *q*, to produce the usual abbreviation of *que* (*q;*); either the change was made sometime after *adeo qui* was transmitted to **R**, or **R**'s scribe, like Buck, did not notice the correction.

[29] Griffin 2013, 221.

Or to put it another way, when a master inflicts an *iniuria* on a slave, he does not do so as master but as one human being wronging another: cf. *Clem.* 1. 18. 2 *cum in seruum omnia liceant, est aliquid quod in hominem licere commune ius animantium uetet.* That is why S. rounds the matter off by making the complementary point: 'Does a master receive a benefit from a slave? Not at all: one human being receives a benefit from another.' Responding to the abstract and hypothetical character of the opening formulation, *atqui* shifts the emphasis to the actual and concrete, introducing a statement that is 'contrary, but not contradictory, to what precedes' (*OLD* s.v. 2): 'yet [there is no need to consider the matter merely abstractly, for] there *is* someone appointed...' Griffin and Inwood nicely capture the force of *atqui*: 'But we actually have an official to hear cases....'

In §22. 4, the perfect subjunctive introduced by the twelfth-century manuscripts is certainly correct, and S.'s point perhaps emerges more clearly with a period after *dedit* and a colon after *acceperis*, drawing out the fact that *ne...acceperis* is a negative command, in which *ne* + perfect subjunctive is regular (*NLS* §126): 'In short, that one did what it was in his power to do: he gave a *beneficium* to his master. Do not receive it from a slave [i.e., as from a *seruus*, not a *homo*]: that is in *your* power.' In both clauses *potestas* refers precisely to what Griffin called the 'area of freedom' within which both parties to the transaction can act from choice as rational beings.

3. 23. 2 Claudius Quadrigarius in duodeuicensimo annalium tradit, cum obsideretur Grumentum et iam ad summam desperationem uentum esset, duos seruos ad hostem transfugisse et operae pretium fecisse. Deinde urbe capta passim discurrente uictore illos per nota itinera ad domum in qua **seruierant** praecucurrisse et dominam suam **ante se** egisse; quaerentibus quaenam esset, dominam et quidem crudelissimam ad supplicium ab ipsis duci professos esse.

seruierant N : serui erant DPEγ, *Fick.*
ante se Npc : ante Nac, *Gertz p. 213*

We have another error in **N** caused by *scriptura continua*, in this case the result not of a mistaken division between words but of the failure to divide: the point of the story is that the two were still slaves (*erant*) at the time that they were performing their heroics, not that they had been slaves (but no longer were). As for *ante se*, Gertz retained **N**'s original reading, pointing to Verg. *G*. 3. 552 (*Tisiphone Morbos agit ante Metumque*), but the fact that he had to look to Vergil for a parallel goes to the nub of matter: for beyond one passage in Caesar (*BC* 1. 51. 4 *ante missis equitibus*) and another in Varro (*LL* 6. 82 *speculator quem mittimus ante*), *ante* as an adverb of place with a verb of motion occurs only in poetry (thus, in Cicero, only at *Arat.* 12 *piscis paulo praelabitur ante*), and not very commonly even there (cf. *TLL* 2. 128. 42–55). The superscript addition of *se* is certainly early (**R** has it) and possibly scribal, to judge from the colour of the ink and the letter forms.

3. 23. 4 In tanta confusione captae ciuitatis cum sibi quisque consuleret, omnes ab illa praeter transfugas fugerunt; at hi, ut ostenderent, quo animo facta esset prior illa transitio, a uictoribus ad captiuam transfugerunt personam parricidarum ferentes; quod in illo beneficio maximum fuit, tanti iudicauerunt, ne domina occideretur, uideri dominam occidisse. **Non est, mihi crede, condicio seruilis animi** egregium factum fama sceleris emisse.

condicio seruilis *Hos.* : non dico seruilis N >*1503, Pinc.*
  non est seruilis *1515–1585* (*mauult Grut. p. 537*)
  non, dico, est seruilis *Lips.‡*
  non, dico, seruilis *1649‡, Gundermann ap. Buck 1908, 57*
  indicium seruilis *Mück 1890, 27*
  non dico seruilis ⟨sed uilis⟩ *Pré.* (*prob. Alexander 1950–2, 19*)

Gertz printed *non est seruilis*, the text of most sixteenth-century editions, but in his apparatus wrote, 'quid lateat, nescio', and with the latter sentiment I wholeheartedly agree. Yet I am certain that any version with *dico* cannot be correct. S. uses *non dico* primarily with *sed* to coordinate contrasting clauses or predicates, though he does use *non dico...sed...*to coordinate contrasting phrases (*EM* 14. 11 *hae litterae, non dico apud bonos sed apud mediocriter malos, infularum loco sunt*) or even nouns (*EM* 88. 12 *ius non dico hominis sed populi fuerit potes expedire?*, *EM* 124. 7 *quod secundum naturam est, quod contigit protinus nato, non dico bonum sed initium boni*). But he never uses the phrase within a clause he has already begun with *non est*, nor so far as I have been able to discover does any other writer of classical Latin; and in this last regard what is true of *non dico* is, with one exception, true of *non est*.[30] It also seems to me extremely unlikely that *dico* could stand as a second parenthetical insertion (so Lipsius, Gronovius, Gundermann) directly after *mihi crede*.

But I must print something, and it seems to me marginally more likely that *non dico* originated as a jotted alternative to *non est*, as a rhetorically forceful way to begin the sentence, than that the string of letters preserves the traces of *condicio*, *indicium*, or the like: *Non est, mihi crede,* {*non dico*} *seruilis animi egregium factum fama sceleris emisse*—'It is not, believe me, characteristic of a servile spirit to have purchased....' I will also mention Hosius' conjecture in the apparatus, as the best alternative to this approach.

3. 26. 1–2 Cenabat Paulus praetorius in conuiuio quodam imaginem Tib. Caesaris habens ectypa et eminente gemma. **(2)** Rem ineptissimam fecero si nunc uerba quaesiero quemadmodum dicam illum matellam sumpsisse: quod factum simul et Maro ex notis illius temporis uestigatoribus notauit et seruus eius **quoi** nectebantur **insidiae ei ebrio anulum extraxit. Et cum Maro** conuiuas testaretur

---

[30] Cic. *Verr.* 2. 1. 10 *non est, non est in hoc homine cuiquam peccandi locus*, where the second *non est* is pragmatically equivalent to *mihi crede* in the present passage.

admotam esse imaginem obscenis et iam subscriptionem conponeret, ostendit in manu sua seruus anulum. Si quis hunc seruum uocat et illum conuiuam uocabit.

quoi *Gruter p. 538* : quo N > 1515 (*def. Buck 1908, 58*), cui M, *Eras.*, 1529‡, quando G insidiae Npc : insidias Nac, in⟨sidiae. is sub⟩sidians *Pré.*
quod factum... et seruus eius, quoi... insidiae, ei ebrio anulum extraxit. Et cum Maro... conponeret, ostendit... anulum. *dist. Hos.* : quod factum... et seruus eius, quoi necteban-tur insidiae. Ei ebrio anulum extraxit, et cum Maro... conponeret, ostendit... anulum. *dist. Alexander 1934, 54 (cf. Alexander 1950–2, 20)*

To take the second issue first: the standard punctuation, retained by Hosius, is that of **N**, which places full stops after *extraxit* and *seruus anulum*. Alexander proposed placing a full stop after *insidiae*, because he accepted Préchac's objection—'nec satis enucleate per *simul* uerbum sententiis *et... notauit, et... extraxit* coniunctis'—but rejected Préchac's characteristically improbable solution. But the articulation of the sentence—*simul et A et B*, where A and B are two different actions per-formed by two different subjects simultaneously—is faultless; and since the *seruus* must be the implied subject of *extraxit* and hence of *ostendit*, Alexander had to explain away the appearance of *seruus* after the latter by claiming that it 'has the special force "for all he was a slave" '.[31] He would have done better to point out that his proposal would not require the third-person pronoun to refer to the same person in different oblique cases in the same clause, which S. does not do else-where. But Latin certainly admits the usage: so Asconius, in a passage remarkably similar to ours, *Mil.* 35. 6 C. *in uia Appia occisum esse anulumque eius ei morienti extractum...*, and cf., e.g., Cic. *Verr.* 2. 2. 95 *eodemque ei tempore de eadem re lit-terae complures a multis eius amicis ac necessariis adferuntur...*, *Clu.* 21 *interim uenit index ad Dinaeam... qui nuntiaret ei filium eius, M. Aurium, uiuere....* It is also pertinent that S. otherwise admits sentence-initial *ei* only when it has a strongly deictic force as a correlative pronoun.[32]

As for the relative pronoun between *eius* and *nectebantur*, Buck argued that **N**'s *quo* should be retained as an instrumental ablative referring to *anulum*, but the sentence's structure makes that very improbable. Gruter's *quoi* is easier, relative to *quo*, than *cui*, and there is good reason to believe that S. admitted that form of the pronoun: it is the form **N** offers at 6. 7. 1, 6. 8. 1 (*aliquoi*), 6. 14. 3, 6. 43. 3, and it has been accepted in four other passages where the dative is needed but the primary manuscripts read *quo, quod,* or *quot* (3. 33. 4 *quoi* Gertz [*quo* **N**], *Clem.* 2. 2. 2 *quoi* Gertz [*quod* **N**], *Vit. beat.* 23. 2 *quoi* Madvig [*quot* **A**, *quo* γ],

---

[31] The proposal first appeared in Alexander 1934, the explanation of *seruus* in Alexander 1950.
[32] *Clem.* 2. 7. 1 *ego ut breuiter tamquam in alieno iudicio dicam*: '*Ei* [Erasmus, *et* N] *ignoscitur qui puniri debuit...*', *Ira* 3. 22. 3 '*nunc*' *inquit* '*male dicite Antigono, cuius uitio in has miserias incidisti; ei autem bene optate qui uos ex hac uoragine eduxit*', *EM* 118. 6 *Tu ista credis excelsa quia longe ab illis iaces; ei uero qui ad illa peruenit humilia sunt.*

Brev. 10. 3 *quoi* Gruter [*quo* ω]).[33] For the use of *quoi* and similar forms in early imperial inscriptions, cf., e.g., *SCPisone* (20 CE, *quoi*, *quoius*), *Lex Irnitana* (Spain 91 CE, *quoi*), *CIL* 3. 2609 (Dalmatia 101–30 CE, *quoi*), *CIL* 11. 1828 (Italy s. I[in.], *quoius*), *AE* 1979 no. 434 (Germania Superior 31–100 CE, *quoi*), *CIL* 10. 3969 (Capua, Augustan?, *quoiquam*), *CIL* 10. 5809 (Latium s. I[1/2], *quoius*).

3. 27. 4 Honeste fecit Caesar quod ignouit, quod liberalitatem clementiae adiecit: quicumque hoc audierit exemplum necesse est Caesarem laudet, sed cum seruum ante laudauerit. **Non expectas,** ut tibi narrem manu missum, qui hoc fecerat; nec tamen gratis: pecuniam pro libertate eius Caesar numerauerat.

non N : num *1605 (prob. Watt 1994, 226)*

The flat declarative statement, 'You're not waiting for me to tell you…', seems odd (Griffin and Inwood's 'You do not have to wait to hear…' is too much to extract from the simple indicative). Lipsius' *num*—'You're not waiting for me to tell you…, are you?' (sc. because you've already anticipated the outcome)—is preferable: as Watt points out, *num* was corrupted to *non* in some witnesses near the start of the next sentence (3. 28. 1 *post tot exempla, num* [**N**, *non* ψ *recc. plerique*] *dubium est…*).

3. 28. 3 Neminem despexeris, etiam si **circa** illum obsoleta sunt nomina et parum indulgente adiuta fortuna. Siue libertini ante uos **habentur** siue serui siue exterarum gentium homines, erigite audacter animos et quidquid in medio sordidi iacet transilite: expectat uos in summo magna nobilitas.

circa N : citra *Shackleton Bailey 1970, 361–2* | ante uos N, *1605‡* : ante nos Fç₂ç₃ç₁₅ >*1585*, autem nobis aui *Pinc.* | habentur ç₁‡ : habent N, sunt *vel* latent *Shackleton Bailey 1970, 361–2* (latent *et Watt 1994, 227*)

The image of a man surrounded (*circa illum*) by the names of his ancestors is not problematic after the evocation, immediately preceding, of the ancestor masks and family trees prominently displayed in people's homes (3. 28. 2 *imagines in atrio exponunt et nomina familiae suae longo ordine ac multis stemmatum inligata flexuris in parte prima aedium conlocant*). The verb in the following *siue*-clause is a different matter: I can squeeze sense neither from **N**'s *habent* nor from the *habentur* of several *recentiores* that became the print vulgate (Basore's 'Whether your line before you holds freedmen or slaves…' does not so much translate the Latin on the Loeb's left-hand page as paraphrase what S. must have meant). *sunt* is the wrong tense and *latent*, closer to *habent*, is unsatisfactory precisely because

---

[33] At 4. 8. 1 *quoi* (Gertz, *quod* **N**) *primum inuenta seminum uis*, either *quoi* must be accepted or more extensive corruption must be assumed (see the discussion ad loc.); ambiguity reigns at 4. 37. 1 *quod* (**N**, *quoi* Gertz) *ut nuntiatum est*, where I will print *quoi*. Cf. also 4. 7. 2 where *quom*, introduced by Hosius (*quod* **N**), is preferable to *cum*.

the 'names' are not hidden: they constitute *quidquid sordidi in medio iacet* that 'you' must 'leap across'. Rather than obelize *habent* I will print the stopgap *erant*.

3. 29. 5 Adspice trabes siue proceritatem aestimes altissimas, siue crassitudinem spatiumque ramorum latissime fusas: quantulum est his conparatum illud quod radix tenui fibra conplectitur? Tolle radicem: nemora non surgent nec tanti montes uestientur. Innituntur fundamentis suis **templa excelsa urbis**, tamen quae in firmamentum totius operis iacta sunt latent.

altissimas N, *Eras. p. 272* : -mam ς₂ς₃ *>1529*

tolle…uestientur *post* adspice…conplectitur *coll. Haase, ante* adspice *coll.* N

templa excelsa urbis *Hos.* ('*fort.* et stelae *vel* cellae' *in app.*) : templa et illa urbis N,

   templa et illa urbis moenia ψ, *1490‡* (uerbis *pro* urbis *1475, 1478*)

   templa et alia urbis *Grut. p.* 539 ('nescio quomodo mihi semper suspecta fuerit uox *illa*, nuncque etiam magis sit, quod uerbum *moenia* non repererim in antiquissimo Naz. libro')

   templa et †illa urbis *Gertz* ('*fort.* insulae urbis' *in app.*)

   templa et culmina urbis *J. Müller 1892, 5*

   templa et tecta urbis *E. Thomas 1893, 290*

   et templa illa urbis *Buck 1908, 58–9*

   templa et sacella urbis *Rossbach 1907, 1488*

   templa aemula urbis *Kronenberg 1907, 28*

   templa et urbes; illa *Pré.*

   templa tot illa urbis *Birt 1928, 51*

   templa et pilae urbis *Brakman 1928, 152*

   templa et illa ⟨fastigia⟩ urbis *Alexander 1950–2, 20*

   templa, ed⟨ita⟩ illa urbis *Mazzoli 1974, 75*

   templa et alia ⟨aedificia⟩ urbis *Watt 1994, 227*

That the sentence *Tolle…uestientur* was misplaced in **N** I take to be certain: the whole *trabes* must be mentioned before the root. The sentence was omitted at some point, because of a *saut du même au même* (-*tur*…-*tur*), and after being added in a margin was reinserted in the wrong place. What happened after *templa* is a problem of an entirely different order.

Here simply listing the many lines of attack that have been taken helps to make clear that obelization—the route chosen by Gertz alone among editors—is the only methodologically sound decision, because we cannot certainly, or even very probably, pinpoint the source of the problem. Is *et* the villain? (So variously Buck, Birt, and Mazzoli.) Or is some other word lurking behind *et illa*? (So Hosius, Kronenberg, and Préchac.) Or behind *illa* alone? (The most popular choice: Gruter, Müller, Thomas, Rossbach, Brakman, Gertz in his apparatus, Hosius in his.) Or should another noun be supplied for *illa* to modify, and if so, should it precede *urbis* (Alexander) or follow (ψ and the print vulgate)? Or is it some combination of these? (So Watt, replacing *illa* with *alia* and adding *aedificia*.) Printing *templa* †*et illa*† *urbis* leaves the core of S.'s thought and (probably) isolates the problem; I will also mention in the apparatus the suggestion of Thomas—because *templa* and *tecta* occur together so often, in both prose (e.g., *Helv.* 10. 7, Cic. *Cat.* 1. 12, 2. 29, 3. 2, 22, Liv. 5. 18. 12, 42. 3. 7, Quint. 8. 3. 68) and verse (e.g., *Herc. Fur.* 1288, Verg. *Aen.* 1. 632, Ov. *F.* 2. 672)—before resorting to *alii alia* and a reference to the list found here.

3. 31. 1–2 Puta me uitam pro uita reddidisse: sic quoque munus tuum uici, cum ego dederim sentienti, cum sentiens me dare, cum uitam tibi non uoluptatis meae causa aut certe per uoluptatem dederim, cum tanto maius sit retinere spiritum quam accipere quanto leuius mori ante mortis metum. (**2**) Ego uitam dedi statim illa usuro, **tu** nescituro an **uiueret**; ego uitam dedi mortem timenti, tu uitam dedisti ut mori possem; ego tibi uitam dedi consummatam, perfectam, tu me expertem rationis genuisti, onus alienum.

tu (1°) Npc : *om.* Nac
uiueret N >*1515, Grut. p. 539, 1649‡* : uiuerem *1529–Lips.*

After being omitted in **N** between *usuro* at the end of one line and *nescituro* at the start of the next, *tu* was added in the margin just before the latter, almost certainly by the scribe himself. There is another stumble at the end of the same short clause, where the scribe—if the fault was his, not his exemplar's—was less alert. Though one might argue that the participles in the phrases *statim illa usuro* and *nescituro an uiueret* refer to indefinite third parties ('to someone who...')—and hence reject Erasmus' *uiuerem* in favour of *uiueret*—it is difficult to see the justification for doing so, when from the outset the passage is cast in terms of exchanges between an 'I' and a 'you', and when *tu nescituro an uiuerem* is answered within the space of eleven syllables by *tu uitam dedisti ut mori possem*.

3. 31. 5 Deinde ut nihil aliud dicam quam bonis artibus me studuisse **et cursum ad rectum iter uitae derexisse**, in ipso beneficio tuo maius quam quod dederas recepisti: tu enim me mihi rudem, imperitum dedisti, ego tibi filium qualem genuisse gauderes.

et...derexisse *Gertz* : ut...direxissem N (*def. Buck 1908, 59, sed* de- *mauult*), ut...dirigerem ψ, *1529‡*, ut...dirigentem >*1503*, dirigere *1515*, uel...derexisse *Pré.*

Buck defended the construction found in **N** on the ground that a pluperfect subjunctive can be used in a consecutive clause to denote an action completed before the event described in the main clause.[34] Rather: 'of the tenses of completed action, the pluperfect subjunctive in consecutive clauses is necessarily rare.

---

[34] 'Nun ist aber bei konsekut. *ut*...der Konj. Plusquamperf. möglich, wenn ein bereits vor dem Eintritt des im Hauptsatz Ausgesagten vollendetes Ereignis bezeichnet sein soll.'

It may, however, follow a pluperfect indicative of the main clause, or an imperfect that denotes a long continued state, without implying priority to the time of the main action' (*NLS* §163). As Gertz saw, the original infinitive, *derexisse*, gained an -*m* before *in*, and *et* inevitably became *ut*.

3. 35. 1–2 Iam tempus est quaedam ex nostra, ut ita dicam, moneta proferre. Qui id beneficium dedit quo est aliquid melius potest uinci. Pater dedit filio uitam, est autem aliquid uita melius: ita pater uinci potest quia dedit beneficium quo est aliquid melius. **(2)** Etiamnunc qui dedit alicui uitam, si et semel et iterum liberatus est **mortis periculo**, maius accepit beneficium quam dedit; pater autem uitam dedit; potest ergo si saepius periculo mortis liberatus a filio fuerit maius beneficium accipere quam dedit.

mortis periculo Npc2*(?)Qpcψ‡ : mortis Nac, a periculo mortis Npc1*, *Pinc.*, morte is *Pré.*

Gertz, Hosius, and Préchac were the first editors to report **N**'s text here, but each of their reports contains inaccuracies; the most serious of these is Hosius' suggestion that the initial correction in **N** might have been *a morte*, of which there is not a trace.[35] The facts are these: **N** originally had only *mortis*, which was taken over by **R** and transmitted to the later tradition, where it reappears in the less interpolated medieval manuscripts (**CQacM**);[36] subsequently, *a p(er)iculo* was written above the letters *ortis* with a line running from *a* to the space in the text between *est* and *mortis*, indicating the intended insertion point (the ink of the line is the same colour as the ink of the added phrase), producing a reading that was subsequently suggested independently by Pincianus; at a still later point, *a* was canceled, leaving it unclear whether the intended reading was *periculo mortis* (as in the clause that follows, *potest ergo*…) or *mortis periculo* (as the location of *periculo* would suggest); in any case, the latter phrase appears in the more densely populated branch of the tradition, ψ, whence it reached **Q** by contamination before becoming the vulgate reading of the *recentiores* and printed editions.

After all that, what S. wrote is remains uncertain. Préchac's suggestion could be attractive but for the fact that when S. uses correlative *is* with *qui*—as he does over thirty times—it always precedes the relative pronoun. On the other hand, writing either *periculo mortis* or *mortis periculo*, as the following parallel clause prompts one to do, rather glaringly leaves the error without a ready explanation. I will print *periculo mortis*, regarding it only as a reasonable stop-gap, not a probable solution.

[35] Gertz's app. crit.: 'mortis **N**[1], *omisso* periculo, *quod add. ug.* (*ex* **D**?), a periculo mortis **N**[2](?)' (where '*ug.*' denotes the print vulgate and '**D**' is Gertz's catch-all *siglum* for the *recentiores* he knew from Fickert's apparatus). Hosius' app. crit.: 'periculo **GP** *om.* **NRM** a morte *ut uid.* **N**[2], a per. mortis **N**[3].' Préchac's app. crit.: 'morte is *nos* : mortis| **N**[1] a periculo mortis **N**[2] *edd. ex seq. uerbis*' (where '|' indicates, correctly, that *mortis* stands at the end of a line).

[36] **C**'s closest companion in the φ-family, **B**, contains only excerpts of *Ben.* and omits all but the first sentence of 3. 35.

3. 36. 3 'Hoc agite, optimi iuuenes! Proposita est inter parentes ac liberos honesta contentio, dederint maiora an receperint. **(3)** Non ideo uicerunt, quia occupauerunt; sumite modo animum, qualem decet, et deficere nolite: uincetis optantes. Nec desunt tam pulchro certamini duces, qui ad similia uos cohortentur ac per uestigia sua ire ad uictoriam saepe iam **partam** ex parentibus iubeant.

partam ς₁₇, 1529‡ : paratam N, pactam ς₂, peractam >1515

partam, presumably a conjecture by Erasmus (there is no note), was anticipated in one of the *recentiores*; it remained the vulgate until Fickert ousted it in favour of *paratam*, which he knew from several manuscripts, including **G**. After Haase restored *partam* it has remained in the text and is certainly correct. The metaphor *uictoria parta* (the passive is more common, but cf. Val. Max. 2. 7. 2 *uictorias et... tropaea peperit ex eo hoste*, Liv. 7. 34. 13 *ex Sidicinis Campanisque uictoriam pepererunt*, 30. 14. 7 *uictoriam sibi peperit*) is a particular favourite of Livy (fifteen times), but its use is well attested elsewhere, including *Const. sap.* 19. 4 *uos* [= the not-yet wise]... *rem geritis, sapienti parta uictoria est*;[37] it is guaranteed here by *ex parentibus*, cf. Val. Max. and Livy 7. 34. 13, just quoted, with Livy 3. 71. 1 *uictoriam... ex hostibus partam. uictoria* is securely paired with *parare* only at Tac. *Germ.* 30. 2 *parare uictoriam* and Petr. *Sat.* 15. 9 *uictoria... parata* (guaranteed by the metre); it is probably correct also at Frontin. *Strat.* 1. 11. 2 *praeclara uictoria... parata est.*[38]

3. 37. 4 Manlius... ad tribunum plebis qui patri suo diem dixerat uenit: petito tempore... stringit occultatum sinu ferrum et 'Nisi iuras' inquit 'te diem patri remissurum, hoc te gladio transfodiam. In tua potestate est utro modo pater meus accusatorem non habeat.' Iurauit tribunus nec fefellit et causam **actionis omissae** contioni reddidit.

actionis N, 1529mg., 1557mg. (*dub. Grut. p. 540*: 'quod non temere damnauerim. perputent tantum sapientiores utrum hic magis conueniat') 1649‡ (*Gron. p. 139*) : accusatoris ς₁₉ >1605 (accusationis ς₅ς₈ς₁₆)
omissae *Will. Polyhistor p. 141. 43 Ouellette Fick.* : emissae N >1503, remissae Hς₆ς₁₆ς₁₉, 1515‡

When in 363 BCE the tribune Marcus Pomponius brought charges against T. Manlius Capitolinus Imperiosus (dict. 363), the latter's son, T. Manlius

---

[37] Besides Livy and Valerius Maximus cf., e.g., Cic. *Phil.* 14. 1, *Off.* 1. 35, *Att.* 10. 9a. 1 (Caelius), Caes. *BG* 5. 43. 3, *BC* 3. 82. 1, Sall. *Iug.* 82. 3, Suet. *Nero* 54, Tac. *Hist.* 1. 57. 2, *Ann.* 14. 36. 5.

[38] In his Teubner edition Ireland prints *parata*, the reading of the oldest intact manuscript (Lond. Harl. 2666, s. IX^in.), against *patrata* and *peracta*, the readings of later witnesses (cf. the *peractam* printed in the earliest editions of S. in the passage under discussion), and Oudendorp's emendation, *parta*. Conversely, *parata* was read at Liv. 5. 6. 1 in the Oxford edition of Conway and Walter, on the strength of the *codex Upsalensis* and two *recentiores*; *parta*, accepted previously by Weissenborn, was restored by Ogilvie in his more recent Oxford edition.

Imperiosus Torquatus (cos. 347), persuaded Pomponius, at sword-point, to drop the case: the tribune 'gave a promise under oath and kept his word, and before the assembled people he explained why the case had been dropped'. By the twelfth century N's impossible *emissae* had been corrected to *remissae*, which became the vulgate reading after it was printed in 1515. Fickert kept *remissae* in his own text, but since he knew of *emissae*, again from G, he suggested 'fortasse legendum *omissae*' in his note, and the suggestion was taken up by Gertz, Hosius, and Préchac; and in this they were all anticipated by the great historian of early medieval England, William of Malmesbury,[39] whose excerpt of this passage in his *Polyhistor* reads *actionis omissae*. It is natural to suppose that *o* could become *e* in minuscule script, and *actionem omittere* is a well-attested idiom for dropping or dismissing an action at law (e.g., Tac. *Hist.* 4. 44 *eos qui coeptam, deinde omissam actionem repeterent* and often in the *Digest*). But in fact *o* and *e* are only rarely interchanged in N, while *s* and *r* are often hardly distinguishable in its style of minuscule:[40] initial *r* could easily have been lost after terminal *s*, and *actionem remittere* is also a well-attested idiom (e.g., *Dig.* 2. 4. 11. pr. *si paeniteat libertum et actionem remittat*, 17. 1. 12. 1, 34. 3. 7. 6, 9. pr., 47. 2. 54. 1). Given those facts, and given that S. just previously wrote *diem…remissurum* to express the same idea—*dies* and *actio* being effectively equivalent in the context—I will print *remissae*.

---

[39] William died sometime after Christmas 1142, leaving his *Historia Novella* unfinished (a promised fourth book appears not to have been written); the *Polyhistor*, which 'consists of stories from Latin literature interspersed with William's introductions and comments', cannot be dated, and the excerpts that follow Seneca, from Macrobius' *Saturnalia* and Nennius' *Miracula Brittaniae*, 'are different from what precedes them…, suggesting that the end of the original *Polyhistor* may have come before that point' (Ouellette 1982, 18 and 25).

[40] On the interchange of *o* and *e*, see Appendix 2 n. 2. For the confusion of *s* and *r*, cf. 1. 9. 2 *nihil re adiuturus*, where N's *re* became *se* in R, nonsensically; and 4. 27. 1 *dicitur* (Npc, *-mur* Nac) *timidus proprie natura etiam ad inanes sonos pauidus*, where Gertz (relying on Kekulé's report, cf. Introduction n. 19, and followed by Hosius and Préchac) believed that N's original reading was *dicimus* and accordingly altered *timidus* and *pauidus* to *timidos* and *pauidos*. But the reading is certainly *dicimur*, as can be seen if one compares the last letter's flatish finishing stroke with the arched strokes of the neighbouring s's. Cf. *Clem.* 1. 12. 3 *cum quaeremus* (Madvig), where N's reading left Gruter uncertain: 'Naz(arianus) habet *consequeremur*, aut certe *consequeremus*, nam uix possum discernere utrum ultima litera accipienda pro R, an uero pro S. Sed tamen magis uidetur S' (he was right).

Notes to Book 4

4. 2. 1–2 In hac parte nobis pugna est cum Epicureis, delicata et umbratica turba in conuiuio suo philosophantium, apud quos uirtus uoluptatum ministra est, **illis paret**, illis deseruit, illas supra se uidet. 'Non est' inquis 'uoluptas sine uirtute'. (2) Sed quare ante uirtutem est? De ordine **putas disputationem esse**? de re tota et de potestate eius ambigitur. Non est uirtus, si sequi potest; primae partes eius sunt, ducere debet, imperare, summo loco stare; tu illam iubes signum petere.

illis paret Npc : illas para Nac, illas parat *Mazzoli 1974, 76–7*
putas disputationem esse G *Agric. p. 272, 1557‡* : disputas disputationem esse Npc1 (dispo- Nac *bis*) >*1503* (i.e., disputas?...esse)
    disputas? disputatio enim est Npc2* (*ss. man. post.*)
    disputas? disputationem esse oportet *1515, 1529*
    disputas? disputatio est ς₅, *Pinc.*
    in his putas d- esse *Gertz (Pré.)*
    disputas? ⟨putas⟩ d- esse *Alexander 1950–2, 21*

Before bringing rank into the discussion explicitly—*De ordine putas...?*—S. uses metaphors of hierarchy to convey the Epicureans' ranking of *uoluptas* before *uirtus*: *uoluptatum ministra...illis deseruit, illas supra se uidet.* **N**'s corrected text, *illis paret*, is consistent with those metaphors; Mazzoli's *illas parat* is not.[1] In what follows, retaining **N**'s *disputas* (changed from *dispo-* by the scribe) requires that significant surgery be performed on *disputationem esse*, whether by adding *oportet* or by changing the case of the noun and the form of the verb (the version written in **N** by a late correcting hand is more elegant than the version of ς₅ and Pincianus). But given the ease with which *putas* could become *disputas* by antici-pation before *disputationem*, reading *putas* with **G** and Agricola is preferable both to those measures and to Gertz's attempt (inevitably welcomed by Préchac) to salvage something of *dis* with *in his*.

4. 3. 1 Inserenda haec, mi Liberalis, fuerunt quia beneficium de quo nunc agitur dare uirtutis est et turpissimum id **causa ullius alterius rei** dare quam ut datum

---

[1] **N**'s corrector wrote *i* above the *a* of *illas* and *et* above the second *a* of *para* before the text was transmitted to **R**; but probably because he put an expunction point only under the latter *a*, the *i* above *-as* was subsequently erased. Alexander (1950–2, 21) thought that S. should have written *Non est...uoluptas sine uirtute sed ante uirtutem* before *Sed quare ante uirtuem est*, but he decided that 'it is perhaps Seneca, not a scribe, who has imposed a burden on the reader here in the matter of effecting a transition'. The burden, however, is surely minimized if not eliminated by the preceding metaphors.

sit. Nam si recipiendi spe tribueremus, locupletissimo cuique non dignissimo daremus; nunc uero diuiti importuno **pauperem praeferimus**. Non est beneficium, quod ad fortunam spectat.

causa ullius (illius Nac) alterius rei Npc : u- a- r- causa *Siesbye ap. Gertz p. 216*
pauperem N : ⟨bonum⟩ pauperem *Gertz ibid.*
praeferimus ς₁ς₆‡ : praeferamus Nac, praeferam Npc (*Pré.*)
ad fortunam N : fortunam *1585‡*

Gertz allowed the transmitted order to stand in his text but in his notes approved Siesbye's preference for *ullius alterius rei causa*:

> nam apud Senecam certe nullum aliud exemplum inuenitur, quo is uerborum ordo, quem N hoc loco exhibet, defendi possit, eaque, quae ex aliis scriptoribus prosae orationis adferuntur, ualde dubia sunt (cfr. Maduigii Emend. Liuian. p. 474), ut unum illud supersit, quod Sueton. Aug. 24 reperitur, si modo hoc uerum est.

I set to one side whatever examples of *causā* + following genitive might be found in the texts of other authors (I did accept Suet. *Aug.* 24. 1—[*Eques*] *duobus filiis adulescentibus causa detrectandi sacrimenti pollices amputasset*—but would now want to rethink that decision): the fact that sixty times elsewhere in his prose works S. has occasion to use the construction, always with the genitive preceding, persuades me that he used it here too. I assume that *causa* was lost through inadvertence and reinserted in the wrong place. Note that the order found in genitive + *causā* is no less fixed in the equivalent phrase *meā causā* ('for my sake', 'on my account') and its siblings: *causā tuā / nostrā / vestrā* occur nowhere, and *causā meā* or *suā* is found—outside Plautus and Terence (in Terence only once: *Eun.* 1071)—in contexts that might suggest the usage was colloquial (Phaedr. *Fab.* 1. 22, Quint. *DMin.* 275. 6, 344. 10, [Quint.] *DMai.* 15. 7).

Gertz also persuades me that *bonum* (lost after -*tuno*) is wanted with *pauperem*, not for merely formal balance with *importuno*, but because not just any *pauper* would do. Bestowing a *beneficium* is a moral act demanding that an ethical judgement be made of the recipient: e.g., 4. 9. 3 *si turpi datur, nec honestum esse potest nec beneficium*; Gertz compares 4. 10. 5, a little farther on, *Ad animum tendit aestimatio mea; ideo locupletem sed indignum praeteribo, pauperi uiro bono dabo.*

As for the verb immediately following, there is no reason to prefer the reading *praeferam* that was produced in **N** by correction: it is unlikely to be correct if regarded as a future indicative, since S. uses future after *nunc* very rarely and then generally when he speaks of something he is about to do *qua* author (e.g., *Ira* 3. 1. 1 *Quod maxime desiderasti, Nouate, nunc facere temptabimus…*, *Otio* 2. 1 *nunc probabo tibi…*); if it is taken to be subjunctive, there is no reason to prefer it to **N**'s original reading, *praeferamus*.[2] The *recentiores'* reading, *praeferimus*,

---

[2] Préchac preferred *praeferam*, which he mistakenly took it to be the original reading of **N** (Hosius, also mistakenly, ascribed it to Gruter). But the suspension stroke for -*us* was certainly written first in

would appropriately make a normative assertion after the preceding counterfactual condition ('If we were bestowing benefits with the expectation of a return, we would give to all the wealthiest people, not the most worthy; but now we prefer [sc. as we should]....'): but there would be reason to doubt the form even if it were transmitted from antiquity, because (as Nigel Holmes has observed) S. nowhere else uses the first-person plural present indicative of *fero* or its compounds, a form that was all but completely avoided by Cicero too.[3] **N**'s *praeferamus*, regarded as a hortatory subjunctive, also provides a fitting sequel to the counterfactual: 'If we were bestowing benefits with the expectation of a return, we would give to all the wealthiest people, not the most worthy; but now [sc. given that that is not our motive] let us prefer....' For a similar use of *nunc uero* + subjunctive following a counterfactual condition, cf. *Tranq. 7. 5 Vix tibi esset facultas dilectus felicioris, si inter Platonas et Xenophontas... bonos quaereres...: nunc uero in tanta bonorum egestate minus fastidiosa fiat electio.*

4. 4. 2 Hoc qui dicit [sc. non dare deum beneficia] non exaudit precantium uoces et undique sublatis in caelum manibus uota facientium priuata ac publica, quod profecto non fieret, nec in hunc furorem omnes **profecto** mortales consensissent adloquendi surda numina et inefficaces deos, nisi nossemus illorum beneficia nunc oblata ultro, nunc orantibus data....

profecto (2°) *del. Mur.*

Muretus was generally too ready to approach emendation in the spirit of a prose composition instructor, producing what he thought an author should have written, but at least two considerations persuade me that he was right to delete the second *profecto* here: neither S. nor any other writer of classical Latin repeats the adverb in successive clauses within the same sentence; and in **N** the second *profecto* sits directly beneath the first, where it was probably generated by the scribe's wandering eye.[4]

---

the same pale ink as the text, then later canceled by a stroke in darker ink (similarly Gruter p. 541). Griffin and Inwood also prefer *praeferam*, on the ground that 'it is the fact of our giving by choice to the poor that is needed to refute the supposition that we give in hopes of a return' (p. 210 = Griffin 2013, 234): but if the idea of actual fact were crucial to the refutation, it would be best to retain *praeferimus*, for actual fact is no more represented by an intention (*praeferam*, read as future) than it is by an exhortation (*praeferamus*).

[3] Holmes 2004; the only occurrence in Cicero is *Flacc.* 3 *sed quoniam, iudices, multa nos et in nostris rebus et in re publica defellerunt, ferimus ea quae sunt ferenda*, where, Holmes notes, '*feremus* would be an easy conjecture' (I can add: as would *feramus*).

[4] Note also: though other writers of Latin prose place *profecto* directly after a form of *omnis* (Cic. *Or.* 119 *omnia profecto*, Liv. 25. 38. 10 *ex omni profecto saeuitia*, Quint. *DMin.* 297. 6 *omnibus profecto*), in S.'s prose works *profecto* appears only as the first or second word in its clause (half a dozen times, including the first *profecto* here) or directly after the verb it emphasizes (*Pol.* 16. 3 *amisi Germanicum fratrem, quem quomodo amauerim intellegit profecto quisquis cogitat quomodo suos fratres*) or at the boundary between object and subject (*NQ* 7. 1. 7 *conglobatam* [sc. *flammam*]...*nec stabili inditam corpori profecto iam mundus turbine suo dissipasset*).

A similar slip seems to have occurred on the next page in **N**.

4. 5. 3 Flumina haec amoenissimis flexibus campos cingentia, illa praebitura commercio uiam uasto et nauigabili cursu uadentia, ex quibus quaedam **aestatis** diebus mirabile incrementum trahunt ut arida et feruenti subiecta caelo loca subita uis aestiui torrentis inriget? Quid **medicatorum torrentium uenae**? quid in ipsis litoribus aquarum calentium exundatio?

aestatis N : statis 1515‡
torrentium N : fontium *Kronenberg 1923, 46, Axelson 1933, 67*

We can take the second issue here first, since it is comparable to the matter just discussed: the phrase *medicatorum torrentium uenae* is just very odd, and the oddness does not simply lie in the appearance of *torrentium* so soon after *torrentis*.[5] As Axelson observed, *torrens* in S. denotes a more or less temporary outpouring—for example, a river's seasonal inundation (so *aestiui torrentis* in this passage: see below, and note the contast at *EM* 40. 8 *perennis sit unda, non torrens*)—to which one can add that *uena* as a geological term generally refers to a subterranean phenomenon, whereas *torrentes* rush along the surface; and as both Axelson and Kronenberg observed (it appears independently), S. must be referring to what he otherwise calls 'medicinal springs': *Prov.* 2. 1 *medicatorum uis fontium*, *NQ* 3. 25. 10 *medicatorum fontium riuos* (cf. also *uenasque fontium* later in this book, §25. 2). Coming so soon after *torrentis...*and *-torum, fontium* would have been vulnerable to change through an error of perseveration; that the scribe came to write it at the end of a line in **N** directly under the first syllable of *torrentis* probably doomed it.[6]

Now to return to the phrase *aestatis diebus*, a sentence earlier in S.'s list of the many god-given *beneficia* manifested in nature: the list begins at 4. 5. 1—'*Non dat deus beneficia.' Vnde ergo ista quae possides, quae das, quae negas, quae seruas, quae rapis?*—and continues as one item after another is added, with a noun in the nominative at or near the start of each sentence. The point here is twofold: first, *aestatis* is otiose, given that *aestiui torrentis* is soon going to provide the same information in a more richly detailed setting; more important, since S. is referring to the seasonal, life-giving inundations provided by certain rivers, the phrase introduced in Erasmus' first edition—*statis diebus*, 'on certain / fixed days'—bears directly on the theme of divine providence central to S.'s argument: *Quid enim aliud est natura quam deus et diuina ratio toti mundo partibusque eius inserta?* (§7. 1). For the phrase, compare Pliny on the summer rising of the Euphrates (*NH* 5. 90):

---

[5] S. does not always avoid such repetitions: e.g., 4. 6. 5 *surgentem aetatem...surgenti iuuentae*, cf. Albrecht (2008), 77–8.

[6] Cf. also the discussion of 7. 15. 3.

> Increscit autem et ipse Nili modo **statis diebus** paulum differens ac Mesopotamiam
> inundat sole optinante xx partem Cancri [= 13 July]; minui incipit in Virginem
> e Leone transgresso [= 24 August], in totum uero remeat in xxix parte Virginis
> [= 21 September].

The phrase is well attested (e.g., four more times in Pliny) but still uncommon
enough to provoke a puzzled reader to add the initial diphthong and produce a
more familiar word that works in the passage.

4. 6. 1 Si pauca quis tibi donasset iugera, accepisse te diceres beneficium: inmensa
terrarum late patentium spatia negas esse beneficium? Si pecuniam tibi aliquis
donauerit et arcam tuam, quoniam tibi id magnum uidetur, impleuerit, beneficium uocabis; tot metalla ⟨**deus**⟩ **defodit**, tot flumina **emisit terra, super quae
decurrunt sola, aurum** uehentia; argenti, aeris, ferri inmane pondus omnibus
locis **obruit**, cuius inuestigandi tibi facultatem dedit, ac latentium diuitiarum in
summa terra signa disposuit: negas te accepisse beneficium?

deus defodit *Hos.* (*dein* deus fodit *Festa 1900, 433*) : defodit N (*def. Buck 1908, 61–2 et,
metri causa, Kronenberg 1923, 46–7*)
flumina emisit terra JV : flumine misitera Nac
    flumina emisit aera Npc
    e- in aera *1475‡*
    e- arenas *Pinc.*
    haeret Grut. p. 542 ('tantum pronuncio, locum insanum, locum mutilum')
    e- in arena *Lips.* (*def. Kronenberg 1923, 46–7*), e- per ea *Madvig 1871–84, 2:412*
super quae decurrunt N : s- q- decurrant ς₁₉
    s- q- decurrit ς₄
    super quam decurrunt ς₅ς₆
    super quas decurrunt *Pinc.*
    quae decurrunt super *Skutsch ap. Hos.*
sola, aurum ψ‡ (*Madvig 1871–84, 2:412*) : solarum Nac
    uel um *ss.* Npc* (*i.e.,* uel solum, *man. post., sic* M)
    solaurum R, sol aurum CQac
    solum aurum QpcM
    solidi auri *Pinc.* (*resp. Grut. p. 542*)
    solidum aurum *Haase*
    sal, aurum *Gundermann ap. Buck 1908, 61–2*
obruit *Gertz* : obrutum N

The theme of divine beneficence continues, exemplified first by the gift of *inmensa
terrarum late patentium spatia*, contrasted with the paltry *pauca...iugera* that
some mortal might give, then, in a much longer sentence, by the immeasurable
gift of mineral wealth in its various forms, contrasted again with a relatively
mingy human gift, an *arca* full of *pecunia*. S.'s point in that long sentence is generally clear, though the exact form in which he has cast it is obscured by a relatively

minor problem near the start of the apodosis and by the substantial corruption in N's text that soon follows—*flumine misitera super quae decurrunt solarum*—which leaves me uncertain that we can recapture the *ipsissima uerba*. That being the case, I will propose what I take to be a plausible stop-gap.

To start with the sentence's backbone—five third-person singular perfect active verbs, *defodit, emisit* (which must be lurking in *flumine misitera*, as N's early corrector saw), *obruit* (Gertz's necessary correction of *obrutum*, without which *pondus* lacks a construction), *dedit*, and *disposuit*—and what seems to me a necessary premise: all five verbs have the same subject. If that is the case, then JV's superficially attractive *flumina emisit terrā* must be set aside (*terra* might be the subject of *defodit* but certainly not of the verbs that follow) and Haase's supplement, *deus*, must be accepted as the appropriate subject of all the verbs. Next, two corrections of errors derived from the misreading of *scriptura continua*: along with *emisit* N's corrector rightly extracted *flumina* from *fluminemisitera*—the only plausible candidate for the role of *decurrunt*'s subject—and *sola aurum* must be extracted from *solarum*, allowing *aurum uehentia* to look back to *flumina*, defining the rivers as 'gold-bearing' (in his note Lipsius remarks, 'Tagus olim, Pactolus, hodie flumina Noui orbis').

That leaves two remaining questions: what to make of the last three letters of *fluminemisitera*? and what to make of *super quae decurrunt sola*? Though discarded above, the reading of JV, when viewed differently, provides the answer to the first question: *flumina emisit terrā*, cf. EM 79. 12 *emissus his tenebris* and especially NQ 2. 57. 3 *calidi fumidique natura emissa terris in nubes incidit*. Finally, since *quae decurrunt* must look to *flumina*, asking 'What to make of *super quae decurrunt sola?*' amounts to asking 'What to make of *super*?' Its proper function would surely be to govern *sola*, 'over the (earth's) surfaces', but it cannot perform that function placed where it is. That leaves a choice between transposing *super*, as Franz Skutsch suggested to Hosius—on the assumption that it was omitted, then misplaced when the correction was made—or regarding *sola* as an 'accusative of the space traversed' with *decurrunt*—'rivers that traverse the (earth's) surfaces, bearing gold'[7]—and ejecting *super* as a superscript note above *sola* (or, God knows, *quae*) that worked its way into the text. Neither of these alternatives is clearly more probable than the other: I will print Skutsch's suggestion. So we emerge with *tot metalla ⟨deus⟩ defodit, tot flumina emisit terra quae decurrunt super sola, aurum uehentia*: 'the god buried so many minerals [or, mines], sent forth from the earth so many rivers that traverse the earth's surfaces, bearing gold ....'

4. 8. 1 Hunc [sc. deum] et Liberum patrem et Herculem ac Mercurium nostri putant: Liberum patrem, quia omnium parens sit, **quoi** primum inuenta

---

[7] Cf. Sen. *Contr.* 9. pr. 4 *cursores…id* [sc. *spatium*] *saepe decurrunt in exercitationem quod…decursuri in certamine*, or the metaphor at Cic. *Sen.* 83, *decurso spatio* [sc. *uitae*], with *OLD* s.v. 8.

seminum uis est **consultura per uoluptatem**; Herculem, quia uis eius inuicta sit quandoque lassata fuerit operibus editis, in ignem recessura; Mercurium, quia ratio penes illum est numerusque et ordo et scientia.

quoi primum inuenta seminum uis est consultura per uoluptatem *Grut. p. 542* : quod primum inuenta seminum uis est, consultura per uoluptatem N >*1529*

　　quod ab eo primum inuenta seminum uis est, consultura per uol- *Eras. p. 273*
　　('uetustum exemplar') *1557‡*

　　quod per eum inuenta seminum uis est consultura per uol- *Lips.*

　　quod primum inuenta seminum uis est ** consultura per uol- *Haase*

　　quod primum inuenta seminum uitis [*gen. sing.*] consitura peperit uol- *Madvig 1871–84, 2:412–13*

　　quoi primum inuenta seminum [sc. humanorum] uis est et consitura per uol- *Gertz pp. 218–19*

　　quod primum inuenta seminum uis est ⟨ei⟩ [*uel* ⟨ei⟩ est] consultura per uol- *Rossbach 1888, 119 n. 16*

　　quoi primum inuenta seminum uitis [*nom. sing.*] est consolatura per uol- *Busche 1917–18, 467–9*

　　cui primum inuenta seminum uis est ⟨uitae⟩ consultura per uol- *Basore* ('he who first discovered the seminal power that is able to subserve life through pleasure')

　　quoi primum inuenta seminum uis est consultura per uol- ⟨uitae perpetuitati⟩ *Pré.* ('celui à qui remonte la première invention de la puissance séminale chargée de pourvoir par la volupté à la continuation de la vie')

　　quoi primum inuenta seminum uis est ⟨coniugio⟩ consultura per uol- *Alexander 1950–2, 21* ('by whom first was discovered the seminal power destined, under the call of pleasure, to take thought for physical union [and so for the perpetuation of life]')

Some expression of agency is needed, to connect Liber as *pater* to the action described in the clause, and I take Gruter's *quoi* here, as *datiuus auctoris*,[8] to be the most probable solution, given that we can be confident it was a form S. used (cf. the discussion 3. 26. 1–2) and given the ease with which this less common form could become *quod* after *quia*; other solutions require different kinds of intervention, from the relatively simple *ab eo* or *per eum* or *ei* to Madvig's thorough rewriting. As for the more serious problem—what to do about *consultura?*—the participle promises to give sense appropriate to the context—'that would look after / see to the needs of', denoting the motive of the benevolent *parens*—and gives a firmer foundation for a solution than Busche's *consolatura* or Madvig's and Gertz's *consitura*, a hapax legomenon imported from Cic. *Rep.* 1. 29. 2. *consulere* in the required sense never occurs absolutely, and Haase's marking of a lacuna rightly indicated that a supplement is needed, most probably a noun in the dative: Basore's simple *uitae* is an adequate stop-gap, which I will print after *consultura*.

---

[8] Cf. Pinkster 2015, 247–9.

4. 9. 1 . . . plurima beneficia ac maxima in nos deus **defert** sine spe recipiendi, quoniam nec ille conlato eget nec nos ei quidquam conferre possumus; ergo bene- ficium per se expetenda res est. Vna **spectatur** in eo accipientis utilitas, ad hanc accedamus sepositis commodis nostris.

defert *Gertz* (*qui et* ad nos *pro* in nos) : refert N, confert Ipc $\varsigma_1\varsigma_6$‡, re⟨uera con⟩fert *Pré.* spectatur $\varsigma_{1\ddagger}$: expec- N (*def. Buck 1908, 62*), expetatur *Pré.*

That neither *beneficium deferre* nor *beneficium referre* is among the expressions S. uses for 'bestow a *beneficium*' is perhaps surprising, but it is true, and the lack is telling, given how often he invokes the idea in the treatise. On the other hand, the idiom that some *recentiores* introduced here and that the printed editions retained before Gertz—*in aliquem beneficium conferre*—is quite common; that fact, together with *conlato* and *conferre* following in the sentence, strongly suggest that *confert* is what he wrote here. Préchac's attempt to salvage N's *re-* would be worth considering if it helped to explain how *uera con* would have been lost, but it does not. Perhaps the scribe's eye was simply caught by *re-* a dozen letters farther on, in *recipiendi*.

If *spectatur*, in the next sentence, were the reading transmitted from antiquity, no one would think to replace it. But since we know that it is not ancient and have reason to suppose that *expectatur* is, and since the latter can have a sense—'hope for' (*TLL* 5. 1895. 25–1898. 82)—appropriate to the context (e.g., *EM* 88. 17 *secunda expecto, malis paratus sum*), Buck was right to argue that replacing it is unjustified; for the same reason N's *expectat* can also be restored to the text at 4. 13. 3 *Beneficium eius commodum expectat cui praestatur, non nostrum*, where it has also been displaced in the printed editions by *spectat*.[9] Here *expectatur* expresses the one hope a benefactor can decently entertain; hortatory *accedamus* urges us to act to realize it.

4. 9. 2–3 'Praeterea quaeritis ⟨**ubi et quomodo detis**⟩ **beneficium**, quod non esset faciendum, si per se beneficium dare expetenda res esset, **quoniam**, quocumque loco et quocumque modo daretur, beneficium erat'. **(3)** Honestum propter nullam aliam causam quam propter ipsum sequimur; tamen, etiam si nihil aliud sequen- dum est, quaerimus, **cui** faciamus et quando et quemadmodum; per haec enim constat. Itaque, cum eligo, cui dem beneficium, id ago, ut quandoque beneficium sit, quia, si turpi datur, nec honestum esse potest nec beneficium.

⟨ubi et quomodo detis⟩ beneficium *Gertz* (*iam* ubi et qui [*adv.*] dandum [*uel* detis] *Stephanus 1586b, 16*) : beneficium N >*1529*

---

[9] Cf. also the discussion of 5. 13. 1–2. Buck mentioned *expetatur* as a possibility but discarded it; Préchac took it up. It is open to the same objection as *spectatur*, and one more: since S. has just said that *beneficium*—'doing good', the act of bestowing a benefit—'should be sought for its own sake', his use of the same verb to urge the seeking of *utilitas*—even that of another—would at least be awkward.

> cui detis *Eras. p. 272* ('sic uetustus codex'), *1649‡*
> cui *1557*
> cui dandum sit *1585, 1605*
> quomodo detis *Mur.* ('certe tale quid deest' *Gron. p. 142*)
> beneficio locum *Hos. in app.*
> quoniam *Gertz* : que enim N
> > quae enim R‡ *Eras., Pré.*
> > quod Npc* (ss. man. post. ?, q̊ *in mg.*)
> > quae ψ >*1492, Pinc., 1557, prob. Grut. p. 543*
> > *om. 1503–1529, 1585, 1605*
> > quia enim *dub. Grut., recip. 1649* ('Gruterus ex Naz.' *perperam Gron. p. 143*)
> cui *Hos.* (*post* cui id *Gertz*) : quid N

Gertz got matters right enough in his first two interventions here to make his suggestions worth printing. Erasmus seems to have been the first to notice that something was missing in the *textus receptus* between *quaeritis* and *beneficium*, and Muretus was the first to see that the something needed was not a retro-spective *cui*—looking back to *diligenter eligendos quibus beneificia demus* at the start of §9. 2—but something that would look ahead to *quocumque loco et quocumque modo daretur*. Stephanus' refinement of Muretus' *quomodo* was then improved by Gertz, who replaced adverbial *qui* with *quomodo* and pre-ferred *detis* to *dandum*, providing a clear *ratio corruptelae* after *quaeritis*. As for *quoniam*, neither **R**'s *quae enim*, derived from **N**, nor the *quod enim* of **N**'s corrector will do, since S. writes those phrases only when *quae* or *quod* is an interrogative adjective (respectively *Marc.* 3. 4, *EM* 26. 3, and *Ira.* 2. 7. 2, 3. 42. 1, *EM* 30. 17), and he never writes Gruter's hesitant *quia enim* ('suspicio mihi scribendum'), which is largely confined to comic texts.[10] *quae* is a trivialization of **R**'s reading that arose in the ψ-family of medieval manuscripts and became the print vulgate: *quoniam* provides the explicit causal link that is wanted after *quod non esset faciendum*.

I doubt, however, that Gertz's *cui id* (not improved by Hosius' *cui*) is correct. It occurred to him because S. will round off this paragraph by returning to the choice of a recipient: *itaque cum eligo cui dem beneficium* at the end of §9. 3 returns to '*Dicitis*' inquit '*diligenter eligendos, quibus beneficia demus...*' at the start of §9. 2. But we are not there yet.[11] The immediate concern is the constituent elements of the *beneficium*—*per haec enim constat*—and among these the 'what' certainly deserves a place. As a secondary matter, note that when the benefi-ciary—the 'for whom'—is under discussion, the verbs S. uses are *dare* and *donare*, not *facere*.

---

[10] Gronovius took over *quia enim* in his edition because he misread Gruter's note ('Gruterus ex Naz.'), which itself misreported **N**'s original reading as *qui enim*.

[11] Griffin and Inwood make a similar point (pp. 210–11): 'Seneca only reverts to the issue of choos-ing a beneficiary...with *Itaque, cum eligo, cui dem* (9. 3), and only returns to it properly at 10. 3.'

4. 10. 1 Depositum reddere per se res expetenda est; non tamen semper reddam nec quolibet loco nec quolibet tempore. Aliquando nihil interest utrum infitier an palam **reddam**. Intuebor utilitatem eius cui redditurus sum et nociturum illi depositum negabo.

reddam : ⟨non⟩ reddam *Watt 1994, 227–8*

infitiari means the same thing in the realm of *credita* as it does in the realm of *beneficia*:[12] a denial, typically disingenuous, that one has received what one has received. Concerning the transmitted text, Watt observes, 'It is difficult to imagine circumstances in which it makes no difference whether I deny having received a deposit or openly return it: there must be something wrong with the text.' Inserting *non* before *reddam* solves the problem by restoring what was in all likelihood a single letter (*ñ*) lost after -*m*: if it does not serve the other party's interest for me to return the thing he left in my keeping—if, say, he deposited a sword when sane but demanded it back when mad (Cic. *Off.* 3. 95, cited by Watt)—I not only may but should decline the request, whether by denying that the deposit had been made or by a frank refusal. *negabo* covers both possibilities.[13]

4. 11. 3 Atqui ut scias rem per se expetendam esse bene facere, aduenis modo in nostrum delatis portum **statim** abituris succurrimus, ignoto naufrago nauem qua reuehatur et damus et **struimus**.

statim Nac : & statim Npc
struimus N >*1503, prob. Grut. p. 543*: instruimus ς₁₅, *1515‡, Axelson 1933, 55 (metri causa; prob. Alexander 1950–2, 21)*

et statim is an early, probably scribal correction in **N**, and I think the conjunction is wanted, to enable the double antithesis to emerge more clearly: not just *delatis* vs. *abituris* but also *modo* vs. *statim*.[14] As for *struimus*, Axelson noticed that the transmitted text caused the end of the sentence to have the same rhythm as the second half of a pentameter ($\overline{}\,\smile\,\smile\,\overline{}\,\smile\,\smile$), an effect that a careful writer of rhythmical prose would avoid. *instruimus* provides both better rhythm—$\overline{}\,\smile\,\smile\,\smile\,\overline{}\,\smile\,\smile$ (resolved double cretic = double 1st paean)—and better sense: 'we both give and equip' (*instruimus*) vs. 'we both give and build' (*struimus*).[15]

---

[12] e.g., 1. 1. 3, 2. 23. 2, 35. 3, 3. 13. 1, 6. 27. 3, and cf. 4. 2 on *creditum* vs. *beneficium.*

[13] Rejecting *non*, Griffin (2013, 239) argued that '*infitiari* is, in some unusual circumstances, the proper return and so equivalent, paradoxically, to its diametric opposite, *palam reddere*, which is the correct return in normal circumstances'; but the contrast between 'unusual' and 'normal' circumstances misses the point of *aliquando*, which surely means that 'sometimes'—i.e., on a given occasion, in a particular set of circumstances—*infitiari* and *non reddere* are effectively identical and equally correct.

[14] 'Probably scribal': the inserted ampersand's ink is identical in colour to the surrounding text, and the finishing diagonal stroke has at its end the exuberant little curl characteristic of the scribe in this portion of text.

[15] ς₅, a highly interpolated manuscript dating to 1375, has been cited as the source of *instruimus* by editors since Fickert, who first collated and reported it, but it reads *struimus*, as do all the *recentiores* I have examined save ς₁₅.

4. 12. 3–4 Nemo Tusculanum aut Tiburtinum paraturus salubritatis causa et aestiui secessus, quoto anno empturus sit, disputat; **cui e re sit, tuendum est.** **(4)** Eadem in beneficio ratio est; nam quom interrogaueris, quid reddat, respondebo: bonam conscientiam. Quid reddat beneficium? dic tu mihi, quid reddat iustitia, quid innocentia, quid magnitudo animi, quid pudicitia, quid temperantia; si quicquam praeter ipsas, ⟨ipsas⟩ non petis.[16]

quoto anno N (*cf. §12. 4* quom interrogaueris, quid reddat…) : quotā *aut* quoto nummo *aut* quoto anno disputat *Lips.*, quota annua *Gron. p. 144*, quanto *Bentley* (*Hedicke 1899, 7*), quoto annuo *Fick*.

cui e re sit tuendum est *Hos.* ('s(*iue*) cur' *in app.*) : cum erit tuendum est Nac (*Pré.*)
　ꞁ emerit ꞁ utendum Npc* (*ss. man. post.*)
　cum emerit tuendum est Ipcς₁‡, *Alexander 1937, 58* (*sim. Alexander 1950–2, 22*)
　cui meret id intuendum est *Gertz pp. 221–2*
　cur emat, intuendum est *Klammer 1878, 60*
　cum uenierit aptum, emendum est *J. Müller 1892, 6*
　cum erit utendum, emet *Georgii 1929, 112*
　⟨prout ae⟩cum erit, tuendum est *Mazzoli 1974, 78–9*

S. is elaborating a familiar theme: in giving a *beneficium* one must keep one's eye fixed on what the essential aim of the action is, a thing to be sought *per se*. In the first sentence, no one but Préchac has been satisfied with **N**'s *cum erit tuendum est* (he took it to mean, 's'en présente-t-il un, il ne faut pas le laisser échapper'), but no such unanimity has greeted any proposed solution. A general sense of what is required should be reasonably clear once one recognizes that *quoto anno* in the preceding clause has the same sense as it does at Cic. *Att.* 9. 9. 4 *sciebam enim te quoto anno… solere quaerere*: as Shackleton Bailey translates, '[I was] aware that you generally want to know about price-yield ratio'—that is, how long it will take for the land's yield to compensate for the price. So here S. is saying (in Griffin and Inwood's version, slightly modified), 'No one prepared to buy a villa at Tusculum or Tibur as a healthy summer retreat debates how many years it will take to recoup the cost': the latter consideration is beside the point, and you have to keep your eye on what the aim of your action really is. This is the only thought fully consistent both with what precedes (buying land as a haven, not as an investment) and with what follows (giving a *beneficium* as an action done for its own sake, not for a return that can be expected). Compared with that, the version that became the print vulgate—*cum emerit tuendum est*, 'when he has bought it, it must be looked after'—could not be more inconsequential, while the version Gertz considered in his *Adnotationes* misses the point in a different way, as his paraphrase show ('id est: ei emptori, qui praedium sibi aera merere fructuique et lucro esse uult, hoc spectandum est, quoto anno empturus sit'). In fact among the versions that have been considered, only those of Hosius—'what is it good for,

---

[16]　*praeter ipsas, ⟨ipsas⟩ non petis* is a glittering contribution by Modius 1584, 391.

that's the point that needs attending to'—and Klammer—'why is he buying it, that's the point…'—are on the right track: Hosius' version, being much closer to the traces in **N**, is the one I will print, while citing Klammer's in the apparatus. For the sense of *tueri* here, 'attend to'—retaining contact with the verb's primary sense, 'watch over' (hence 'maintain', 'protect'), while approaching the force of *intueri*—compare *Brev.* 14. 1 *Soli omnium otiosi sunt qui sapientiae uacant, soli uiuunt; nec enim suam tantum aetatem bene tuentur: omne aeuum suo adiciunt.*

4. 13. 1 Vobis uoluptas est **inertis otii facere corpusculum** et securitatem sopitis simillimam adpetere et sub densa umbra latitare tenerrimisque cogitationibus, quas tranquillitatem uocatis, animi marcentis oblectare torporem et cibis potionibusque intra hortorum latebram corpora ignauia pallentia saginare;

inertis otii Npc >*1557, prob. Grut. p. 544, 1649‡* : -ti otii Nac, inerti otio *Pinc., 1585, 1605*
facere N, *1475–1557, 1649‡* : ł farcire Npc* (*ss. man. post.*), *1557mg., prob. Grut., agnosc. Lips.,* assuefacere *Pinc., 1585, 1605,* iacere *Lips.,* fouere *Hos. in app.,* ⟨deliciis assue⟩facere *Watt 1994, 228*
corpusculum Npc (-colum Nac) >*1503, Pinc., 1585‡, Grut.* : crepusculum *1515, 1529, 1557,* opusculum *Madvig 1871–84, 2:413–14 (Gertz),* facere ⟨compos⟩ corp- *Koch 1874, 14–15*

I could imagine that S. wrote *Vobis uoluptas est inertis otii*—'For you, pleasure is a matter of / the realm of idle sloth'—and I could imagine that he wrote (say) *Vobis uoluptas est farcire corpusculum*—'For you pleasure amounts to stuffing your miserable body'—but I could not imagine putting in the text something like *Vobis uoluptas est inertis otii, farcire corpusculum,* even if *farcire corpusculum* did not anticipate and spoil *corpora…saginare.* As for the transmitted text, with *facere corpusculum,* attempts to make it yield sense are well intentioned—'You count it pleasure to surrender your miserable body to sluggish ease' (Basore), 'Your idea of pleasure is to give your contemptible body over to idle sloth' (Griffin and Inwood)—but in fact they more closely approximate the text as emended by Pincianus, *inerti otio assuefacere corpusculum.* That emendation, or Watt's, or another like them would make fine sense, but I am not sufficiently confident of S.'s intended meaning to put one or another in the text, even as a stop-gap. I suspect that there is a brief lacuna before or after *facere*; be that as it may, I will put a dagger in the text before the infinitive, mention Pincianus' *assuefacere* in the apparatus, and let *alii alia* suffice, with a reference to this discussion.

4. 18. 2 Fac nos singulos, quid sumus? praeda animalium et uictimae ac **bellissimus** et facillimus sanguis; quoniam ceteris animalibus in tutelam sui satis uirium est, quaecumque uaga **nascebantur** et actura uitam segregem, armata sunt, hominem **imbecilla ⟨cutis⟩** cingit, non unguium uis, non dentium terribilem ceteris fecit, nudum et infirmum societas munit. **Duas ⟨deus⟩ res dedit**, quae **illum obnoxium** ualidissimum facerent, rationem et societatem; itaque, qui par esse nulli posset, si seduceretur, rerum potitur.

bellissimus Nac >*1557, prob. Grut. p. 545* : ɫleuissimus Npc* (*ss. man. post.*), delectabilis ac be- F, uilissimus *1585, 1605*, imbecillissimus *1649‡* (imbecillimus *Dale. adn.*)

nascebantur Nac >*1529* (*Grut. p. 545*) : nascuntur Npc* (*ss. man. post.*), Eras. p. 272 ('melius'), *1557‡*

imbecilla cutis cingit ς₁₂, *Madvig 1871–84, 2:414* : inbecilla cingit Nac

    inbecillitas cingit Npc* (*man. post.*), *1529–1605*

    imbecilla uis cingit ς₃ς₄ς₇pc >*1515* (imbecilla cingit uis ς₅, inbecilianis [< inbecilla uis] cingit ς₂)

    imbellia cingt *Grut. p. 545, 1649*

    tutela *Hos. in app.*

    inbecilla ⟨cutis pro tegmine⟩ *Pré.*

duas ⟨deus⟩ res *Haase* : duas res Nac, natura *post* res Npc* (*ss. man. post.*), deus illi *post* res *Gertz*

illum obnoxium Nac *Gron. p. 146, 1649‡* : illum -io Npc

    illum ex obnoxio ς₆, *Lips.*

    illum obnoxio quolibet >*1515*

    illum obnoxio cuilibet *1515mg.*

    illum ceteris obnoxium ς₄

    illum obnoxium ceteris *Eras., 1529–1605*

    illum a noxio quamlibet ualido securum *Pinc.*

    illi obnoxium *Grut. p. 545*

That S. never uses the superlative forms of *bellus* does not count for nothing, but it counts for less than the fact that no Roman writer is on record as using any form of *bellus* to modify *sanguis*. **N**'s late corrector made a not bad guess with *leuissimus*, but Muretus' *uilissimus* is better—in fact, given the confusions of *e* / *i* and *b* / *u* that are so common in **N** (cf. 7. 2. 2 *uilium* Npc : *bi-* Nac and Appendix 2), it all but counts as the transmitted reading—and the sense snaps snugly into place: for powerful predators, human blood is as cheap as it is easy; cf. *Clem.* 1. 1. 3, where a different sort of predator is represented as praising himself for demonstrating *summa parsimonia etiam uilissimi sanguinis* (sim. Curt. 8. 7. 4, cf. Tac. *Ann.* 1. 76. 3 *Drusus… uili sanguine nimis gaudens* sc. at gladiatorial shows).

In place of the imperfect, *nascebantur*, the same late corrector introduced *nascuntur*, which does seem a more suitable companion for the other present-tense verbs in this generalizing context: that is presumably why Erasmus judged it *melius*. But there is a reason to prefer *nascebantur*, beyond the consensus of the manuscripts (Gruter's reason) and even beyond the fact that it is difficult to see how or why the suitable *nascuntur* would have become *nascebantur*: the imperfect has an inceptive sense that perfectly fits the observation S. is making—'whatever creatures were by birth / by nature going to be [cf. *OLD* s.v. 12–14] nomadic and destined to live their lives apart were provided with weapons.'

In the next case, however, that corrector made a better guess with *imbecillitas*. S. is very fond of the word, especially when speaking of human *imbecillitas*, whether physical or moral (cf. *Ira* 3. 42. 3, *Brev.* 11. 1, 14. 1, *EM* 53. 12, 59. 6, 82.

23, 91. 6, 92. 25, 113. 27, 116. 5), and in fact references to such weakness frame *De beneficiis* itself, with 1. 1. 9 *Hos* [sc. *deos*] *sequamur, quantum humana imbecillitas patitur* and 7. 27. 3 *Est istuc graue uitium, est intolerabile et quod dissociet homines, quod concordiam, qua imbecillitas nostra fulcitur, scindat ac dissupet.* In the latter place the *graue uitium* is of course ingratitude, and S. is making very much the same point he makes here, on the way ingratitude corrodes the social bonds that make us safe despite our weakness. If our *imbecillitas* can be spoken of metaphorically there as being 'propped up', it can be spoken of metaphorically here as 'enveloping' or 'clothing' us, probably with a nod at a secondary meaning of *cingere*, 'to arm for battle'.

As for the last crux, an express subject is wanted, *deus* and *natura* are the only plausible candidates, given the action described, and the former is preferable, placed where Haase put it. Gertz's *illi* is not needed after *res*, with the demonstrative so close to hand in the final relative clause, and that demonstrative should be *illi* as Gruter saw. With *illi obnoxium* the objective complement stands where it belongs, *obnoxium* ('subservient') anticipates the metaphors of *dominium* and *imperium* to come in the next sentence (see just below), while *ualidissimum* maintains the stress previously placed on the physical might of the animal kingdom. *illi* was simply assimilated to the two following accusatives.

4. 19. 1–2 Deos nemo sanus timet: furor est enim metuere salutaria, nec quisquam amat quos timet. Tu denique, Epicure, deum inermem facis, omnia illi tela, omnem detraxisti potentiam et ne cuiquam metuendus esset proiecisti illum **extra metum. (2)** Hunc igitur **insaeptum** ingenti quidem et **inexplicabili** muro diuisumque a contactu et a conspectu mortalium non habes quare uerearis; nulla illi nec tribuendi nec nocendi materia est; in medio interuallo huius et alterius caeli desertus sine animali, sine homine, sine re ruinas mundorum supra se circaque se cadentium euitat non exaudiens uota nec nostri curiosus

metum N, *Pinc., resp. Grut. pp. 545–6* : mundum *Mur.*, metam *Lipsius 1585b, 34, prob. Grut. (Gundermann ap. Buck 1908, 63)*, motum *1649*
insaeptum N, *Grut. p. 546, 1649* : saeptum ς₁ >1605, *Castiglioni 1920, 172*, inceptum ς₁₀ς₁₃, intersaeptum *Madvig 1871–84, 2:414–15*
quidem N : quodam 1585‡ (*prob. Georgii 1929, 112*)
inexplicabili Npc (-uili Nac) (*def. Alexander 1950–2, 23*) : inexpugnabili *Weyman 1900, 1211*, inexuperabili *Georgii 1929, 112*

To say that Epicurus 'cast god beyond fear' so that 'no one would have to fear him' comes very close to saying nothing. *metam* would be simple, but 'boundary' by itself is insufficient. Muretus' *mundum* is not much more difficult—it implies *mundum* > *metum* through an error of perseveration after *metuendus*—and respects Epicurean orthodoxy. It is when the 'ramparts of the *mundus* fall away' that 'the essence of divinity is revealed' (Lucr. 3. 15–16, 18 *moenia mundi*

| *discedunt...apparet diuum numen*), because the gods inhabit the imperishable *intermundia*—'the space between our heaven and another', as S. is about to say— where they 'avoid the debris of collapsing worlds'; cf. 7. 31. 3 (alluding to Epicurus) *alius illos* [sc. *deos*] *extra mundum suum proicit*.

In the following sentence neither *quidem* nor *inexplicabili* needs to be troubled: *ingenti* does not need the qualification that *quodam* would provide ('some sort of huge...', 'a huge, so to speak...'), and *inexplicabili* is a very Senecan way to say 'baffling' (5. 19. 9, *EM* 74. 6—where it again keeps company with *ingens*—95. 29, 101. 9). *insaeptum* is different: I am reluctant to alter a hapax legomenon simply because that is what it is; on the other hand, the idea of 'walling in' / 'blocking off' is common enough that the verb should be attested somewhere else if it had a real existence.[17] Rather than choose Madvig's *intersaeptum* I will print *saeptum* and suppose that *in-* was the product of anticipation before *ingenti...inexplicabili*, as Castiglioni suggested and as Eduard Fraenkel noted in the margin when he was proofreading the article '2. *insaeptus*' for the *TLL*.[18]

4. 21. 4 Quomodo est disertus etiam qui tacet, fortis etiam **qui conpressis mani- bus uel etiam adligatis**, quomodo gubernator etiam, qui in sicco est, quia con- summatae scientiae nihil deest, etiam si quid obstat, quo minus se utatur, ita gratus est etiam, qui uult tantum nec habet huius uoluntatis suae ullum alium quam se testem.

qui conpressis manibus uel etiam adligatis N : qui *del. Madvig 1871–84, 2:415, post* adliga- tis *add.* est *Wesenberg ap. Gertz p. 224,* iacet *J. Müller 1892, 7,* qui compressis man⟨et man⟩ ibus u- e- a- *Pré.,* qui...adligatis ⟨manet⟩ *Alexander 1950–2, 23*

Something must be amiss here, and the sequence *qui tacet...qui in sicco est* suggests that the problem does not lie with *qui*. Though Alexander recognized that Préchac's *manet* was as usual paleographically driven, he nonetheless wished to retain it, following *alligatis* for the sake of the clausula (double cretic). But there is no need to suppose anything more than *est* was lost—probably a single letter, *e* with a suspension stroke, like the *est* that follows *quomodo* at the start of the sentence—and *adligatis est* rounds off the clause satisfactorily with a cretic + spondee.

4. 21. 6 Si uero bonam fidem perfidiae suppliciis adfici uidet, non descendit e fastigio et supra poenam suam consistit: 'Habeo' inquit, 'quod uolui, quod petii; nec paenitet nec paenitebit nec ulla iniquitate me eo fortuna perducet, ut hanc

---

[17] *OLD* s.v. *insaepire* 'to hedge in', 'enclose'; Gruter thought *in-* has an intensifying force ('quod uer- bum si admittimus, non negabit...sed uero affirmabit magis: quemadmodum *inuinctum* pro *ualde uincto* ponitur...').

[18] *TLL* 7. 1823. 69–71: '*saeptum* Castiglioni et Ed. Fraenkel in plagulis *in* ex sequentibus errore praereptum censentes.'

uocem audiat: "quid mihi uolui? quid nunc mihi prodest bona uoluntas?"' Prodest
et in eculeo, prodest et in igne; qui **si singulis** membris admoueatur et paulatim
uiuum corpus circumeat, licet ipsum cor plenum bona conscientia **stillet**: place-
bit illi ignis, per quem bona fides conlucebit.

si singulis Npc (si *ss. pr. man., ut uid.*) : singulis Nac, qui singulis…circumeat licet *dist.*
Gertz, qui singulis…circumeat ⟨licet⟩, licet ipsum *Pré.* (*prob. Alexander 1950–2, 23*)
cor ς_{14} : corpus N‡ (*e corpus praeced.*)
stillet N : ustilet *Cornelissen 1870, 14*

The addition of *si* before *singulis* was certainly an early correction—*si singulis* is
R's text—and I would say it is almost certainly scribal, to judge from the colour of
the ink and the letter forms. If that is the case, the scribe evidently caught his slip
when he turned his eye back to his exemplar, and there is no need to doubt the
conjunction's authenticity. Near the end of the sentence *stillet* is certainly sound,
but the meaning is 'melt' (sc. in the fire), not 'drip with blood' (Basore, Griffin and
Inwood): *OLD* s.v. 1b '(of a melting or dissolving solid)', cf. *NQ* 3. 29. 7 (of lique-
fying soil) and *destillare* at *EM* 24. 5 and 66. 51, of the flesh 'melting from' Mucius
Scaevola's right hand as he holds it in Porsenna's flame.

4. 22. 2–3…pulchritudo [sc. honesti] animos circumfundit et delenitos admira-
tione luminis ac fulgoris sui rapit. **(3) At multa hoc commoda oriuntur, et tutior
est uita melioribus amorque et secundum bonorum iudicium aetasque secu-
rior quam innocentia, quam grata mens prosequitur.** Fuisset enim iniquissima
rerum natura, si hoc tantum bonum miserum et anceps et sterile fecisset. Sed
illud intuere, an ad istam uirtutem, **quae saepe tuta ac facili aditur uia**, etiam per
saxa et rupes et feris ac serpentibus obsessum iter fueris iturus.

at multa…oriuntur *interlocutori dat Eras.*, at multa…prosequitur *eidem dat Alexander
1950–2, 23–4*
hoc N[19] : hinc $\varsigma_1\varsigma_6$‡, ab hoc *Gertz*
est N : *del. Haase*
amorque et N >1490 (*Grut. p. 546*), 1605‡ : amarque et 1492, amatque et 1503, 1515, atque
1529, 1557, et 1585 (*om.* amorque…aetasque: *adn. praerancidam ad loc. scripsit Mur.,*[20]
resp. Grut. p. 546)
quae saepe tuta ac facili aditur uia *Gertz* (*iam* quae saepe tuta ac facili uia aditur ς_{12}) : quae
saepe tuta ac facili daturus Nac[21]

---

[19] There is a small erasure before *hoc* in **N**, more likely the remnant of an errant punctuation mark
than a letter.
[20] 1585, 37: 'Comprehensionem hanc iam ante deprauatam ab aliis, magis etiam deprauauit
Erasmus qui utinam a Seneca abstinuisset manus. Minore negatio [sic] pleraque restituerentur.'
[21] **R** has **N**'s uncorrected text, which is then found in most of the later medieval manuscripts; of the
few that innovate, the only versions worth reporting are those of **G**, which took an independent line in
fashioning a more or less readable text, and **H**, which had some currency among the *recentiores* and
became the text of the printed editions through Erasmus'.

quae saepe tuto ac facili aditur Npc* (*ss. man. post.*) *1557‡, unde* quae saepe tuto ac
facile aditur *Haase*
quae saepe tuto ac facili datura uiam G
quae saepe tuto ac facili datur Hς₁ >*1529*
quae saepe e tuto ac facili aditur *Eras. p. 272* ('in uetusto [sc. codice]')
quae saepe tuta ac facili aditur ς₁₆ς₁₇, *Pinc.* ('ut subintelligatur *uia* graeco more')
quae saepe [*abl. sing.*] tuta ac facili datur *Buck 1908, 64*
quo es saepe tuta ⟨uia⟩ ac facili aditurus *Pré.*
quae saepe tuto ac facili datur usui *Mazzoli 1974, 82*

It was at the start of §20 that we last heard the imaginary interlocutor insist on the
practical advantages of gratitude—'*Sed inest*' inquit '*huic bono etiam utilitas aliqua*'—and the opening of this passage reads more smoothly if he is brought back
to speak here—but only *At multa hoc commoda oriuntur*, as Erasmus saw, not all
of *At multa...prosequitur*, as Alexander suggested.[22] After S. lyrically evokes
the ravishing beauty of the *honestum*, the interlocutor objects, 'But many practical advantages arise from this source'.[23] To which S. replies, in effect, that what
is true of gratitude in this regard is true of virtue in general: 'Yes, better people
in fact enjoy a safer way of life, the affection and favourable opinion of good
men, and a less troubled span of years that innocence and a grateful disposition
attend. For the universe would have been dreadfully unfair if...'. But then he
brings the discussion back to the principle that virtue must be pursued irrespective of the obstacles ('But consider this...'). The interlocutor's irruptions
are not always explicitly marked by *inquit* or the like (cf., e.g., 3. 14. 1, 3. 17. 1, 3.
30. 1, 3. 35. 4, 4. 5. 1).

The last sentence's crux is among those in which the thought intended is clear
in general terms—one can often achieve virtue safely and easily—but the words
S. chose to convey it are lost behind the archetype's corruption (here, at least *daturus*): we are left to select a form of words that can provide a plausible stop-gap, to
be branded as such in the apparatus, even if we cannot be even reasonably confident that the words match S.'s. I am fairly sure that some variation on *daturus* will
not give us what we need: virtue is not 'being given', as the versions of the early
editions, Buck, and Mazzoli would have it (the latter two attempts seem especially
implausible), and I do not think it is going to 'provide a way', as G's version was
meant to suggest. A late correcting hand often active in N introduced a version
with *aditur*:[24] it was first printed in Curio's edition of 1557, after Erasmus reported

---

[22]   Erasmus wrote ad loc., '*At...conuenit obiicienti ab aduerso, Et tutior* est respondentis accidere
in omni genere uirtutis' (1529, 42). This understanding of the passage shows that Haase was mistaken
to seclude *est*.

[23]   Gertz's addition of *ab* is probably unnecessary (cf. *TLL* 9. 999. 54–69, though most instances of
oriri + ablative are concerned with ancestry), but I would sooner print *ab hoc* than the *hinc* of the
recentiores and print vulgate.

[24]   This corrector is Kekulé's 'm. sec.'—i.e., second after the early corrector whose work was already
present in the text transmitted to R, in addition to the scribe's self-corrections—whom Kekulé dated

it (doubtless from **N**) in the critical appendix inserted after *Epistulae Morales* in his edition of 1529 and Pincianus blended it with his version of the passage. For our limited purpose this is more promising. The main candidates are the reading of the corrector, with Haase's adjustment of *facili* to *facile* to provide a familiar adverbial form; Erasmus' version, which allows the corrector's *tuto ac facili* to stand preceded by *e*;[25] and Gertz's version (anticipated in one of the *recentiores*), which allows **N**'s *tuta ac facili* to stand but requires the insertion of *uia*. There is not much to choose among them: I will print Haase's version of the corrector's text.

4. 27. 1–3 Timidus dicitur aliquis quia stultus est, et hoc malos sequitur quos indiscreta et uniuersa uitia circumstant; dicitur timidus proprie natura etiam ad inanes sonos pauidus. Stultus omnia uitia habet sed non in omnia natura pronus est: alius in auaritiam, alius in luxuriam, alius in petulantiam inclinatur. (2)...Non hoc dicimus sic omnia uitia esse in omnibus, quomodo in quibusdam singula eminent, sed malum ac stultum nullo uitio uacare; ne audacem quidem timoris absoluimus, ne prodigum quidem auaritia liberamus. (3) Quomodo homo omnes sensus habet, nec ideo tamen omnes homines aciem habent Lynceo similem, **sic, qui stultus est, ⟨non⟩ tam acria** et concitata habet **omnia, quam quidam quaedam**. Omnia in omnibus uitia sunt, sed non omnia in singulis extant: hunc natura ad auaritiam impellit; hic uino, hic libidini deditus est aut, si nondum deditus, ita formatus, ut in hoc illum mores sui ferant.

sic qui stultus est ⟨non⟩ tam acria ς₅ς₆ς₁₇ς₁₈, *Pinc.*, *1557‡*, *prob. Grut. p. 547* : sic stultus est
tam acria Nac, qui *add.* Npc
   sic ⟨hic⟩ stultus est, ⟨tamen⟩ non tam *Pré.*
   sic qui stultus est ⟨omnium uitiorum particeps est, non tamen⟩ tam *Shackleton Bailey*
   1970, 362
   sic stultus ⟨omnia uitia habet nec tamen qui stultus⟩ est tam *Mazzoli 1974, 82–3*
omnia, quam quidam quaedam Npc (*pr. man. vel man. eiusdem aet.*) : omnia, quam quidem Nac, omnia ⟨uitia⟩, q- q- q-, ⟨omnia tamen habet⟩ *Gertz*

S. is elaborating the familiar Stoic principle that the non-wise—the *stulti*, who are also *mali*—are not free from any vice: even if a *stultus* is not (say) ungrateful at any particular moment, his moral imperfection disposes him to ingratitude, as a 'wrathful' person's disposition inclines him to actual fits of anger. All the corrections in **N**—the addition of *qui* after *sic*, *quidam quaedam* for *quidem*— were made, if not by the scribe, then certainly by a contemporary hand, and all

to the thirteenth or fourteenth century (Gertz 1876, iv). Writing a faint but legible hand in pale ink, he was certainly working at a time far enough removed from **N**'s creation that some elements of its script were challenging: for example, in the case of ligatures joining *t* to a following vowel (so *ti* = **ꝗ**) he commonly wrote a small, faint *t* above the ligature.

[25] Judged *bonum* by Gruter, who however added, 'ego hic Harpocratem imitor & labrum indice signo' (p. 546).

were transmitted to **R**. All that is needed to make the sense complete is the *non* supplied in a number of *recentiores*: given that S. already stated the principle clearly in the paragraph's second sentence, *Stultus omnia uitia habet*, I cannot join Gertz and more recent critics in thinking that it needs restating a few sentences later.

4. 27. 5 Quomodo male filiae suae consulet qui illam contumelioso et saepe repudiato **collocauit**, malus pater familiae habebitur qui negotiorum gestorum damnato patrimonii sui curam mandauerit, quomodo dementissime testabitur qui tutorem filio reliquerit pupillorum spoliatorem, sic pessime beneficia dare dicetur quicumque ingratos **eligit** in quos peritura conferat.

collocauit Npc : collogauit Nac, collocauerit *Gertz*, collocabit *Buck 1908, 65*
eligit N : -get *Feldmann 1887, 21*

It is not *mandauerit* and *reliquerit* in the succeeding examples that convince me that something is wrong with *collocauit* but the illogic of its relation with the future tense of *consulet*. Yet having decided that *collocauit* cannot stand, I think *mandauerit* and *reliquerit* argue in favour of Gertz's correction, which implies an error almost as easy as Buck's *collocabit*. By contrast, I do not think that the relation between *dicetur*…and *eligit* compels the change to *eleget*, though I will add '*fort. recte*' in the apparatus, given that *-et* and *-it* are so frequently confused in **N**.

4. 28. 5–6 In iis exige censuram et personarum aestimationem quae separatim tamquam digno dantur, non in his quae promiscue turbam admittunt. Multum enim refert utrum aliquem non excludas an eligas. Ius et furi dicitur, pace et homicidae fruuntur, sua repetunt etiam qui aliena rapuerunt, percussores et domi ferrum exercentes murus ab hoste defendit, legum praesidio qui plurimum in illas peccauerunt proteguntur. (**6**) Quaedam non poterant **ceteris** contingere, nisi uniuersis darentur; non est itaque, quod de istis disputes, ad quae publice inuitati sumus. Illud, quod iudicio meo ad aliquem peruenire debebit, ei, quem esse ingratum sciam, non dabo.

ceteris N >*1557 (prob. Grut. p. 547), 1649‡* : certis *Pinc., 1557mg., 1585, 1605, Gertz,* rectis *Courtney 1974, 105*

S. is wrapping up a paragraph that began with an interlocutor's objections and his own reply:

> 'Di quoque' inquit 'multa ingratis tribuunt'. Sed illa bonis parauerunt, contingunt autem etiam malis quia separari non possunt.

If *ceteris* here were correct, it would have to mean 'Some things could not fall to the lot of the rest [sc. beyond the malefactors I have just mentioned] unless they were given to all at once'. That seems less than ideally lucid; in any case, it is wrong to tie the thought to the sentence just past. Rather, in concluding the topic, S. is looking back to where it began: as in §28. 1 he wrote, 'Ita quae refers [sc. gifts of the gods like sunlight and the seasons] pro uniuersis inuenerunt, excerpere singulos non potuerunt', so here he must have written, 'Quaedam non poterant certis ['individuals': *OLD* s.v. 3] contingere, nisi uniuersis darentur', with *certis* playing the part that *singulos* did previously.[26] For the confusion, in reverse, cf. 2. 30. 1 *in cetera* (**N**), which became *incerta* in some *recentiores*.

4. 31. 5 Hominem tam palam obscenum ad fasces et ad tribunal admisisti? Nempe dum ueterem illum Scaurum senatus principem **cogitas et** indigne fers subolem eius iacere.

cogitas et *Gertz* : cogitasset Nac >*1529*, cogitas Npc*, HG, *Pinc.*, *1557‡*

Gertz's solution here produces the best outcome, treating *Nempe dum* ... as a continuation of the preceding thought and *cogitas et indigne fers* as members of a compound predicate in the *dum*-clause: 'Did you really admit...? No doubt [you did], while thinking of...and resenting....' But the report of **N** needs a small clarification. Relying on Kekulé's collation of **N**, Gertz recorded its reading as *cogitas. sẽ*, and put his emendation in the text; Hosius recorded **N** as reading *cogitasset*, and printed *cogitas et*, with attribution to Gertz.[27] Both reports contain part of the truth: **N**'s original reading was *cogitasset* (the reading passed on to **R** and most of the later manuscripts), and sometime after **R**'s text was produced, a reader did put a punctuation mark after *cogitas*, producing *cogitas. sẽ*. But that same reader—to judge by the colour of the ink—also drew a line under *sẽ*, with the intention of canceling those letters: hence my report above that *cogitas* is the corrected reading of **N** not reflected in **R**.

4. 32. 1–2 ⟨Idem facere⟩[28] deos ueri simile est, ut alios indulgentius tractent propter parentes auosque, alios propter futuram nepotum pronepotumque ac longe sequentium posterorum indolem. Nota enim illis [sc. dis] est operis sui series omniumque illis rerum per manus suas iturarum scientia in aperto semper est, nobis ex abdito subit et quae repentina putamus illis prouisa ueniunt ac familiaria. (2) 'Sint hi reges quia maiores eorum **non** fuerunt, quia pro summo imperio habuerunt iustitiam, abstinentiam, quia non rem publicam sibi sed se rei publicae dicauerunt. Regnent hi quia uir bonus quidam ante proauus eorum fuit qui

---

[26] Thus Griffin and Inwood, 'Certain things cannot accrue to particular people unless they are given to all and sundry', tacitly correcting Hosius.

[27] Strictly, Hosius attributed *cogitasset* to **O**, his *siglum* for 'consensus codicum **NRGMP** aut omnium aut ceterorum', correctly adding that **G** reads *cogitas* (so too **H**, the twelfth-century copy from Cherbourg). Préchac recorded *cogitasset* for **N** and printed *cogitas et* without attribution.

[28] That there is a lacuna before *deos* is certain; that S. wrote *idem facere deos* (Madvig 1871–84, 2:415–16) is not, but it must convey what he had in mind, and *idem* is more apt than Mazzoli's *melius* (1974, 83), to say nothing of Muretus' *Deos uidere est*. Compare, in a similar context, *Prov.* 3. 4 *Idem facit fortuna: fortissimos sibi quaerit, quosdam fastidio transit*.

animum supra fortunam gessit, qui in dissensione ciuili—quoniam ita expediebat rei publicae—uinci quam uincere maluit.

non N : *om.* ς₄ς₅ς₆ς₁₉, boni *Gertz*

S. is explaining that the gods sometimes favour the apparently undeserving thanks to their ability to take a very long view, which sometimes causes them to reward a person in the present because their ancestors' desert went unrewarded: 'Let these be kings because their ancestors were not....' The suppression of *non* found in some *recentiores* is presumably intentional and results from a misunderstanding; if so, the error is remarkably short-sighted, since *pro summo imperium habuerunt iustitiam...* in the next clause makes plain that they were not *reges*. Gertz's *boni* is correct as a matter of fact, since it is clear that the people referred to were in fact good, but it unsubtly makes explicit what S. leaves implied in his quasi-paradoxical formulation. The same point emerges more straightforwardly in §32. 3, *At ego scio alii me istud dare, alii olim debitum soluere*: 'But *I* know that I am granting this to one man but paying what was once owed to another.'

4. 32. 3–4 'Hic corpore deformis est, adspectu foedus et ornamenta sua traducturus: iam me homines accusabunt, caecum ac temerarium dicent, nescientem quo loco quae summis atque excelsissimis debentur ponam. At ego scio alii me istud dare, alii olim debitum soluere. **(4)** Vnde isti norunt illum quondam gloriae sequentis fugacissimum, eo uultu ad pericula euntem, quo alii e periculo redeunt, numquam bonum suum a publico distinguentem? "Vbi" inquis "iste aut quis est?" **Vnde uos scitis?** Apud me istae expensorum acceptorumque rationes dispunguntur, ego, quid cui debeam, scio; aliis post longam diem repono, aliis in antecessum ac prout occasio et rei publicae meae facultas tulit.' Ingrato ergo aliquando quaedam, sed non propter ipsum dabo.

Vnde uos scitis? >*1557* (Vbi inquis iste? aut quis est unde uos scitis? C) : Vnde, uos scitis. N, *del. Mur.*, 1585, 1605 (*prob. Grut. p. 548*), 'Vnde?' Nescitis *Lips.*, 1649‡, *Wesenberg ap. Gertz*, Vnde noscitis *Fick.*

In this continuation of the passage just treated the words *Vnde uos scitis?* (punctuated in N with a comma after *Vnde* and a period after *scitis*) have encountered some heavy weather in the text's editorial history: after being treated correctly as a question in the earliest editions, their deletion by Muretus was approved by Gruter, then Lipsius' conjecture replaced them in Gronovius' edition and Fickert's conjecture in his own, before Haase restored them. The trouble is perhaps due to the fact that *Vnde isti norunt...?* and *Vnde uos scitis?* represent a rhetorical gesture of which S. is almost uniquely fond, in which *unde* effectively = 'how?' and the indicative verb of knowing shades into 'can / could know.' So in the first example here, S. speaks from the point of view of the divinity who is aware that human beings, with their limited knowledge, will criticize him for being capricious (*iam me homines accusabunt...*), unjustly: *At ego scio .... Vnde isti norunt...?*, 'But *I* know .... How can *they* know...?' And so in the second example, to the question, 'Where is that [good man you refer to] or who is he?', the god replies, 'How can you know? *I* am the one who keeps the accounts... *I* know what I owe, and to whom.'[29] Cf. *Cons. Marc.* 22. 1 *Quereris, Marcia, non tam diu filium tuum uixisse quam potuisset? Vnde enim scis an diutius illi expedierit uiuere, an illi hac morte consultum sit?*, EM 17. 8 *Tu uero, siue aliquid habes, iam philosophare (unde enim scis an iam nimis habeas?), siue nihil*, NQ 6. 1. 11 *Vnde scis an melior eorum locorum condicio sit in quibus iam uires suas fortuna consumpsit et quae in futurum ruina sua fulta sunt?* It happens that—apart from one passage in the elder Pliny (*NH* 8. 10)—I have encountered this type of question used in this way only in the *Controversiae* of S.'s father (2. 3. 7 [Junius Gallio], 2. 6. 2 [the elder Arellius Fuscus]).

4. 34. 3 'Si promiseris' inquit 'te daturum beneficium et postea ingratum esse scieris, dabis an non? Si facis sciens, peccas, das enim cui non debes dare. Si negas, et hoc modo peccas, non das ei cui promisisti. **Conscientia** uestra hoc loco titubat et illud superbum promissum, numquam sapientem facti sui paenitere nec umquam emendare quod fecerit nec mutare consilium.'

conscientia N : constantia *Lips.*

I cannot say that Lipsius' conjecture here is necessary, but I think it is very probably right. As he remarks in his note, *constantia* is exactly the issue here, and not many words farther on S. expressly rejects the *inconstantiae crimen* (§35. 3 *Tunc fidem fallam, tunc inconstantiae crimen audiam, si cum eadem omnia sint quae erant promittente me non praestitero promissum*). Further, the interlocutor S. here conjures up is being not just recalcitrant but rather cutting (*illud superbum promissum*), and *constantia... titubat* suits the tone; it is also clear that 'waver' is just what *constantia* should not do, whereas the pertinence of *conscientia* here, and what it would mean for it to waver, are less evident.

4. 34. 5 Imprudentium ista fiducia est fortunam sibi spondere; sapiens utramque partem eius cogitat; scit, quantum liceat errori, quam incerta sint humana, quam multa consiliis obstent; ancipitem rerum ac lubricam sortem suspensus sequitur, consiliis **certis incertos euentus expendit. Exceptio** autem, sine qua nihil destinat, nihil ingreditur, et hic illum tuetur.

certis incertos Npc1 : *n. l.* Nac (-ti- *et* -to- *in ras.*), certus, incertus (*sine* expendit) Gundermann *ap.* Buck 1908, 65–6
exceptio *sub* expendit *in mg. inf. add.* Npc2* (*man. post.*), exc⟨ipit. Exc⟩eptio Pré.

---

[29] Basore's translation here catches the nuance a bit more faithfully ('"Where", you ask, "is this man, or who is he?" But how could you know these things?'), Griffin and Inwood a bit more freely ('"Where", you ask, "is that man or who is he?" You have no way of knowing').

This innocent-seeming passage presents one of the deeper puzzles in the text. Fol. 64[r] in **N** ends with *euentus exceptio au(tem)*, the last word abbreviated, with punctuation between *euentus* and *exceptio*; *expendit* is a supplement added beneath *euentus* in the lower margin, and the *-ti-* of *certis* and *-to-* of *incertos* both stand in erasures. The crux resides in the fact that the latter corrections were made before— probably, long before—*expendit* was added. Gruter tentatively ascribed *expendit* to **N**'s scribe, and Hosius in his first edition wrote 'suppl. pr. corr. (?) in **N**';[30] but Buck was certainly correct both to point out that—unlike *certis incertos*—*expendit* does not appear in **R** and the later manuscripts and to attribute it to the later correcting hand that used a pale ink (the *t* is clearly by the same hand that so frequently elucidated **N**'s *t*-ligatures).[31] One could add that whoever wrote *expendit* did not make the ideal choice, since the verb typically is used of literally or figuratively weighing things already on hand, not outcomes lying in the uncertain future.[32] As for Gundermann's suggestion that *certis incertos* was originally *certus incertus*, traces of what might have been a *u* are visible in the first erasure, but the *to* written in the second erasure has entirely obscured what originally stood there.

In this muddle it is best to be guided by the scribe's original punctuation of the text, with marks (.[7]) after both *sequitur* and *euentus* isolating *consiliis...euentus* as a discrete unit of sense. That fact in turn argues rather strongly in favour of Gundermann's suggestion: on the one hand, it is difficult to see what other combination could produce an equally serviceable sense-unit; on the other hand, it implicitly but convincingly explains how *consiliis certis incertos euentus* was generated. Puzzled by the syntax of *certus incertus*—very likely because he failed to see that *euentus* is a genitive—a reader decided to provide *sequitur* with a second object, and to throw in an instrumental ablative for good measure. *consiliis certus incertus euentus* might be an editor's motto; in any case, that is what I will print.

4. 35. 1 Promisi beneficium nisi si quid incidisset quare non deberem dare. Quid enim, si quod illi pollicitus sum **patria sibi dare** iusserit? si lex lata erit, ne id quisquam faciat, quod ego me amico meo facturum promiseram?

---

[30] Gruter p. 549: 'at enim non temerarium est quod additur in optimo Nazar. eadem, ut mihi uidetur, subscriptum manu: incertos euentus expendit: fere enim suspicor uocem eam hinc excidisse, ideoque in locum suum restituendum.' Hosius' 'pr. corr.' = 'primus corrector in **N** eiusdem fere aeui, quo codex scriptus est' (*Hos. 1* xxvi = *Hos. 2* xxxiv).

[31] Cf. n. 24 in this chapter; the same hand also altered the punctuation mark originally inserted between *euentus* and *exceptio* (a dot on the baseline with a short diagonal stroke above it, .[7]) by erasing the diagonal and adding a stroke in lighter ink beneath the dot; strokes of the same sort, in the same ink, were added many times on this and the surrounding pages. In his second edition Hosius changed the apparatus to read 'suppl. **N**[3] (?), vd. Buck p. 16; 65' (**N**[3] = 'correctores posteriores codicis **N**') but retained *expendit* in the text.

[32] Cf. 3. 8. 3 *Quis inter se ista* [sc. *beneficia* of different magnitudes] *comparabit? Quis expendet?, Ira* 1. 19. 8 *Haec* [sc. approaches to punishment, just mentioned] *cui expendenda aestimandaque sunt, uides quam debeat omni perturbatione liber accedere ad rem summa diligentia trantandam, NQ* 3. 25. 5 *Quamcumque uis rem expende et contra aquam statue, dummodo utriusque par sit modus.*

patria HOFpc‡ : -riam N (*Gundermann ap. Buck 1908, 66*), in patriam *Hos. in app.*
sibi dare N, *prob. Grut. p. 549* : non sibi dare HOpcς₂, sibi non dare Ipcς₃ *>1503*, sibi me
dare *1515‡*, sibi nos dare *Lips.*, me sibi dare *Gertz*

patria is wanted—S. is thinking of public authority trumping personal connection, as *lex* in the next sentence shows—and as editors since 1515 have generally
seen, a first-person pronoun is as much in place here with *dare* as it is with *factu-*
rum in what follows. I also agree with Gertz that *me* should precede *sibi*, where
the last letter of the transmitted *patriam* is probably a vestige of *me*, left by another
misreading of *scriptura continua*.

4. 37. 2 Narrauit Philippo naufragium suum, auxilium tacuit et protinus petit ut
sibi cuiusdam praedia donaret. **Ille quidam** erat hospes eius, is ipse a quo receptus erat, a quo sanatus.

quidam *1585‡* : quidem N

In this edifying anecdote, one of Philip of Macedon's soldiers, rescued after ship-
wreck by a beneficent *hospes*, betrays his saviour by fraudulently persuading the
king to give him the man's property. *ille quidam* does not occur outside Plautus,
and there only in one passage of *Cistellaria*:[33] Muretus' emendation became established as the vulgate but was rightly ejected by Fickert, only to be reinstated by
Gertz, whom Hosius followed.

   In contrast, Gertz had the correct impulse in the following passage, at the end
of the anecdote, by which point Philip has learned the truth and deprived the
soldier of his ill-gotten gains.

4. 37. 4 Dignus quidem fuit cui non inscriberentur illae litterae sed insculperentur, qui hospitem suum **nudo** et naufrago similem **in id ⟨in⟩ quo** iacuerat ipse
litus expulerat.

nudo N : nudum *Will. Polyhist. p. 142. 19*, Gertz *p. 229*
in id ⟨in⟩ quo *Will. Polyhist., 1478‡* : in id quod Nac (*Bourgery 1922, 407*), in id quo
Npc, *1475*

William of Malmesbury, who elsewhere showed himself to be a shrewd emender
of classical Latin texts, here anticipated two later conjectures.[34] The second
has been the vulgate text since it first appeared in the edition of 1478, and I take it
to be uncontroversial. The first was also tentatively proposed by Gertz ('*cum in*
solo adiectiuo "naufrago" *imago sita esse uideatur*'), and I believe that it, too, is
correct: *nudo et naufrago similem* (as though for *nudo naufrago similem*) is rather
awkward, while *nudum et naufrago similem* is a very Senecan structure, offering

---

[33] *Cist.* 737, 739; *illa quaedam* does not occur at all.
[34] For William's impact on the text of Suetonius' *De vita Caesarum*, see Kaster 2016a, 122–33
(in broader strokes, Kaster 2016b, xxxi–xxxiv).

paired predicate modifiers, the second slightly weightier than the first, with the emphasis appropriately placed on *naufrago*. Reaching *nudum*, a scribe simply saw *naufrago* coming into view.

4. 37. 5 Sed uidebimus quis modus poenae seruandus fuerit: auferendum utique fuit quod summo scelere inuaserat. Quis autem poena eius moueretur? **Id** conmiserat propter quod nemo misereri misericors posset.

id Nac : qui id Npc (qui *add. ss.*), Rpc (*edd.*), quid Rac

qui was an early addition in **N**, but **R**'s scribe bobbled slightly in copying it, writing *quid* before adding a small superscript *i*. *qui id* thereafter was the reading of the manuscripts and all the editions before Gertz, who removed *qui*; he was followed by Hosius. It is helpful here to compare 5. 11. 1 *qui gratiam refert debet impendere, sicut qui soluit pecuniam*: in this case the second *qui* was initially omitted in **N**, then added above the line, where the scribe of **R** found it and passed it along to all later copies, and it has never been questioned because it is plainly needed. Having compared side-by-side colour digital images of the two passages in **N**, I can say that the same hand wrote both: the size and shape of the letterforms are identical in both additions, and the only discernible difference is the shade of the ink, which is a bit paler in the addition made in the passage under discussion—but so is the ink of the text on that page. In short, there is a very good chance that both additions were made by the scribe. The addition in this case, it is true, is not as clearly necessary: the text printed by Gertz and Hosius is obviously intelligible, and *eius* could simply resume the implied subject of *inuaserat*. But I think it more likely that S. also intended *eius* to be correlative with *qui*, binding together what are in fact two halves of a single thought, and giving the moral of the tale—to my ear—a very Senecan rhythm.

4. 38. 2 Age, si Philippus possessorem illum eorum litorum reliquisset, quae naufragio ceperat, non omnibus miseris aqua et igni interdixerat? '**Potius**' inquit 'intra fines regni mei **tu litteras** istas **oculis inscribendas** durissima fronte **circumfer.** I, ostende, quam sacra res sit mensa hospitalis; praebe in facie tua legendum istuc decretum, quo cauetur, ne miseros tecto iuuare capital sit. Magis ista constitutio sic rata erit, quam si illam in aes incidissem.'

potius Nac : potius est Npc‡
tu litteras *Gertz* : et litteras N >*1515*, te lit- *1529*‡, {et} litteras *Siesbye ap. Gertz p. 229*, i et litteras *Madvig ibid.*, et ⟨litus⟩ litteras *Pré.*
oculis N (*def. Pré., Alexander 1950–2, 25*) : foculis *Lips.*, aculeis *Gertz*, acubus *Skutsch ap. Hos.*, oculis ⟨omnium⟩ *Alexander 1934, 54–5* [*v. seq.*], omnibus ⟨ingratis⟩ *Watt 1994, 228–9*
inscribendas N : ingerendas *Hermes ap. Hos.*, seruandas *Alexander 1934, 54–5*, inscribendas ⟨inscriptas⟩ *pensitavit Alexander 1950–2, 25*
circumfer. I *Gertz* (circumfer *iam Madvig*) : circumferri N, circumferre *1529*‡

To take *potius* first. The text of **N**—*potius est… et litteras… circumferri*, with the early correction *est*—was passed to **R** and ultimately became the text of the printed editions before Erasmus' edition of 1529: the reading that he established—*potius est… te litteras… circumferre*—was the vulgate before Gertz. There is a serious problem with that text, however, to which Gertz drew attention: ' "potius est" sequente accusatiuo cum infinitiuo uix recte pro eo, quod est "satius est", dicitur.' In fact predicative *potius* with infinitive or accusative + infinitive is vanishingly rare and all but non-existent when not accompanied by *quam* coordinating a comparison:[35] the fact that at *NQ* 3. pr. 5 S. writes, 'quanto satius est, sua mala extinguere quam aliena posteris trader! quanto potius, deorum opera cele-brare quam Philippi… latrocinia!', tends to confirm Gertz's point, not undermine it. I will not print Gertz's emendation, however. Coaxing *tu* out of *et* is not easy, while *circumfer. I* is too obviously an attempt to explain *circumferri*, and not very Senecan besides: S. several times juxtaposes *i* closely with a second imperative in his prose works, but when he does he invariably writes *i nunc et* (6. 35. 5, *Brev.* 12. 8, *Helv.* 6. 8, 10. 10, *EM* 88. 37, *NQ* 1. 16. 3). Madvig's *potius… i et litteras… circumfer* is preferable, the intervening words providing the buffer between the imperatives otherwise provided by *nunc*. After *i* was swallowed by *mei*, *circumferri* was probably produced to provide an infinitive that seemed to be wanted with *potius*.

As for the absurd *oculis inscribendas*, it is not rescued by Préchac's citation of Cicero on Epicurean optical theory (Cic. *ND* 1. 108 *Vos autem non modo oculis imagines sed etiam animis inculcatis*), still less by Alexander's citation of Jeremiah (17:1 'The sin of Judah is written with a pen of iron and with the point of a diamond; it is graven upon the table of their hearts'). *inscribendas* is guaranteed by §37. 3 *stigmata inscriberet* and §37. 4, just previously discussed. The latter also shows why Gertz's *aculeis*, just the sort of unexpected word that would be vulnerable to corruption, should be adopted in place of *oculis*, just the word that corruption would produce: the previous thought that the malefactor 'deserved to have the letters… carved into him' is here answered by 'those letters that should be inscribed with spikes / barbs / needles'.[36]

4. 40. 2 Quid enim regi, **quid pauper{i quid}** diuiti reddam, utique cum quidam recipere beneficium iniuriam iudicent et beneficia subinde aliis beneficiis one-rent? quid amplius in horum persona possum quam uelle? Nec enim ideo beneficium nouum reicere debeo, quia nondum prius reddidi. Accipiam tam libenter,

---

[35] See *TLL* 10. 340. 44–57; without comparison only Liv. 38. 5. 10 *potius uisum est Amphilochis… ferre opem*, Quint. 5. 10. 124 *potius fuerit esse contentum*.

[36] As Griffin notes (2013, 256), Philip should be understood to have ordered the miscreant's fore-head to be tattooed, with ἀχάριστος or the like; *insculperentur* and *aculeis inscribendas* raise the stakes, from tattooing (which could be removed) to gouging and permanent disfigurement (*non inscriberen-tur illae litterae sed insculperentur*).

quam dabitur, et praebebo me amico meo exercendae bonitatis suae capacem materiam; qui noua accipere non uult, acceptis offenditur.

quid pauper ς₂ >*1492, 1585‡* : quid pauperi quid N
    pauper, quid G
    quid ς₆
    quid pauper quid *1503, 1515, 1529*
    quid principi, quid *Pinc., 1557 (prob., ut uid., Grut. pp. 550–1)*
    quid pauper inquit *Pré.*

I suspect that **N**'s text is more likely the result of intentional alteration than mechanical error: someone introduced an unwanted *quid* and changed *pauper* to the dative because he mistook the sentence's form and S.'s intended meaning. If that is so, the apparent economy of the correction that became the vulgate after Muretus deleted a string of five consecutive letters counts for less than the passage's rhythm and rhetorical structure; and that in turn makes me think that the text of **G**, juxtaposing *pauper* with the first dative, is more likely to be what S. wrote.

Notes to Book 5

5. 1. 1 In prioribus libris uidebar consummasse propositum, cum tractassem quemadmodum dandum esset beneficium, quemadmodum accipiendum. Hi enim sunt huius officii fines: quidquid ultra moror, non seruio materiae sed indulgeo, quae quo ducit sequenda est, non quo inuitat. Subinde enim nascetur **quo lacessat** aliqua dulcedine animum, magis non superuacuum quam necessarium.

quo (3°) N >*1515 (Grut. p. 551)* : quod G, *1529‡*

quod lacessat had stood in the text since Erasmus' edition of 1529, before Haase replaced it with **N**'s *quo*, known from Gruter's report. Gertz saw that some explanation was wanted (p. 230):

> ut tollatur ambiguitas…, hic dicam in **N** esse: 'subinde enim nascetur, *quo* lacessat aliqua dulcedine animum', in qua scriptura 'materia' subiecti loco auditur, ablatiui autem 'quo' et 'dulcedine' diuersa significatione cum uerbo iunguntur….

Perhaps: but then what do *superuacuum* and *necessarium* modify? Surely the subject of *nascetur* and *lacessat*: 'for frequently there will arise an issue—pertinent rather than essential—to provoke the mind with some sweet beguilement' (with *magis non superuacuum quam necessarium* compare the next sentence, *perseueremus…scrutari etiam ea quae…conexa sunt, non cohaerentia*). **N**'s scribe confused *quo* and *quod* in the clause immediately preceding (*quo* Npc : *quod* Nac): it appears that he did it again here, in reverse.

5. 1. 4 Ipse usque eo abes ab omni iactatione, usque eo statim uis exonerare quos obligas ut quidquid in aliquem confers uelis uideri non praestare sed reddere, ideoque plenius ad te sic data reuertentur: nam fere secuntur beneficia non reposcentem et ut gloria fugientes magis sequitur, ita fructus beneficiorum gratius **respondet** per quos esse etiam ingratis licet.

respondet Qψ (*Hos. 2, post Stangl 1909, 131, Baehrens 1912, 326*): respondit N, respondet quam illis ς₂ >*1503*, respondet illis ς₅, *1515‡*, ⟨iis⟩ respondet *Gertz (Hol. 1)*

Hosius initially followed Gertz in supplying the correlative pronoun between *gratius* and *respondet* but omitted it from his second edition, persuaded that it was unnecessary by Stangl and Baehrens, the latter citing 2. 23. 1 *quomodo danti in tantum producenda notitia est muneris sui in quantum delectatura est cui datur, ita accipienti adhibenda contio est*. But that is a rather different context, since *cui datur* just = *accipientem* and by itself provides a stand-in for the participle's object, whereas *per quos… licet* plays a much more complex syntactic and semantic role. In any case, where the pronominal idea is as intimately bound to *gratius* as it is to *respondet*, and when *iis* could have dropped out so easily after *-ius*, it seems perverse to insist that S. abstained from employing the correlative as he does hundreds of times elsewhere in his prose works.

5. 1. 5 Propositum optimi uiri et ingentis animi tam diu ferre ingratum donec feceris gratum. Nec te ista ratio decipiet: **succumbunt** uitia uirtutibus si illa **non cito** odisse **properaueris**.

succumbunt : -bent Gertz
non cito ς₅, *1585‡* : concito N, cum cito ς₂ς₁₃ *>1515*, quam cito K ς₃ς₁₅ (*om.* odisse)
properaueris (prosp- Nac) Npc, *1529‡* : praeparauerit ς₂ *>1515*, praeparaueris ς₁₁

Gertz was probably not correct to introduce the future tense here. S. allows a future or future perfect in the protasis to be accompanied by a present indicative in the apodosis when he frames a generalizing or gnomic condition such as the one we have here, and the instances are numerous enough that we should think twice before emending a stylistic trait out of existence: see the discussions of 1. 2. 2 and 1. 2. 3, and from the other prose works cf., e.g.:

> *Ira* 2. 34. 1 *mures formicaeque, si manu admoueris, ora conuertunt;*

> *Marc.* 12. 2 *si confessa fueris percepisse magnas uoluptates, oportet te non de eo quod detractum est queri;*

> *Brev.* 8. 2 *Si corporis dotes… conseruauerimus…, si non subierimus… seruitutem, si corpori grata eo nobis loco fuerint quo sunt in castris auxilia…, ita demum utilia sunt menti;*

> *Pol.* 6. 1 *potest et illa res a luctu te prohibere nimio, si tibi ipse renuntiaueris nihil eorum… posse subduci;*

> *EM* 71. 35 *si quicquam ex studio… laxauerint, retro eundum est.*

Contrast the discussion of 7. 24. 2 *Post hoc quisquis properauerit, sero dat*, where I believe Gertz was correct to print the *dabit* that Wesenberg suggested to him.

As for *non cito*, which occurred independently to Muretus and at least one other reader, as a replacement for the transmitted but impossible *concito*, I can only say that I agree entirely with Gruter: 'ipse hic non habeo diuinatorum arteis [sic]. solum dixerim Mureti emendationem mihi non satisfacere. nam quo minus hic toleremus uocem cito impedit illud *properaueris*' (p. 551). I will print *non cito* and indicate in the apparatus that I regard it as a *pis aller*.

5. 3. 1 Lacedaemonii uetant suos pancratio aut caestu decernere, ubi inferiorem ostendit uicti confessio. **Cursor cretam prior contigit: uelocitate illum**, non

animo antecessit; luctator ter abiectus perdidit palmam, non tradidit. Cum inuic-
tos esse Lacedaemonii ciues suos magno aestimarent, ab iis certaminibus
remouerunt, in quibus uictorem facit non iudex nec per se ipse exitus, sed **uox
cedentis et tradere iubentis.**

cursor N : cursor ⟨hic⟩ *Watt 2001, 232*
illum N (*def. Alexander 1950-2, 26-7*) : ille *Gertz*, alium *Pinc., 1557mg., 1585‡*, aemulum
Kronenberg 1907, 285, illum ⟨alterum⟩ *Castiglioni 1920, 174*
cedentis ρ (*def. Alexander 1950-2, 27*) : caedentis N, cadentis *Gertz* (*prob. Busche
1917-18, 470-1*)
tradere N : parcere *Madvig 1871-84, 2:417*, tardare *Busche 1917-18, 470-1*
iubentis Npc : -betis Nac, uolentis *Watt 2001, 232-3*

Had S. written *Cursor cretam prior contigi: uelocitate illum, non animo antecessi*,
I doubt that anyone would trouble over the role or identity of *illum*, as the person
I was measuring myself against: *prior* in itself implies 'than another'. I do not
think that the change of person should make a difference in this regard, especially
in view of S.'s readiness to invoke the '*ille* of the anonymous other', as I called it in
my discussion of 2. 11. 2; the use of *ille* at 1. 14. 3 and 6. 9. 1, cited there, is
pertinent here as well.

 The disgrace of defeat derives not from the fact of defeat, the actual outcome
(*ipse exitus*), but from the defeated party's spoken acknowledgement of the fact,
when he has no choice but to cry, 'Uncle!'[1] *Victi confessio* in the first sentence
reappears as *uox cedentis* in the last, and *tradere* tells us what the *uox* was: the
person yielding says, 'Trade [sc. palmam]!', bidding (*iubentis*) the contest's super-
visor to hand over the prize to the victor (cf. *luctator... perdidit palmam, non tradidit*, just preceding).

5. 4. 2-3 Nam si turpe est beneficiis uinci, non oportet a praepotentibus uiris
accipere beneficium quibus gratiam referre non possis—a principibus dico, a
regibus, quos eo loco fortuna posuit ex quo largiri multa possent pauca admodum et imparia datis recepturi. **(3)** Reges et principes dixi, quibus tamen potest
opera nauari et quorum illa excellens potentia per minorum consensum ministe-
riumque constat. **At** sunt quidam extra omnem subducti cupiditatem, qui uix
ullis humanis desideriis continguntur; quibus nihil potest praestare ipsa fortuna.
Necesse est a Socrate beneficiis uincar, necesse est a Diogene, qui per medias
Macedonum gazas nudus incessit calcatis regiis opibus....

constat Npc : constant Nac
at *Hos.* : et Nac (*def. Buck 1908, 67*), *del.* Npc, *om.* R‡, *sed Gertz*

---

[1] This version of 'I give up!' seems to be a North Americanism, probably dating to the late nineteenth century. Fanciful aetiologies circulate, including the claim that it is as old as the Roman empire,
when bullies would force their victims to cry, 'Patrue!'

The deletion of *&* before *sunt* in **N** was made early: the conjunction is absent in **R** and in all later manuscripts, and no conjunction stood in the printed editions until Gertz's *sed*. The issue arises at the boundary between two categories of people to whom it is difficult or impossible to make an appropriate return, the *praepotentes* (kings, princes, and such) and near-sages like Socrates and Diogenes who are 'withdrawn from all desire': since the contrast between the two categories is obviously strong, either *sed* or *at* would be appropriate, and superior to *et*. But the corrector's act gives me pause. *&* was canceled by a diagonal stroke, rising from left to right, in the same colour ink as the text, and it is identical to the diagonal stroke that was used to cancel the misplaced *n* that turned *constat* into *constant* immediately preceding. It is the difference between the two corrections that gives me pause: for whereas *constant* is an obvious error and the deletion of *n* was an obvious move to make, whatever else one might say about *&*, it is not obviously wrong. So why was it deleted? I very strongly suspect that the ink of the canceling strokes is the same colour as the text in both cases because it was the scribe who made these corrections, and that he deleted *&* because he saw that it was not in his exemplar after all. I will print *sunt quidam* and place it at the beginning of a new paragraph: compare 2. 23, where *sunt quidam* is similarly used to introduce a new category (those *qui nolint nisi secreto accipere*) that by editorial convention stands at the beginning of a new paragraph and new chapter. The paragraph here will continue until §5. 2, where S. introduces—also without a conjunction—the next category of those to whom it is difficult to make an adequate return, parents.

5. 5. 4 Saepe necesse est ante alia beneficia petamus quam priora reddidimus, nec ideo non petimus aut turpiter, **quia non reddituri debebimus**, quia non per nos erit mora, quominus gratissimi simus, sed interueniet aliquid extrinsecus, quod prohibeat: nos tamen nec uincemur animo nec turpiter his rebus superabimur, quae non sunt in nostra potestate.

petimus N : petemus *Madvig 1871–84, 2:417*
turpiter N : turpiter petimus ς_{1},
quia non reddituri debebimus R : quian red- deb- N, quasi non reddituri, debebimus *Madvig 1871–84, 2:417*, non *del. Gemoll 1890, 14–15*
sed N : si *Gertz*

We can suspend judgement on Madvig's *petemus*, which was motivated by his other alteration here, and on Gertz's *si* (for *sed*, often written as *ſ;*), until we have dealt with the main crux in the passage, which resides in the four words in bold above. Since there is a tangle of negatives, especially in *nec ideo non petimus aut turpiter*, perhaps expressing the point positively can help to clarify matters: we often must seek new favours before we've made a return on previous favours, but we can make the request, and honorably, because…we will not be obliged to make a return? Obviously not. The thought is rather:

We make the request, and honourably, because we <u>will</u> be obliged to make a return, and nothing that's up to us will hinder our being very grateful. If some external cause intervenes to prevent [making a return], we will not be defeated in respect of our good intention (*animo*) nor will any disgrace attach to being overcome by circumstances beyond our control.

Three changes are required to produce this straightforward text, amounting to the change of no more than three letters. First, with Gemoll delete *non* after *quia*, which is to say, read *quia* for N's *quian*, from which R produced *quia non*: whether the *n* is mere textual flotsam or was intended to represent *non* (i.e., *ñ*), it should not be there; if it began as *non* (whether or not abbreviated), it was introduced mistakenly by a scribe who had just written *nec...non...* and saw *quia non* coming into view two words farther on.[2] Then read Gertz's *si*, but punctuate with a period after *simus*, joining the conditional clause to what follows, which addresses the consequences of circumstance overcoming good intentions. This produces a better structure than Madvig's proposed solution—*nec ideo non petemus aut turpiter, quasi non reddituri, debebimus*, causing *turpiter* to modify *debebimus*—and is at least as economical.[3] I take the two causal clauses, *quia...quia...*, to modify *nec...non petimus aut turpiter* independently, in the sort of asyndetic parallelism of which S. is so fond, and of course I understand *reddere* or *ne reddamus* with *prohibeat*.

5. 6. 6 Socrates parem gratiam Archelao referre non posset **si illum regnare uetuisset?** Parum scilicet magnum beneficium a Socrate accipiebat, si ullum dare Socrati potuisset.

si illum regnare uetuisset Npc, *1529mg.* : si illum regnare uetuisset si illum regnare tuisset Nac, si illum regnare docuisset ς₁ >*1503*, si illum negare docuisset *1515*, si illum docuisset regnare *1529‡*, si illum re⟨rum naturam i⟩gnorare vetuisset *Courtney 1974, 105–6*

Despite the emendations that have been attempted, the problem posed by the first statement here is not textual but interpretive; it perhaps helps to recognize that it is the first of two ironic, quasi-paradoxical epigrams that complement each other. The second suggests that the opportunity to do a favour for Socrates was the greatest favour Archelaus could hope to receive from Socrates; the first suggests that Socrates could have shown adequate gratitude to the king by causing him to cease being king—that is, by causing him to lay aside the trappings and exercise of power and their inevitably corrupting influence. Or as Basore put it, 'if he had taught him the true values of life'.

---

[2] For a vivid example of perseveration and anticipation at work simultaneously, cf. 5. 7. 6–8. 1, where between *beneficium sibi dedit* and *natura prius est* N's scribe added *natura sibi dedit*.

[3] For another apparent instance of *fi > f*, cf. the discussion of 7. 19. 8; for *f > fi*, cf. the discussion of 2. 13. 2. Independently of this puzzle, there is no need to join Madvig in reading *grati* for *gratissimi*.

5. 8. 2 Quomodo nemo se portat, quamuis corpus suum moueat et transferat, quomodo nemo, quamuis pro se dixerit, adfuisse sibi dicitur nec statuam sibi tamquam patrono suo ponit, **quomodo {si} aeger**, cum cura sua conualuit, mercedem a se non exigit, sic in omni negotio, etiam cum **aliquid, ⟨quod⟩** prodesset sibi, fecerit, non tamen debebit referre gratiam sibi, quia non habebit, cui referat.

aeger *Haase* : si aeger N (*def. Buck 1908, 67*)
aliquid ⟨quod⟩ prodesset sibi *Dale. adn.* (*e cod. German.*), *Madvig 1871–84, 2:408 n. 1* :
aliquid prodesset sibi Nac
   a- prodesse s- Npc, R >*1503, prob. Pinc.*, 'mss. mei quinque' *Grut. p. 552, 1649‡*
   aliquis sibi profecerit Kς15
   aliquis probe fecerit *1515–1605*
   aliquid probe sibi *Lips.*
   aliquis quod prodesset sibi *dub. Madvig 1871–84, 2:408 n. 1*
   alii quod prodesset, sibi *Gundermann ap. Buck 1908, 67–8*

S. is continuing to discuss the topic first raised in 5. 7, whether people can properly be said to bestow *beneficia* on themselves; the discussion continues through 5. 11. Here comparison with the places where S. does write *quomodo si…sic…* shows why Haase was correct to seclude *si* here: 6. 6. 3 *Quomodo si quis scriptis nostris alios superne inprimit uersus, priores litteras non tollit sed abscondit, sic beneficium superueniens iniuria adparere non patitur*, EM 9. 5 *Quomodo si perdiderit Phidias statuam protinus alteram faciet, sic hic faciendarum amicitiarum artifex substituet alium in locum amissi.* Buck's claim that *cum cura sua* is 'kausal oder instrumental' is one of his more desperate attempts to save N's credit.

A bit farther on, the supplement *quod* seems as secure as the seclusion of *si*, and certainly more straightforward than the jettisoning of *prodesset* to which most other attempts to produce sense have been forced (the exception, Gundermann's *alii quod*, is more ingenious than convincing). The more difficult question is whether the need for *aliquis*—evidently felt no later than the twelfth century—is similarly compelling. Madvig's *aliquis quod* might look like a step too far, but it at least serves a diagnostic purpose, since it implies a useful framing of the problem: which is more likely, that *aliquis* became *aliquid* by assimilation when *quod* was still in the text, or that S. left the subject of *fecerit…debebit…habebit…referat* implied after making the subject of *conualuit…exigit* explicit? I am going to gamble on the former, especially since the shift from the specific example of the sick man's self-cure to the generalized *in omni negotio* suggests that a generalized subject, *aliquis*, is wanted.

5. 10. 1 Beneficium est praestitisse aliquid utiliter, uerbum autem 'praestitisse' ad alios spectat. Numquid non demens uidebitur qui aliquid sibi uendidisse se dicet, quia uenditio alienatio est et rei suae iurisque in ea sui ad alium translatio? Atqui quemadmodum uendere sic dare aliquid a se dimittere est et id quod tenueris habendum alteri tradere. Quod si est, beneficium nemo sibi dedit quia nemo dat sibi; alioqui duo contraria **in uno coeunt**, ut **sit idem** dare et accipere.

alioqui *Grut. p. 552, prob. Lips.*, *1649‡* : aliqui Nac, aliquid Npc *>1605*
uno N *>1557, prob. Grut. p. 552, 1649‡* (*cf. Axelson 1933, 81–2*) : unum *1585, 1605*
sit idem ç₅ç₆, *Grut. p. 552* : id sidem Nac, id idem Npc, id idem est ç₄, idem *>1503*, idem sit *1515‡*

I take Gruter's *alioqui*, approved by Lipsius and thereafter the vulgate, to be uncontroversial. In the phrase *in uno coeunt* **N** and all the manuscripts after it have the ablative, including the four relied on by Gruter (**N** itself among them), who accepted a version of the text containing *in uno*. That evidently persuaded Gronovius to restore *in uno* to the text, after Lipsius approved Muretus' *in unum*; the latter reading was also rejected by Axelson, on the ground that 'Bekanntlich begegnet auch in der besten Latinität mitunter *in* mit Akkusativ, wo der Abiativ normal wäre'. That might be true of the best Latin in general, but where the idea is specifically 'coming together in one [place *vel sim.*]', *in unum coire* is the choice without exception, including the choices made elsewhere by S. himself: *NQ* 4a. 2. 3 *duobus in unum coituris amnibus*, 7. 8. 1 *quiquid umidi aridique... in unum coit*, cf., e.g., Liv 6. 3. 7, 7. 36. 12, 25. 35. 6, 26. 41. 22, Plin. *NH* 37. 152.

'Suspicor emendandum', Gruter wrote, in introducing *sit idem*, where the printed editions had felt their way gradually toward *idem sit* after **N**'s impossible text was passed along to the medieval manuscripts, and as is evident from the *recentiores* the same suspicion had moved at least one earlier reader. Confirmation of a sort is provided by the correct report of **N**, first found in Préchac's apparatus—'ut id *idem [s eras.] N¹ ut id idem N²*'—after Gruter, Gertz, and Hosius all reported that the manuscript simply read *id idem*.[4] That appears to be the reading at first glance, but on closer inspection one notices an usual amount of space separating *d* and *i*. On still closer inspection the impress of an upright ſ can just be seen on the hair-side surface: *id sidem* in place of *sit idem*.

5. 10. 3–4 Idem ipso uocabulo adparet, in quo hoc continetur, 'bene fecisse': nemo autem sibi bene facit, non magis quam sibi fauet, quam suarum partium est. Diutius hoc et pluribus exemplis licet prosequi. **(4) Quidni? cum** inter ea sit habendum beneficium, quae secundam personam desiderant. quaedam, cum sint honesta, pulcherrima, summae uirtutis, nisi in altero non habent locum. Laudatur et inter maxima humani generis bona fides colitur: num quis ergo dicitur sibi fidem praestitisse?

quidni ç₅ç₆, *cod. Pinc.*, *Mur.*, *1585‡* (*prob. Grut. p. 553*) : quid N *>1557* (*def. Buck 1908, 68–9*), qui π, *del. Skutsch ap. Hos.*, quo id (*vel* in quid) *Pré.*

---

[4] Of the three, only Gruter had firsthand knowledge of the manuscript; Gertz and Hosius were relying on collations made by others, cf. Introduction n. 19 and Chapter 6 n. 1, respectively.

Gruter regretted some of Muretus' habits—as here, his passing off as his own a reading he owed to Pincianus—but he recognized merit when he saw it;[5] the reading is also found, beyond the *codices nonnulli* cited by Pincianus, in some of the *recentiores* I have examined. *Quidni* is one of the adverbs S. especially likes to brandish in driving home what he takes to be an obvious truth (nearly ninety times, including another *Quidni? cum*...—or better, *Quidni, cum*...?—a bit earlier, in §10. 2), and it is certainly apt here. Buck defended *quid*, preferring to understand *quid?*, standing in isolation.[6] But S. uses *quid?* as Buck suggests more than fifty times, and it is followed by a complete sentence every time but one (*NQ* 6. 8. 2 *Quid, cum uides Alpheon*...?).

5. 11. 3–4 (3) Beneficium est quod potest, cum datum est, et non reddi; qui sibi beneficium dat non potest non recipere quod dedit: ergo non est beneficium. Alio tempore beneficium accipitur, **alio redditur**; *** **(4)** In beneficio et hoc est probabile, hoc suspiciendum, quod aliquis, ut alteri prodesset, utilitatis interim suae oblitus est, quod alteri dedit ablaturus sibi; hoc non facit qui beneficium sibi dat. **(5)** Beneficium dare socialis res est, aliquem conciliat, aliquem obligat; sibi dare non est socialis res, neminem conciliat, neminem obligat, neminem in spem inducit, ut dicat: 'Hic homo colendus est; illi beneficium dedit, dabit et mihi'. **(6)** Beneficium est, quod quis non sua causa dat, sed eius, cui dat; is autem, qui sibi beneficium dat, sua causa dat; non est ergo beneficium.

lac. post redditur *stat. Haupt 1875–6, 2:274* : alio redditur; ⟨at hic non alio tempore accipitur, alio redditur⟩ *Pré.*

S. is rounding off his discussion of 'self-favouring' with five short proofs: the first and last take the form 'Proposition A, Proposition B, *ergo* C'; the third and fourth take the form 'Proposition A, Proposition B', leaving the conclusion (*ergo non est beneficium*) implied; the second presents only 'Proposition A'. Haupt concluded that there was a lacuna:[7]

> prima sententia et tertia plenae et perfectae sunt, sed deest ratiocinatio in secunda nec potest dubitari quin post illa *Alio tempore beneficium accipitur, alio redditur* Seneca dixerit in beneficio quod quis sibi ipse det unum esse dandi reddendique tempus, itaque diuersum esse illud beneficium a beneficio quod recte ita dicatur.

Anyone who has followed S. through this topic would certainly be able to understand what should follow *Alio tempore beneficium accipitur, alio redditur*, and it is

---

[5] Gruter p. 553: 'uidetur tacite hanc emendationem sibi adscribere Muretus; at eam eruit e codicibus suis Pinc. meis uocabulum *ni* prorsus exulat. sed male tamen'.

[6] 1908, 69: 'als überleitende Frage...= *quid uis, quid mirum?* Noch eine andere Auffassung ist möglich: *quid? = cur?*, eine allgemein bekannte Verwendung; die Antwort folgt in dem *cum...desiderant*'.

[7] Haupt considered only the first three *sententiae*, but the second appears all the more anomalous if all five are taken together.

possible that S. left the rest of the syllogism implied. On balance, however, I think it likely that as in the third and fourth *sententiae* he spelled out at least Proposition B, something along the lines of Préchac's supplement, which would easily be lost by *saut du mêmê au même*: I will print *beneficium quod quis sibi dat simul accipitur et redditur* as a stop-gap.

5. 12. 2 Quid enim boni est nodos operose soluere, quos ipse, ut solueres, feceris? Sed quemadmodum quaedam in oblectamentum ac iocum sic inligantur, ut eorum solutio imperito difficilis sit, quae **illi**, qui **implicuit**, sine ullo negotio **paret**, quia conmissuras eorum et moras nouit, nihilo minus illa habent aliquam uoluptatem (temptant enim acumen animorum et intentionem excitant), ita haec, quae uidentur callida et insidiosa, securitatem ac segnitiam ingeniis auferunt, quibus modo campus, in quo uagentur, sternendus est, modo **creperi** aliquid et confragosi obiciendum, per quod erepant et sollicite uestigium faciant.

illi N >*1515 Fick.* : ille *1529*‡
implicuit B, ς₁₆, *1515*‡ : explicuit N (quae ille qui explicuit *Mazzoli 1974, 84–5, v. inf.*), ea plicuit *Gertz in app.*
paret B, *Fick.* : spirat N >*1503*
    patet Kς₁₅ς₁₆mg.ς₂₁
    separat *1515*‡
    'altioris aliquid procul dubio latet mendi' *Grut. p. 553*
    aspirat *Rossbach 1907, 1489*
    extricat *Skutsch ap. Hos. 1*
    se aperit *Hos. in app.*
    {spira} it *Pré.*
    explicat *Shackleton Bailey 1970, 362* (*sic et Watt 1994, 229*)
    ⟨in⟩spiciat *Mazzoli 1974, 84–5*
creperi *Grut.* ('forte', *in appendice, p. 990*) *Lips.*, *1649*‡ (*resp. Axelson 1933, 96 n. 32*) : crebri N >*1557* (*def. Mazzoli 1974, 85–6*)
    taetri ς₁₄ς₂₁
    recti *1515mg., 1529mg.*
    scabri *Pinc., 1557mg., 1585, 1605*
    asperi *Alexander 1934, 55*

The passage provides a transition to the treatment of two Stoic paradoxes—that no one is ungrateful (5. 12–14) and that everyone is ungrateful (5. 15–17)—which S. presents as puzzles to exercise the mind. The form of the text with *implicuit* and *paret* is first found in a twelfth-century manuscript that preserves one of the two sets of medieval excerpts of *De beneficiis* that were in circulation; it was first printed by Fickert. *implicuit* appears inevitable, despite Mazzoli's attempt to salvage *explicuit*.[8] *paret* is a different matter. Though it allows **N**'s *illi* to stand and is

---

[8] Gertz's *plicuit* is ruled out because that form of the perfect in the simplex *plicare* is unattested before the *Vetus Latina* (*TLL* 10. 2440. 47–50).

closer to **N**'s *spirat* than several alternatives that have been proposed, it is rather poor in both syntax and sense: it requires *quae* to refer to *solutio* when it would better resume *eorum*;[9] and it produces questionable sense with *parere* = 'obey' / 'comply with' (a *solutio* that obeys?), while *parere* = 'be visible' / 'evident' (as though the simplex of *adparere*) is not plausible, since where not exclusively poetic (S. uses it at *Ag.* 457) it is a legalism (*TLL* 10. 1373. 5ff.). A much better solution is provided by *separat*—even closer to *spirat* than *paret*—and *ille*—lost to the recurrent *i* / *e* confusion in **N**—that together allow *quae* to resume *eorum* and serve as the common object of *implicuit* and *separat*: 'the inexperienced person finds it difficult to undo those [knots] that the person who entwined them separates with no trouble.'

Near the end of the same very long sentence Lipsius' *creperi* has been the vulgate since Gronovius put it in the text in place of **N**'s *crebri*, which cannot (*pace* Mazzoli) produce acceptable sense. Yet the sense of *creperi*—'obscure' / 'doubtful'—does not make it an ideal choice, either; and the argument that Axelson brought against it is compelling:

> Wie der Artikel des Thes. l. Lat. an die Hand gibt, begegnet *creper* zuerst bei Pacuvius, Accius und Lucilius, dann bei den beiden Archaisten Varro und Lukrez, ist danach lange aus der Literatur verschwunden, um später gerade dort aufzutauchen, wo man es von vornherein erwartet, nämlich bei Apuleiüs (einmal), und findet schliesslich bei ganz späten, verkünstelten Schönschreibern wie Symmachus und Ennodius eine spärliche Verwendung (ausserdem, bezeichnenderweise, bei Grammatikern und Glossographen).[10]

As an alternative, Pincianus' *scabri* is not bad (cf. *Ira* 3. 35. 5 *scabras lutosasque semitas*), but Alexander's *asperi* is better: cf. 5. 24. 1 *asperrimus locus in quo ex rupibus acutis unica illa arbor eruperat, Ira* 2. 13. 1 *arduum in uirtutes et asperum iter, Helv.* 6. 4 *deserta loca et asperrimas insulas* (sim. *NQ* 4a. 2. 3), 11. 5 *in solitudinibus asperrimis, EM* 66. 44 *illud plana et molli uia ierit, hoc aspera, NQ* 2. 28. 2 *aspera saxa et eminentia.*

5. 12. 3 Dicitur nemo ingratus esse; id sic colligitur: 'Beneficium est, quod prodest; prodesse autem nemo homini malo potest, ut dicitis Stoici; **ergo beneficium non accipit malus, *** ingratus est**. Etiamnunc beneficium honesta et probabilis res est; apud malum nulli honestae rei aut probabili locus est, ergo nec beneficio;[11] quod si accipere non potest, **ne reddere quidem** debet, et ideo non fit ingratus…'.

---

[9] Thus Griffin and Inwood write '<u>knots</u> are formed in such a way that <u>they</u> are difficult to solve for an unskilled person, but <u>yield</u> without any effort to the person who entangled them' (underlining added), which gets at the basic idea but cannot be derived from the text of Hosius that they are translating.

[10] Compare the discussion of 1. 5. 2 *parui pendunt*.

[11] **N** made a hash here with a blundering dittography, *ego aut beneficium nec* [Npc, *ne* Nac?] *beneficio* (cf., e.g., 5. 14. 3 *ingratus est quisquam ingratus est* for *ingratus est quisquam*): the simple solution,

ante ingratus *lac. stat. Haase, qui* nullus itaque malus *suppl.* : malus. ingratus. | est etiam nunc N[12]

malus. ergo non est ingratus H (*iam* ergo ingratus non est *Vinc. Bell., Spec. Hist. 5. 29, Spec. Doct. 4. 49*)

malus (:) ingratus est. quomodo etiamnunc ς₂ >*1503*

malus: itaque nec ingratus est? quomodo etiamnunc *1515*

malus: itque nec ingratus est. Etiamnum *1529‡*

malus: ingratus est etiamnunc? *Fick.*

igitur non ingratus est *Pré.*

ne reddere *Gertz* : nec reddere N (*Pré.*)

The presence of a lacuna is beyond reasonable doubt, despite Buck's attempt to defend N's text.[13] That it is not a large lacuna is clear enough: for example, Vincent of Beauvais, who twice closely paraphrased the passage, completed the syllogism in each case with *ergo ingratus non est*, and in the direct tradition a form of the missing words is first found in a manuscript dated to the second half of the twelfth century (**H**), within a generation of Vincent's death in 1164. Something along the same lines is next found in the Basel edition of 1515, from which Erasmus removed the unwanted question mark and *quomodo* in his edition of 1529. I will print Haase's supplement, *malus: ⟨nullus itaque malus⟩ ingratus est.*

A bit farther along the question arises whether Gertz was correct to replace **N**'s *nec* with *ne*. We can approach the answer first by considering S.'s rare uses of *nec… quidem* beyond *De beneficiis*:

Pol. 2. 1 si cogitaueris nihil profuturum dolorem tuum, **nec** illi quidem quem desideras **nec** tibi…

NQ 6. 24. 2 Nam in nostris quoque corporibus cutis spiritum respuit **nec** est illi introitus nisi per quae trahitur, **nec** consistere quidem a nobis receptus potest nisi in laxiore corporis parte…

In both of these passages it is clear that *nec… quidem* is in place when it is preceded or followed by another *nec* with which it forms a pair at the same level of syntax, 'neither…nor….' In *De beneficiis*, **N** reads *ne…quidem* in forty-five places where it clearly appropriate; beyond that, there are these four places besides the present where a question arises:

ergo nec beneficio, is found already in some of the *recentiores* (e.g., ς₁ς₆ς₁₂); Préchac (*ergo {haut bene fictum} nec beneficio*) and Mazzoli (1977, 76: *ergo ⟨etiam si erogo⟩ ut beneficium, nec beneficio*) proposed more fanciful fixes.

[12] The presentation of the text in **N**—with punctuation after both *malus* and *ingratus* at line-end and *est etiam nunc* at the start of the next line—became in **R** *malus. ingratus est etiamnunc*, which was reproduced in the later medieval manuscripts in ways that do not affect the main point under discussion here (malus: ingratus est etiam. nunc CπGUKF, malus. ingratus est. etiamnunc QIJV).

[13] 1908, 69: 'Die Ausg. nehmen nach "malus" eine Lücke an; dies ist unnöting, wenn man liest "malus; ingratus est?"' In the proposition *prodesse autem nemo homini malo potest*, S. leaves it to the reader to understand the antecedent premises: all who are not *sapientes* are *stulti*, and every *stultus* is also *malus*.

1. 1. 8 Eodem animo beneficium debetur, quo datur, et ideo **non est neglegenter dandum**: sibi enim quisque debet, quod a nesciente accepit; **ne** [N, nec *1475‡*] **tarde quidem**, quia, cum omni in officio magni aestimetur dantis uoluntas, qui tarde fecit, diu noluit....

1. 4. 1 Sed ne faciam, quod reprehendo, omnia ista, quae ita extra rem sunt, ut **ne circa** [*Gertz* : nec circa N, *Pré.*] rem quidem sint, relinquam....

7. 14. 6 Contra nunc illud pone: si oblitus esset accepti beneficii, si **ne** [*1529‡* : nec N, *Pré.*] temptasset quidem gratus esse, negares illum gratiam rettulisse....

7. 18. 1 De altero beneficii genere dubitatur, quod si accipere non potui nisi sapiens, **ne** [*1605‡* : nec N >*1585, Pré.*] reddere quidem nisi sapienti possum....

In the first of these passages **N**'s *ne* should stay: the pattern is very much like *NQ* 3. 27. 12, where Hine's Teubner reads *non uacabat timere mirantibus; ne dolor quidem habebat locum*, with the reading of the more generally reliable manuscripts (*ne* ZHW[1] : *nec* FρU) and punctuation that draws out the clauses' antithetical character and the 'diminishing' effect of the second.[14] In the remaining passages, which bear no relation to the *nec...nec...*pattern noted above, **N**'s *nec* was orrectly rejected in favour of *ne* by Gertz, Erasmus, and Lipsius. The same conclusion is valid for Gertz's *ne* here.

5. 12. 4 'Etiamnunc, ut dicitis, bonus uir omnia recte facit; si omnia recte facit, ingratus esse non potest. Malo uiro beneficium nemo dare potest. Bonus beneficium reddit, malus non accipit; quod si est, nec bonus quisquam ingratus est nec malus. Ita ingratus in rerum natura est nemo, **et hoc inane**.' (5) Unum est apud nos bonum, honestum...

ingratus...nemo, et hoc inane Npc (nemo...inane *om. Nac, add. in mg. inf. pr. man.*) >*1515* : est nomen, et hoc inane *Eras., 1529‡*
    ingratum est nomen inane *Grut. p. 533*
    est nemo. at hoc inane *Ruh.*
    nemo. et ⟨nomen est⟩ hoc inane *Madvig ap. Gertz (Hos.)* (*contra* nomen *v. Buck 1908, 69*)
    et hoc inane ⟨uerbum est⟩ *Mazzoli 1974, 86–7*

The various attempts to make **N**'s text yield sense by adding *nomen* (*vel sim.*), like Buck's claim that the text is sound ('Doch ist der Gedanke auch ohne dasselbe [sc. *nomen*] vollständig: *hoc* (d. h. der Begriff *ingratus*) *inane* "das ist etwas Inhaltloses"; *inane* ist substantiviert zu denken'), are forced and unpersuasive. I will obelize *et hoc inane* and indicate in the apparatus that *hoc inane* might well have begun as

---

[14] A similar effect could be achieved in both passages by reversing the order of the clauses, thus: *non est tarde dandum, nedum neglegenter; non dolor habebat locum, nedum uacabat timere.* Oltramare's Budé reads *nec* at *NQ* 3. 27. 12, which causes the passage to conform to the pattern found at *Pol.* 11. 2. 1 and *NQ* 6. 24. 2. On *ne* vs. *nec quidem* see H.–S. 450, TLL 9. 321. 8–22.

a marginal comment on the value of the proof—left by someone who found futile the idea that there are no ingrates—which gained an *et* when it was incorporated in the text.[15] At §15. 1 the corresponding proof that all people are ingrates simply ends, *omnes ergo ingrati sunt.*

5. 12. 6 Quemadmodum stomachus morbo uitiatus et colligens bilem quoscumque accepit cibos mutat et omne alimentum in causam doloris trahit, ita **animus scaeuus** quidquid illi conmiseris id onus suum et perniciem et occasionem miseriae facit. Felicissimis itaque opulentissimisque plurimum aestus subest minusque **se inueniunt** quo in maiorem materiam inciderunt qua fluctuarentur.

scaeuus *Iuret. p. 105 (resp. Axelson 1939, 12)* : aecus N, caecus Qψ (*def. Buck 1908, 69, prob. Alexander 1950–2, 29*), aequus C (*Gundermann ap. Buck*), malus ς₄, aeger *Pré.* (*prob. Aexelson 1950–2, 29*), saucius *Mazzoli 1974, 87–8*
se N (*Pré.*) : sedem *Koch 1874, 16 (sed u. E. Thomas 1900, 207 n. 161, Buck 1908, 69)*

The conjectures *scaeuus* and *sedem* (for *se*) were mistakenly introduced by Gertz and retained by Hosius, though the latter did restore *se* in his second edition. *scaeuus* in the required sense ('perverse' *vel sim.*) is attested before the time of Gellius and Apuleius (who adored the adjective) only at Sall. *Hist.* 1 *Or. Lepidi* §5 *scaeuos iste Romulus*; with *animus caecus*, the right choice here, compare Cic. *Fin.* 4. 65 *Platonem quoque necesse est, quoniam nondum videbat sapientiam, aeque caecum animo ac Phalarim fuisse?*, Liv. 40. 13. 5 *sed caecus criminandi cupiditate animus…*, Quint. 1. 10. 29 *Ac si quis tam caecus animi est ut de aliis dubitet.* As for *minus… se inueniunt* = 'they are less settled', compare the elder S.'s use of the same metaphor to describe the inexperienced speakers who find themselves *bouleversés* the first time they leave the declaimer's auditorium and enter the forum, *Contr.* 3. pr. 13 *uix se inueniunt, adsuerunt enim suo arbitrio diserti esse* (cf. Petr. *Sat.* 47. 2 *multis iam diebus uenter mihi non respondit, nec medici se inueniunt*, 119. 1 (24) *quaerit se natura nec inuenit*, all cited by Buck 1908, 69 n. 1, cf. Schmeling 2011, 198).

5. 13. 1–2 Sunt animi bona, sunt corporis, sunt fortunae: illa animi bona a stulto ac malo submouentur, ad haec admittitur quae et accipere potest et debet reddere et si non reddit ingratus est. Nec hoc ex nostra tantum constitutione: Peripatetici quoque, qui felicitatis humanae longe lateque terminos ponunt, aiunt minuta beneficia peruentura ad malos: haec qui non reddit ingratus est. **(2)** Nobis **itaque** beneficia esse non placet quae non sunt animum factura meliorem; commoda tamen illa esse et **expetenda** non negamus.

itaque N : utique *Gertz*
expetenda Qψ : expectanda N

[15] This resembles what Ruhkopf had in mind by printing *At hoc inane*: but he closed the interlocutor's remarks after *natura est nemo* and took *At hoc inane* to be a remark by S.

According to the Stoics (*ex nostra constitutione*) the *stulti ac mali* cannot receive *animi bona*, though they have available *bona corporis* and *bona fortunae* (subsequently called *commoda* in the last clause here): if they receive advantages of the latter sort and make no return, they count as *ingrati*. S. then notes by the way that the *Peripatetici* have a more relaxed view, before resuming the main line of the discussion: *nobis itaque*.... Gertz's *utique* is plausible but unwanted, since *itaque* here has the force of 'Well then,...', picking up from where the speaker left off before a parenthetical remark (*OLD* s.v. 2). Near the end of the sentence the reading of most of the medieval manuscripts, *expetenda*, is specious, but **N**'s *expectanda* means 'are to be hoped for' (*OLD* s.v. 3) and should be retained (cf. the discussion of 4. 9. 1).

5. 14. 1–3 Cleanthes uehementius agit. 'Licet' inquit 'beneficium non sit quod accepit, ipse tamen ingratus est quia non fuit redditurus etiam si accepisset'. **(2)** Sic latro est, etiam antequam manus inquinet, quia ad occidendum iam armatus est et habet spoliandi atque interficiendi uoluntatem: exercetur et aperitur opere nequitia, non incipit. Sacrilegi dant poenas quamuis nemo usque ad deos manus porrigat. **(3)** 'Quomodo' inquit 'aduersus malum ingratus est quisquam {ingratus est}, cum malus dare beneficium non possit?' Ea scilicet ratione, quia **ipsum, quod accepit, beneficium non erat, sed uocabatur; ⟨qui⟩** accipiet ab illo aliquid ex his, quae apud imperitos ⟨**in pretio**⟩ sunt, quorum et malis copia est, ipse quoque in simili materia gratus esse debebit et illa, qualiacumque sunt, cum pro bonis acceperit, pro bonis reddere.[16]

aperitur GIpcJV : -ietur N
ingratus est quisquam Ipcς₁ς₆ : i- est q- ingratus est N, ingratus est quisquam? ingratus est cum ψ, quisquam ingratus est? ingratus...JV
malus dare *Feldmann 1887, 22* : male dare N, malo d- ψ, malo dari ς₁ς₁₅‡, a malo dari *Haupt 1875–6, 2:275*, ille dare *Gertz*
ipsum...uocabatur ⟨qui⟩ *ante* accipiet *coll. Gertz pp. 234–5, Hos., ante* Sacrilegi (*sup.*) N (*cf. Buck 1908, 69–70, Pré., prob. Alexander 1950–2, 30*), ipsum...uocabatur *delend. censet Feldmann 1887, 22*
aliquid HIpcς₁ : ait quid N
⟨in pretio⟩ *add. Madvig 1871–84, 2:417–18 (prob. Hermes 1874, 30, Feldmann 1887, 22–3, Pré., Alexander 1934, 55, et Alexander 1950–2, 30) : om.* N, bona sunt *add. Pinc., 1557‡*
quorum et malis copia est *Feldmann 1887, 23* : quorum si m- c- est N, *1529mg., 1557mg.* (et si), *1605‡*, si *obel. Gertz*
    quo tamen si m- c- est ς₂ >*1503*
    cui tamen etsi (tametsi *Muretus 1580, 300*) malus est ς₈, *1515–1585*
    quorum m- c- est (*del.* si) *Haase, sim.* quorum m- c- est (si *ante* accipiet *coll.*) *Hermes ap. Hos.*

---

[16] Because of the large number of corruptions involved in the passage, I thought it more straightforward to present the text I intend to print rather than the text of Hosius' second edition, as I otherwise do in these discussions.

quorum saepe m- c- est *Gertz p. 235*
quorum scilicet m- c- est *H. J. Müller 1881, 46–7*
(quorum scilicet malis copia) et *Alexander 1950–2, 30* (*si hoc genus placet, melius*
(quorum scilicet malis copia est) ⟨et⟩)
acceperit ρ : acci- NR, accipiet ς₂ (acceperit pro bonis *om.* γ)

N's text here suffered a number of obvious corruptions, several of which were already corrected before the era of the printed book (*aperitur, ingratus est quisquam, aliquid, acceperit*). Others were addressed in the nineteenth century and do not require discussion here: Feldmann's *malus dare* (requiring change of a single letter in N's text, but rejected by Hosius in favour of Haupt's suggestion), Madvig's palmary supplement, *in pretio* (rejected by Hosius but approved by Gertz and others), and Müller's *scilicet*, which I think preferable to Feldmann's *et* printed by Hosius, in place of **N**'s *si*, which Haase deleted and Gertz obelized. But there is still a core issue that requires some clarification.

In §13 S. explained that even though *stulti ac mali* are incapable of receiving a *beneficium* truly so called—a thing that benefits the *animus*—they can receive material *commoda* that in common parlance are called *beneficia* (§13. 2 *Quaedam, etiam si uera non sunt, propter similitudinem eodem uocabulo conprehensa sunt*), and they will be *ingrati* if they do not make a suitable return for such advantages. At the beginning of §14 S. turns to a different argument, owed to Cleanthes: though *stulti* cannot receive a *beneficium* truly so called, they would not make a return even if they were to receive one, just because they are *stulti ac mali* and so dispositionally inclined to ingratitude; just so, in the two examples that follow, the *latro* is a *latro* and the *sacrilegus* a *sacrilegus* just because they have the inclination or intention to commit robbery and sacrilege, whether or not they are actively engaged in robbery, or actually laying hands on the gods, at any given moment. But in **N** the clause in bold above stands between these two examples and addresses a different point entirely, concerning things that are not true *beneficia* but are so called in common parlance. Buck and Alexander claimed that the clause represents an interlocutor's response to the preceding example, but the inconsequence seems to me obvious: not only does it address a different point, but the subject of *accepit* could only be taken to be last third-person singular entity mentioned, the *latro*—an absurdity, since the bandit is not introduced as a receiver of *beneficia* but as an example of a dispositionally vicious person. Either the clause is an interpolation and should be deleted (so Feldmann) or it has been shifted from its proper place in the text, presumably because it was at some point omitted and then ineptly reinserted (so Gertz).

In favour of the former explanation is the fact that it is a complete thought, not a fragment: omissions that are mechanically generated by *saut du même au même* tend to consist of fragmentary phrases and coincide with complete clauses only in those cases where the first or last words of two successive clauses resemble each other. But Gertz's transposition of the clause presumes exactly that explanation, according to which a scribe's eye jumped from *quia* to *qui accipiet*, omitting *quod accepit…qui*. Given that fact, and that the clause is quite apt where Gertz put it, I take that to be the preferable explanation. Had the clause begun as a marginal note that was drawn into the text, it would more likely have been written next to the remark in §13. 2 quoted just above, *Quaedam…eodem uocabulo conprehensa sunt*, where it would be more obviously apposite.

5. 14. 5 Aes alienum habere dicitur et qui aureos debet et qui corium forma publica percussum, quale apud Lacedaemonios fuit quod usum numeratae pecuniae praestat. Quo genere obligatus es, hoc fidem exolue. **(5)** Quid sint beneficia, an et in hanc sordidam humilemque materiam deduci magnitudo nominis clari debeat, ad uos non pertinet, **in alios quaeritur uerum**. Vos ad speciem ueri conponite animum et dum honestum discitis, quidquid est, in quo nomen honesti iactatur, id colite.

in alios quaeritur uerum (uerbum Nac) Npc, *Pinc.*, *agnosc. Grut. p. 554, Lips. 1649‡* : in alios quaeritur. uerum. uos CQ

  in alios quaeritur. uerum uos HPOWUJF (in alios quaeritur. uos uerum Kç₁₅)
  in aliis quaeritur. uerum ç₁₆ç₁₉
  sed ad alios. uerum ç₇
  sed ad alios. uerum uos ç₉
  sed ad alios utrum nos ç₈
  sed alios uerum ç₅
  in alios quae sunt uerum ç₂
  sed ad alios spectat. uerum >*1557*
  ad alios specta uerum *Mur., 1605*
  ⟨nec⟩ in alios q- u- Gertz (*resp. Alexander 1950–2, 31*)
  inter philosophos q- u- *Niemeyer 1899, 442*

Material advantages, S. has said, are not true *beneficia* but are commonly understood and spoken of as such, and so a return in kind is owed (§13). As for what (true) *beneficia* are, and whether that great and shining name should be lowered to the level of *sordida humilisque materia*, 'that does not pertain to you [sc. the non-wise], the question is directed to others [sc. the wise]. But *you* adjust your thinking to match the semblance of the truth…'; for the contrast, cf. Paenaetius as quoted at *EM* 116. 5:

  Eleganter mihi uidetur Panaetius respondisse adulescentulo cuidam quaerenti an sapiens amaturus esset. 'De sapiente' inquit 'uidebimus: mihi et tibi, qui adhuc a sapiente longe absumus, non est committendum ut incidamus in rem commotam…'.

The clauses *ad uos non pertinet, in alios quaeritur* are best understood as having the same subject: *quaeritur* simply looks to the questions that have just been asked. *in* 'indicat[es] persons toward whom behaviour, feelings, etc., are directed'

(*OLD* s.v. *in* 11): there is no need to alter it or to interpret it in a hostile sense (e.g., Basore, 'your search for the truth is to the detriment of others'). *uerum* should not be taken to anticipate *ueri* in the phrase *speciem ueri*, but should be construed as the conjunction—the part it played in some *recentiores* and the editions before Muretus—with a period after *quaeritur*, the text that is found in several medieval manuscripts in the π- and γ-families.

5. 15. 4–6 Accepti ab illa [*sc.* re publica] exercitus in ipsam conuertuntur, et imperatoria contio est, **(5)** 'Pugnate contra coniuges, pugnate contra liberos! Aras, focos, penates armis incessite!' Qui ne triumphaturi quidem inire urbem iniussu senatus deberetis quibusque uictorem exercitum reducentibus curia extra muros praeberetur, nunc ciuibus caesis perfusi cruore cognato urbem subrectis **intrate** uexillis. **(6)** Obmutescat inter militaria signa libertas, et ille uictor pacatorque gentium populus remotis procul bellis, omni terrore conpresso, intra muros obsessus aquilas suas horreat.

intrate N : -tis Gertz

Before Haase, editors did not use punctuation to indicate where the *imperatoria contio* ended; Haase placed everything from *pugnate* to *horreat* between quotation marks. Gertz thought this absurd, since the relative clauses—with *qui... triumphaturi* and *quibus... reducentibus curia... praeberetur*—must refer to the *imperatores*: 'num igitur imperatores hac contione se ipsos adloquuntur?', Gertz asked. Taking *qui ne... uexillis* to be an example of *apostrophe*, S. addressing the generals, he concluded that *intratis* was needed for *intrate*, and resumed quotation marks with *Obmutescat... horreat*, S.'s representation of the triumphant generals' thoughts. To judge from his punctuation, reproduced here, Hosius evidently regarded as valid Gertz's point about the relative clauses but thought that S., in a vigorous *apostrophe*, was fully capable of wielding a sarcastic imperative ('enter the city... let liberty fall silent...'). He was right.

5. 16. 4 Ingratus Cn. Pompeius, qui pro tribus consulatibus, pro triumphis tribus, pro tot honoribus, quos ex maxima parte inmaturus inuaserat, hanc gratiam rei publicae reddidit, ut in possessionem eius alios quoque induceret quasi potentiae suae detracturus inuidiam, si, quod nulli licere debebat, pluribus licuisset; dum extraordinaria concupiscit imperia, dum prouincias, ut eligat, distribuit, **dum ita cum tertio** rem publicam diuidit, ut tamen in sua domo duae partes essent, eo redegit populum Romanum, ut saluus esse non posset nisi beneficio seruitutis.

16. 4 dum ita cum tertio *Grut. p. 554* (cf. *Buck 1908, 70, Alexander 1950–2, 31*) : dum ita dum tertio N

    dum ita γ
    dum ita triumuiris Ipcς$_1$‡
    dum ita triumuir *Lips.*

> dum ita cum ⟨altero et cum⟩ tertio *Wesenberg ap. Gertz*
> dum ita cum socero *Skutsch ap. Hos.*
> tum iterum, tum tertium *Hense ap. Badstübner 1901, 26*
> dum ita tripertito *Badstübner ibid.*
> dum ita duum tertio *Gundermann ap. Buck 1908, 70–1*
> dum iterum, dum tertio *Hos. in app.*
> dominis tribus *Pré.*

Gruter's simple correction of the obvious error in **N** is satisfying, and the many attempts to disambiguate or otherwise modify *tertio* have been unnecessary. Like the cameos of other famous 'ingrates' in Rome's history that fill §16, the long sentence on Pompey picks out his career's highlights, and as S. begins the segment on the so-called first triumvirate, he already has the complete thought in mind: knowing that he is going to refer to Caesar and his marriage connection with Pompey in the *ut*-clause (*in sua domo duae partes*), he simply alludes to Crassus as *tertio* in the *dum*-clause.

5. 18 'In infinitum ius' inquit 'me obligas, cum dicis: "et nostris"; itaque pone aliquem finem. Qui filio beneficium dat, ut dicis, et patri eius dat: **primum, de quo quaero**. Deinde illud utique mihi determinari uolo: si et patri beneficium datur, numquid et fratri? numquid et patruo? numquid et auo? numquid et uxori et socero? Dic mihi, ubi debeam desinere, quousque personarum seriem sequar.'

> et patri eius dat N : et patri eius: est primum? *Hos. in app.*
> de quo QpcπWUIpcK, *1529, 1557* : de quod N (*agnosc. Grut. p. 555*)
>> dic quod JV
>> id quod ς₄
>> uide quod ς₁₂
>> quidem quod ς₁₃
>> de hoc quidem ς₁₆ς₁₇
>> de quo uado ad quem [*vel* qui] currit ς₂ *>1515*
>> de eo ς₅ς₆
>> de quo ad quem currit *cod. Pinc.*
>> de quo usque ad quem currit *Pinc.*
>> unde, quo *Mur.*‡
>> id est quod *Gertz*
>> quod ⟨dicis uerumne sit⟩ quaero *Courtney 1974, 106*

Versions proliferated among the *recentiores*, the wildest among them the one that passed to the first printed editions.[17] *de quo*, the minimal change relative to **N**'s *de quod*, is probably correct, and I take it that 'that is the first part of my question' (Griffin and Inwood) or 'this is the first question I raise' (Basore) is what S. intended;

---

[17] The fourteenth-century manuscript in which it first appears represents a strain in the tradition that contributed countless bad readings to 1475 and its immediate descendants: see Introduction n. 14.

but even making generous allowance for Senecan abruptness, I do not think that meaning can be derived from the words transmitted. I will punctuate with a question mark after *eius dat*, as *quaero* seems to prompt ('The person who gives a *beneficium* to a son, according to you, gives it also to his father?'), and print Gertz's *id est:…eius dat? primum ⟨id est⟩ de quo quaero*, lit. 'this is the first point about which I ask.'

5. 19. 1 'Dissimilia ponis exempla, quia, qui agrum meum colit, agro beneficium non dat sed mihi; et qui domum meam, quo minus ruat, fulcit, **praestat** mihi, ipsa enim domus sine sensu est; debitorem me habet, quia **nullum** habet; et qui agrum meum colit, non illum, sed me demereri uult. Idem de seruo dicam: mei mancipii res est, mihi seruatur; ideo ego pro illo debeo. Filius ipse beneficii capax est; itaque ille accipit, ego beneficio laetor et contingor, non obligor.'

praestat N : ⟨id⟩ praestat *Gertz*
nullum N : non illam *J. Müller 1892, 12–13*, ⟨in ea⟩ nullum *Alexander 1937, 59*

S. generally provides *praestare* with an express object, and *id* after *fulcit* would be easily lost. But he also allows the verb to stand alone, when an object can be easily inferred from the context: e.g., 1. 7. 3 *at hic quod dedit, magnum est, sed dubitauit, sed distulit, sed, cum daret, gemuit, sed superbe dedit, sed circumtulit et placere non ei, cui praestabat, uoluit*. That is the situation we have here, with *beneficium non dat* in the preceding example.

For what follows, Basore's translation—'because it has none, he makes me his debtor', making *domus* the subject of *habet* and taking *nullum* to modify *sensum* understood—does some violence to the Latin, since the subject of the second *habet* must be the same as the subject of the first, while Griffin and Inwood—'He counts me as his debtor because he has no other'—give *nullum* a sense it cannot have: when S. means 'no other', that is what he says (5. 7. 2 *de nullo queri possum alio quam de me*, Brev. 20. 3 *senectutem ipsam nullo alio nomine grauen iudicant quam…*, NQ 7. 4. 3 *faces quae nullo alio inter se quam magnitudine distant*). Alexander's *in ea* is clever, after *quia*, but Müller's *me habet, quia non illam* [i.e., *ñillam*] *habet*, is preferable.

5. 19. 4–5 Quid ergo? Oro te, non dicis, 'Filium mihi donasti et si hic perisset uicturus non fui'? Pro eius uita beneficium non debes cuius uitam tuae praefers? Etiamnunc cum filium tuum seruaui, ad genua procumbis, dis uota soluis tamquam ipse seruatus, illae uoces exeunt tibi, (5) '**Nihil mea interest an me seruaueris**; duos seruasti, immo me magis'.

mea interest an me N : me interest an me >*1503*, interest, mea an me *1585‡* (*prob. Gron.* p. 158), interest, meum an me *Lips.*, ⟨filium⟩ an me *Shackleton Bailey 1970, 363*

We are mulling over the question whether or not someone who bestows a *beneficium* on a son by saving his life *ipso facto* bestows one on the father. Shackleton

Bailey observes, 'For the father to disclaim any interest in his own life defeats the reasoning. And in any context *nihil…magis* would be balderdash.' I do think there is a certain tension or inconsequence in the thought, but I do not see that it is remedied either by Muretus' and Lipsius' transpositions or by adding *filium*: for then the father would be disclaiming any interest in whether his own or his son's life was saved. If we ignore for the moment the last three words—*immo me magis*—I think that we can see that the point turns on the contrast between *me* and *duos*: that you saved *my* life doesn't matter to me (the father says), it's that you save *both* our lives. S. could perhaps have found a better way of putting the point, and the last three words—conveying how utterly the father's well-being depends on his son's—are an exuberant afterthought that was probably better omitted.

5. 20. 6 Dicet aliquis: 'Quid tanto opere quaeris cui dederis beneficium, tamquam repetiturus aliquando? Sunt qui numquam iudicent esse repetendum, et has causas adferunt: indignus etiam repetenti non reddet, dignus ipse per se referet. **Praeterea**, si bono uiro dedisti, expecta, ne iniuriam illi facias adpellando, tamquam sua sponte redditurus non fuisset; si malo uiro dedisti, plectere; beneficium uero ne corruperis creditum faciendo. Praeterea lex, quod non iussit repeti, uetuit'.

praeterea N : propterea *Gertz*

As Gertz saw, the sentence in question develops a further reason for not overtly seeking the return of a favour, one based logically on the premises just stated; it is not adding another, formally unrelated reason ('besides'), as does the *praeterea* that introduces the last sentence here. A glimpse of the latter might have influenced the scribe, causing him to write *praeterea* for *propterea*, but confusion of the two words is in any case not uncommon: a secure instance occurs at 7. 12. 4 *Habeo in equestribus locum, non ut uendam, non ut locem, non ut habitem, in hoc tantum, ut spectem; propterea* (Muretus, *praeterea* N) *non mentior, si dico habere me in equestribus locum.*

5. 21. 1 'Sed lex' inquit 'non permittendo exigere uetuit'. Multa legem non habent nec actionem, **ad quae** consuetudo uitae humanae omni lege ualentior dat aditum.

ad quae *1585‡ (Grut. p. 555)* : adque Nac, atqui Npc

adque for *ad quae* barely counts as a corruption, and Muretus' emendation, approved by Gruter, might very well be correct. And yet: *atqui*, which reappears in **R**, is a very early correction and possibly scribal;[18] it implies the two most common confusions that occur in the manuscript (*i/e* and *t/d*); and it is one of S.'s

---

[18]   A couple of pages farther on, in §§22. 4–23. 2 (f. 82ʳ), the same hand—beyond removing several obvious errors—changed *periendi* to *feriendi* and *iniuriam* to *in iniuriam*, both of them non-obvious corrections that suggest comparison with a manuscript, very possibly the archetype's exemplar. Its record there encourages me to print its correction at 5. 23. 2 *Quare desperas* [Npc, -res Nac] *antequam*

most favoured adverbs (nineteen times elsewhere in the work, in nine of which it appears in **N** as *adqui* before correction, cf. pp. 194–5). I will take the chance of printing it, while adding '*fort. recte*' next to *ad quae* in the apparatus.

5. 21. 2 'Sed ex beneficio' inquit 'creditum facis'. Minime: non enim exigo sed repeto, et ne repeto quidem sed admoneo. **Num** ultima quoque me necessitas in hoc aget, ut ad eum ueniam cum quo mihi diu luctandum sit? ⟨Si⟩ quis tam ingratus est ut illi non sit satis admoneri, eum transibo nec dignum iudicabo qui gratus esse cogatur.

num ultima quoque *Fick.* : nam ultima quoque N >*1557* (*resp. Mur.*)
   ne…quidem *1585*‡
   ne ultima quoque *1649*
   nam…⟨non⟩ in hoc *Haase*
   nam ⟨uix⟩ *Castiglioni 1920, 174* (*prob. Alexander 1950–2, 31–2*)

The question: when and in what form is it right for a benefactor to seek some return in a moment of need? The crux is the phrase *ad eum uenire*, which is too ambiguous to make S.'s point ideally clear, since that point turns on the relation between *admoneo* and *ad eum ueniam*: if they refer to the same action on the needy benefactor's part, **N**'s text can be retained; if *ad eum ueniam* denotes a more urgent action than *admoneo*—say, 'making a direct approach' (Griffin and Inwood: 'calling on someone')[19]—then some negative expression is wanted. The repetition of *admonere* (*ut illi non satis sit admoneri*) after *ad eum ueniam* confirms that a contrast is being drawn, but Fickert's *num ultima quoque*, accepted by Hosius, could provide what's needed only if it meant something like 'Even extreme necessity will not bring me to approach him directly…, will it?' But it cannot: after *num* the collocation 'X *quoque*' regularly means 'X too', not 'even X' (e.g., Cic. *Clu.* 62 num Fabricios quoque innocentis condemnatos existimes…?, Liv. 31. 18. 2 'Num Abydeni quoque…ultro intulerunt arma?, Plin. *Ep.* 8. 17. 1 num istic quoque immite et turbidum caelum?). The best solution is Haase's *non in hoc*, accepted by Gertz, which implies only the loss of *ñ* before *in*: '"But you're making a favour into a loan". Not at all: I am not demanding but requesting, and not even requesting but reminding. For even extreme necessity will not bring me to approach directly someone with whom I'll have a long struggle. If someone is so ungrateful that being reminded is not enough, I'll pass him by….'

5. 22. 1 Multi sunt qui nec negare sciant quod acceperunt nec referre, qui nec tam boni **sunt** quam grati nec tam mali quam ingrati, segnes et tardi, lenta

---

temptes? Quare properas et beneficium et amicum perdere?, where I take **N**'s original reading to be an error of anticipation before *temptes*.

[19] Cf. §22. 1, where *non adpellabo sed commonefaciam* seem to correspond, respectively, to *ad eum uenire* and *admonere*.

nomina, non mala; hos ego non adpellabo, sed conmonefaciam et ad officium aliud agentes reducam.

If each relative clause depends on *multi sunt* independently of the other—as seems to be clear, for the sentence would still be intelligible if either were absent— *qui...sunt* should be *qui...sint*.

5. 24. 1–2 Causam dicebat apud diuum Iulium ex ueteranis quidam paulo uiolentior aduersus uicinos suos, et causa premebatur. 'Meministi' inquit 'imperator, in Hispania talum extorsisse te circa Sucronem?' Cum Caesar meminisse se dixisset, 'Meministi quidem sub quadam arbore minimum umbrae spargente cum uelles residere feruentissimo sole et esset asperrimus locus, in quo ex rupibus acutis unica illa arbor eruperat, quendam ex commilitonibus paenulam suam substrauisse?' **(2)** Cum dixisset Caesar: 'Quidni meminerim? et quidem siti confectus, quia impeditus ire ad fontem proximum non poteram, repere manibus uolebam, ⟨**nisi com**⟩**milito**, homo fortis ac strenuus, aquam mihi in galea sua adtulisset.'

⟨nisi com⟩milito BH (nisi cum- K, *sic et cod. Will. Polyhist. p. 142. 29*), 1490‡ : milito N
  promilitio ψ (*praeter* GK)
  nisi P. Militio *Pinc.*
  nisi Militio *Rossbach 1888, 18 n. 14, 146*
  nisi pro militio *cod. Pinc.*
  ⟨ni bonus com⟩milito *Pré.*
  ⟨nisi idem com⟩milito *Shackleton Bailey 1970, 363*
  ⟨auidus ni ibi com⟩milito *Mazzoli 1974, 88–9*

Both *nisi* and *com-* are plainly needed to fill a small gap in the text, and both already are found in several of the twelfth-century γ-manuscripts and the excerpt that William of Malmesbury inserted in his *Polyhistor*.[20] Neither Préchac's *bonus* nor Shackletion Bailey's *idem* is equally necessary, but the latter helps to tie the anecdote's narrative together, and it is something S. could have written: I will include it in the supplement.

5. 25. 5 Moneri uelle ac posse secunda uirtus est. Equus obsequens facile et parens huc illuc frenis **leniter** motis flectendus est. Paucis animus sui rector optimus; proximi sunt, qui admoniti in uiam redeunt: his non est dux detrahendus.

est. equus (equos [nom.] *Gertz in app.*) obsequens facile et parens *Rubenius ap. Gron. 1658, 188, Madvig 1871–84, 2:419* : est. || quos obsequens facet et parere N, quos obsequentes

---

[20] In a rare departure from good sense, Pincianus got it into his head that *Publius Militio* was the soldier's name, having found *nisi pro militio* in one of his *codices*: he therefore not only promoted the reading *nisi P. Militio* here but also proposed replacing *quidam paulo uiolentior* and *quendam ex commilitonibus* with *quidam Publius Militio* and *quendam P. Militionem* earlier in the passage and *militi* with *Militioni* at the end of §24. 3, where most ψ-manuscripts have *militio*.

facit et parce > *1515*, quo obsequentes faciat et parent *Eras.*, quo obsequentes facias, parere *Gron. p. 161*

leniter ς₆ς₁₆ς₁₈, *1529‡* : leuiter N > *1515*, *Gron. p. 161*

Rubenius' emendation, which occurred independently to Madvig, is among the most brilliant to have been made in the text, and I have nothing to add;[21] my more pedestrian interest here is the adverb that follows. *leniter* occurs in several of the *recentiores* and became the vulgate reading after Erasmus put it in his text. Gronovius, who kept *leniter* in his edition, favoured **N**'s *leuiter* in his *Notae* of 1649, and he was right to do so: if S. can use that adverb to describe how a king 'lightly moved' a curtain aside (*Ira* 3. 22. 2 *leuiter commouit*) he could use it here to evoke a light flick of the reins; so similarly of old age 'gently releasing' a person (*EM* 30. 12 *leuiter emitteret*), of rivers 'gently released' (*NQ* 3. 15. 8 *amnes... leuiter emissi*), and of the wind 'gently pressing' upon clouds (*NQ* 2. 23. 1 *uento... leuiter urgente*).

---

[21] Albert Rubens, the eldest son of Peter Paul Rubens, contributed another brilliant emendation at 6. 35. 5, *uoti tui an uis?* (uotituis anuis Nac, uoti tui sanuis Npc (R), uoti tui. sanius CQψ > *1515*, *Pinc.*, *1649‡*, uoti tui? sanus *Eras.*, *1529, 1557*, uoti tui, si animus ei *Pinc.*, uotum? sanus *1585, Lips.*).

Notes to Book 6

6. 1 Quaedam, Liberalis, uirorum optime, exercendi tantum ingenii causa quaeruntur et semper extra uitam iacent; quaedam et, dum quaeruntur, oblectamento sunt et quaesita usui. Omnium tibi copiam faciam; tu illa, utcumque tibi uisum erit, aut peragi iubeto aut ad explicandum ludorum ordinem induci. **Quin his** quoque, si abire protinus iusseris, non nihil actum erit; nam etiam quae discere superuacuum est, prodest cognoscere. Ex uultu igitur tuo pendebo; prout ille suaserit mihi, alia detinebo diutius, alia expellam et capite agam.

quin his *Pinc.* : in his N, *Pré.*, his ς₅, *1475‡* (in *del. Haase*), quia his *Lips.*, illis *Gertz*

In his prose works S. uses *quin* as a subordinating conjunction vastly more often than as an introductory adverb, most commonly after an expression (or negation) of doubt—*(non) dubium est quin...*—or restraint—*uix sibi temperant quin...*—or after *nihil / non multum abest*. He writes *quin* at the start of a sentence rarely and only to introduce a question—'Why not...?'—usually strengthened by *potius*: 6. 30. 2 *Quin potius eum potentem esse uis, cui plurimum debes, ⟨et⟩ beatum?* (sim. *Ira* 3. 43. 1, *Brev.* 2. 4, 27. 6, cf. also *Otio* 1. 4). If *quin* were archetypal, Lipsius' *quia* would be worth considering; but since we know it is not, it is better to regard **N**'s *in* as an intrusion after *induci* than to suppose with Gertz that *illis* became *in his*. *in* was omitted in ς₂, which here as often elsewhere uniquely corresponds to the *editio princeps*, and *his* became the vulgate reading. Fickert introduced Pincianus' *quin*, which was reintroduced by Hosius after Haase and Gertz dismissed it.

6. 2. 1–2 An beneficium eripi posset quaesitum est. Quidam negant posse, non enim res est sed actio. Quomodo aliud est munus, aliud ipsa donatio,... ita aliud est beneficium ipsum, aliud quod ad unumquemque nostrum beneficio peruenit. **(2)** Illud incorporale est, inritum non fit; materia uero eius huc et illuc iactatur et dominum mutat. Itaque **cum eripis**, ipsa rerum natura reuocare, quod dedit, non potest. Beneficia sua interrumpit, non rescindit: qui moritur, tamen uixit; qui amisit oculos, tamen uidit.

cum eripis Npc (cum *add. in mg. ante* eripis *pr. man.*) : eripis Nac
 post eripis *lac. stat.* Gertz ('cum eripis ⟨alicui quod dedisti, beneficii materiam non ipsum beneficium ei eripis⟩' *in app., exempli gratia*)
 eripi ⟨putas⟩ *Castiglioni 1920, 175*
 cum eripis, ⟨rem non beneficium eripis⟩ *Albertini 1923, 161 n. 7*

cum ⟨eripis materiam, non⟩ eripis ⟨ipsam rem⟩ *Pré.*
cum eripit ipsa rerum natura, reuocare... *Alexander 1934, 55* (*sim. Alexander 1950–2, 33*)
cum ⟨eripis, hanc tantum⟩ eripis *Mazzoli 1974, 90–9*

That Gertz was correct to posit a lacuna is, I think, beyond a reasonable doubt: other considerations aside, *eripis* desperately needs an object. S. uses *eripere* just over one hundred times in the *philosophica*, only once without an express object nearby for an active form, or subject for a passive form: *Ira* 3. 28. 4 *multum autem interest utrum aliquis uoluntati meae obstet an desit, eripiat an non det*. But there two different actions—taking away and withholding—are being contrasted abstractly; here, where what one is actually taking away constitutes the very question under discussion, it is wholly implausible that *eripis* should stand in isolation. It might be that the loss antedates the writing of **N**, where initially *itaque* stood at the end of one line, *eripis* at the start of the next, and the scribe, noticing that he had omitted *cum*, added it in the margin next to *eripis*, in the same ink and letter-size used in the text: had the scribe himself omitted more than *cum*, that would perhaps have caught his eye at the same time as the overlooked conjunction.[1] On the other hand, noticing the omission of *cum*, then adding it, might have been just the distraction that caused the scribe's eye to jump from one *eripis* to another, which is the likely cause of the larger omission.

Be that as it may, a supplement along the lines of those proposed by Gertz and Préchac is needed, though I do not think either of those proposals is very attractive, Gertz's because it says more than it needs to and is too long, Préchac's because it uneconomically posits two distinct omissions.[2] I will print *itaque cum eripis* ⟨*materiam, beneficium non eripis*⟩: *ipsa rerum natura reuocare quod dedit non potest*.

6. 8. 1 Beneficium aliquis nesciens accipit, nemo a nesciente. Quomodo multos fortuita sanant nec ideo remedia sunt, **et in flumen** aliquoi cecidisse frigore magno causa sanitatis fuit, quomodo quorundam flagellis quartana discussa est et metus repentinus animum in aliam curam auertendo suspectas horas fefellit nec ideo quidquam horum, etiam si saluti fuit, salutare est, sic quidam nobis prosunt, dum nolunt, immo quia nolunt; non tamen ideo illis beneficium debemus, quod perniciosa illorum consilia fortuna deflexit in melius.

et N (*def. Buck 1908, 72*) *Hos.* 2 : ut *Siesbye ap. Gertz Hos. 1*, et...fuit *post* discussa est *coll. Rossbach 1888, 120 n. 17*

---

[1] That *cum* was originally omitted is not noted in the apparatus of Gertz, Hosius, or Préchac, in the case of the first presumably because it was not reported in Kekulé's collation (for a similar deficiency, cf. the discussion of 2. 14. 5). The omission by Hosius, who relied on new collations by F. de Duhn and O. Rossbach (1900, vi), and Préchac, who made a fresh collation himself (1921, vi), is perhaps more surprising.

[2] At seventy characters (spaces included) Gertz's supplement is twice as long as the average line in **N**. Albertini's suggestion would better be *cum eripis* ⟨*rem, beneficium non eripis*⟩.

Gertz accepted Siesbye's correction, *ut* for *et*. Hosius followed Gertz in his first edition but shifted ground in his second, evidently persuaded by Buck's argument: each of the two limbs of the comparison, *quomodo...quomodo...*, contains three elements, the only difference being that in the first the sequence is 'allgemeiner Satz—Schlusssatz—Beispiel' (*quomodo—nec—et*) while in the second the sequence is 'Beispiel—Beispiel—Schlusssatz' (*quomodo—et—nec*), with a negative conclusion and *et* = 'and so' in both cases.

I initially resisted this argument, on the ground that the presence of an 'allgemeiner Satz' in the first comparison should motivate the use of *ut* to introduce the illustrative example, and that the absence of such a generalizing sentence in the second comparison explained the difference in their use of conjunctions. Or to put it another way, I reasoned that if the second comparison had the same structure as the first, they would look like this:

> quomodo multos fortuita sanant nec ideo remedia sunt, ut in flumen aliquoi cecidisse frigore magno causa sanitatis fuit,

> quomodo quibusdam uis uel terror saluti est nec ideo salutaris, ut quartana alicui flagellis discussa est et metus repentinus animum in aliam curam uertendo suspectas horas fefellit,

> sic quidam nobis prosunt...

But it turns out that Siesbye and I were wrong: for in the scores of places where S. uses *quomodo...sic / ita...* to coordinate an analogical argument's components, he never uses *ut* to subjoin an example illustrating the premise introduced by *quomodo*.

6. 8. 2 An existimas me debere ei quicquam, cuius manus, cum me peteret, percussit hostem meum, qui nocuisset, nisi errasset? Saepe **testis**, dum aperte **peierat**, etiam ueris testibus abrogauit fidem et reum uelut factione circumuentum miserabilem reddidit.

testis *Agric. p. 273, 1557–1605* : hostis N *>1529, def. Lips., 1649‡*
peierat *1515‡* : perierat N *>1503 (Pré., cf. Lucan. 6. 749)*

Lipsius' defended N's *hostis*, on the ground that it denotes 'aduersarius noster, hostilis animi notus testis', and persuaded Gronovius to restore it to the text, but for S., as for Latin more generally, a *hostis* is always a 'public' enemy, the opposiite of a *civis*. Vogel rightly restored *testis*, Fickert ousted it once again, then Gertz restored it, it seems for good (it was accepted even by N's most devoted champions, Buck and Préchac). As for *perierat*, the fact that S.'s nephew appears to have used that form (6. 749 *Stygias qui perierat undas*, noted at *OLD* s.v. *peiero* but ignored at *TLL* 10. 985. 44–8) gives cause for pause (it was accepted here by Préchac), but for S. *perierat* is only the pluperfect indicate of *perire* (*Ira* 1. 11. 5,

18. 4, 2. 33. 6, *EM* 81. 1); *peierare* otherwise appears only twice, in the tragedies (*Tro.* 612 *peierat*, *Phoen.* 589 *peierassem*).

6. 8. 4 Aduersarius meus, dum contraria dicit et iudicem superbia offendit et **in unum testem temere ⟨rem⟩ demittit, causam meam erexit**; non quaero, an pro me errauerit: contra me uoluit.

in unum testem temere ⟨rem⟩ demittit, causam *Madvig 1871–84, 2:419* : in unum testem deme re demittit, causam N
    in unum testem demere dimittit, causam C
    in unum testem temere dimittit, causam Qψ (t- dimicat G) *Pinc., 1557mg., resp. Mur., prob. Lips.*
    unum testem temere dimittit, causam ς₁ *>1605*
    in unum testem tenere causam dimittit ς₁₂
    minimum testem temere dimittit *dub. Grut. p. 559*
    in unum testem de me rem demittit *Ruh. p. 260*
    in unum testem temere demittit causam *Buck 1908, 72–3*
    in unum testem de me reo demittit *Gundermann ap. Buck*
meam Gπ‡ : mea N (*Buck 1908, 72–3*)

The text's documentary record here is unsettled, to say the least: Ruhkopf's *in unum testem de me rem demittit* was not bad, but Madvig's version is better, replacing the rather lame *de me* with the *temere* found in most of the twelfth-century manuscripts, a detail that (as Buck noted) meshes nicely with *superbia*. Buck preferred to construe *causam* with *demittit* and retain N's *mea*, taking it to signify *mea argumenta* in contrast to the 'opposing arguments' (*contraria*) of the *aduersarius*. That interpretation cannot stand—since *contraria dicit* is one of the opposing advocate's *faux pas*, it must mean 'makes contradictory statements'— but *mea* could nonetheless denote 'my interests', and Buck's version is certainly worth mentioning in the apparatus. For *rem in aliquid demittere* = 'to let the issue (of a case) rest (on certain evidence)' *OLD* s.v. 8b cites this passage and *Digest* 12. 2. 34. 9 (Ulpian) *cum res in iusiurandum demissa sit* (cf. *TLL* 5. 493. 27–33); Miriam Griffin notes that 'the idea that it is unjust to rely on one witness to convict someone is credited to Q. Mucius Scaevola in the Republic (Val. Max. 4. 1. 11…) and finally became a rule of law: *Dig.* 48. 18. 20, *CT* 11. 39. 3 = *CJ* 4. 20. 9 (Emperor Constantine in AD 334).'[3]

6. 9. 3 Non est beneficium, nisi quod a bona uoluntate proficiscitur, nisi illud adcognoscit, qui dedit. **Profuit aliquis mihi, dum nescit: nihil illi debeo; profuit, cum uellet nocere**: imitabor ipsum.

profuit (1º) aliquis…illi debeo N : profuit…dum nescit ⟨dum non uult⟩; nihil illi debeo *Castiglioni 1920, 175*, profuit…debeo; ⟨profuit dum non uult: nihil illi debeo⟩ *Pré.*

---

[3] Griffin 2013, 295.

profuit (2°) cum uellet (-lit Nac) nocere N : profuit, ⟨dum non uult: nec huic debeo; profuit,⟩ cum uellet nocere *Gertz*

The various proposed supplements are intended to take account of the category 'not wishing', as distinct from 'ill-wishing', I think unnecessarily. The setup—*non est beneficium...quid dedit*—concerns acting with good intention and acting with awareness of the *beneficium* as such; the sequel concerns acting without awareness and acting with bad intention. S. contented himself with the chiasmus.

6. 13. 3–4 'Puta' inquit 'aliter fieri non posse me magistratum, quam si decem captos ciues ex magno captiuorum numero redemero: nihil debebis mihi, cum te seruitute ac uinculis liberauero? atqui mea id causa faciam.' **(4)** Aduersus hoc respondeo: 'Aliquid istic tua causa facis, aliquid mea: tua, quod redimis, ⟨**mea, quod me redimis;**⟩ tibi enim ad utilitatem tuam satis est quoslibet redemisse. Itaque debeo, non quod redimis me, sed quod eligis; poteras enim et alterius redemptione idem consequi, quod mea. Vtilitatem rei partiris mecum et me in beneficium recipis duobus profuturum. Praefers me aliis; hoc totum mea causa facis.'

mea quod me redimis *Madvig 1871–84, 2:420, iam* mea quod me eligis SB (mea quod eligis ς₁₉, *cod. Pinc., 1557–1605, prob. Grut. p. 559*) : *om.* N

S. has been discussing a question of central importance: in what circumstance does an action that person A performs *sua causa* oblige person B to feel grateful if he benefits from the same action? In §13. 1–2, S. answered the question this way:

> Non sum tam iniquus ut ei nihil debeam qui cum mihi utilis esset fuit et sibi. Non enim exigo ut mihi sine respectu sui consulat, immo etiam opto, ut beneficium mihi datum uel magis danti profuerit, dum modo id qui dabat duos intuens dederit et inter me seque diuiserit. **(2)** Licet id ipse ex maiore parte possideat, si modo me in consortium admisit, si duos cogitauit, ingratus sum, non solum iniustus, nisi gaudeo hoc illi profuisse quod proderat mihi.

Unsurprisingly, the answer depends upon A's intentions: if the benefit to B is merely incidental, the latter is under no obligation, but if A acted with the conscious intention of benefiting both herself and B—'with an eye on two people' (*duos intuens*), 'with thought for two people' (*duos cogitauit*)—then B is indeed obliged to be *gratus*. If this thought is kept in mind in turning to §13. 3–4, I believe we can see why Madvig's supplement—inspired by the supplement *mea, quod* (*me*) *eligis* found in some *recentiores* and printed editions—is incorrect precisely because *redimis* does not entail the focused intentionality that *eligis* necessarily implies. Or to put it another way, *mea, quod me redimis* cannot be sound when S. is going to write, ten words later, *debeo, non quod redimis me, sed quod eligis*: the 'I' who is speaking here can say that the ransomer acted *mea causa* only if the ransomer had 'me' in mind as a beneficiary—*si duos cogitauit*: hence the statement *praefers me aliis: hoc totum mea cuasa facis* with which the passage ends. I do think a supplement is needed here, to satisfy the expectation aroused by *aliquid… tua causa facis, aliquid mea*; but the supplement should be *mea, quod me eligis*, for consistency with the preceding sentences and to anticipate the clauses *sed quod eligis* and *praefers me aliis* that are to come.

6. 15. 1 'Isto modo' inquit 'nec medico quicquam debere te nisi mercedulam **dicis** nec praeceptori, quia aliquid numeraueris; atqui omnium horum apud nos magna caritas, magna reuerentia est'.

dicis N : dices *1529‡*

Yet another confusion of *i* and *e* surely accounts for N's *dicis* here, with future perfect indicative in the *quia*-clause stating a factual reason in a causal sequence. *dices* was the vulgate from Erasmus on; Fickert reintroduced *dicis* without giving a reason, and it was retained thereafter.[4]

6. 16. 1–2 Quare et medico et praeceptori plus quiddam debeo nec aduersus illos mercede defungor? Quia ex medico et praeceptore in amicum transeunt et nos non arte, quam uendunt, obligant, sed benigna et familiari uoluntate. **(2)** Itaque medico, si nihil amplius quam manum tangit et me inter eos, quos perambulat, ponit sine ullo adfectu facienda aut uitanda praecipiens, nihil amplius debeo, quia me non tamquam amicum uidet, sed tamquam **imperatorem**.

imperatorem N (*def. Buck 1908, 73–4*) : spectatorem Ppc (*man. post.*)
  amicus uidet sed tamquam imperator *Mur.*[5]
  emptorem *uel* inuocatorem *Pinc.* (emp- *1557mg.*, *Pré.*, inuoc- *prob. Alexander 1950–2, 34*)
  intemperantem *Grut. p. 991* (*in appendice*)
  interpellatorem *Madvig 1871–84, 2:420*
  imperantem *Gertz*
  'erat cum coniciebam *pariatorem*' *Hos.* [sc. one who squares an account]
  pariaturum *Georgii 1929, 113*
  imper<i> a⟨udi⟩torem *Walter 1943–4, 192*
  imperitiorem *Mazzoli 1974, 91–2*

Anyone wishing to follow Hosius and Buck in retaining N's *imperatorem* and assigning to it the meaning ' "Besteller" oder "Auftraggeber" ' (so Buck) can derive

---

[4] Fickert's note—'*dicis* = RGVTDHW **T-E1. E2.–Vo** = *dices*'—might suggest that he was impressed by the way the manuscripts lined up behind *dicis*: beyond **R** (= our **G**) and **V** (= ς₅), the manuscripts are *recentiores* in Milan (**D**) and Wolfenbüttel (**RW**); **TH** were then in the possession of individual scholars, and the other symbols denote the printed editions, **T-E1.** = *1478–1515*, **E2.–Vo** = *1529–Vog.*

[5] Next to the reading given here, Muretus noted 'olim'; the reading he actually favoured was one he found in a book given to him by Antonius Constantinus: *quia me non tamquam amicum sed tamquam quemlibet alium uidet.*

no comfort either from S.'s other uses of the noun (just under forty times, always 'military commander') or from the company this passage keeps at *OLD* s.v. 1a, which cites Hosius' text under the general heading 'a person who gives orders', along with three passages from Plautus and a fragment of the elder Cato; *TLL* 7. 554. 33–41 cites the same evidence and circumspectly notes, '*fort. add.*: Sen. *benef.* 6, 16, 2…sed tamquam [imperator]em (imperantem *Gertz, ci. alii alia*)'. Pincianus' *emptorem* and Gertz's *imperantem* are the most plausible alternatives: since S. begins the chapter by including the *medicus* among those who 'sell' their skills (*artem, quam uendunt*), since the metaphor is repeated soon after (§16. 4 *quod uendiderunt, quod emimus*), and since if *emptorem* became *imptorem*—as could all too easily happen—*imp(er)atorem* would surely follow (*per = p* with a stroke through the descender), that is the better choice.

6. 19. 2, 4 'Quid ergo?' inquit, 'si princeps ciuitatem dederit omnibus Gallis, si inmunitatem Hispanis, nihil hoc nomine singuli debebunt?' Quidni debeant? debebunt autem non tamquam proprium beneficium, sed tamquam publici partem….**(4)** Primum, cum cogitauit Gallis omnibus prodesse, et mihi cogitauit prodesse; eram enim Gallus et me, etiam si non mea, publica tamen nota conprendit. Deinde ego quoque illi non tamquam proprium debebo, sed **tamquam commune munus; ⟨unus⟩** ex populo non tamquam pro me soluam, sed tamquam pro patria conferam.

tamquam NQ, *Eras., 1649‡* : *om.* RCψ *>1585, quomodo Pinc., 1605 (vid. seq.)*
commune munus; ⟨unus⟩ ex populo *Fick.* : commune munus ex populo N *>1515,* commune; unus ex populo *Eras., 1529–1585* (commune unus ex populo *dist. 1649*), sed quomodo unus ex populo *Pinc., 1605*

If the emperor grants citizenship to all the inhabitants of a province, what does a newly enfranchised individual owe him? Erasmus' emendation of the transmitted text was adopted in all subsequent editions save Lipsius' (Gronovius modified the punctuation in his text), until Fickert introduced his elaboration, which editors through Préchac accepted. But this is another case in which S.'s usage is clear and decisive, showing Fickert's change to be a case of gilding the lily: *munus* appears over sixty times in the work, in all but three instances as a thing bestowed (cf. a few lines farther on, §19. 5 *istius muneris, quod uniuersis datur*), never as a thing owed.[6] S. means, 'My obligation to him will be not personal but communal; as one of the populace I will not pay a debt as though on my own behalf but will contribute as though on my homeland's behalf.'

6. 23. 1 Adice nunc, quod non externa cogunt deos, sed sua illis **in lege** aeterna uoluntas est. Statuerunt, quae non mutarent; itaque non possunt uideri facturi

---

[6] The exceptions: at 1. 12. 3 and 7. 20. 3 *munus* = 'gladiatorial / theatrical show'; at 7. 14. 4, 'duties' (*muneribus…functus est*).

aliquid, quamuis nolint, quia, quidquid desinere non possunt, perseuerare uolu-
erunt, nec umquam primi consilii deos paenitet.

in lege F$\varsigma_1\varsigma_6\varsigma_{15}$ >1515, *Madvig 1871–84, 2:420*: in legem N, *1529‡* (*Pré.*), obel. *Gertz*
    sua illos in lege aeterna uoluntas [sc. cogit] *Feldmann 1887, 23*
    sine lege *Badstübner 1901, 26*
    sua: illis in legem aeterna uoluntas est dist. *Buck 1908, 74*

'Add to this that external factors do not force the gods, but their own eternal will
takes the place of law for them': so Griffin and Inwood, as though *in lege* = *pro
lege*. But while S. must intend to say something very much like that, it cannot be
derived from the Latin of Hosius' edition that they are translating. Madvig was
correct to say that the transmitted reading *in legem... uoluntas est* could not mean
'their will is for a law [i.e., has the force of law] for them' ('Voluntatem esse *in
legem* (intelligunt, opinor, *pro lege*), Latinum non est'), but that did not stop Lejay
and Buck from assigning that meaning to the phrase.[7] On the other hand, I am
fairly sure that I do not know what it means to say that the gods' will is entirely in
(an / the) eternal law (so Madvig: 'Deorum uoluntas tota est in lege aeterna eaque
continetur'), and I understand why Gertz placed a dagger before *in legem*. But in
the end I side with Badstübner, who correctly supposed that *lex* here must correspond to *externa* in the preceding clause, as a constraint upon will and action that
the gods simply do not need and to which they are not subject ('Wie die folgen-
den Worte "Statuerunt..." zeigen, haben die Götter bei Anbeginn aller Dinge
einmal gewollt, und dieser Wille ist ewig und unabänderlich ohne Gesetz'): *uoluntas* corresponds to the *primum consilium* mentioned at the end of the passage
quoted here, which is *per se* sufficient, forever and unalterably. 'Their own might
holds them to their purpose' (§23. 2 *uis sua illos in proposito tenet*).

6. 23. 6 Vide, quantum nobis permiserit, quam non intra homines humani
imperii condicio sit; uide, in quantum corporibus uagari liceat, quae ⟨**non**⟩ **coercuit** fine terrarum, sed in omnem partem sui misit; uide, animi quantum audeant,
quemadmodum soli aut nouerint deos aut quaerant et **mente in altum elata**
diuina comitentur: scies non esse hominem tumultuarium et incogitatum opus.

⟨non⟩ coercuit UIK >*1492, Pinc., 1557‡* : coercuit N, *1503–1529* (*agnosc. Grut. p. 561*), non
cohiberet ς_{19}, ⟨ne⟩ coercuit ⟨quidem⟩ *Pré.*
in altum elata diuina *Haupt 1875–6, 3:377, Hermes 1874, 24* : in altum dat adiuina Nac, in
altum data diuina Npc (*def. Axelson 1939, 31, Alexander 1950–2, 35*)

The first correction is obviously necessary and was made no later than the twelfth
century. *in altum elata*, which occurred independently to Haupt and Hermes, is a

---

[7] The phrase *in legem* is rare—e.g., *in legem et ordinem uenire*, *in legem cadere / incidere* ('to be
subject to a law'), *in legem deflectere* ('to shift a matter so that it is subject to one law rather than
another'), *in legem iurare*, *in legem orationem habere*—and never occurs with a stative verb.

very nice idea, accepted by Gertz and Hosius, and if it were the transmitted text no one would think to disturb it. But I am persuaded by Axelson that it was unnecessary: to show that the expression *in altum data* is Senecan he cited *EM* 76. 25 *liberis* (sc. *animis*) *et in universum datis*, and *data* here is more generally in line with the sense of *dare* = 'put', 'place', 'cause to go' (*OLD* s.v. 19).

6. 24. 2 Adulescentibus quoque ac iam potentibus sui, si remedia metu aut intemperantia reiciunt, uis adhibetur ac **seueritas**. Itaque beneficiorum maxima sunt, quae a parentibus accepimus, dum aut nescimus aut nolumus.

seueritas *Koch 1874, 16 (resp. Kronenberg 1923, 47)* : seruitus N (*def. Axelson 1939, 175–6, Alexander 1950–2, 35*)

Koch's conjecture was motivated above all by the sense—'Non *seruitus* adhibetur adulescentibus parum modestis a parentibus, si modo non omnem caritatem exuerunt, sed *seueritas*'—and he pointed to 5. 5. 2, where *seueritas, admonitiones,* and *diligens custodia* are parental traits that children come to appreciate only when they have matured (*cum iam aetas aliquid prudentiae collegit et adparere coepit propter illa ipsa eos amari a nobis debere propter quae non amabantur*), a point similar to the one made here. Kronenberg rejected *seueritas* because it ruined the double cretic clausula provided by *-betur ac seruitus* and said that *seruitus* denoted no more than *necessitas*, citing *NQ* 2. 24. 3 *Si igni permittes ire quo uelit, caelum…repetet; ubi est aliquid quod eum feriat et ab impetu suo auertat, id non natura sed seruitus iussit.*[8] But a metaphor applied to fire does not provide an adequate demonstration that *seruitus* applied to a human being could mean anything other than servitude. Axelson, who also objected to the rhythm of *seueritas*, thought he had the evidence needed in *Ira* 2. 21. 1–2, a passage precisely on child-rearing:

> Plurimum, inquam, proderit pueros statim salubriter institui; difficile autem regimen est, quia dare debemus operam ne aut iram in illis nutriamus aut indolem retundamus. (2) Diligenti obseruatione res indiget; utrumque enim, et quod extollendum et quod deprimendum est, similibus alitur, facile autem etiam adtendentem similia decipiunt. (3) Crescit licentia spiritus, seruitute comminuitur; adsurgit si laudatur et in spem sui bonam adducitur, sed eadem ista insolentiam et iracundiam generant: itaque sic inter utrumque regendus est ut modo frenis utamur modo stimulis.

But so far from supporting the argument in favour of *seruitus*, the passage undermines it, since *seruitus* and *licentia*—'servitude' and 'licence'—represent extremes equally removed from the recommended middle way along which 'reins' and 'goads' provide proper guidance. Absent evidence that *seruitus* can have a more

---

[8] Reading Schultingh's *iussit* with Hine, for *eius fit* or *eius sit*.

nearly neutral sense comparable to *necessitas*, I will print *seueritas*, admitting a lesser but acceptable clausula (*-betur ac seueritas* = ditrochee + cretic) for the sake of making sense.

6. 25. 4 Quid, si gubernator a dis tempestates infestissimas et procellas petat, ut gratior ars sua periculo fiat? quid, si imperator deos oret, ut magna uis hostium circumfusa castris fossas subito impetu conpleat et uallum trepidante exercitu **uellat** et in ipsis portis infesta signa constituat, quo maiore cum gloria rebus lassis profligatisque succurrat?

uellat *Gertz* : bellat Nac, con|uellat Npc

Gertz appears to have preferred *uellat* just because he knew that it was closer to the original reading of **N**.[9] He probably did not know (because Kekulé's collation probably did not report) that *con* had been added in a space left at the end of a line before a new line began with *bellat*, in ink the same colour and shade as the main text but with slightly thinner letter-forms;[10] he certainly did not know that *bellat* became *conuellat* early enough for the latter to be taken over by **R**; and even if he had known, he could not have known the significance of that fact, since **R**'s pivotal role in transmitting the archetype's text was first recognized a generation later by Buck. In S.'s lexicon *uellere* can denote the vigorous action of a cyclone uprooting a tree (*NQ* 7. 5. 1), but it primarily denotes actions of lesser scope and force: the plucking of a hair, from a head (*Tranq.* 8. 3), beard (*EM* 114. 21, *NQ* 1. 17. 2), or armpit (*EM* 56. 2), or, metaphorically, of someone groping for words (*EM* 40. 10 *singula uerba uellenti*); with this last contrast *EM* 40. 2 *solet magno cursu uerba conuellere, quae non effundit…sed premit et urget*, of the philosopher Serapio's forceful and rapid speech. *conuellat* is clearly the more appropriate word; and since the addition of *con* was a non-obvious correction, I suspect that it was motivated by a comparison with **N**'s exemplar (compare, e.g., the discussion of 5. 4. 2–3).

6. 28. 1–2 'Si uota' inquit 'ualuissent, et in hoc ualuissent, ut tutus esses'. Primum certum mihi optas periculum sub incerto auxilio. Deinde utrumque certum puta: quod nocet prius est. (**2**) Praeterea tu condicionem uoti tui nosti: me tempestas **occupauit** portus ac praesidii dubium. Quantum tormentum existimas, etiam si accepero, eguisse? etiam si seruatus fuero, trepidasse? etiam si absolutus fuero, causam dixisse? Nullius metus tam gratus est finis, ut non gratior sit solida et inconcussa securitas.

---

[9] p. 249: 'scripsi: 'uallum trepidante exercitu uellat'. N m. pr. 'bellat' habet, s. m. 'conuellat', id quod uulgo editur et frequentius usurpatur; sed tamen etiam simplici uerbo in hac re Latini usi sunt; cfr. Liuii lib. IX, 14, 9.'

[10] On line-end as a locus of textual upset, cf. the discussions of 2. 5. 3, 6. 2. 1–2, 7. 28. 3; cf. 4. 39. 3 concoxerim R, con|codixerim N (di *in ras.*).

occupauit N : -bit *Gertz*

Where the confusion of *-uit* and *-bit* is concerned, the question *Vtrum in alterum abiturum erat?* cannot be decisive. But there are two positive reasons why I think Gertz was right. The first is provided by *nosti*: the point is that 'you' know *now*, while for 'me' the resolution still lies in the future. The other reason is provided by *accepero... seruatus fuero... absolutus fuero* immediately following, with which *occupabit* makes a better fit than *occupauit*.

6. 30. 2 Quin potius eum potentem esse uis cui plurimum debes ⟨et⟩ **beatum?** quid enim, ut dixi, uetat te referre etiam summa felicitate praeditis gratiam? cuius plena tibi occurret et uaria materia. Quid? Tu nescis debitum etiam locupletibus solui?

⟨et⟩ beatum Ipcς₁‡ : beatum N, ac beatum G, beatum *ante* esse uis (*pro* potentem) *Grut. p. 562*, beatum⟨que⟩ *Gertz* (*Brakman 1909, 35*)

Absent a more extreme remedy like Gruter's, which it is difficult to justify, a conjunction is certainly needed, and none of those that have been provided has any more authority *a priori* than the others.[11] That being so, the best choice is Gertz's *-que*, since the loss of *q;* before *quid* implies a slightly easier *ratio corruptelae*, and *-bes beatumque* gives a rhythm that is slightly preferable (cretic + troche vs. *et / ac beatum* = ditrochee).

6. 33. 3 Nescis, quantum sit pretium amicitiae, si non intellegis multum te ei daturum, cui dederis amicum, rem non domibus tantum, sed **saeculis** raram, quae non aliubi magis deest, quam ubi creditur abundare.

domibus tantum, sed saeculis N (*def. Buck 1908, 74–5*)
> hominum aetatibus tantum, sed domibus *Badstübner 1901, 26–7*
> d- tantum, sed insulis *Lejay 1901, 130*
> d- tantum ⟨singulis⟩, sed saeculis *Pré.*
> d- tantum, sed sacculis *Alexander 1950–2, 36–7* ('moneybags', *coll. 2. 10. 1, EM 87. 18*)
> hodie tantum, sed saeculis *Watt 1994, 229*

The juxtaposition of place (*domibus*) and time (*saeculis*) has been a stumbling block here, as some conjectures make plain by trying to harmonize the fields of reference (Lejay, Watt, and I suppose Alexander). But I suspect that the generalizing plurals have also contributed to the perceived difficulty:[12] had S. written

---

[11] To adopt Gruter's suggestion, one would have to suppose that *potentem* began as a gloss and then supplanted the word it was explaining; but *beatum* is not the sort of word that cries out for explanation, and *potens* would not be a plausible choice if it did (it does not appear, for example, as a gloss on *beatus* in Goetz's *Corpus Glossariorum Latinorum*).

[12] Though I think Buck's defense of the transmitted text is essentially correct, note how his paraphrase sidesteps the plural *domibus*: 'So steht also der immerhin noch enge "Kreis eines Hauses

amicum, rem non domo Caesaris tantum sed saeculo nostro raram, it probably would have seemed no more odd than, say, *Marc.* 2. 2 *duo tibi ponam ante oculos maxima et sexus et saeculi exempla*. I see no need to alter the transmitted text.

6. 34. 1 Consuetudo ista uetus est regibus regesque simulantibus populum ami-corum **discribere, et proprium** superbiae magno aestimare introitum ac tactum sui liminis et pro honore dare, ut ostio suo propius adsideas, ut gradum prior intra domum ponas, in qua deinceps multa sunt ostia, quae receptos quoque excludant.

discribere *Gertz* : de- N
et proprium Nac : est proprium Npc‡

Gertz's *discribere*, 'distinguish, separate', is an advance over **N**'s *describere*, 'write down'; that is less clearly true of his decision (followed by Hosius and Préchac) to abandon the vulgate's *est* for *et*, a step he took, I suspect, just because he knew that *et* was the original reading of **N**. But *est* is an early correction, the *ſ* having been added above and between *e* and *t* in the same style and colour ink as the main text; it was received and transmitted by **R** to the later manuscripts and printed editions; and it gives the thought the same structure and emphasis as, e.g., the second *est* at 7. 27. 3 *Est istuc graue uitium, est intolerabile et quod dissociet homines, quod concordiam, qua inbecillitas nostra fulcitur, scindat ac dissupet.*

6. 35. 4 'Ista' inquit 'festinatio **nimium grati est**!' Id apertius exprimere non pos-sum, quam si repetiuero, quod dixi: Non uis reddere acceptum beneficium, sed effugere. Hoc dicere uideris: 'Quando isto carebo? quocumque modo mihi labo-randum est, ne isti obligatus sim'. Si optares, ut illi de suo solueres, multum abesse uidereris a grato; hoc, quod optas, iniquius est: execraris enim illum et caput sanctum tibi dira precatione defigis.

nimium grati *Madvig ap. Gertz* (*post* nimia festinatio grati *Haase*) : nimiam ingrati Nac, nimia in- Npc (*Pré.*)
   nimia festinatio ingrati γ‡
   nimia, non ingrati *J. Müller 1892, 15–16* (*prob. Alexander 1950–2, 37*)
   animi ingrati est? *Kruczkiewicz 1877, 436*
   nimia ⟨ia⟩m ingrati est? *Buck 1908, 75*
   nimia non grati est? *Hos. in app.*
   animi grati est? *Kronenberg 1923, 47*

Madvig's suggestion would be acceptable if *nimium* denoted 'very', without a sug-gestion of excess. But though that sense occurs (*OLD* s.v. 2), it is rare, almost

oder Haushalts" gegenüber den *saeculis* "ganzen Generationen". Der Gegensatz ist also ein örtlicher und zeitlicher.'

exclusively found in Plautus, Terence, and Cato, and certainly non-Senecan: adverbial *nimium* and *nimius* occur nearly one hundred times in the *philosophica*, always with sense of 'too (much), excessively', and even in an utterance that will be shown to be misguided, the thought of being 'too grateful' is as out of place as the thought of being 'too beneficent'. On balance, N's corrected reading is preferable, produced by the diagonal stroke, canceling *m*, that seems to be a characteristic of scribal correction (cf. the discussion of 5. 4. 2–3): the imagined interlocutor asks the naïve question, 'Is that extravagant haste the mark of an ingrate?', only to receive S.'s withering reply. Near the bottom of the same page (§35. 5 *ad infitiationem*), where the scribe wrote *adinfini* at the end of one line and *tiationem* at the start of the next, strokes of the same sort cancel the letters *ni*, erroneously added by the scribe when he first incorrectly anticipated that *infi* would have a more familiar sequel.[13]

6. 37. 3 Quemadmodum illi seruauerunt bonorum ciuium officium, qui reddi sibi penates suos noluerunt clade communi, quia satius erat duos iniquo malo adfici quam omnes publico, ita non seruat grati hominis adfectum qui bene de se merentem **difficultatibus uult** ⟨**opprimi**⟩ quas ipse summoueat, quia, etiam si bene cogitat, male precatur. Ne in patrocinium quidem, nedum **in gloriam est** incendium extinxisse, quod feceris.

post difficultatibus *add.* opprimi ψ‡ (*prob. Grut. p. 564*) : difficultatibus uult N (*prob. Gron. pp. 169–70*), uult ⟨affici⟩ *post* submoueat *add.* S, ⟨distringi⟩ difficultatibus uult *Gertz* (*recip. Pré., prob. Alexander 1950–2, 37*)
in gloriam est Gς₁ (in gloriam Qψ) *resp. Axelson 1939, 53* : in gloriam quidem N, in gloriam reputandum est ς₁₂, in gloriam ⟨satis⟩ est *Madvig ap. Gertz*, in gloriam cedet *Gertz*, in gloriam cui dem *Pré.*, in gloriam cuidam *Alexander 1950–2, 37* (*qui et* fecerit *pro* feceris)

We have in both cases the certain loss of a verb form. In the first, the sense of the medieval supplement *opprimi* is blameless, though its loss cannot be readily explained: Gertz's *distringi* aimed at providing a more paleographically plausible stop-gap (*dist-...diff-*), though I find the sense a bit bland ('distracted': cf., e.g., 5. 23. 1 *occupationibus...districtus*, sim. *EM* 106. 1, *Brev.* 7. 3 *districtus animus*, *Helv.* 12. 2 *animus...in pauciora distringitur*): *distrahi* might be a shade better (psychologically 'torn', e.g., 7. 19. 3 *hi...quot cupiditatibus tot crucibus distrahuntur*, *EM* 51. 9 *inter tot adfectus distrahar*, *Tac. A.* 2. 40 *Tiberium anceps cura distrahere*). In the second case, I think Axelson was right to suppose that

---

[13] Also on the same page in **N**: at §35. 5—*Nemo, ut existimo, de immanitate animi tui dubitaret si aperte illi paupertatem, si captiuitatem, si famem ac metum imprecareris; at quid* (ς₆ >1605 : aliquid quid Nac, aliquid Npc, 1649‡, atqui quid *Gertz*) *interest, utrum uox ista sit uoti tui an uis? Aliquid enim horum optas*—Gertz based his conjecture on the text of **N** before correction; but since the same diagonal strokes were used to cancel the second *quid*, apparently when the scribe immediately realized his blunder, *quid* cannot serve as the basis of correction, and *at quid*, first found in some *recentiores*, is probably correct.

N's *in gloriam quidem* came about when an ineptly repeated *quidem* drove out the verb; if so, we have no idea what the verb was, and any paleographically based solution is unlikely to be right. *in gloriam est* is no more attractive here than *in legem... est* was at 6. 23. 1, previously discussed; Madvig's *in gloriam satis est* might just be acceptable (cf. 4. 18. 2 *ceteris animalibus in tutelam sui satis uirium est*, NQ 2. 5. 2 *quantum in nutrimentum sui satis est*, 3. 27. 3 *in exitium mortalium satis est*) if we had any reason to take *est* as a starting point. Gertz's *cedet* gives better sense, in an idiom—with *in* + accusative, 'produce' / 'turn into' / 'result in' (OLD)—that is solidly Senecan (e.g., EM 28. 2 *in inritum cedit... iactatio*, 78. 3 *in remedium cedunt*, sim. Tranq. 9. 3, EM 114. 1 *in proverbium cessit*, Const. sap. 5. 6 *in praedam cesserat*); and here I can offer nothing preferable as a stop-gap.

6. 38. 3 Miles bellum optat, si gloriam; agricolam annonae caritas erigit; eloquentiae pretium **excitat** litium numerus; medicis grauis annus in quaestu est; institores delicatarum mercium iuuentus corrupta locupletat; nulla tempestate tecta, nullo igne laedantur: iacebit opera fabrilis. Vnius uotum deprensum est, omnium simile est.

eloquentiae pretium excitat *Grut. p. 991* ('olim', *in appendice*) *Wesenberg ap. Gertz* (*qui exceptat obel.*) : e- p- exceptat N (*def. Buck 1908, 75–6:* 'eine Reihe von Prozessen erwirbt rednerischen Ruhm')

    e- p- expectat SBVI*ss.*

    excepta lite non numerares ς₅*mg.*

    e- p- exoptat ς₂ς₅ *>1515*, e- exoptat p- *1605–49*

    e- exceptat p- *Eras., 1529, 1557*

    eloquentiae principes exoptant *Pinc.* (*cum* litium numerum)

    eloquens captat pretium ex litium numero *Mur.*

    eloquentiae expectat pretium e litium numero *Stephanus 1586a, 208–9*

    eloquentia pretium exoptat, litium numerum *Lips.*

    exaltat *Bentley (Hedicke 1899, 7)*

    disceptat *Madvig 1871–84, 2:421*

    accendit *Cornelissen 1870, 15*

    exaggerat *Thurot 1874, 52*

    ex⟨tendit inex⟩pectatus *E. Thomas 1893, 293*

    extentat *Pré.*

To defend **N**'s text Buck must ascribe to *pretium*, *exceptat*, and *numerus* meanings that they do not readily bear, and even then the sense is questionable ('A series of trials acquires oratorical renown'?). *exceptat* is certainly corrupt, and Thomas's conjecture has the merit of drawing attention to the fact that without modification *numerus* must struggle to provide by implication what *annonae caritas* and *grauis annus* supply expressly in the examples that precede and follow. Gruter's tentative *excitat*, which Wesenberg independently suggested to Gertz, is the only suggestion I find at all tempting;[14] but though it is a verb S. uses scores of times, to rouse people (or, in *NQ*, natural phenomena) to action, or to arouse emotional states, or to raise buildings, nowhere is it found in a context or with a sense at all comparable to the context we have here and the sense we need.[15] As often, the general point S. is making is not in doubt, but in this case I cannot see a truly plausible form of words to insert as a stop-gap. Reluctantly, I will join Gertz in placing an obelus before *exceptat*, but only before, because I am not confident that corruption is confined to the verb.

6. 39. 1 Sed non, quidquid reprehendendum, etiam damnandum est, sicut hoc uotum amici, quod in manibus est, male utentis bona uoluntate et in id uitium incidentis, quod **deuitat**; nam dum gratum animum festinat ostendere, ingratus est.

quod deuitat *Siesbye ap. Gertz* : quod euitat N (*def. Axelson 1939, 32–3*), uitat *Alexander 1950-2, 38*

Axelson was right to insist that *euitat* is not only blameless, it has a preferable sense, 'shun' vs. 'dodge' (cf. 3. 5. 2 *uerba priora quasi sordida et parum libera euitant*, *EM* 93. 12 *quid autem ad rem pertinet quam diu uites quod euitare non possis?*). Alexander, who had a tendency to approach rhythm the way Préchac approached paleography, contended that '(t)he clausula points clearly to *uitat*. The use of the verb is conative: "is trying to avoid." No doubt, as Axelson...says, *euitare* is the preferable word in that sense, but the clausular argument takes precedence where the use of *euito* is not mandatory.' But I believe that gets the weighting wrong: an archetypal reading that provides just the right sense should be a candidate for emendation on rhythmical grounds only if the rhythm it produces is one the author is known to have shunned; the cretic + trochee produced by *-tis quod euitat* certainly does not meet that criterion. Consider an issue that arises a bit farther along in the text:

6. 40. 2 Si mihi non desideranti redderes, ingratus esses; quanto ingratior es qui desiderare me cogis! Expecta! Quare subsidere apud te munus meum non uis? Quare obligatum moleste ⟨te⟩ **fers**? Quare quasi cum acerbo feneratore signare rationem parem properas?

te fers *Gruter p. 565* (*propter rhythmum resp. Bourgery 1913, 104, sim. Castiglioni 1922, 219 n. 1, Alexander 1950-2, 38, Watt 1994, 229-30*) : fers N, te *post* quare *coll. Gertz*

---

[14]   Gruter: 'ueniebat quidem in mentem olim....uerum cur excidisset illa uox omnibus nota? tollo itaque manum de tabula, iubeoque coniiciant quibus id Apollo indulsit Palatinus.' Bentley's *exaltat* requires a verb that is vanishingly rare in pre-Christian Latin; Madvig's *disceptat* would be attractive if only it could mean 'determines'; Cornelissen's *accendit* makes fine sense but is too far from the *ductus litterarum*; and so on.

[15]   The entry in *OLD* s.v. *excito* 7c 'to raise in value', 'send up' cites only this passage.

The pronoun is plainly needed, and Gruter put it where he did on paleographical grounds ('ut pronomen illud absorptum fuerit a praecedente uoce'); but a series of critics in the last century condemned the choice on rhythmical grounds, because it replaced S.'s preferred cretic plus spondee with a less preferred double spondee. Placing *te* where Gertz placed it restores the preferred rhythm, and that is all to the good; but *te* belongs where Gertz placed it because, as Watt pointed out, that is where Wackernagel's law—published sixteen years after Gertz's edition—says the unstressed pronoun should stand.[16]

6. 41. 1 Ipsam hanc cupiditatem primo quoque tempore liberandi se meminerimus ingrati esse: nemo enim **libenter** reddit quod inuitus debet, et quod apud se esse non uult, onus iudicat esse, non munus.

libenter N : ⟨non⟩ libenter *Watt 2001, 233*

Watt wrote, 'I have inserted before *libenter* the negative which the sense seems to demand. S. here repeats what he has already said at 4. 40. 5 *qui nimis cupit soluere inuitus debet, qui inuitus debet ingratus est.*' But this mistakes the force of *libenter*. S. means that when a person makes a return for something he wishes he did not owe (*inuitus debet*), he might experience relief at so doing—as he would feel relief at casting off an unwanted *onus*—but he does not experience the gladness and pleasure that come from performing a virtuous act that is choiceworthy *per se*. Or to put it another way: returns are properly made in the same spirit in which benefits are properly bestowed. Compare §42. 2: '*Quid ergo? Si nulla interuenerit occasio, semper debebo?*' *Debebis, sed palam debebis, sed libenter debebis, sed cum magna uoluptate apud te depositum intueberis.*

6. 41. 2 Quanto melius ac iustius in promptu habere merita amicorum et offerre, non ingerere, nec obaeratum se iudicare, quoniam beneficium commune uinculum est et inter se duos adligat! Dic: 'Nihil moror, quominus tuum reuertatur; opto, hilaris accipias. Si necessitas alterutri nostrum inminet fatoque quodam datum est, ut aut tu cogaris beneficium recipere aut ego ⟨**alterum**⟩ **accipere**, det potius, qui solet. Ego paratus sum....'

⟨alterum⟩ accipere *Gertz* : accipere N (*def. Buck 1908, 76*)

Here I think Buck has the better of it: *recipere* and *accipere* stand in clear contrast, and the context makes plain that it is a new benefit that the recipient is accepting. Less important but still to the point, the supplement implies no *ratio corruptelae*.

6. 42. 2 'At uereor ne homines de me sequius loquantur'. Male agit qui famae, non conscientiae gratus est. Duos istius rei iudices habes, illum ⟨**quem non debes timere, et te,**⟩ quem non potes.

---

[16] Cf. the discussion of 7. 27. 1 *uideberis tibi* ⟨*uidere*⟩ vs. ⟨*uidere*⟩ *uideberis tibi*.

illum ⟨quem non debes timere, et te⟩ quem non potes *Gertz pp. 252–3* : illum quem non potes N

　illis queri non potes JV

　quos fallere non potes H

　illum quem non potes ⟨et quem potes⟩ I*mg.*, ς₁, *cod. Pinc.*

　illum quem uitare potest, alterum quem uitare non potes ς₈ς₁₆ς₁₇

　illum ⟨quem potes et⟩ quem non potes >*1503*

　illum quem potes *1515, 1529* (al. non potes: sed neutrum placet *1529mg.*)

　illum quem fallere non potes et quem potes ς₁₈

　⟨te⟩ quem non potes ⟨fallere, illum quem potes⟩ *Eras.*

　⟨te⟩ quem non potes ⟨fallere, et illum quem potes⟩ *1557‡*

　'aliquid hic latet, quod non ego protraho' *Grut. p. 565*

　illum quem non potes fallere et quem potes *cod. Lips.*

　quem ⟨potes fallere [effugere *Buck 1908, 76–7*], et te, quem⟩ non potes *Haase*

The realization that *potes* needs an infinitive is first attested in the twelfth-century manuscripts, with the book from Cherbourg providing *fallere*. After some further fits and starts, Erasmus saw the essential shape of the problem, and the version he proposed in his note became the vulgate starting with Curio's edition of 1557, which added *et* before *illum*. Gertz then brought us as close as we can come to the *ipsissima uerba*, by inserting *debes* in place of the first *potes* and by recognizing that *fallere* missed the paragraph's true concern: for from the outset of §42, where S. addresses *mi Liberalis*, it is the latter's (supposed) worry—*uerentis et aestuantis ne in ullo officio sis tardior…sollicitudo…anxietas…uereor*—that is front and centre. I will make one tweak: the supplement would better be represented as *illum quem non ⟨debes timere, et te quem non⟩ potes*, because in cases of *saut du même au même*, it is typically the second member of the look-alike pair that is omitted, when the scribe confuses a string he has already written with one he has not yet reached.

Notes to Book 7

7. 1. 1 Reliqua hic liber cogit, et exhausta materia circumspicio non quid dicam sed quid non dixerim; boni tamen consules quidquid **ibi** superest, cum tibi superfuerit.

ibi *Haase* : tibi N >*1503 agnosc. Grut. p. 566, om. 1515‡*

It is of course not implausible that an original *ibi* became *tibi* in anticipation of what follows; but is equally plausible that *super-* became *tibi super-* in anticipation of what follows. A further consideration causes me to prefer the latter explanation: given that S. has just written *hic liber cogit*, if a locative expression were wanted with *quidquid superest*, I would expect it to be 'here', not 'there'.

7. 2. 4 Hanc uoluptatem aequalem, intrepidam, numquam sensuram sui taedium percipit hic, quem deformamus **cum maxime**, ut ita dicam, diuini iuris atque humani peritus. Hic praesentibus gaudet, ex futuro non pendet; nihil enim firmi habet, qui in incerta propensus est. Magnis itaque curis exemptus et distorquentibus mentem **nihil sperat aut cupit nec se mittit in dubium suo contentus.**

cum *Pinc., 1585‡, prob. Grut. p. 567* (quom *Skutsch ap. Hos.*) : quem NπF, qui γς₅ >*1557*, uel qui Q, quam CHK *cod. Pinc.*, quoniam…peritus hic *Gundermann ap. Buck 1908, 77* nihil Qψ‡ : et nihil N (*def. Buck 1908, 77, recip. Pré.*), est; nihil *Gertz*

At issue in this passage and the next is the *uoluptas* enjoyed by the sage, who surely distinguishes what is base from what is honourable. Here *qui* and *quam* appear in the later manuscripts as attempts to derive sense from the *quem* bequeathed by **N**, but Pincianus' *cum* must be right: *cum maxime*, here in the sense 'just now', is one of S.'s favourite idioms, and though the phrase typically precedes the verbal idea it modifies (whether finite verb or participle), S. does postpone it elsewhere too (7. 27. 1 *captae cum maxime ciuitatis*, EM 23. 10 *nemo hoc praestat qui orditur cum maxime uitam*).[1]

---

[1] Harry Hine has pointed out to me another anomaly, the placement of *ut ita dicam*, which typically stands either in the midst of the phrase it qualifies (e.g., 3. 35. 1 *ex nostra, ut ita dicam, moneta*) or before, preceded by *et* (e.g., Clem. 2. 3. 1…*ne una finitio parum rem comprehendat et, ut ita dicam, formula excidat*). A small lacuna before the expression here cannot be ruled out—e.g., ⟨constans et⟩, *ut ita dicam,…peritus*; yet comparable phrasing can be found at 5. 7. 4 *Nempe reprenditur adsentator et aliena subsequens uerba, paratus ad falsa laudator: non minus placens sibi et se suspiciens, ut ita dicam, adsentator suus.*

The end of the passage quoted is more interesting. In most of the twelfth-century manuscripts *et* disappears from the place it had before *nihil*, and *nihil* became the print vulgate, questioned only by Gertz, whose *est*, however, is very awkwardly placed. But *et nihil…nec…*was defended by Buck, and I believe he was correct. The thought is 'both A and not B', where in this case A = two verbs, B = one: 'freed from great anxieties that mangle thought, he both has no hopes or wants and does not submit to doubt.' Compare, e.g., 6. 29. 1 *quos* [sc. *gratos*] *illi et habere contingat nec experiri necesse sit*, 7. 19. 8 *si uero sanguine…non tantum gaudet sed pascitur, si et suppliciis…crudelitatem exercet nec ira sed auiditate quadam saeuiendi furit.*[2]

7. 2. 5–6 Et ne illum existimes paruo esse contentum, omnia illius sunt, non sic quemadmodum Alexandri fuerunt, cui quamquam in litore rubri maris steterat **plus deerat quam qua uenerat**: illius ne ea quidem erant quae tenebat aut **uicerat, cum** in oceano Onesicritus praemissus explorator erraret et bella in ignoto mari quaereret. **(6)** Non satis adparebat inopem esse qui extra naturae terminos arma proferret, qui se in profundum inexploratum et inmensum auiditate caeca prorsus inmitteret?

qua uenerat N, *1529‡* : quia ue- R (cum ue- Q), inue- UIK, acquisierat ς₁ *>1515*, qua uenerat ⟨erat⟩ *Watt 1994, 230*
uicerat, cum…quaereret. non *dist. edd.* : uicerat. cum…quaereret, non *dist. Watt 1994, 230*

quam qua uenerat was the locus of some turmoil in the manuscripts and early printed editions, starting from **R**'s certainly nonsensical *quia* for **N**'s *qua*. But though *illi…plus deerat quam qua uenerat* seems compressed, it is an intelligible Latin idiom: though Alexander stood on the shores of Arabia, 'more was lacking to him than as far as he had come', i.e., 'than all the territory he had covered to that point'; compare *OLD* s.v. *qua* 4b and the texts cited there. The point is glossed after the colon: he did not truly possess even what was in his grasp or what he had conquered.

About the sequel, Watt remarked, 'The *cum* clause is nowadays always taken with what precedes, with which it does not go at all well. I think that it goes with what follows; so the translation of Thomas Lodge (1614).' The punctuation Watt found wanting is the legacy of **N**—a lesser pause (a simple point) following *uicerat* and *erraret* and a stronger pause (.⁷) following *quaereret*—which became the pattern followed in the printed editions.[3] But Watt was clearly right: Alexander's steersman, 'wandering on Ocean', was the one 'bearing arms forth beyond the

---

[2] On the correct reading at 7. 19. 8, *si et suppliciis…* for *sed et suppliciis…*, see the discussion later in this chapter.

[3] On the same page in **N** the mark .⁷ appears after 7. 2. 3 *quies* and *aestimauimus*, 7. 2. 4 *pendet*, *propensus est*, and *contentus*, after all of which save the first modern editors insert a strong mark of punctuation (colon or period). The first five editions, through Venice 1503, punctuate with a comma

bounds of nature'. I will place a period after *uicerat* and a comma after *quaereret*, and allow the sentence to straddle the boundary conventionally drawn between §2. 5 and §2. 6 (the same sort of boundary-straddling occurs at 1. 1. 5–6, 2. 24. 2–3, 4. 15. 2–3, 5. 15. 4–5, 5. 19. 4–5, 6. 16. 4–5, 6–7, 6. 21. 2–3).

7. 4. 3 Fines Atheniensium aut Campanorum uocamus, quos deinde inter se uicini priuata terminatione distinguunt; et **totus ager utique ullius rei publicae est**, pars deinde suo domino quaeque censetur; ideoque donare agros nostros rei publicae possumus, quamuis illius esse dicantur, quia aliter illius sunt, aliter mei.

utique ullius *Hos.* : aut ullius N, *1529* (et totus…censetur *om. 1475–1515*), *ante* aut *obel. Gertz*

aut illius G, illius aut illius Gpc
illius aut huius ς₅
illius *cod. Pinc.*
huius aut illius *Eras., 1557‡*
ante unius *Madvig ap. Gertz pp. 255–6*
alicuius *Werth 1891, 45*
Apulicus *Feldmann 1887, 24*
publicus *Skutsch ap. Hos.*
aut huius aut illius *vel* alterutrius *Rossbach 1907, 1488*
quamuis ullius *Buck 1908, 77–8*
aut cultus *Gundermann ap. Buck (de quo* 'mallem "saltus"' ' *Hos. in app.)*
totius *Brakman 1909, 35*
haut ullius *Pré. (resp. Axelson 1939, 3)*
ante *(Madvig)* alicuius *(Werth) Alexander 1950–2, 39*
antiquitus *Courtney 1974, 106*

N's corrupt text suggests that S. most likely intended something like 'the territory as a whole belongs to this or that commonwealth, then each parcel is assigned to its owner'. In that case, the most straightforward solution is the one sketched by the correction in **G**, *illius aut illius*, which is preferable to the *illius aut huius* of ς₅ or Erasmus' conjecture, *huius aut illius*, which became the vulgate after 1557. S. tends to pair *hic* and *ille* to denote 'this…that' in the sense of 'the one…the other' ('the former…the latter', etc.), referring to determinate entities previously mentioned or readily understood: e.g. *Ira* 2. 17. 2 *Nec latronem oportet esse nec praedam, nec misericordem nec crudelem: illius nimis mollis animus, huius nimis durus est*, EM 37. 1 *Deridebit te, si quis tibi dixerit mollem esse militiam et facilem. Nolo te decipi. Eadem honestissimi huius et illius turpissimi auctoramenti uerba sunt:* 'uri, uinciri ferroque necari' (i.e., the 'oath' of the *militia uirtutis* and that of the *ludus gladiatorius*). For 'this…that' in the sense of 'one or another unspecified

(in the form of a colon, :) after *uicerat* and a period after *quaereret*; the Venetian editions (1490–1503) also place a comma (:) after *erraret*, omitted in the editions of 1475 and 1478.

entity', as here, he tends to repeat *ille*: e.g., 1. 14. 3 *Accepi idem quod ille, sed ultro. Accepi quod ille, sed ego intra breve tempus, Ira 3. 26. 4 Quid illius pallorem, illius maciem notas?* Repeated *illius* also implies a slightly more straightforward *ratio corruptelae*: I will print *totus ager aut ⟨illius aut⟩ illius rei publicae.*

7. 6. 1 In omnibus istis, quae modo rettuli, uterque eiusdem rei dominus est. Quo modo? quia alter rei dominus est, alter usus. Libros dicimus esse Ciceronis; eosdem Dorus librarius suos uocat, et utrumque uerum est: alter illos tamquam auctor sibi, alter tamquam emptor adserit; **ac recte** utriusque dicuntur esse, utriusque enim sunt, sed non eodem modo. Sic potest Titus Liuius a Doro accipere aut emere libros suos.

ac OV, *cod. Pinc., 1557‡* : ad Nac, at Npc >*1529 (def. Buck 1908, 78),* sic ς₁₂, ita *Gertz p. 256*

The key word here is *adserit*: each person lays a claim that from his perspective is decisive; *but in fact* the books are rightly said to belong to both. The correction of *ad* to *at* in **N** is early and probably scribal: the *d* was canceled by the same diagonal stroke already encountered several times, and the *t* was added above the line in the same colour ink and same graceful form as the *t*'s in the surrounding text.

For the same reason, we find a similar issue a little farther on:

7. 7. 3 Hic respondetur omnia quidem deorum esse, sed non omnia dis dedicata, in iis obseruari sacrilegium quae religio numini adscripsit; sic et totum mundum deorum esse inmortalium templum, solum quidem amplitudine illorum ac magnificentia dignum, tamen a sacris profana discerni, **non omnia** licere in angulo cui fani nomen impositum est quae sub caelo et conspectu siderum licent.

non omnia Nac : et non omnia Npc (*pr. man.*) (*def. Buck 1908, 78, recip. Pré.*)

Because *&* was certainly inserted by the scribe, and because the thought expressed by *non omnia*…elaborates and clarifies *a sacris profana discerni*, I will print *et non omnia.*[4]

7. 6. 3 Quid eius sit, quid non sit, sine **diminutione** imperii quaeritur; nam id quoque quod tamquam alienum abiudicatur aliter illius est. Sic sapiens animo uniuersa possidet, iure ac dominio sua.

diminutione N : de- *Gertz*

A tiny point. The noun is spelled with both *di-* and *de-* in manuscripts generally, and in **N** especially, with its fluid interchange of the vowels, the reliability of the

---

[4] In the same sentence Muretus inserted *et* before *tamen*, presumably (he does not comment) because *tamen* is typically postpositive, and there *et* remained until Hosius removed it in his first edition, correctly: for *tamen* standing first in its clause cf. 1. 1. 10, 2. 29. 5, 4. 39. 4, 6. 34. 4, 7. 4. 6, 12. 3.

spelling here approaches zero. But since we know that the verb was *deminuere*, I will impose the form *deminutio* here, as editors of the other prose works have done when some or all of the manuscripts read *di-*.[5] This happens to be the only place in the work where either noun or verb appears.

7. 8. 1 Ergo cum animum sapientis intuemur potentem omnium et per uniuersa dimissum, omnia illius esse dicimus, **cum ad hoc ius cottidianum**, si ita res tulerit, capite censebitur. Multum interest, possessio eius animo ac magnitudine aestimetur an censu. **(2)** Haec uniuersa habere de quibus loqueris abominabitur. Non referam tibi Socraten, Chrysippum, Zenonem et ceteros magnos quidem uiros, maiores quidem quia **in laudem** uetustorum inuidia non obstat.

cum ad hoc N (*def. Buck 1908, 79*) : cum autem hoc *Haase,* qui ad hoc *Gertz,* 'an "*cum…censeatur*"?' *Hos. in app.*
laudem N : laude *Madvig ap. Gertz*

Buck's defends *cum ad hoc*—'Nun ist aber *ad hoc ius cott.* = *ad iudices* "vor den Richtern" oder = *secundum hoc ius cott.*'—but that misses the point, because *hoc ius cottidianum* is being contrasted with *animum sapientis,* as Haase saw: 'when we consider the sage's *animus…,* when we consider this everyday *ius* of ours…' (cf. *animo* vs. *censu* in the following sentence). I will print *at cum hoc* (cf. *EM* 28. 4, 84. 6, *NQ* 1. 1. 5, 1. 2. 9, 2. 19. 1 , 7. 1. 2). And because *in* + accusative with *obstare* is a non-existent construction (for 'get in the way of' or any other sense of the verb), I will also print Madvig's *in laude*: 'where the praise of venerable men is concerned (*in* = "in respect of", *OLD* s.v. 41), envy offers no opposition.'

7. 8. 2–3 Paulo ante Demetrium rettuli, quem mihi uidetur rerum natura nostris tulisse temporibus ut ostenderet nec **illum a nobis corrumpi nec nos ab illo corripi posse**, uirum exactae (licet neget ipse) sapientiae firmaeque in iis quae proposuit constantiae, eloquentiae uero eius quae res fortissimas deceat, non concinnatae nec in uerba sollicitae sed ingenti animo prout impetus tulit res suas prosequentis. **(3)** Huic non dubito quin prouidentia et talem uitam et talem dicendi facultatem dederit ne aut exemplum saeculo nostro aut conuicium deesset.

corrumpi N : corripi *Grut. p. 568*
corripi N (*def. Buck p. 79*) : corrigi *Grut. p. 568* (*resp. Lips., Alexander 1950–2, 40, Griffin 2013, 329*)

The first change Gruter proposed here was certainly mistaken, and the second has found little more favour: though accepted by Préchac, *corrigi* was spurned by

---

[5] *Const.* 5. 4 deminutio *Mur.* : di- *codd.* ; *EM* 58. 22 deminutio *OvMV* : di- δ, 85. 5 deminutionem *V* : di- *Qδ; NQ* 1. pr. 3 deminutio *Z Mur.* : di- *cett,* 1. 15. 2 deminutionem *Gertz* : di- *codd.*

Lipsius ('Frustra enim aut stulte Natura hominem gignat ostentque, a quo corrigi non possimus'), was found to be 'very dull indeed' by Alexander, and was rejected by Griffin (correlating the infinitives *corrumpi* and *corripi* with the providential purpose stated in the next sentence, *ne aut exemplum… aut conuicium deesset*). But while I would not ordinarily expect to find myself on Préchac's side of such a divide, I cannot help but believe that the framing provided by *illum a nobis… nec nos ab illo…*, which could hardly be more emphatically antithetical, requires that the second infinitive be clearly the opposite of *corrumpi*, something *corripi* is not. As for the divine purpose to which Lipsius and Griffin refer, if such a paragon's inability to correct 'us' served to reveal to us just how very bad we are—a lesson obviously not lost on S. —then the divine aim would appear to have been achieved.

7. 12. 5–13 Idem inter amicos puta fieri: quidquid habet amicus, commune est nobis, sed illius proprium est, quia tenet; uti iis illo nolente non possum. 'Derides me' inquis; 'si, quod amici est, meum est, liceat mihi uendere.' Non licet; nam nec equestria, et tamen communia tibi cum ceteris equitibus sunt. **(6)** Non est argumentum ideo aliquid tuum non esse, quia uendere non potes, quia consumere, quia mutare in deterius aut melius; tuum enim est etiam, quod sub lege certa tuum est.

13 *** accepi, sed certe non minus. Ne traham longius, beneficium maius esse non potest; ea, per quae beneficium datur, possunt esse maiora et plura, in quae **se denique** beneuolentia effundat et sic sibi indulgeat, quemadmodum amantes solent, quorum plura oscula et conplexus artiores non augent amorem, sed exercent.

ante accepi *lac. stat. Haase, ante* ne te[6] *Mur. : lac. denegat Pré. (app. ad loc.)*
se denique *Gertz pp. 257–8* : sed qui N
    sed si ç₁₁ç₁₈
    sunt qui UIK (*recc. plerique*)
    si ea ç₂ >1515
    se ç₁₀ç₂₁, 1529–1605
    se undique *Lips., 1649‡*
    se et qui *Pré.*
    sit qui *Mazzoli 1974, 95–6*

There is certainly a lacuna after the last words of §12: Préchac attempted to avoid that conclusion by placing §13 before §12,[7] but as Miriam Griffin pointed out, the way S. introduces a new question at the beginning of §14. 1 (*haec quoque… quaestio profligata est in prioribus*) rules that possibility out: the distinction drawn

---

[6] The *editio princeps* printed *nec te traham*, a text found earlier in ç₂; from 1529 on, the vulgate was *ne te traham*, which is found in several other *recentiores* (ç₃ç₄ç₅). N's *ne traham*, first printed by Fickert, is correct.
[7] Followed by Abel 1987, 28.

in §13, between the *beneficium* properly understood and the material means of its conveyance, was in fact discussed *in prioribus* (1. 5–7), but the principle that friends have all things in common (§12) does not appear earlier.[8] The loss is too great for us to be certain what argument S. developed; Griffin tentatively suggested something along these lines: 'All of what is held in common between friends is held by each, but each can possess and be given different amounts of it. For [as the text resumes] though a benefit cannot be more or less, the means by which a benefit is conveyed can be.'[9]

In what follows, **N**'s corrupt *in quae sed qui beneuolentia effundat* resulted in the chaotic versions of the medieval and humanist manuscripts; the first intelligible version—*in quae se*, found among the *recentiores*[10]—enjoyed some popularity after Erasmus adopted it, but it was displaced in the vulgate by Lipsius' *se undique*.[11] I do not think that Gertz can be faulted for rejecting that adverb as being a bit more exuberant than the context calls for ('parum mihi quidem aptum uidetur, cum significare debeat "omnimodo"'), but I cannot say that I find his *denique*—'in short'—more convincing.[12] Being unable to provide anything better of my own, I will print *se †quit†*.

7. 14. 1–3 Quaeritur an qui omnia fecit ut beneficium redderet, reddiderit. **(2)** 'Vt scias' inquit 'illum non reddidisse, omnia fecit ut redderet: adparet ergo non esse id factum cuius faciendi {non esse} occasionem non habuit. Et creditori suo pecuniam non soluit is qui ut solueret ubique quaesiuit nec inuenit.' **(3) Quaedam** eius condicionis sunt ut effectum praestare debeant; quibusdam pro effectu est omnia temptasse ut **efficerent**. Si omnia fecit, ut sanaret, peregit partes suas medicus; etiam damnato reo oratori constat eloquentiae officium, si omni ui usus est; laus imperatoria etiam uicto duci redditur, si et prudentia et industria et fortitudo muneribus suis functa est.

faciendi occasionem QUIK‡ (*Grut. p. 570*)˙ : faciendi non esse occasionem Npc (accas|sionem Nac), faciendi nouissime occasionem *Mazzoli 1977, 77–8*[13]

---

[8] Griffin 2013, 330.   [9] Ibid., 316.

[10] Beyond the manuscripts noted above, Gruter also attributed it to his (now unknown) *codex Coloniensis*.

[11] He refers to 'scripti quidam' as reading *in quae sunt qui* (the reading of Gruter's 'Palatinus secundus' and 'tertius' = ς_{20} and ς_{19}) and to his own 'liber' as reading *inique sunt qui*.

[12] p. 258: 'Etenim adparet beneuolentiam non ita solum se effundere, ut maiora et plura det, sed etiam ita, ut pulchriora, ampliora, frequentiora (cfr. V, 2, 2) praebeat similiterque datorum pretium multis modis augeat; itaque plures conparatiuos Seneca ponere potuit, sed hos simul conplexus est dicendo: "in quae se *denique* effundat." '

[13] The words *non esse* must be the legacy of a reader who thought that *non habuit* should be construed with what follows. Beyond a period after *ut redderet*, N's text was originally unpunctuated in this vicinity: a period (.˙: cf. the discussion of 7. 2. 5–6) was later added after *habuit* (I will use a comma), in an ink noticeably darker than the surrounding text, evidently by the same hand that inserted the same period several other times on the page and used a virgule to resolve *soluitis* into *soluit is* in the next line.

quaedam N : quidam *Gertz* (*p. 258, prob. Alexander 1950–2, 41*)
efficerent *1515‡* : -ret N >*1503*, efficeres *Shackleton Bailey 1970, 363*

To the question, 'Can someone who has done all he could to make an adequate return be said to have made one?', the imaginary interlocutor says, 'Certainly not!'; S. says, 'It depends'—hence the parallel constructions with which §14. 3 begins. To take the second issue first, where my premise is that N's *efficeret* is flawed in any case: Shackleton Bailey conjectured *efficeres* because he was certain that *quibusdam* is neuter; and he probably was certain of that because of *quaedam*. Yet as Alexander pointed out, since the three examples that illustrate the principle stated in *quibusdam...efficerent* have a *medicus,* an *orator,* and an *imperator* as their agents, it should follow that those agents all resume the idea of *quibusdam.* And if *quibusdam* is masculine, it seems, if not certain, then highly likely that the indefinite pronoun with which it is parallel should be masculine too: hence Gertz's *quidam,* which links both the idea of obligation (*debeant*) and the act of producing an outcome (*effectum praestare*) to human agency, which is where they belong.

7. 15. 1 Ad summam puta, cum captus esses, me pecuniam mutuatum rebus meis in securitatem creditoris oppositis nauigasse **hieme tam saeua** per infesta latrociniis litora, emensum, quidquid periculorum adferre potest etiam pacatum mare; peragratis omnibus solitudinibus, cum, quos nemo ⟨non⟩ fugiebat, ego quaererem, tandem ad piratas perueni; iam te alius redemerat: negabis me gratiam rettulisse? etiamne, si in illa nauigatione pecuniam, quam saluti tuae contraxeram, naufragus perdidi, etiamne, si ⟨in⟩ uincula, quae detrahere tibi uolui, ipse incidi, negabis me rettulisse gratiam?

tam saeua N : iam saeua *Gruter p. 570, 1605‡,* tum saeua *Castiglioni 1920, 175–6* (*prob. Alexander 1950–2, 41*)

In promoting Castiglioni's *tum,* Alexander affected bewilderment at the role of *tam* in the phrase *hieme tam saeua:* 'I have no idea what *tam* is doing in the phrase *hieme tam saeva*; it has no correlation of any kind.' Certainly *tum,* like Gruter's *iam,* makes fine sense, and no one would think of disturbing either adverb if it happened to stand in N. But of course the non-correlative, merely intensifying use of *tam*—'such a...' / 'so (very)...' (here, 'when the winter (weather) was so ferocious')—is common, and the text is strewn with examples: besides *tam propensa uoluntas et cupida* near the end of this chapter, see, e.g., 1. 1. 9 *hac tam effusa...benignitate* [Lipsius, *necessitate* N], 1. 4. 5 *tam bellis puellis,* 2. 20. 2 *tam magnum pretium,* 2. 24. 2 *tam ualde uis,* 2. 26. 2 *tam exiguo dignum me iudicauit,* 3. 6. 1 *tam inuisum uitium,* 3. 36. 2 *certamen tam optabile.* In that light, the conjecture of *tum* for *tam* appears unnecessary; the infrequency with which *a* and *u* are interchanged in the paradosis represented by N (Appendix 2 n. 2) makes it less than likely as well.

7. 15. 3 'Duas' inquit 'res ille tibi praestitit, uoluntatem et rem; tu quoque illi duas debes.' Merito istud diceres ei, qui tibi reddidit uoluntatem otiosam, **huic uero {debes et}, qui et** uult et conatur et nihil intemptatum relinquit, **id non potes** dicere; utrumque enim praestat, quantum in se est.

<u>huic uero qui et</u> uult et conatur et nihil intemptatum relinquit, <u>id non potes</u> dicere *Hos.*
    <u>huic uero debes & qui</u> uult…relinquit, <u>et non potest</u> dicere Nac
    <u>huic uero debes & qui</u> uult…relinquit, <u>sed non potes</u> dicere Npc
    <u>huic uere debes et qui</u> uult…relinquit, <u>sed non potest</u> dicere R >*1503*
    <u>huic uere diceres sed qui</u> uult…relinquit, <u>non potes</u> dicere ς₅ς₆
    <u>huic uere debes et qui</u> uult…reliquit, <u>sed non potes</u> dicere *1515*
    <u>huic uere debes qui et</u> uult…reliquit, <u>sed non potes</u> dicere *1529*
    <u>huic uero qui</u> uult…relinquit, <u>non potes</u> dicere *Pinc.*
    <u>huic uero qui et</u> uult…relinquit, <u>non potes</u> dicere *1557‡*
    <u>huic non debes qui et</u> uult…relinquit: utrumque enim…(*om.* <u>non potes dicere</u>) *Fick.*
    <u>hic uero debet; sed qui</u> uult…relinquit, <u>ei non potes</u> dicere *Gertz pp. 258-9*[14]
    <u>huic uero debenti, qui</u> uult et…relinquit, <u>ei non potes</u> dicere *Feldman 1887, 24*
    <u>huic uero qui debens et</u> uult…relinquit, <u>id non potes</u> dicere *Pré.*
    <u>huic uero et ⟨non⟩ debes, qui</u> uult et conatur et nihil intemptatum reliquit, <u>et non potes</u> dicere *Alexander 1937, 59-60* (sim. *Alexander 1950-2, 41-2*)
    <u>huic uero: 'debes', ei qui et</u> uult…relinquit, <u>non potes</u> dicere *Mazzoli 1974, 96-7*

R sent matters off in the wrong direction for most of seven centuries by miscopying **N**'s *uero* as *uere* and by overlooking the correction of *potest* to *potes*.[15] Beyond that, the key turning points in the passage's history are obvious: Erasmus' *qui et* for *et qui*, Pincianus' deletion of both *debes* and *sed*, and Curio's decision to blend both innovations (as he often did) to produce what became the vulgate version in 1557. Equally obvious is the key issue: what to do about *debes*? Clearly, retaining some form of *debere* requires further significant adjustments: for example, Mazzoli must change the structure of the sentence, in a way that seems to me impossibly awkward, by making *huic uero: 'debes'* follow so swiftly and redundantly upon *merito istud diceres ei*; Alexander must transpose *et* to precede *debes* and insert *non*, to produce a version that—with *et non debes* and *et non potes*—is no less awkward, because in this context *potes* actually means nothing other than *debes*; and Gertz, whose version is perhaps the most attractive, must change *huic* to *hic*, *debes* to *debet*, *et qui* to *sed qui*, and *et non* to *ei non*—and while none of the alterations is difficult taken individually, their accumulation does lengthen the odds. But none of these scholars had seen **N**: if they had, their urge to retain *debes* might have been tempered by the knowledge that in the manuscript *debes &* sits directly under *duas debes*, both of them at line-end and separated only by a line

[14] *hic uero ultro* and *hic uere* were variations on Gertz's text offered, respectively, by J. Müller 1892, 17–18, and Georgii 1929, 113–14.
[15] I say 'overlooking' because **R** does reflect the change of *et* to *sed* in **N**, and it is plain that the same hand canceled both the *t* of *potest* and the *t* of *et*, before adding superscript *ſ* and *d*.

ending with *reddidit*.[16] In short, I believe that Erasmus was right to read *qui et*, Pincianus was right to delete *debes* as an interloper, and—because *dicere* wants an object corresponding to *istud*—Hosius was right to read *id* for **N**'s original *et*: it is his text that I will retain.

7. 19. 2 Reddere est id, quod debeas, ei, cuius est, uolenti dare. Hoc unum mihi praestandum est; ut **quidem habeat**, quod a me accepit, iam ulterioris est curae; non tutelam illi, sed fidem debeo, multoque satius est illum non habere, quam me non reddere.

quidem habeat *1529‡* (*prob. Grut. p. 571*) : quidam debeat N, quidam habeat *>1515*, custodium debeam eius *Pinc.* (*1557mg.*), quidam id habeat *Grut. p. 571* (*Pré.*)

In §16. 1 **N** had *habeo* where *debeo* was wanted; here, where *habeat* is wanted, it falls, curiously, into the opposite error. But should it be preceded by **N**'s *quidam* or Erasmus' *quidem*? The latter is a bit bold, because *quidam* seems blameless. But the pronoun is also otiose—there being no difficulty in understanding some general third-person singular subject from the context—whereas *quidem* gives just the emphasis that is wanted, 'that he in fact have…': cf. *Pol.* 18. 6 *Satis praestiterit ratio, si id unum ex dolore quod et superest et abundat exciderit: ut quidem nullum omnino esse eum patiatur nec sperandum ulli nec concupiscendum est*, EM 52. 20 *Testari uultis attendere uos mouerique rerum magnitudine? Sane liceat: ut quidem iudicetis et feratis de meliore suffragium, quidni non permittam?* There is some risk that in choosing *quidem* one is making the author say what one thinks he should have said, but in this case it is a risk I am willing to run.

7. 19. 4 'Tale' inquit 'illi beneficium, quale accepisti, non potes reddere; accepisti enim a sapiente, stulto reddis.' **Non; reddo illi, quale nunc potest recipere, nec per me** fit, quod deterius id, quod accepi, reddam, sed per illum, **cui, si** ad sapientiam redierit, reddam, **quale ⟨accepi⟩, dum** in malis est, reddam, quale ab illo potest accipi.

Non, reddo illi…recipere, nec per me…*dist.* N (*Eras.* p. 75) : non reddo CQV *>1557*, nam reddo Ipcç₃ç₅, nunc reddo *Pinc.*, immo reddo *Mur.* (*ex paraphrasi Erasmi male intellecta*), non reddo illi…recipere? nec per me…*dist. Gertz*
cui si N *>1503, 1529‡* : cum (*uel* ei si) *Madvig 1871–84, 2:422–3*, cui nisi *Gertz* (*dein reddam quale post* in malis est *del., cf. pp. 260–1*)
quale ⟨accepi⟩ *1529* : quale N, quale dum in malis est reddam? quale…accipi *dist.* ψ, quale ⟨donauit⟩ *Pré.*, quale ⟨olim dedit⟩ *Mazzoli 1977, 79–80*

---

[16] Strictly, *reddedit* Nac, *reddidit* Npc. For similar interpolations attributable to the *mise en page* in **N**, see the discussions of 4. 4. 2 and 4. 5. 3.

N's text is essentially sound save in the vicinity of *quale... dum*. Hosius' overactive punctuation, reproduced above, does not help to clarify the structure of the thought, but that is easily remedied:

> Non, reddo illi quale nunc potest recipere, nec per me fit quod deterius id quod accepi reddam, sed per illum. Cui si ad sapientiam redierit, reddam quale ⟨accepi⟩; dum in malis est, reddam quale ab illo potest accipi.

There have been two attempts to sidestep the need to acknowledge that a verb was lost after *quale*. In one branch of the medieval manuscripts repunctuation was used to provide a patch:

> ...sed per illum, cui si ad sapientiam redierit, reddam. Quale dum in malis est reddam? Quale ab illo potest accipi,

which is clever, but *reddam* is left rather stranded. Gertz tried a different approach, reading *nisi* for *si* and deleting *reddam quale*:

> ...sed per illum, cui, nisi ad sapientiam redierit, reddam, quale, dum in malis est, {reddam quale} ab ilio potest accipi,

but that amounts to avoiding the need to acknowledge one flaw at the cost of positing two others, and it spoils the symmetry of the thought besides. Erasmus' *accepi*, which I will print, does not so much as hint at a *ratio corruptelae*, but that consideration is outweighed by the epigrammatic pointedness of *quale accepi... quale...potest accipi*; and though the conjectures of Préchac and Mazzoli seem intended to suggest a *saut du même au même*, insofar as each employs a word beginning with *d* before *dum*, that is not terribly persuasive, and *quale donauit* (or *olim dedit*)...*quale...potest accipi* is limp.

7. 19. 5, 7 'Quid? si' inquit 'non tantum malus factus est, sed ferus, sed inmanis, qualis Apollodorus aut Phalaris, et huic beneficium, quod acceperas, reddes?' Mutationem sapientis tantam natura non patitur....**(7)** Deinde interrogo, utrum iste ferus sit animo tantum, an et in perniciem publicam excurrat? Proposuisti enim mihi **Phalarim et ⟨alterum⟩ tyrannum, quorum** si naturam habet intra se malus, quidni ego isti beneficium suum reddam, ne quid mihi cum illo iuris sit amplius?

Phalarim et ⟨alterum⟩ tyrannum, quorum *Hos.*
    Phalarim et tyrannum (tyrr- Nac), q- N (*Buck 1908, 81, Stangl 1910, 1070*)
    Phalarim et tyrannum, q- H, *ss. .s.* appollodorum
    Phalarim .s. appollodorum et tyrannum, q- O
    Phalarim et tyrannum Apollodorum, q- JVς₂ς₁₁ς₁₈
    Apollodorum et Phalarim tyranum, q- *1529‡*[17]

---

[17] I omit the editions down to Basel 1515, which all have some version of the monstrous *autem prohalatum et titanum quorum.*

> Phalarium {et} tyrannum, quoius *Gertz*
> Phalarim et Apollodorum, quorum *Rossbach 1888, 122*
> Phalarim et ⟨Cassandreum⟩ tyrannum *Brakman 1909, 35*
> Phalarim tyrannum et Apollodorum *Pré.*

S. also pairs the two tyrants as exemplars of extreme savagery at *Ira* 2. 5. 1, but as Muretus noted, 'Phalaris quidem uolgo notus est, Apollodorus non item': whereas Phalaris' name was the byword for ferocious tyranny, in the Latin Middle Ages—or earlier still —probably not one reader in 100 could have identified Apollodorus as tyrant of Cassandreia in the third century BCE; and as Rossbach saw, that is why **N**'s text reads as it does. S. wrote *Phalarim et Apollodorum*, a reader helpfully wrote *tyrannum* above the second name, and eventually the name was replaced by the gloss. Compare the process that we see at work along similar lines, but to the opposite effect, in two twelfth-century manuscripts of the π-family: in **H** a reader wrote the gloss *s(cilicet) apollodorum* above *tyrannum*, and in **O** we see *.s. apollodorum et tyrannum* standing in the text after *Phalarim*. Had an alert reader come along and recognized that *phalarim et apollodorum* must be the men to whom S. is referring, he might even have deleted *et tyrannum* and inadvertently restored what S. had written. But as we see in some other twelfth-century manuscripts and *recentiores*, what emerged instead was *Phalarim et tyrannum Apollodorum*.

7. 19. 8 Si uero sanguine humano non tantum gaudet, sed pascitur, **sed et** suppliciis omnium aetatium crudelitatem insatiabilem exercet nec ira sed auiditate quadam saeuiendi furit, si in ore parentium liberos iugulat, si non contentus simplici morte distorquet nec urit solum perituros, sed excoquit, si arx eius cruore semper recenti madet, parum est huic beneficium non reddere. Quidquid erat, quo mihi cohaereret, intercisa iuris humani societas abscidit.

sed et N : {sed} et *Gertz*, si et *Gruter p. 572 (e cod. Col.)*, et si ⟨caede⟩ et *Kronenberg 1907, 287*, sed {et} *Castiglioni 1920, 176*

The passage is continuous with the preceding, elaborating the theme *non tantum malus…sed ferus*. A survey of the contexts in which S. writes *sed et* persuades me that those who thought it out of place here were right. On the one hand, there are the instances where *sed et* = 'but also / even X' or 'but X too' and the force of *et* falls heavily on the word following, e.g., *EM* 12. 6 *angustissimum habet dies gyrum, sed et hic ab initio ad exitum uenit, ab ortu ad occasum*, *NQ* 5. 16. 4 *ab oriente hiberno eurus exit, quem nostri uocauere uulturnum—et Liuius hoc illum nomine appellat in illa Romanis parum prospera* [detail follows]…; *Varro quoque hoc nomen usurpat—sed et eurus iam civitate donatus est* (sim. *EM* 49. 3, 102. 18, 124. 21 [*et* by conjecture]). On the other hand, there are the more numerous instances where *sed et* is in contrast to a preceding negative, *non* or *non tantum* or the like, e.g., 6. 13. 5 *nec desidero illud mihi tantum dari, sed et mihi* (*sim. NQ* 1. pr. 7, 2. 53. 2, 4b. 13. 5, 6. 5. 3, *Tranq.* 3. 5 [*et* by conjecure], *Vit. beat.* 9. 1 *non enim hanc* [sc. *uoluptatem*] *praestat, sed et hanc, NQ* 2. 38. 3 *non cum fato pugnant sed et ipsae in lege fati sunt*). We have a preceding *non* here too, of course, but its force is fully discharged in the focused antithetical phrases *non tantum gaudet, sed pascitur*. I think the solution lies not in deleting *sed* or *et* but in regarding this as another instance where *ſi* was misread as *ſ;* = *sed*, a slip no doubt encouraged by the *sed* immediately preceding.[18] I will print Gruter's emendation, derived from his *codex Coloniensis*: *Si uero sanguine*..., *si et suppliciis*...*nec ira*..., *si in ore parentium*..., *si non contentus*...*sed excoquit*..., *si arx eius*....

7. 19. 9 Si praestitisset quidem aliquid mihi sed arma patriae meae inferret, quidquid meruerat perdidisset et referre illi gratiam scelus haberetur. Si non patriam meam impugnat sed suae grauis est et sepositus a mea gente suam **exagitat, abscindit** nihilo minus illum tanta prauitas animi, **etiam** si non inimicum, inuisum mihi efficit, priorque mihi ac potior eius officii ratio est quod humano generi quam quod uni homini debeo.

abscindit Npc (ad- Nac) 'melius' *Grut. p. 572* : abscidit ς2ς5ς6ς19‡, ac scindit *Gertz p. 261*
etiam N : ⟨et⟩ etiam *Haase*

After **N**'s corrected reading, *abscindit*, became *abscidit* in some *recentiores*—no doubt under the influence of *abscidit* at the end of §19. 8 (see above)—it found its way into the *editio princeps* and held sway in the printed editions until *abscindit* was restored for good by Fickert. But more problematic than the choice of verb is the punctuation. **N** was originally unpunctuated here, but a point was soon inserted between *exagitat* and *abscindit*;[19] that punctuation was carried over into the printed editions, though it is doubly problematic. First, *tanta prauitas animi* must be the subject of *efficit*, and it can only very awkwardly be the subject of both *abscindit* and *efficit*. Haase was apparently the first editor to recognize this problem, so he inserted *et* before *etiam*. But this did nothing to address the second problem, one of sense: 'such great perversity of mind nonetheless tears that one off / away'—from what? Seeing the problem of sense ('sububscura est significatio'), Gertz attached the verb to the preceding sentence, reading *suam exagitat ac scindit*.[20] That is far better, but I do not think it is correct: why—unlike the ten other predicates in this passage—does this one require two verbs? and why do the two verbs denote actions of such different kinds and intensities, the relatively

---

[18] Cf. the discussion of 5. 5. 4; for *ſ* misread as *si* in **N**, see the discussion of 2. 13. 2.

[19] The point is in the same dark ink as the *b* that changed *adscindit* to *abscindit*; both changes was made early enough to stand in the text transmitted to **R**.

[20] In his first edition Hosius agreed with Gertz on the punctuation but rejected his conjecture—printing *exagitat abscindit* and producing thereby a very awkward pair of asyndetic verbs—then returned to the text of the vulgate before Haase in his second edition.

mild 'harass', 'persecute' vs. the very violent 'rend'? If one is doing the latter, the former has already been left far behind. I conclude that *abscindit* is an interloper, a *Doppelgänger* of the foregoing *abscidit* that ended up occupying a place where it does not belong.

7. 20. 4–5 Sed haec **rara nequitia est semper portenti loco habita**, sicut hiatus terrae et e cauernis maris ignium eruptio; itaque ab illa recedamus, de iis loquamur uitiis, quae detestamur sine horrore. **(5)** Huic homini malo, quem inuenire in quolibet foro possum, quem singuli timent, reddam beneficium, quod accepi. Non oportet mihi nequitiam eius prodesse; quod meum non est, redeat ad dominum. **Bonus sit an malus, quid ⟨differt⟩?** diligenter istud excuterem, si non redderem, sed darem.

rara UpcIpcJV‡ : rare N
nequitia est N : nequitia est et Ipcς₅sς₁₈, nequitia est rara et ς₃, est nequitia et *Gertz p. 261*, nequitia et *Castiglioni 1920, 176 (prob. Alexander 1950–2, 43)*
quid ⟨differt⟩? *Gertz (p. 261)* : quid N >*1503*
    bonus an malus, quid? JV (*Fick., Buck 1908, 82, Pré.*)
    qui…DP *1515*
    redeat domum bonus an malus. quam… *1529‡*
    quam *del. vel* quidni? *Pinc.*
    quid ⟨ad me⟩? *Madvig 1871–84, 2:423 (Rossbach 1907, 1487)*
    quid ⟨attinet⟩? *Brakman 1909, 35–6*
    quid ⟨mea⟩? *Stangl ap. Hos.*
    quid ⟨eligam⟩? *Mazzoli 1977, 80*

The transmitted text leaves the participial phrase *semper…habita* unacceptably isolated; insertion of *et* produces one of S.'s favourite structures, modifier + noun *et* + modifier. Castiglioni's solution, praised by Alexander, is elegant and worth citing in the apparatus, but I am reluctant to do without the archetype's *est*, after which *&* could so easily have been lost by haplography. Of the remaining alternatives, the version found in some *recentiores* seems to me preferable to Gertz's: the structure of the former—*haec rara nequitia est et semper…habita*— is neater than *haec rara est nequitia et semper…habita*, which Gertz chose only because he thought it helped to explain N's *rare* (i.e., *rara est > rara ē > rarae > rare*).

At the end of the passage only diehard believers in **N** like Buck and Préchac have lately (i.e., within the last century or so) thought that the text was more or less sound as it stood (in S., *quid?* stands thus isolated only when another question follows, never at the end of a sentence). If as it appears something has dropped out, the loss must be slight, since the general relation between *bonus sit an malus* and *diligenter istud excuterem* is plain, and any of the proposed stop-gaps (except, perhaps, Mazzoli's) would do. Gertz thought that *differt* would more easily be lost before *diligenter* than Madvig's *ad me*: perhaps, but the scribe's eye could have jumped as easily from *quiD* to *Diligenter*, and it is best to minimize the distance it would have to jump; Madvig's 'What does it matter *to me*?' (cf. *NQ* 6. 32. 4) is also more to the point.

7. 24. 2 Num illos castigare mollius potuit? 'Emissem' inquit 'pallium, si nummos haberem.' Post hoc quisquis properauerit, sero **dat**; iam Socrati defuit. Propter acerbos exactores repetere prohibemus, non, ut numquam fiat, sed ut parce.

dat N : dabit *Gertz* (*Wesenberg suadente*)

Unlike generalizing or gnomic conditions in which a present tense in the apodosis consists comfortably with a future or future perfect in the protasis, this quasi-conditional sentence (*quisquis* = *si quis*) contemplates an actual response to a specific circumstance: here the future perfect in the protasis is most appropriately answered by a future in the apodosis. For the distinction, cf. the discussions of 1. 2. 2, 1. 2. 3, and 5. 1. 5.

7. 26. 1 'Sed nihil' inquit 'proficimus; dissimulat, oblitus est: quid **facere debeam?**' **Quaeris** rem maxime necessariam et in qua hanc materiam consummari decet, quemadmodum ingrati ferendi sint: placido animo, mansueto, magno.

quid facere debeam? quaeris *1515‡* : q- f- debeam quaeris N >*1503* : q- f- debeo? iam quaeris *Gertz p. 261*, q- f- debeam ⟨quaero⟩. quaeris *Pré.*, ⟨dic⟩ q- f- debeam? (*immo*, debeam.) *Kronenberg 1923, 47* (*coll. 5. 18, EM 117. 21*)

Gertz's premise—that we should have either *Quid faciam?* (cf. 7. 31. 2 'Non est relata mihi gratia: quid faciam?') or *Quid facere debeo?*—is valid ('What am I to feel obliged to do?' is a possible thought, but not one really suited to this context). If we take it that S. wrote *debeam* in an indirect question, then a governing verb has been lost and Kronenberg's suggestion is attractive. If we take it that S. wrote *debeo*, then *debeam* is more likely due to accident than intentional alteration: not many readers, seeing the straightforward *Quid facere debeo?*, would think to themselves, 'Hold on, should that not be a deliberative subjunctive?' In that case, Gertz's solution—*debeo iam* > *debeam*—is fairly elegant, if perhaps a tad mechanical: I will print it but add '*fort. melius*' next to Kronenberg's conjecture in the apparatus.

7. 26. 4 Quis est istorum tam firmae mentis ac solidae, ut tuto apud eum beneficia deponas? Alius libidine insanit, alius abdomini seruit; alius lucri totus est, cuius summam, non uias, spectat; alius inuidia laborat, alius caeca ambitione et in gladios inruente. Adice torporem mentis ac senium et contraria huic inquieti pectoris agitationem tumultusque perpetuos; adice aestimationem sui nimiam et tumorem, ob quae contemnendus est, insolentem. Quid contumaciam ⟨**dicam**⟩ in peruersa nitentium, quid leuitatem semper aliquo transilientem?

quid contumaciam ⟨dicam⟩..., quid leuitatem *Gertz* : quid contumaciam..., quid leuitatem N, loquar *post* transilientem *add.* B*Img.*ς₁‡, quid? contumaciam...quid? leuitatem *Pré.*

Some *recentiores* inserted *loquar* at the end of the last sentence here: because that supplement was incorporated in the *editio princeps* and was then passed along without change in the vulgate text, Gertz, as the first editor to take full account of **N**, was also the first to recognize that something was amiss.[21] He does not include this passage among those discussed in his *Adnotationes*, presumably because he took it to be obvious that a verb was needed; it was not, however, obvious to Préchac, whose 'solution' again ignores the way S. (but not only S.) uses 'Quid?'[22] But the relation between these two questions is exactly analogous to the relation between *alius inuidia laborat* and *alius caeca ambitione et in gladios inruente* earlier in this passage: absent *laborat* a reader could probably infer from the context what S. was driving at, but no one could seriously contend that a verb did not need to be supplied. The verb Gertz supplied, and the place he chose to put it (*-ciam -cam*), look just right. Note that a very similar issue arises soon after:

7. 27. 1 Si tibi uitae nostrae uera imago succurret, ⟨**uidere**⟩ **uideberis** tibi captae cum maxime ciuitatis faciem, in qua omisso pudoris rectique respectu **uires in concilio sunt uelut signo ad permiscenda omnia dato. Non igni, non ferro abstinetur**; soluta legibus scelera sunt; ne religio quidem, quae inter arma hostilia supplices texit, ullum impedimentum est ruentium in praedam.

⟨uidere⟩ uideberis tibi *Gertz* : uideberis (-biris N*ac*) tibi N*pc*, uideberisque tibi ς₈, uideb-eris tibi uidere I*pc*ς₁‡
uires...sunt uelut...omnia dato. non igni...*dist. Eras.* : uires...sunt, uelut...omnia dato, non igni...N, uictores...sunt [etc.] *Koch 1874, 17–18,* uictores...eunt. uelut...dato [etc.] *Feldmann 1887, 24–5*
concilio N : consilio HVς₅ς₆ς₁₅ς₁₇‡

In the text of the same *recentiores*, *uidere* was inserted after *tibi*, and that text again became the vulgate, which I think in fact has a bit more in its favour than Gertz's *uidere uideberis tibi*. The latter seems to imply a simpler *ratio corruptelae*, which I imagine explains Gertz's choice (he does not make the point explicit), but that advantage is perhaps only apparent—with *uideberis tibi uidere*, a scribe who had written *tibi* might look up to see the next word, *uide-*, and skip it out of confusion with the *uide-* he had already written—and the latter phrasing has a weightier advantage of its own: it allows the unstressed pronoun to stand second in its clause, as Wackernagel's law says it should.[23] Note that though S. does not

---

[21] Erasmus and Gruter knew **N**'s text here, but neither comments on it.
[22] Cf. the discussion of 7. 20. 4–5.
[23] Cf. the discussion of 6. 40. 2 *Quare te obligatum moleste fers?* vs. *Quare obligatum moleste te fers?*

juxtapose the active infinitive with a finite passive form of *uidere* elsewhere, the idiom appears frequently in Cicero, across the genres of his prose, to evoke a scene captured by the mind's eye, as here.[24] In what follows, Koch's and Feldmann's emendations are unnecessary: the thought that (military) 'might' is present in the place of assembly and deliberation is aptly chilling, and it is appropriately linked, by Erasmus' repunctuation, to the prospect of utter chaos (*ad permiscenda omnia*).

7. 28. 3 Fortasse uitium, de quo quereris, si te diligenter excusseris, in sinu inuenies. Inique publico crimini irasceris, stulte tuo: ut absoluaris, ignosce. Meliorem illum facies ferendo, utique peiorem exprobrando. Non est, quod frontem eius indures; sine, si quid est pudoris residui, seruet. Saepe dubiam uerecundiam uox conuiciantis clarior rupit. Nemo id esse, quod iam uidetur, timet; **deprenso pudor demitur**.

deprenso pudor demitur *Haupt 1875–6, 2:275* : deprenso (-praenso Nac) pudore | emitur N (*Buck 1908, 82*), deprehensus pudore emittitur ς₃ >*1503*, deprehensus pudor amittitur *1515‡*, deprehensus pudor emittitur ς₄ς₅, *Rossbach 1907, 1487*

Haupt contributed several excellent emendations to the text, and this is among the best.[25] As often, the problem arises in **N** at line-end, where *pudor* was assimilated to *deprenso* and a letter was lost at the beginning of the verb when it was written at the start of a new line.[26] It was recognized no later than the twelfth century that *pudore* should be *pudor* and that some verb denoting 'loss' was lurking in *emitur*, so that these final three words could epigrammatically comment on and confirm the statement with which it is paired: 'No one fears to be that which he is already seen to be: when someone has been caught out, his sense of shame is lost'—that is, *pudor* has a primarily prophylactic force, and when it is lost, the malefactor develops the 'hard face' just mentioned as an outcome to be avoided (*Non est, quod frontem eius indures*).[27] A version with *pudor* and *emittitur* began to circulate (*deprenso pudor emittitur* **H**, printed by Préchac), and another (regrettably, with *deprehensus*) became the vulgate after 1515.[28] In his contribution Haupt provided a verb that both entailed a slighter corruption than any previously suggested and better responded to S.'s lexicon for the 'stripping away'

[24] e.g., *Inv.* 2. 171, *De or.* 2. 33, *Fin.* 5. 4, *Sen.* 71, *Am.* 41; *Att.* 7. 1. 2, *Fam.* 4. 4. 3, 9. 15. 2; *Div. Caec.* 45, *Agr.* 2. 94, *Cat.* 4. 11, and a vivid passage of the lost *pro Gallio* twice quoted by Quintilian (8. 3. 66, 11. 3. 165).
[25] Cf. esp. 7. 30. 1 *quod explicari pertinacia ⟨potuit, uiolentia⟩ trahentis abruptum est* (explicari pertinacia trahentis N, explicauit per- tra- ψ, explicatur per- tra- H, explicauit mora per- tra- Ipc, ς₁, *1475‡, alii alia*).
[26] About Buck's defense of **N**'s text—'Damit bedeutet *deprenso pudore emitur*: die Unterdrückung des Ehrgefühls ist der Preis hiefür'—the less said the better.
[27] On the significance of *frons* here, and the significance of the *os durum* or *ferreum*, cf. the discussion of 2. 1. 2.
[28] Besides the later versions cited in the apparatus, note *deprenso pudor adimitur* ς₁₇, *depre(hen)so pudor eripitur* ς₈ς₁₆, *deprehensus pudore pudor emittitur* ς₂, cf. also *deprenso pudore pudor emitur* JV.

of an affective disposition or state like shame or fear or desire: cf. *EM* 48. 9 *quid...cupiditates demit?* 58. 3 *quid ex his metum demit?*

7. 29. 1 'Perdidi beneficium.' Numquid quae consecrauimus perdidisse nos dicimus? Inter consecrata beneficium est, etiam si male respondit, bene conlatum. Non est ille qualem sperauimus: simus nos quales fuimus ei dissimiles. **Damnum non tunc factum: adparuit**; ingratus non sine nostro pudore protrahitur, quoniam quidem querella amissi beneficii ⟨non⟩[29] bene dati signum est.

non tunc factum: adparuit N : nunc tunc f- a- ς₉, *cod. Pinc., 1557*, tunc factum nunc apparuit *Pinc., 1585‡*, non nunc f- a- *Haase*, non tunc factum ⟨est cum⟩ app- *Madvig 1871–84, 2:423–4*[30]

Everything turns on the meaning of *tunc*, which I believe must look to *Non est ille qualem sperauimus*, and the moment when 'we' learned that our beneficiary was not the person we hoped he would be: our loss only became evident then, but it actually occurred when we bestowed the *beneficium*, the point S. states expressly at the start of §30: *Stulte non nosti detrimenti tui tempora: perdidisti, sed cum dares, nunc palam factum est.* On that understanding, *non tunc factum* is sound, and it is not necessary to spell the thought out here, as Madvig's conjecture does. I am less certain about the abrupt juxtaposition of *factum* and *adparuit*: I will let it stand but suggest '*fort.* ⟨sed⟩ adparuit' in the apparatus.

7. 30. 2 Quae ratio est exacerbare eum, in quem magna contuleris, ut ex amico dubio fiat non dubius inimicus et patrocinium sibi nostra infamia quaerat, **nec dicere**: 'Nescio quid est, quod eum, cui tantum debuit, ferre non **potuit**; subest aliquid'? Nemo non superioris dignitatem querendo, etiam si non inquinauit, adspersit: nec quisquam fingere contentus est leuia, cum magnitudine mendacii fidem quaerat.

dicere *Madvig* ('willkürlich', *Buck 1908, 82–3*) : desit N (*prob. Gron. p. 177, Buck 1908, 82–3*), desit qui dicat Ipcς₁‡, desit ⟨uox⟩ *Rossbach 1888, 147*, desit ⟨nescius qui dicat⟩ *Pré.*, derit *Alexander 1950–2, 44–5*
debuit N : detulit *J. Müller 1892, 18*
potuit N : potuerit *Wesenberg ap. Gertz*

There is nothing to be gained from importuning your beneficiary to make an appropriate return: you will only alienate him, with the result that he will protect his own name by blackguarding you (*patrocinium sibi nostra infamia quaerat*), complaining about your behaviour and casting aspersions on your *dignitas*

---

[29]   The needed negative has been provided since the *editio princeps*; Préchac printed ⟨hau⟩ bene, but S. never uses *haud* or *haut*—much less *hau*—in his prose works.

[30]   Some *recentiores* offer versions that have no chance of being correct: *non tunc apparuit factum* ς₂, *non tecum factum* ap- ς₈ς₁₆ς₁₉, *non tunc* ap- ς₁₅.

(*Nemo non superioris dignitatem querendo... adspersit*). Thus the thoughts that surround the words between quotation marks, and *pace* Madvig, who thought that the words were the benefactor's,[31] they must reflect the thinking of someone who has heard and is trying to make sense of the embittered beneficiary's complaints: in Griffin and Inwood's translation, 'I don't know why he couldn't stand someone to whom he owes so much. Is there something behind it?' So *dicere* provides no help, and we are back to **N**'s *desit*, which despite Gronovius and Buck is not sufficient by itself (similarly Alexander's *derit*): it would require, in effect, that the quotation serve as the verb's subject, but among the many scores of imagined quotations that S. weaves into his text, that is something they never do. Rossbach's *uox* seems attractive, since S. frequently uses *uox est* or the like with an appositive quotation, but he reserves that idiom for sententious 'sayings' or 'utterances' that are deemed worthy of quotation and remembrance (e.g., 5. 15. 3, *Clem.* 2. 1. 1, *Prov.* 3. 3, *Ira* 1. 11. 3, 33. 2, *EM* 87. 5, 89. 19–20), a category to which the present instance does not belong. *desit* ⟨*qui dicat*⟩, a legacy of some *recentiores* that became the print vulgate, is an adequate stop-gap: cf. 6. 4. 5 *iudex sedet qui dicat...*, 7. 21. 1 *fuit qui diceret...*, sim. *Const.* 6. 2–3, *Helv.* 16. 6, *EM* 94. 8.

As for the words between the quotation marks, Griffin and Inwood's translation also brings out two salient features of the utterance that are obscured by Hosius' punctuation, preserved here, though the obscurity did not begin with Hosius but extends back to the *editio princeps*. First, a question mark should stand on both sides of the closing quotation mark, since we have a question—'subest aliquid?'—within a question—'Quae ratio est...?' Second, the punctuation of 'Nescio quid est, quod...' is apparently meant to suggest that *nescio quid* functions as an indefinite pronoun—'There's something or other that...';[32] that in turn would suggest that we do not have an indirect question here; and that in turn would salvage the integrity of **N**'s *potuit* (Fickert sought to achieve the same end by simply omitting *nescio*). But that is unsatisfactory for two reasons: on the one hand, it leaves *quod* without a function in its clause, the object of *ferre* being *eum*; on the other hand, S. uses *quid est quod* with the idiomatic sense = 'why...?' several times elsewhere, and when he does, the subjunctive invariably follows (*EM* 13. 6 *quid est quod trepident, quod contagium quoque mei timeant...?*, 102. 6–7 *Quid est quod praedicere uelim?...Quid est quod etiamnunc praedicere uelim? NQ* 3. 4. 1 *Quid est quod illam aut sic impleuerit...aut subinde sic*

---

[31] *Adv.* 2. 424: 'Quae sequuntur, *nescio* cet., non ex scriptoris persona dicuntur, sed ex eius, qui ingratum eum, in quem beneficium contulit, expertus iniuriam sibi factam elevare conatur.' Müller's conjecture similarly mistakes the burden of the complaint.

[32] In fact S. happens to use pronominal *nescio quid* just once in the prose works, at *Apoc.* 5. 2 (reporting Claudius' approach to Olympus: *nuntiatur Ioui...nescio quid illum minari...respondisse nescio quid perturbato sono*), and he is not much more given to *nescio quis* or *nescio qui* (the former not at all, the latter only at *Ben.* 5. 15. 3).

suppleat). With *nescio quid est quod*, then, we have the equivalent of *nescio cur…*, 'I do not know why…', with which Gertz rightly printed Wesenberg's subjunctive: '*Nescio quid est quod eum cui tantum debuit ferre non potuerit: subest aliquid?*'

7. 31. 2 'Non est relata mihi gratia: quid faciam? quod di, omnium rerum optimi auctores, qui beneficia **ignoranti** dare incipiunt, ingratis perseuerant. **(3)** [S. briefly summarizes some wrong–headed views that doubt or deny the gods' beneficence, then:] **(4)** Nihilo minus tamen more optimorum parentium, qui maledictis suorum infantium adrident, non cessant di beneficia congerere de beneficiorum auctore dubitantibus, sed aequali tenore bona sua per gentes popu-losque distribuunt; unam potentiam, prodesse, sortiti spargunt oportunis imbri-bus terras, maria flatu mouent, siderum cursu notant tempora, hiemes aestatesque interuentu lenioris spiritus molliunt, errorem labentium animarum placidi ac propitii ferunt.'

ignoranti N >*1529* : ignorantibus ς₈ς₁₆ς₁₇, *Agric. p. 273, 1557‡*, ignorati *cod. Pinc.*

Haase was the first editor since Erasmus to put *ignoranti* in his text and only the second to refuse the correct reading, *ignorantibus*, found in several *recentiores* and first proposed by Agricola;[33] after Gertz restored *ignorantibus*, Hosius reverted to *ignoranti*. But the choice should not be controversial. In reporting *ignorantibus* Erasmus gave a formal reason for Agricola's preference—'Rodolphus legit, *igno-rantibus*, ut respondeat ad id quod sequitur, *gratis* [*sic*]'—and that is fine as far as it goes, since the two epithets clearly do respond to one another in referring to categories of (plural) persons, 'the ignorant' and 'the ungrateful'. But aside from that parallel construction there is a very good substantive reason why the singular is out of place in this context: for as S. stresses elsewhere when speaking of the sorts of divine benefactions he has in mind here—the rains, the seas, the stars, the seasons, the *bona* that the gods disperse *per gentes populosque*—they cannot be given to one without being given to all: see especially 4. 28. 1,

> Ita quae refers—diem, solem, hiemis aestatisque cursus et media ueris autum-nique temperamenta, imbres et fontium haustus, uentorum statos flatu—pro uniuersis inuenerunt, excerpere singulos non potuerunt.

Haplography—loss of *b*; (= -*bus*) before *d*—provides a *ratio corruptelae*.

---

[33] Nine years before Haase, Fickert had printed Pincianus' inferior suggestion, *ignorati*, evidently intended in the sense *ignoti*: in fact the confusion *ignoratae* / *ignotae* occurs in the manuscripts of Livy at 29. 16. 4; beyond that passage the participial form is exceedingly rare before the Christian period, and it is never used of persons (cf. *TLL* 7. 1:315. 39–55).

APPENDIX 1

N and Q

In an early study of the transmission of *De beneficiis* and *De clementia* Giancarlo Mazzoli argued that one of the manuscripts of German origin, **M**, represented a line of descent from **N** independent of **R** (1978, 98–109). Four years later he extended his argument to include **Q**, another product of Germany, with a text very similar to **M**'s (1982, 204–10). Reviewing the history of these texts in *Texts and Transmission* (1983, 363–5), and responding only to Mazzoli's earlier paper, Leighton Reynolds dismissed the contention in a footnote.[1] But in 2001 Ermanno Malaspina returned to the question, concentrating on **Q** in *De clementia* (which **M** lacks), and adopted a modified form of Mazzoli's position: the manuscript does reveal the influence of **N** independent of **R**, but that is the result not of descent, but of contamination with a source that had had access to **N**'s text.[2] Having reviewed the evidence that Mazzoli marshalled, now with a view to *De beneficiis* and concentrating again on **Q**—because it is the purer representative of whatever tradition it shares with **M**, and because **M** is lacking after *Ben.* 4. 22. 2—I conclude that Malaspina was correct.

In his paper of 1982 Mazzoli listed seventy-six places in *De beneficiis* that demonstrate 'l'accordo NQ contro R e quasi sempre contro Rρ' (1982, 206). I have examined these passages, adding three others of the same sort (these are marked by an asterisk in what follows), in each case asking the question that I believe must be answered in the affirmative if a passage is to serve as evidence corroborating Mazzoli's thesis: does **Q** here uniquely share with **N** a certainly correct reading that could not be the product of independent conjecture?

In a handful of cases a passage had to be eliminated because **Q** is in fact not aligned with **N** against **R**:

1. 3. 4 nos (Npc, nus Nac) scientia iuuat NR : s- n- i- Q
3. 3. 4 cum maxime N : eum maxime RCQMψ
3. 11. 2 dant Npc*MGpcψ (dand Gac, *ut uid.*) : danti NacRCQ
4. 34. 5 utramque ψQ : utraque NRC

Another relative handful of passages were in one or another way irrelevant to Mazzoli's argument. So in several cases the agreement of **N** and **Q** was produced by correction in **Q**, a fact that obviously could not serve to demonstrate **Q**'s descent from **N**:

2. 2. 1 licet NHJVQpcM : libet RCQψac
3. 24 intellegas Npc*HQpc : -gis NacRCQψac M
4. 23. 1 tepore NJVQpc : NJVQpc : tempore RCQψac
7. 22. 1 sint NQpc : sunt RCQψac‡

---

[1] 1983, 364 n. 5: 'it is perfectly plain that M derives from N via R, as does every other manuscript I have seen. It so happens that M is the only non-abbreviated φ text which had come to light [sc. at the time of Hosius' edition], so that it stands out in Hosius's apparatus as being closer to N than the other manuscripts. The handful of places where it agrees with N against R are probably the result of correction.'

[2] See Introduction n. 12.

Similarly, in these two cases,

> 4. 9. 1 sine Npc* (*man. post.*)HIpcQ : si in Nac, in spe RCψ, non Wpc
> 4. 10. 4 gratus est et ingratus qui reddidit ςₛς₆, *1605‡* : gratus qui reddidit NacCψM : gratus et ingratus q- r- Npc* (*man. post.*), gratus q- r- ingratus Q, gatus non q- r- J, gratus ingratus q- r- Ipc, gratus tuum q- r- V,

a reading entered in **N** as a correction by a much later hand could not aid Mazzoli's argument;[3] in the first passage, furthermore, the correction itself shows that the truth was within the reach of conjecture and so could occur independently to more than one reader, while in the second passage **Q**'s reading is not quite aligned with the corrected text of **N**, and the error in **N**'s original text—the lack of the word *ingratus*—is obvious in the context (*saepe autem et non redditurus gratus ⟨est et ingratus⟩ qui reddidit*) and was independently addressed multiple times by different readers.[4] In a few other cases, the reading shared by **NQ** against **R** is a trivial error also found in at least one other medieval witness:

> 4. 1. 2 eundum RCQpcMψ : eundem NQacI, eandem V
> 4. 37. 4 in id ⟨in⟩ quo *1478‡* : in id quod NacUIJVQ, in id quo NpcRCπGWK
> 5. 6. 1 ne hoc RCπGWJV : nec hoc NUIKQ

In a much larger number of passages, **NQ** do share a good reading lacking in **R**, but they do not share it uniquely: presumptively, therefore, it was either circulating more generally in the medieval tradition, or different readers were able to arrive at it independently by conjecture, or both of these things were true (in most cases the correct reading is obvious in context):

> 1. 3. 8 late patentis NQMUVDpc : late petentis RC
> 1. 5. 2 incurrit Npc (-ret Nac) CQMG : inoccurrit RacJV, occurrit Rpcψ
> 1. 10. 5 emittere NQMHWJV : amittere RCπGUI, admittere K
> 2. 25. 2 quam NQMHEpcγ : quem RCπG
> 2. 35. 3 sic NQMUpcIpc : si RCψ
> 3. 32. 5 gloria e tenebris Npc (-riae tene- Nac) Ipc, gloria etene- QM : gloria et tene- RCψ
> 3. 35. 3 quo magis NQMHγ : quo maius RCπGIac
> 4. 22. 2 sui NQMH (fulgori sui C) : ui (*post* fulgoris) Rψ, uis JV
> 5. 3. 2 uincantur NQHEacJV : uincatur RCψ
> 5. 12. 3 sic NQHIpcJV : si (*ante* colligitur) RCψ
> 5. 16. 4 beneficio NQIpcJVKpc : bene RCψ, penae G
> 5. 22. 1 ego (*bis*) NQK : ergo RCψ, >*1515*
> 6. 2. 2 incorporale NQBHGIpc : corporale RCψ
> 6. 3. 2 armati NQHpcGUpcIpcJpc : armatis RCψ, armamenti V
> 6. 4. 5 sedet N, f; & QIpc : sed RCψ, est sed JVH
> 6. 5. 4 nihilo minus NQJV : minus (*om.* nihilo *post* illo) RCψ, >*1515*
> 6. 9. 2 lis seruauit NQOpcEpcHpcWpcKacIJV : lis serauit RCPGWacKpc, liberauit C, exercuit Ipc, seruauerat U
> 6. 14. 2 mihi NQIpc : tibi RCψ (*dein* tuum *om.* UJV—a fig leaf to cover the absurdity introduced by *tibi*)
> 6. 15. 8 turres NQ(th-)Hpc(tures Hac)γ: turpes RCπW, urbes Eac (*ut uid.*)

---

[3] After the scribe's self-corrections and the work of the corrector who had improved the text by the time it was transmitted to **R**, the next correcting hand probably belongs to the thirteenth or fourteenth century: cf. R. Kekulé in Gertz 1876, iv, and cf. Introduction n. 1.

[4] At 6. 31. 5 Lacones obiecti Ipcς₁ : L- subiecti Npc (laconesubiec|ti Nac) WJVQ, L- subiecit RCπGUIacK, the masc. nom. pl. ending -*ti* omitted by **R** is obviously needed after *Lacones* and was in fact supplied in several other medieval manuscripts.

6. 19. 2 publici NQJV : publice RCψ
6. 23. 1 possunt (2°) NQU : possint RCψ
6. 26. 2 conlata NQK : conlocata RCψ
7. 19. 9 officii NQIpc : officio RCψ
7. 27. 3 qua NQψ : quia RCG

More than half the instances that Mazzoli adduced, then, provide no evidence useful for his argument.

We can turn now to a number of more ambiguous instances: here, on the one hand, the reading is indeed shared uniquely by **NQ(M)** against **RCψ**, where the text of the latter is wrong or problematic; on the other hand, viewed in context the correction does appear to be within the reach of conjecture, as is presumptively demonstrated by the fact that in half of these passages the correction already stands in a printed edition that appeared before Erasmus introduced **N** to the learned world near the end of *Ben.* 4:[5]

1. 7. 1 non in NQ‡ : non RCψM
1. 9. 5 suam NQ‡ : suum RCψM
1. 14. 1 et in illum NQ : in illum et RCψM‡
2. 20. 2 ex institutione NQM‡ : ex stitutione R (exti- C), institutione ψ
*2. 27. 4 quae quondam Npc*QM (q; Nac), *1585*‡ : qua quondam RCψ, *1515–1557*, qua quidam *>1503*
4. 6. 3 lassae NQM, *1515*‡ : lassa RCψ, laxae *>1503*
4. 36. 2 quanti promissi NQ, *1529*‡ : quantum promissi RCψ, *>1503*, quantum promisi DOI, *>1503*, quando promisi *1515*
4. 37. 2 opertis NQ‡ : apertis RCψ
5. 20. 2 doleat aliquis NQ, *1529, 1557* : dole aliquis R, dolere aliquis Cψ, *>1515*, doleat quis *1585*‡[6]
6. 22 agedum NQ, *1515*‡ : agendum RCψ, *>1503*
6. 23. 3 ituri NQ‡ : itura RCψ, ituros *>1515*
*6. 31. 8 potes NQ, *1529*‡ : potest RCψ, *>1515*
7. 16. 4 quia bonus est ς₄ς₁₀ : quia repetit NQ (*post* quia repetit),[7] quia petit Rψ, qui appetit C
7. 27. 2 ex sacro NQ : sacro RC, *1605*‡, sacra ψ, *>1585*[8]
7. 28. 3 iam uidetur NQ : etiam uidetur RCψ, *>1605*[9]
7. 31. 5 tepente NQ, *1515*‡ : repente RCψ, *1492, 1503* (rapente *>1490*)

Such passages, where **Q** might but need not owe its text to **N** independently of **R**, seem to require a verdict of *non liquet*.

---

[5] Five of the passages were printed correctly in the *editio princeps*, another three in the Basel edition of 1515. It is in his note on 4. 36. 2, listed here, that Erasmus first cites **N**: 'Longobardicum uetustissimum, quanti promissi mei, quae germana est lectio' (1529, 42).

[6] The sentence is as follows: *Non est spectandum an doleat aliquis beneficio accepto sed an gaudere debeat.* The reading of **Cψ**, *dolere*, is certainly conjectural, the work of someone who inferred that the reading transmitted from **R**, *dole*, was the remnant of an infinitive parallel with *gaudere*; but a more alert reader, seeing *debeat*, would have been able to conjecture *doleat*.

[7] Here the point is that **R**'s *petit* could mechanically be altered to *repetit* after the words *quia repetit* that precede.

[8] *sacra* is a 'correction' that is construable in its grammar but absurd in the context: *Hic ex priuato, hic ex publico, hic ex profano, hic ex sacro rapit…*; the retention of *sacro* from Lipsius on is almost equally puzzling.

[9] A temporal sense, 'already', is wanted here (*Nemo id esse, quod iam uidetur, timet; deprenso pudor demitur*), which *etiam* cannot provide.

But then there are just over twenty cases where I think the debt is unambiguously clear: in most of these passages the text of **RC**ψ presents an 'uncorrectable' error beyond the reach of conjecture—especially transposition and omissions—such that the exact nature or even the existence of the error is visible only because an independent witness—the reading of **NQ**—is available for comparison:

1. 1. 10 si licet NQ, *Pinc.*, *1557* : scilicet RCψ, *1529*, *om.* *>1515*, si et licet *1585‡*
2. 25. 2 et luceat NQ (et licet M), *1649‡* : ut luceat RCψ, *>1605*
3. 32. 5 maius NQ : maius illum RV, illum maius C, maius ullum Mψ‡
4. 11. 1 gesta res NQ : res gesta RCψM‡
5. 6. 1 mensuram iam NQ : mensuram RCψ‡
5. 6. 6 procederet NQ : procedere RC, procedere solitus erat ψ (s- p- e- K)‡[10]
5. 8. 5 hoc exemplum habet NQ : habet hoc exemplum RCψ‡
5. 9. 4 nobis beneficium NQ : b- n- RCψ‡
5. 17. 4 uide quam ingrata NQ : quam ingrati uide RCψ, quod ingrati uide JV, quam ingrata uide HIpc (uide *post* ingrata *vel* ingrata sit *coll. edd.*)
5. 21. 2 me necessitas NQ : necessitas RCψ‡
5. 25. 1 ex magna necessitate NQ : necessitate RCψ‡
5. 25. 3 tacendum erat NQ : tacendum RCψ‡[11]
*6. 4. 3 ac si ni(c)hil NQ : *om.* RC, licet ψ, quasi non ς_1‡
6. 6. 1 licet mihi NQ : licet me RCψ‡, licet K
6. 10. 1 aliquid facere NQ, *1529‡* : aliquid RC, alicui ψ, *>1515*
6. 14. 4 emi NQ, *1529‡* : enim RC, ei ψ, *>1515*
6. 17. 1 manus suas locanti NQ : locanti RCψ, se locanti ς_5‡
6. 19. 4 tamquam commune NQ (*Eras. adn.*), *1649‡* : commune RCψ, *>1605*
6. 21. 4 tibi illud occurrat N (illud tibi occurrat Q)[12] : tibi occurrat RCψ‡
6. 23. 2 ob aliud NQς_{12},[13] *1649‡* : obaudio RCψ, ideo ς_1, *>1605*
7. 19. 7 se malus NQ, *1529‡*: malus RCψ, *1475, 1478* (malos *1493–1503*, muros *1515*)
7. 22. 1 oblitus es NQ : oblitus RCψ, non oblitus Ipc$\varsigma_2\varsigma_3\varsigma_{20}$‡

That such errors were indeed 'uncorrectable' in the sense suggested above is made evident by the fact that only a small minority of them were in fact corrected in the early editions, and only one of them—the first—was corrected by a critic who had no knowledge of **N**: the others were corrected either by Erasmus in the latter part of the text, where he could refer to the 'Lombard book' (5. 20. 1, 6. 10. 1, 6. 14. 4, 7. 19. 7), or by Gronovius (2. 25. 2, 6. 19. 4, 6. 23. 2), relying on the knowledge of **N** that he derived from Gruter's *Animaduersiones* (1594, 530, 561).

To close with a specific example, consider 5. 25. 1, on the question whether or when one should seek (*repetere*) a return of *gratia* for a *beneficium*:

---

[10] The sentence (describing Socrates) is *Vir facetus et cuius per figuras sermo procederet…maluit illi nasute negare*: *procederet* was perhaps within reach of medieval conjecture, though the context provides no explicit cue for the subjunctive (contrast the case of 5. 20. 2 *doleat aliquis* at n. 6 in the previous list); in any case ψ's reading shows what medieval conjecture in fact produced.

[11] An alert reader could infer from the following clause, *si inter sapientes uiueremus*, what sort of verb was wanted, but such a reader would more likely choose *esset*—the reading in fact found in several *recentiores*—than *erat*.

[12] The placement of *illud* could have resulted from the errant insertion of a superscript correction in an ancestor of **Q**.

[13] ς_{12}, one of the rare fourteenth-century representatives of φ, is not otherwise conspicuous as the source of exceptional conjectures: perhaps the source here is not **N** but **Q**.

Repetam itaque, quia hoc aut ex magna necessitate [**NQ**, *necessitate* **RCψ**] *facturus ero aut illius causa a quo repetam.*

I wager that it would be very rare reader indeed who would feel the need, unprompted, to add *ex* before the blameless-seeming causal ablative *necessitate*, parallel with *causa*. I wager further that not one reader in ten thousand would be moved to put *magna* between *ex* and *necessitate* without the prompting, specifically, of **N**.

I believe that these last cases, especially, put it beyond reasonable doubt that **Q**'s text bears the mark of **N**'s influence independent of **R**. But I also believe it to be beyond reasonable doubt that that influence was not the result of direct descent from **N**: twenty-two cases are as nothing in a manuscript that otherwise so clearly bears the impress of **R**, and their distribution—clustering densely in Books 5 and 6—is hardly what one expects to see in one manuscript that is descended from another. I take it, then, that the evidence points to corrections, of a not very systematic sort, entered at one or more points in **Q**'s lineage from one or more sources that had access to **N**. If you ask at what points these corrections occurred and from what sources, I frankly say that I have no idea. But the three hundred years that separate the writing of **Q** from the writing of **R**—years for which the paradosis has left no record at all—were time enough for far stranger things to happen.

Orthographica

This appendix gathers much of the evidence for the most characteristic blunders embedded in **N**'s text and the environments in which they tend to appear. As blunders, usually obviously so, most readings reported here will be omitted from my edition's critical apparatus. But this appendix, combined with that apparatus and the *Appendix critica* that will also appear in the edition, will provide the most complete account yet available of this uniquely important manuscript.

The appendix begins with the most common interchanges of vowels (*e*/*i*, *o*/*u*), then the most common interchanges of consonants (*c*/*g*, *t*/*c*, *t*/*d*, consonantal *u*/*b*), then other familiar categories or causes of error: dittography, haplography, anticipation, perseveration, errors of aspiration, and an illustrative selection of corruptions caused by the misreading of *scriptura continua*. The appendix concludes with a large selection of errors, under the heading 'Miscellaneous', that do not belong to the preceding categories and cannot be explained by the presence of some visual cue or other commonly recognized cause.[1] For the vocalic interchanges, I thought it useful—if only for clarity's sake—to list separately those that occur in word-stems and those that occur in inflectional endings. Unless otherwise indicated, the reading preceding an entry's square bracket is the reading of **N** after correction.

The lists that follow show that vocalic and consonantal interchanges are not random events but tend to cluster in certain environments. Some examples:

- Interchanges of *e* and *i* are by far the most common kind included in this survey.[2] To take an important sub-class here, instances of *e* written for *i* in word-stems cluster very densely in the reduplicated perfect stems of *disco* and the compounds of *sto* and *do* and in the present stems of the compounds of *capio*, *cado*, and *lego*;[3] but among nouns such interchanges do not commonly occur except in *fides* (*fede*, etc.) and occasionally the oblique cases of *uir*. In desinences *e* is written for *i* by far most commonly

---

[1] Note that some interchanges one might expect to find—for example, among consonants, the labial stops *p* and *b*—actually occur quite infrequently: *p* for *b* in forms of *publicus* only (3. 15. 3 publicae] puplicae Nac, 25 publica (*bis*)] pup- (*bis*) Nac, 26. 1 publica] pup- Nac; 4. 28. 4 publicauit] pup- Nac, 32. 4 publico] pup- Nac; 7. 16. 2 publicum R] pup- N, 26. 5 publicum] pup- Nac); *b* for *p*, 3. 26. 1 excipiebatur] excibi- Nac (*ut vid.*); 4. 12. 2 proscriptum...proscriptionis] -scrib- (*bis*) N; 6. 15. 3 prius] brius Nac; 7. 2. 2 opibus] obi- Nac. Conversely, interchanges of *e* and *ae* (or *e caudata*) are so common that their inclusion here would overwhelm all other categories.

[2] The frequency with which *i* and *e* and, to a lesser extent, *c* and *g* (see below) are interchanged suggests that a copy in capital script was a near ancestor of **N**, at least for the text of *Ben.*; that is consistent with the infrequent interchange of, e.g., *e* and *o* or *a* and *u*, letters very like each other in minuscule script but very unlike in capital (*e* for *o*, 3. 1. 2 obsolescunt] obse- Nac, 6. 38. 1 poterat] peteat Nac, 7. 28. 1, 2 memoria] meme- Nac; *o* for *e*, 1. 1. 9 demus] do- Nac, 3. 36. 2 honesta] honoste Nac, 4. 2 re tota] rotata Nac, 9. 1 ille] illo Nac, *ut vid.*, 19. 3 colere] colore Nac, 5. 20. 7 nouissime] -mo Nac, 7. 2. 1 eoque] eo quo Nac; *a* for *u*, 3. 38. 1 summum] -mam Nac, 4. 32. 3 debitum] -tam, 5. 21. 2 num Fick.] nam N; *u* for *a*, 1. 6. 2 neutram] -trum Nac, 1. 9. perspicuuam] -uum Nac, 2. 6. 2 nam] num Nac, 3. 6. 2 dandam] -dum Nac, 4. 27. 5 illam] -lum Nac). Note that Malaspina 2016, xxiii–xxiv, draws the opposite conclusion for *Clem.*: it might be that the two texts converged on **N** from different sources.

[3] Similarly, *i* for *e* occurs especially frequently in the perfect stems of the compounds of *capio* and *lego*.

(and unsurprisingly) in the *-is* ending of third declension and the *-it* of the third person perfect indicative and the third person present indicative ending of third— but not fourth—conjugation verbs (2. 11. 5 nutrit] nutr& Nac is very much an outlier). And while interchanges of *e* for *i* are everywhere in Books 1–3, the same confusion is less common—by a factor of four—in Books 4–7.[4]

- *t* is written for *d* most frequently in *ad* (as preposition or prefix), *aliud*, *(ali)quid, apud* (almost always), *illud, istud*, nouns and adjectives ending in *-dus*, and *pudor* and its cognates; *d* is written for *t* most often in *at* (*atque, atqui*), third declension nouns in *-tudo*, and *inquit*. Without such clusters, the entries below would be very much shorter.
- Though *t* is also written for *c* fairly frequently, the instances are largely confined to nouns and verbs cognate with *scire* and third declension nouns with the nominative singular ending *-cio*; *c* is hardly ever written in place of *t*.[5] A similar asymmetry is found in the case of *b/u*: *b* is written for consonantal *u* a good deal more frequently than *c* is for *t*, but only one third as often as *u* is written for *b*.

Awareness of such marked patterns and tendencies might serve to constrain some efforts at conjectural emendation and help to guide others.

e for *i*

Stem

Book 1: 2. 2 quia] q;a Nac, 3. 3 tria] trea Nac, 5. 4 condidit] condedit Nac, 9. 5 recolligere] recolle- Nac, 10. 4 sacrilegi] sacre- Nac, 11. 3 terribilius R] terre- N.

Book 2: 2. 2 intercidamus] -cetamus Nac, 5. 4 perdidit] -dedit Nac, 11. 3 quid (2°)] qued Nac, 12. 1 distinctum Rpc] des- N, 14. 2 submisse] -messe Nac, 14. 5 accidere] acce- Nac, 17. 1 fide] fede Nac, 21. 3 pericliter] pere- Nac, 24. 4 praestiteris] -steteris Nac, 25. 1 reddidit] reddedit Nac (*corr. man. post.*), 31. 1 fides] fedes Nac, 32. 1 excipere] exce- Nac, 35. 5 minantibus] men- Nac.

Book 3: 1. 2 accidere] acce- Nac, 1. 2 accidit] acce- Nac, 1. 4 intercidit] inter cedit Nac, 3. 4 intercidant] -cedant Nac, 4. 2 incidere] ince- Nac, 5. 1 didicisse] dede- Nac, 5. 1 intercidit] -cedit Nac, 5. 1 excidere] -cedere Nac, 7. 6 reddidit (1°)] redde- Nac, 14. 2 fidem] fedem Nac, 15. 2 fidem] fe- Nac, 15. 3 fidem] fe- Nac, 16. 4 delictorum] delec- Nac, 18. 2 eligit] ele- Nac, 3. 25 fides] fe- Nac, 28. 3 erigite] ere- Nac, 35. 2 accipere (R)] acce-N.

Book 4: 3. 2 distribuere] de- Nac, 11. 3 sterilis] -relis Nac, 14. 1 uirum] uerum Nac, 14. 1 praestitit] -stetit Nac, 31. 3 ancillarum] ance- Nac, 31. 3 dissimulabat] desim- Nac, 37. 1 triginta (R)] -genta N.

Book 5: 7. 5 didicit] dedi- Nac, 9. 4 recipimus] rece- Nac, 10. 1 praestitisse] praeste- Nac, 12. 2 difficilis] defficile Nac, 12. 4 accipit] acce- Nac, 16. 3 edidit] ededit Nac, 20. 7 hominis] homenis Nac, 22. 1 praestiteris] praeste- Nac.

Book 6: 3. 4 diuitem] de- Nac, 4. 2 minime] meni- Nac, 16. 3 didici] de- Nac, 16. 7 maligne] male- Nac, 22 diducta] de- Nac, 31. 11 acciderunt] acce- Nac, 32. 4 fuissent R] fuessent N.

Book 7: 2. 1 dimittere] de- Nac, 4. 2 discripta (*Gertz*)] de- N, 6. 1 accipere] acce- Nac, 9. 1 acciperem] acceperem Nac, 10. 5 familia] fame- Nac, 10. 6 dimitte] de- Nac, 15. 3 eddidit] redde- Nac, 16. 1 reddidisse (ρ)] rededisset Nac (rededisse NpcR), 16. 1 dimittat] de- Nac, 16. 3 accipi] acce- Nac, 18. 2 accipere] acceperi Nac, 19. 1 tradidisse]

---

[4] *i* is written for *e*, in the both stems and desinences, about twice as often in Books 1–3 as in Books 4–7.

[5] e.g., 4. 34. 1 certiora] cerc- Nac, 7. 9. 2 pretiosius] preci- Nac, *ut vid.*, 23. 3 admonitio] -cio Nac, 25. 2 admonitio] -cio Nac.

trade- Nac, 19. 4 accipi] accepi Nac, 19. 6 placidissimis] place- Nac, 19. 9 perdidisset] perde- Nac, 30. 1 perdidisti] perde- Nac.

Desinence

Book 1: 1. 5 auertit] -tet Nac, 1. 7 torsit] torret Nac, 1. 8 fecit] -cet Nac, 1. 13 reddit] redd& Nac, 2. 2 facientis (*gen. sing.*)] -tes Nac, 3. 6 erit] er& Nac, 3. 9 sit] sed Nac, 5. 3 efficit] effic& Nac, 5. 4 hostis (*nom. sing.*)] -tes Nac, 5. 6 uenit] -net Nac, 6. 1 facit] -c& Nac, 6. 1 consistit] -t& Nac, 6. 1 dantis…facientis (*gen. sing.*)] -tes…-tes Nac, 7. 1 respicit] -c& Nac, 7. 1 habuit] -bu& Nac, 7. 1 cupiditatem qui] -temque Nac, 7. 3 dedit] -d& Nac, 9. 4 duxit] -x& Nac, 9. 4 abduxit] -x& Nac, 11. 6 accipientis (*gen. sing.*)] -tes Nac, 13. 1 Orientis (*gen. sing.*)] -tes Nac, 13. 3 hostis (*nom. sing.*)] -tes Nac, 14. 3 dederit] -r& Nac.

Book 2: 1. 2 facit] fac& Nac, 3. 1 corrupit] -p& Nac, 3. 2 fuit] fu& Nac, 3. 3 pluris (*gen. sing.*)] -res Nac, 3. 3 discessit] -s& Nac, 5. 2 dixit] dix& Nac, 5. 3 trahit] -h& Nac, 5. 4 omnis (*nom. sing.*)] -nes Nac, 5. 4 nolentis (*gen. sing.*)] -tes Nac, 6. 1 fecit] fec& Nac, 6. 1 stringit] -g& Nac, 7. 3 noluit] -u& Nac, 8. 1 potuit] -u& Nac, 8. 1 iussit] -s& Nac, 8. 1 dedit] -d& Nac, 10. 2 acceperit] acciperet Nac, 11. 2 tribuerimus] -remus Nac, 11. 2 accepit] accip& Nac, 11. 5 nutrit] -tr& Nac, nutriat Npc* (*man. post.*), 11. 6 facit] -c& Nac, 12. 2 senatoris (*gen. sing.*)] -res Nac, 13. 2 potuit] -u& Nac, 13. 2 descenditque] -detque Nac, 13. 3 ostenderimus] -remus Nac, 14. 1 subsedit] -d& Nac, 14. 5 possit] -s& Nac, 14. 5 occidit] -d& Nac, 14. 5 instruit] -u& Nac, 15. 2 destruit] -u& Nac, 16. 2 deficit] deffic& Nac, 16. 2 sustulerit] -r& Nac, 17. 4 uenerit] -r& Nac, 17. 7 accipientis (*gen. sing.*)] -tes Nac, 18. 1 exigit] -g& Nac, 18. 1 uxoris (*gen. sing.*)] -res Nac, 18. 2 suaserit] suar& Nac, 18. 8 diuisit] diuis& Nac, 20. 1 debuerit] -r& Nac, 20. 3 parentis (*gen. sing.*)] -tes Nac, 20. 3 interfecit] -c& Nac, 22 iudicauerimus] -remus Nac, 25. 1 dixit] dixet Nac, 27. 1 dixi] dix& Nac, 27. 4 respicit] -c& Nac, 29. 4 miserimus] -remur Nac, 31. 1 omnis (*nom. sing.*)] -nes Nac, 31. 2 effecit] -c& Nac, 31. 2 peruenitque] -n&que Nac, 31. 3 tenuit] -& Nac, 32. 3 ludentis (*gen. sing.*)] -tes Nac, 32. 4 effecit (QMψ)] effic& Nac, 34. 1 rettulit (retu- N)] -l& Nac, 34. 3 inpulit] -l& Nac, 35. 3 rettulit (retu- N)] -l& Nac, 35. 4 possit] posse Nac.

Book 3: 1. 3 accepisse] accipesse Nac, 1. 3 reddit] -d& Nac, 2. 2 exigit] -g& Nac, 2. 3 respexit] -x& Nac, 3. 3 gaudentis (*gen. sing.*)] -tes Nac, 4. 2 facit] -c& Nac, 5. 2 dixit] -x& Nac, 11. 2 qui] que Nac, 12. 2 fuerit] -r& Nac, 12. 4 dedit] -d& Nac, 12. 4 fecit] -c& Nac, 12. 4 erit] er& Nac, 14. 2 accipientis (*gen. sing.*)] -tes Nac, 15. 4 redigimus] -gemus Nac, 16. 2 erubescit] erubisc& Nac, 17. 2 obstruxit] -x& Nac, 17. 2 amisit] -s& Nac, 17. 3 percipit] -p& Nac, 18. 2 admittit] -t& Nac, 19. 1 dederit] -r& Nac, 19. 3 potuerit] -r& Nac, 19. 3 quaerentis (*gen. sing.*)] -tes Nac, 19. 4 omnis (*nom. sing.*)] -nes Nac, 19. 4 uicit] -c& Nac, 20. 1 agat] ag& Nac, 21. 2 dixit] -x& Nac, 21. 2 indulsit] -s& Nac, 23. 3 fuit] fu& Nac, 24 promisit] -s& Nac, 26. 2 extraxit] -x& Nac, 27. 2 occurrit] -r& Nac, 27. 4 fecit] -c& Nac, 27. 4 audierit] -r&t Nac, 28. 5 habentis (*gen. sing.*)] -tes Nac, 29. 2 conceditur] -d&ur Nac, 30. 3 rapit] -p& Nac, 33. 2 conspirationi] -ne Nac.

Book 4: 9. 2 quaeritis] -retis Nac, 11. 6 subit] sub& Nac, 20. 2 sint] sent Nac, 23. 3 educit (Npc*)] -cet Nac, 37. 2 habuerit] -r& Nac.

Book 5: 5. 1 inuulnerabili] -le Nac, 6. 7 timeri] -re Nac, 12. 2 difficilis] defficile Nac, 15. 4 sanguini] -ne Nac, 20. 4 ipsi] ipse Nac.

Book 6: 3. 1 parcis] -ces Nac, 9. 2 consecuti] -te Nac, 15. 2 pluris (*gen. sing.*)] -res Nac, 15. 4 pluris (2º) (*gen. sing.*)] -res Nac, 16. 4 pluris (*gen. sing.*)] -res Nac, 21. 2 facit (1º)] -cet Nac, 21. 3 cogenti] -te Nac, 23. 8 impudentis (*gen. sing.*)] -tes Nac, 23. 4 accipimus] -pemus N, inpudentis (*gen. sing.*)] -tes Nac.

Book 7: 7. 2 dicit] -c& Nac, 12. 1 sapientis (*gen. sing.*)] -tes Nac, 19. 3 acceperit (R)] -ret
N, 19. 6 mansuetudinis] -nes Nac, 26. 5 incertissimis] -mes Nac, 27. 2 communis
(*gen. sing.*)] -nes Nac, 27. 3 indignare (1°)] -ri Nac.

i for *e*

Stem

Book 1: 1. 7 accepit] accipit Nac, 1. 8 accepit] -cipit Nac, 2. 1 reprehendas] -hindas Nac,
4. 1 reprehendo] -hindo Nac, 7. 1 recepit] -cipit Nac, 8. 2 accepi] acci- Nac, 9. 5 uendere]
uin- Nac, 11. 1 acceperis] acci- Nac, 13. 2 uestigia] uis- Nac, 13. 3 adulescens] -liscens Nac.

Book 2: 1. 4 facerent] faci- Nac, 5. 2 uerissimum] uiri- Nac, 7. 2 effecit] effi- Nac, 7. 3
cupiditates (*acc. pl.*)] -tis Nac, 7. 3 deprehendere] -hindere Nac, 10. 1 acceperit] acci-
Nac, 10. 2 acceperit] acciperet Nac, 11. 2 accepit] accip& Nac, 14. 2 accepisse] acci- Nac,
15. 1 merces] -cis Nac, 17. 1 denarium (2°)] di- Nac, 18. 3 accepisse] acci- Nac, 18. 5
accepi et] accipi& Nac, 18. 8 seruator es] seruatoris Nac, 21. 5 accepit] acci- Nac, 21. 6
accepi] acci- Nac, 25. 1 effecisti] effi- Nac (*corr. man. post.*), 31. 3 destinauit] di- Nac,
32. 1 accepit] acci- Nac, 32. 1 acceperat] acci- Nac, 32. 4 effecit (QMψ)] effic& Nac, 34. 4
despiciens] di- Nac, 35. 1 beneuole] beni- N, 35. 1 accepit] acci- Nac; cf. 1. 2 se] si Nac.

Book 3: 1. 3 accepisse] accipesse Nac, 3. 4 adulescentiam] aduli- N, 9. 2 excepisse] exci-
Nac, 9. 2 refecisse] refi- Nac, 15. 3 accepisse R] acci- N, 17. 4 acceperit] acci- Nac, 18. 1
reprehensione] -hinsione Nac, 21. 2 excedit] exci- Nac, 22. 1 beneuolentia] beni- N,
23. 3 accepisse] acci- Nac, 29. 8 descendat] discin- Nac, 35. 5 accepi] acci- Nac (*ut vid.*),
37. 2 auderent] audi- Nac, 37. 4 adulescentiam] aduli- N.

Book 4: 5. 1 delicias] di- Nac, 11. 1 beneuolum] beni- N, 11. 1 elegero] eli- Nac, 11. 2
conualescendi] conuali- Nac, 20. 2 intellegit] -ligit Nac, 30. 2 quae res] quaeris Nac, 30. 2
trecenti (*man. post.*)] tricenti Nac, 30. 3 egerunt] egirunt Nac, 37. 1 recollegit] recolli- Nac.

Book 5: 5. 2 adulescentiae] adulis- N, 6. 3 defectio] defic- Nac, 10. 1 uendere] uin- Nac,
10. 2 intellegitur] intelli- Nac, 1219. 5 erubescam] -biscam Nac, 19. 8 accepit (*corr. pr.
man.*)] acci- Nac, 21. 1 consuetudo] consui- Nac, 22. 1 acceperunt] acci- Nac.

Book 6: 2. 3 uero (R)] uiro N, 6. 2 beneficia] beni- Nac, 15. 1 mercedulam] merci- Nac,
15. 5 consuetudine] consui- Nac, 16. 1 mercede] merci- Nac, 24. 2 adulescentibus] adu-
lis- Nac, 34. 2 ueros] uiros Nac.

Book 7: 12. 6 uendere] uin- Nac, 7. 13 beneuolentia (Rac)] beni- N, 19. 3 delegau-
erit (BQpcψ)] deli- N, 19. 6 infectus] infic- Nac, 28. 1 adulescentiam] adulis- N, 29. 1
querella] quaerilla Nac.

Desinence[6]

Book 1: 1. 5 occupationes (*acc. pl.*)] -nis Nac, 1. 9 immortales (*acc. pl.*)] -lis Nac, 1. 10
pertinaces (*nom. pl.*)] -cis Nac, 1. 10 decet] -cit Nac, 3. 2 sorores (*nom. pl.*)] -ris Nac,
3. 2 uirgines (*nom. pl.*)] -nis Nac, 3. 5 iuuenes (*nom. pl.*)] -nis Nac, 3. 6 iudicet] -cit
Nac, 3. 7 uirgines Vestales (*acc. pl.*)] -nis -lis Nac, 3. 10 iubet] iubit Nac, 4. 4 Charites
(*nom. pl.*)] -tis Nac, 5. 3 haeret] -rit Nac, 5. 6 fasces] -cis Nac, 7. 1 essent] -sint Nac,

---

[6] Some instances under this heading—especially third declension masculine/feminine accusative
plural (-*es* vs. -*is*)—may well reflect variations in spelling used by S. Since I tentatively plan to normalize spelling in my edition, printing -*es* for both nominative and accusative plural, I put the variations
on record here. It happens that the certainly incorrect nominative plural -*is* occurs about as often
(twenty-nine times) as the accusative plural -*is* (thirty-one times).

7. 1 dedisset] -sit Nac, 9. 1 uides] -dis Nac, 9. 5 inbecilliores (*acc. pl.*)] -ris Nac, 10. 1 maiores (*nom. pl.*)] -ris Nac, 10. 4 raptores (*nom. pl.*)] -ris Nac, 11. 1 continet] -nit Nac, 11. 4 existimet] -mit Nac, 13. 3 uinceret] -rit Nac, 13. 3 duceret] -rit Nac, 15. 2 fines (*acc. pl.*)] -nis Nac.

Book 2: 1. 4 rogasset] -sit Nac, 1. 4 essent] -sint Nac, 4. 2 remanet] -nit Nac, 4. 3 uoles] -lis Nac, 5. 1 aeque] -qui Nac, 5. 1 quales (*nom. pl.*)] -lis Nac, 5. 2 uoces (*nom. pl.*)] -cis Nac, 7. 2 creditores (*acc. pl.*)] -ris Nac, 7. 2 essent] -sint Nac, 11. 1 posset] -sit Nac, 11. 1 haberes] -ris Nac, 12. 2 detruderet] -rit Nac, 14. 1 licet] -cit Nac, 15. 3 uiresque (*nom. pl.*)] uiris- Nac, 16. 1 refugisset] -sit Nac, 16. 2 urbes (*nom. pl.*)] -bis Nac, 17. 1 deceret] -rit Nac, 17. 1 posset] -sit Nac, 17. 6 imputatores (*nom. pl.*)] -ris Nac, 17. 6 partes (*nom. pl.*)] -tis Nac, 18. 2 debet] -bit Nac, 19. 1 fuisset] -sit Nac, 20. 2 leges (*acc. pl.*)] -gis Nac, 20. 2 esset] -sit Nac, 21. 2 similes (*acc. pl.*)] -lis Nac (*Pré.*), 21. 4 offenderet] -rit Nac, 21. 5 mittentes (*acc. pl.*)] -tis Nac, 21. 6 misisset] -sit Nac, 22 hilares (*nom. pl.*)] -ris Nac, 23. 2 signatores (*acc. pl.*)] -ris Nac, 28. 1 fauet] -uit Nac, 29. 2 neglegentes (*acc. pl.*)] -tis Nac, 29. 5 uirtutes (*acc. pl.*)] -tis Nac, 29. 5 esse te malles] essit emalles Nac, 29. 5 uelles] -lis Nac, 29. 6 inmortales (*nom. pl.*)] -lis Nac, 33. 1 habet] -bit Nac, 35. 4 ille] -li Nac, 35. 4 difficultates (*acc. pl.*)] -tis Nac.

Book 3: 1. 1 displicet] -cit Nac, 1. 2 excuset] -sit Nac, 4. 1 uoluptates (*acc. pl.*)] -tis Nac, 6. 1 maiores (*nom. pl.*)] -ris Nac, 7. 1 rationes (*nom. pl.*)] -nis Nac, 7. 7 disputantes (*acc. pl.*)] -tis Nac, 8. 4 negasset] -sit Nac, 11. 2 debet] -bit Nac. 11. 3 esset] -sit Nac, 12. 4 difficultates (*acc. pl.*)] -tis Nac, 15. 3 uindices (*acc. pl.*)] -cis Nac, 16. 1 plures (*nom. pl.*)] -ris Nac, 16. 1 pauciores (*nom. pl.*)] -ris Nac, 16. 2 nobiles (*nom. pl.*)] -lis Nac, 16. 4 numerare] -ri Nac, 18. 2 amitteret (*Gertz*)] mitterit Nac (-ret Npc), 18. 3 habet] -bit Nac (*ut vid.*), 21. 1 leges (*nom. pl.*)] -gis Nac, 22. 1 esset] -sit Nac, 23. 2 esset (1°)] -sit Nac, 23. 3 habuisset] -sit Nac, 23. 4 ostenderent] -rint Nac, 24 uideret] -rit Nac, 24 esset] -sit Nac, 25 aptasset] -sit Nac, 26. 1 esset] -sit Nac, 26. 2 componeret] -rit Nac, 27. 2 reccideret] -rit Nac, 27. 3 dixisset R] -sit N, 27. 4 laudet] -dit Nac, 28. 2 imagines (*acc. pl.*)] -nis Nac, 28. 2 nobiles (*nom. pl.*)] -lis Nac, 29. 2 esset] -sit Nac, 29. 3 potuisset] -sit Nac, 29. 3 coepisset] -sit Nac, 29. 7 praeferes] -ris Nac, 30. 1 esset (1°) *Gertz*] -sit Nac (-sem Npc), 30. 1 genuisset] -sit Nac, 30. 1 esset] -sit Nac, 30. 2 quale sit] qualisit Nac, 31. 3 exposuisses] -sis Nac, 31. 5 gauderes] -ris Nac, 32. 1 gaudet] -dit Nac, 32. 2 notesceret] -rit Nac, 32. 2 circumfunderet] -rit Nac, 32. 2 discuteret] -rit Nac, 35. 3 indiget] -git Nac, 35. 5 esset] -sit Nac, 35. 5 desideraret] *fort.* -rit Nac, 35. 5 permaneret] -rit Nac, 36. 2 segniores (*acc. pl.*)] -ris Nac, 36. 2 iuuenes (*uoc. pl.*)] -nis Nac, 36. 3 decet] -cit Nac.

Book 4: 1. 3 accessiones (*acc. pl.*)] -nis Nac, 2. 1 uidet] -dit Nac, 2. 2 partes (*nom. pl.*)] -tis Nac, 2. 2 debet] -bit Nac, 3. 2 reges (*nom. pl.*)] -gis Nac, 3. 3 inliberales (*nom. pl.*)] -lis Nac, 6. 4 dices] -cis Nac, 6. 5 uarietates (*acc. pl.*)] -tis Nac, 6. 6 respondent] -dit Nac, 8. 3 esset] -sit Nac?, 9. 1 eget] egit Nac, 17. 4 transeuntes (*acc. pl.*)] -tis Nac, 21. 1 debet] -bit Nac, 24. 1 riget] -git Nac, 25. 2 arentes (*acc. pl.*)] -tis Nac, 26. 2 intemperantes (*acc. pl.*)] -tis Nac, 26. 3 tales (*acc. pl.*)] -lis Nac, 28. 4 urbes (*nom. pl.*)] -bis Nac, 31. 3 faceres] -ris Nac, 32. 2 reges (*nom. pl.*)] -gis Nac, 34. 3 debes] -bis Nac, 38. 1 debet] -bit Nac, 38. 2 reliquisset] -sit Nac.

Book 5: 1. 1 fines] -nis Nac (*ut vid.*), 4. 1 debere] -ri Nac, 4. 4 nollet] -lit Nac, 6. 5 emerget] -git Nac, 7. 6 debet] -bit Nac, 12. 2 solueres] -ris Nac, 15. 5 deberetis] -ritis Nac, 16. 1 duces] -cis Nac, 22. 1 agentes (*acc. pl.*)] -tis Nac, 22. 4 sanabiles (*acc. pl.*)] -lis Nac.

Book 6: 6. 16. 7 posset] -sit Nac, 23. 4 utilitates (*acc. pl.*)] -tis Nac, 27. 3 amitteret] -rit Nac, 27. 3 dubites] -tis Nac, 6. 29. 1 ipse] -si Nac, 29. 1 perseueret] -rit Nac, 31. 2

posset] -sit Nac, 31. 10 posset] -sit Nac, 31. 11 uellet] -lit Nac, 35. 4 solueres] -ris Nac, 35. 5 faceret] -rit Nac, 36. 2 faceret] -rit Nac.

Book 7: 1. 4 omnes (*acc. pl.*)] -nis Nac, 1. 7 torquetur] -quitur Nac, 3. 2 immortales (*nom. pl.*)] -lis Nac, 7. 1 omnes (*acc. pl.*)] -nis Nac, 12. 1 communes (*nom. pl.*)] -nis Nac, 15. 2 fugientes (*acc. pl.*)] -tis Nac, 15. 2 posset] -sit Nac, 16. 1 iudicet] -cit Nac, 18. 1 ille] -li Nac, 18. 2 accipere] -ri Nac, 27. 2 rapientes (*acc. pl.*)] -tis Nac, 28. 2 esset...esset] -sit...-sit Nac.

o for *u*[7]

Stem

Book 1: 1. 4 calumniantes] calom- Nac, 1. 1. 8 custodiat] cos- Nac, 3. 1 extundit] exton- Nac, 3. 9 Eurynomes] eori- Nac (*bis*), 5. 1 consulatum] conso- Nac, 8. 1 consulas] conso- Nac, 14. 2 putet] po- Nac, 15. 6 uoluntate] uolon- Nac.

Book 2: 1. 2 iucundissima] io- N, 1. 3 uerecundia] -condia Nac., 5. 4 uoluntatis] uolon- Nac, 8. 2 rubore] ro- Nac, 10. 4 uoluntate] uolon- Nac, 12. 2 consularis] conso- N, 13. 2 iucunda] io- N, 14. 1 uoluntatem] uolon- Nac, 15. 1 consulendum] conso- Nac, 18. 3 uerecundo] -condo Nac, 25. 2 uoluntas] uolon- Nac.

Book 3: 4. 1 numeremus] no- Nac, 5. 2 humilius] ho- Nac, 9. 3 tabulam] tabo- Nac, 15. 1 custodirentur] cos- Nac, 16. 2 consulum] conso- Nac, 23. 3 uulgaris] uol- Nac, 30. 1 uoluntatis] uolon- Nac, 33. 2 consularibus] conso- Nac, 33. 3 uulgare] uol- Nac, 33. 5 disputabimus] dispo- Nac, 37. 2 urbes] or- Nac.

Book 4: 1. 2 computare] compo- Nac, 2. 3 disputatur] dispo- Nac, 3. 3 quaestuosissime] quaestoo- Nac, 23. 1 umores (Npc1)] omo- Nac (humo- Npc2*), 24. 1 custodiat] cos- Nac, 36. 2 rubori] ro- Nac.

Book 5: 3. 2 custodiunt] cos- Nac, 6. 1 nullo] nolo Nac, 9. 3 numerum] no- Nac, 15. 2 formulam] formo- Nac, 16. 2 consulatus] conso- Nac, 16. 2 trucidationis] troci- Nac, 16. 4 consulatibus] conso- Nac, 17. 2 consulatum] conso- Nac, 19. 6 uoluntarium R] uolon- N, 19. 6 incolumitate] incolo- N, 25. 6 uoluntas] uolon- Nac.

Book 6: 1 uultu] uol- Nac, 6. 15. 1 numeraueris] no- Nac, 16. 2 ambulat] ambo- Nac, 21. 2 uoluntatis] uolon- Nac, 21. 4 uoluntatem] uolon- Nac, 24. 2 nolumus] nolo- Nac, 27. 2 uoluntate] uolon- Nac, 38. 5 consulat] conso- Nac, 43. 3 custodiam] cos- Nac.

Book 7: 7. 2 impune] -pone Nac, 9. 3 luxuria (ρ)] -oria N, 12. 1 singulos R] -golos N, 15. 3 uoluntatem] uolo- Nac, 26. 3 uerecundia] -condia Nac, 26. 4 tuto] toto Nac, 27. 3 luxuriosos (ρ)] luxor- N, 28. 2 consularia] conso- Nac, 28. 3 uerecundiam] -condiam Nac.

Desinence

Book 1: 1. 2. 5 ingratus] -tos Nac, 5. 1 alius (1º)] -os Nac, 5. 4 morbus] -bos Nac, 7. 1 recepturus] -ros Nac.

---

[7] Some instances under this heading may well reflect variations in spelling used by S., in both stems (e.g., *uulgar-* vs. *uolgar-*) and desinences (e.g., -*uus* vs. -*uos*). Since I will usually normalize spelling in my edition (*uulg-*, -*uus*), I put the variations on record here.

Book 2: 8. 1 Tiberius] -os Nac, 18. 8 numeratur] -tor Nac, 21. 6 Rebilus] -los Nac, 29. 4 ictu] -to Nac.

Book 3: 17. 2 morbus] -bos Nac, 19. 2 seruus] -uos Nac.

Book 4: 6. 6 deus] -os Nac, 11. 3 reuehatur] -tor Nac, 20. 2 concitaturus] -ros Nac, 30. 4 percussu] -so Nac, 31. 2 conspectu R] -to N.

Book 5: 3. 1 abiectus] -tos Nac, 9. 1 conpositus] -tos Nac, 9. 3 beneficium] -om Nac, 12. 3 ingratus] -tos Nac, 15. 3 conuentu] -to Nac (ł iustus *ss. man. post.*), 16. 4 inmaturus] -ros Nac, 19. 2 liberatur] -tor Nac, 21. 1 praestandum] -dom Nac, 21. 2 cogatur] -tor Nac, 21. 3 ablaturus] -ros Nac, 24. 3 oculus] -los Nac, 25. 6 contextum] -tom Nac.

Book 6: 2. 1 morbus] -bos Nac, 16. 1 amicum] -com Nac, 16. 5 securus] -ros Nac, 23. 8 minus] -nos Nac, 34. 4 amicus] -cos Nac.

Book 7: 1. 3 magnus] -nos Nac, 1. 5 septimus] -mos Nac, 3. 1 conditur] -tor Nac, 9. 2 coloratur] -tor Nac, 17. 2 malum] -lom Nac, 21. 2 domum] -mom Nac, 30. 1 plurimum] -mom Nac.

u **for** *o*

Stem

Book 1: 3. 4 nos] nus Nac, 6. 2 forma] fur- Nac, 11. 5 opportunitate] oppur- Nac, 12. 3 communis] cum- Nac.

Book 2: 1. 1 monstraturus] mun- Nac, 2. 2 opportunitas] opur- Nac, 3. 2 ignoscitur] ignus- Nac, 9. 1 gloriosum] -usum Nac, 28. 2 fortuna] fur- Nac, 32. 4 lusori] -suri Nac.

Book 3: 7. 3 gloriosa] -usa Nac, 7. 5 formula] fur- Nac, 12. 2 iocundius] iu- N, 15. 3 incorruptos] incur- Nac, 17. 3 iocundissimae] iu- N, 22. 4 fortuna] fur- Nac, 32. 5 potuisse] pu- Nac, 32. 6 possunt] pus- Nac, 38. 1 ignobili] innu- Nac.

Book 4: 4. 3 conplorantes] conplu- Nac, 5. 2 tot (3º)] tut Nac, 5. 2 fortuita] fur- Nac, 6. 2 coloribus] cul- Nac, 6. 6 robustiorem] ru- Nac, 8. 3 fortunam] fur- Nac, 11. 3 auctore] acture Nac, 18. 2 societas] su- Nac, 21. 6 fortuna] fur- Nac, 24. 2 oporteat] opurteam Nac.

Book 5: 2. 2 fortunam] fur- Nac, 6. 1 Diogenes] diu- Nac, 21. 3 pudorem] pudur- Nac, 22. 1 commonefaciam] commune- Nac.

Book 6: 1 3. 2 custoditis] custu- Nac, 29. 2 iocundus] iu- N, 43. 1 custodiuntur] custu- Nac, 43. 3 custodiri] costu- Nac.

Book 7: 26. 4 torporem] tur- Nac.

Desinence

Book 1: 5. 4 raptos] -tus Nac, 15. 2 stimulos] -lus Nac.

Book 2: 14. 1 perniciosos] -sus Nac.

Book 3: 36. 2 stimulos] -lus Nac.

Book 4: 4. 3 querulos] -lus Nac, 6. 5 sonos] -nus Nac, 13. 3 mercator] -tur Nac *ut vid.*, 20. 3 captator] -tur Nac, 26. 2 auaros, luxuriosos, malignos] -us (*ter*) Nac, 27. 5 contumelioso] -osu Nac, 30. 2 Pompeios] -ius Nac, 30. 3 dignos] -nus Nac, 31. 1 deos] -us Nac, 32. 1 alios (1º)] -us Nac.

Book 5: 15. 3 populos] -lus Nac, 21. 3 ingratos] -tus Nac.

Book 6: 16. 5 meos] -us Nac, 30. 1 uoto N] -tu Nac.

Book 7: 1. 4 numeros] -rus Nac, 1. 6 beatosque] -tusque Nac, 10. 1 uolo] -lu Nac, 19. 8 perituros] -rus Nac, 19. 9 humano] -nu Nac, 26. 4 gladios] -dius Nac.

c for g

Book 1: 1. 8 neglegenter] nec- Nac, 1. 9 neglegentesque] nec- Nac, 4. 3 obligati] oblica- Nac, 4. 5 obligatorum] oblica- Nac.

Book 2: 7. 2 obligauit] oblica- Nac.

Book 3: 22. 4 indigere (Npc*)] -dicere Nac, 37. 1 agmina] ac- Nac.

Book 4: 6. 5 uagantibus] uacan- Nac, 9. 3 eligo] elico Nac, 12. 1 regulam...regula] recu- (*bis*) Nac (-c- 1° *corr.*), 37. 1 naufragus] -fracus Nac.

Book 5: 1. 4 obligas (R)] -licas N, 5. 1 obligatus] -catus Nac, 6. 6 figuras] ficu- Nac, 11. 5 obligat] oblicat Nac.

Book 6: 7. 3 largo] larco Nac.

Book 7: 1. 2 recolligo] -co Nac, 2. 1 adfigere (ς₁₂ς₁₆pc)] adficere N, 18. 2 obligare] -care Nac, 21. 1 Pythagoricus (*bis*) R] -coricus (*bis*) Nac (1° *corr.*), 24. 2 castigare] -care Nac, 28. 3 ignosce] icnoce Nac, 31. 3 neglegentiam] nec- Nac, 31. 4 sortiti spargunt] sortitis parcunt Nac.

g for c

Book 1: 1. 9 sacrilegi] sagri- Nac, 4. 1 Graecum] gregus Nac, 4. 4 sacrilegium] sagri- Nac, 8. 1 Socrati] Sog- Nac, 8. 2 Socrates] sog- Nac, 11. 5 delicatos] -gatos Nac.

Book 2: 27. 3 acrior] agri- Nac, 28. 4 uellicare] -gare Nac, 29. 6 conlocauerunt] colloga- Nac.

Book 3: 19. 2 dimicantem] -gantem Nc, 28. 2 conlocant] cologant Nac, 29. 5 crassitudinem] grassi- Nac.

Book 4: 2. 1 delicata] -gata Nac, 4. 1 nec] neg Nac, 9. 2 agricolae] -golae Nac, 22. 2 adliciendas] alligi- Nac (c *ss.*).

Book 5: 6. 1 Socrates] sog- Nac, 6. 2 Socratem...Socrates...Socrati...Socrates] sogr- (*quater*) Nac.

Book 6: 6. 32. 2 Maecenas] mægenas Nac, 35. 4 execraris] -graris Nac, 35. 4 precatione] prega- Nac (*ut vid.*).

Book 7: 1. 7 consecrauit] conseg- Nac, 7. 1 sacrileg- (*ter*)] sagrileg- (*ter*) Nac, 7. 3 sacrilegium] sagri- Nac, 7. 3 sacris] sagris Nac.

t for c

Book 1: 10. 5 sciemus] sti- Nac, 15. 6 scires] sti- Nac.

Book 2: 10. 3 sciat (*ter*)] stiat Nac (*ter*), 11. 4 condicio] -tio Nac, 11. 5 condicio] -tio Nac, 25. 2 conscientia] consti- Nac, 29. 2 scientia] sti- Nac, 31. 4 condicio] -tio Nac, 33. 2 conscientiae] consti- Nac, 34. 3 scientia] sti- Nac, 34. 4 scientia] sti- Nac.

Book 3: 1. 4 conscientiam] consti- Nac, 5. 1 scientia] sti- Nac, 10. 2 conscientiam] consti- Nac, 11. 1 condicionem] -tionem Nac, 11. 2 condicio] -tio Nac, 17. 3 conscientia R] consti- N, 18. 1 condicio] -tio Nac.

Book 6: 15. 6 recessit] r&esit Nac, 42. 1 conuicium] -uitium Nac.

Book 7: 8. 3 conuicium] -uitium Nac, 12. 4 condicione] -tione Nac, 14. 3 condicionis] -tionis Nac, 23. 1 mendacio] -tio Nac.

t for *d*

Book 1: 2. 1 aliud] aliut Nac, 2. 2 illud R] illut N, 2. 3 illud] illut Nac, 2. 4 pudor] putor Nac, 3. 2 ad rem] atrem Nac, 3. 6 illud] illut Nac, 3. 7 apud] aput N (*sic fere semper*),[8] 3. 8 illud] illut Nac, 6. 2 sordida] -ta Nac, 9. 4 sordide] -te Nac, 10. 2 pudicitia] puti- Nac, 10. 5 impendio] -tio Nac, 15. 1 adferent] atf- Nac, 15. 4 pudet] put- Nac.

Book 2: 1. 3 illud] illut Nac, 2. 1 illud] illut Nac, 2. 2 intercidamus] -cetamus Nac, 3. 3 illud] illut Nac, 3. 3 ad] at Nac, 5. 3 quemadmodum] quemat- Nac, 6. 2 aliud] aliut Nac, 8. 2 illud] illut Nac, 9. 1 aliud] aliut Nac, 11. 1 istud] istut Nac, 11. 3 istud] istut Nac, 13. 2 placidaque] -taque Nac, 13. 3 ob id] obit Nac, 21. 1 illud (ρ)] illut N, 21. 4 sordidum] -tum Nac, 21. 5 ludorum] lutorum Nac, 24. 4 illud] illut Nac, 27. 2 ad] at Nac, 30. 2 quando] -to Nac, 35. 1 illud] illut Nac.

Book 3: 1. 4 pudor] putor Nac, 6. 2 illud] illut Nac, 7. 6 illud] illut Nac, 13. 1 illud] illut Nac, 15. 3 at] ad Nac, 16. 3 sordidam] -tam Nac, 18. 1 necessitudo] -tuto Nac, 24 istud] istut Nac, 28. 2 slendidos] -tos Nac, 28. 2 gradus] -tos Nac, 29. 4 gradu] -tu Nac, 30. 1 illud] illut Nac, 31. 5 aliud] aliut Nac, 35. 5 desideraret] desite- Nac, 37. 1 cadentis] caten- Nac.

Book 4: 11. 2 sordida] -dita Nac, 20. 2 adquisitoque] atquisitoque Nac, 36. 1 modus] motus Nac.

Book 5: 2. 2 gradu] -tu Nac, 9. 1 adpetendi] -ti Nac, 12. 6 id] it Nac, 21. 1 ad id] adit Nac.

Book 6: 16. 2 uitanda] -ta Nac, 32. 1 impudicitiae] imputi- Nac, 37. 2 pudet] putet Nac, 38. 3 laedantur] laet- Nac.

Book 7: 12. 1 aliquid (2°)] -quit Nac, *ut vid.*, 14. 5 desiderare] desit- Nac, 14. 6 at] ad Nac, 19. 6 aliquid] -quit Nac, *ut vid.*, 20. 2 desiderauerit] desit- Nac, 26. 1 placido] -to Nac, 26. 2 aliquid] aliquit Nac, 28. 2 candidato] -tato Nac, 31. 2 ad] at Nac.

d for *t*

Book 1: 2. 2 magnitudini] -dudini Nac, 3. 9 datas] dadas Nac, 3. 9 sit] sed Nac, 6. 2 habita] -da Nac, 7. 2 gratius] gradius Nac, 8. 2 inquit] -quid Nac (*sic fere semper*),[9] 9. 2 at] ad Nac.

Book 2: 1. 2 euitemus] euid- Nac, 1. 4 nosmet] -med Nac, 8. 1 aliquot] -quod Nac, 10. 1 confitenti] -denti Nac, 13. 3 magnitudinem] -dudinem Nac, 14. 5 atque R] ad- N, 15. 1 turpitudinem] -dudinem Nac, 17. 3 mittentis] -dis Nac, 23. 2 infitiandi] infidi- Nac, 24. 4 magnitudine] magnidudine Nac, 26. 1 ingratos] -dos Nac, 27. 2 at] ad Nac, 29. 1 magnitudine] -dudine Nac, 32. 3 arti] ardi Nac.

Book 3: 5. 1 geometriam] -driam Nac, 5. 1 magnitudo] -dudo Nac, 5. 2 atque] ad- Nac, 6. 2 atque R] ad- N, 9. 2 ualetudo] -dudo Nac, 16. 1 multitudo] -dudo Nac, 21. 2 at] ad Nac, 27. 1 atque] ad- Nac, 29. 5 crassitudinem] -dudinem Nac, 31. 4 imputas] -das Nac, 33. 4 danti] dandi Nac, 34 35. 4 atqui] adqui Nac.

Book 4: 6. 5 atque] adque Nac, 7. 2 quot] quod Nac, 11. 5 atqui] adqui Nac, 11. 6 at] ad Nac, 14. 4 relinquit] -quid Nac, 17. 3 nequitiam] -dlam (*sic*) Nac, 22. 2 pulchritudo] -dudo Nac, 23. 3 atque (ρ)] adque N, 32. 3 at] ad Nac, 33. 2 serenti...nauiganti] -di...-di Nac.

---

[8] Subsequent instances (twenty-eight times) are omitted; **R** regularly has *apud* in place of **N**'s *aput*.

[9] Subsequent instances (sixty times) are omitted; in all cases *inquit* is supplied by correction in **N**.

Book 5: 8. 3 atque R] ad- N, 9. 2 at] ad Nac, 10. 1 atqui] ad- Nac, 12. 2 quid] quit Nac, *ut vid.*, 17. 3 atqui] ad- Nac, 17. 3 timidi] dimi- Nac, 17. 5 atqui] ad- Nac, 25. 3 petendam] pedendam Nac.

Book 6: atque] ad- Nac, 9. 1 atqui] ad- Nac, 11. 2 atque] ad- Nac, 12. 2 atque] ad- Nac, 13. 3 atqui] ad- Nac, 15. 1 atqui] ad- Nac, 18. 1 atque] ad- Nac, 21. 2 quot] quod Nac, 22 atque] ad- Nac, 25. 2 desideranti] -di Nac, 31. 7 atque] adque Nac, 31. 11 atque] adque Nac.

Book 7: 1. 1 atque] ad- Nac, 2. 4 atque] ad- Nac, 4. 1 atqui] ad- Nac, 7. 1 atque R] ad- N, 19. 2 uolenti] -di Nac, 21. 1 aliquot] -quod Nac, 21. 2 rettulit] redt- Nac.

Consonantal *u* for *b*

Book 1: 3. 10 belle] uelle Nac, 9. 1 liberalitatis] liu- Nac, 10. 2 peccabitur] -uitur Nac, 10. 2 libertas] liu- Nac, 12. 3 hiberna] hiu- Nac, 14. 2 liberalitatem] liu- Nac, 14. 2 libet] liu- Nac, 14. 3 libera] liu- Nac.

Book 2: 1. 2 deliberasse] deliu- Nac, 2. 2 cibi] ciui Nac, 5. 3 liberare] liu- Nac, 7. 2 liberauit] liu- Nac, 8. 2 liberalitas] liu- Nac, 11. 3 narrabit] -uit Nac, 12. 2 liberae] liu- Nac, 14. 2 perseuerabimus] -uimus Nac, 18. 2 censebit] -uit Nac, 18. 7 liberum] liu- Nac, 19. 1 bestiariis] ues- Nac, 20. 2 tractabimus] -uimus Nac, 20. 2 libertatem] liu- Nac, 27. 2 liberauerat] liu- Nac.

Book 3: 7. 2 laudabit] -uit Nac, 8. 1 admiraberis] -ueris Nac, 8. 3 conparabit] -uit Nac, 8. 4 libenter] liu- Nac, 9. 3 aestimabit] -uit Nac, 20. 2 liberum] liu- Nac, 20. 2 iubere] iuu- Nac, 21. 2 cibaria] ciu- Nac, 21. 2 liberalius] liu- Nac, 22. 3 libidinem] liu- Nac, 24 iube] -ue Nac, 26. 2 uocabit] -uit Nac, 27. 1 parabat] -uat Nac, 27. 4 liberare] liu- Nac, 28. 3 libertini] liu- Nac, 29. 1 liberi] liu- Nac, 30. 3 nobilitaui] nou- Nac, 33. 5 disputabimus] -uimus Nac, 36. 2 optabile] -uile Nac, 36. 2 liberos] liu- Nac, 38. 3 praedicabit] -uit Nac.

Book 4: 3. 2 inuiolabiles R] -uile Nac (-les Npc), 5. 3 nauigabili] -uili Nac, 6. 1 uacabis] -uis Nac, 6. 2 uocabis] -uis Nac, 6. 4–5 boues (*bis*)] uobes (*bis*) Nac, 6. 5 pabulum] pauu- Nac, 7. 2 aptabis] -uis Nac, 13. 2 laboriosa] lau- Nac, 17. 4 optabit] -uit Nac, 19. 2 inexplicabili] -uili Nac, 19. 3 conglobauerunt] conglou- Nac, 21. 4 gubernator] guu- Nac, 23. 1 obseruabilem] -uilem Nac, 27. 2 Fabius] fau- Nac, 27. 3 libidini] liu- Nac, 29. 1 monstrabis] -uis Nac, 31. 2 iubebat] -uat Nac, 34. 3 superbum] -uum Nac, 37. 3 liberam (Npc*)] liuerauit Nac (liberauit R), 38. 1 superbae] -uae Nac.

Book 5: 2. 4 renuntiabit] -uit Nac, 5. 1 inuiolabilem (R)] -uilem N, 5. 4 superabimur] -uimur Nac, 6. 1 superbia] -uiae Nac, 6. 6 superbe] -ue Nac, 6. 7 superbo] -uo Nac, 11. 4 probabile] -uile Nac, 12. 3 probabilis Rpc] -uilis N, 19. 4 procumbis] -uis Nac, 20. 4 dilaberetur] dilau- Nac.

Book 6: 11. 2 laudabimus...castigabimus] -uimus (*bis*) Nac, 12. 2 pabulum] pau- Nac, 12. 2 boues] suo bes Nac, 17. 1 gubernatori] guu- Nac, 23. 2 inbecillitate] inue- Nac, 25. 4 gubernator] guu- Nac, 27. 2 bene] uene Nac, 31. 9 labentia] lau- Nac, 36. 1 monstrabit (*Eras.*)] -uit N, 38. 4 libitinarios] liu- N.

Book 7: 9. 5 iurabit N] -uit Nac, 14. 3 debeant] -ueant Nac, 14. 5 acerbus (Qψ)] -uus N, 15. 5 debeo] -ueo Nac, 22. 2 debet] -uet Nac, 23. 3 bonis] uobis Nac, 26. 3 miraberis] -ueris Nac, 27. 3 inbecillitas] inue- Nac, 28. 2 inbecillitatem] inue- Nac.

b for consonantal *u*

Book 1: 4. 4 Iouis (R)] -bi Nac (-bis Npc), 4. 6 nouas] -bas Nac.

Book 2: 10. 1 iuuatur] iuba- Nac, 11. 1 seruaui] -bi Nac, 29. 1 ceruos] -bos Nac, 29. 1 corui] -bi Nac.

Book 3: 3. 1 quod nouis] quodno bis Nac, 6. 2 ueneficii] bene- Nac, 37. 4 inuisi (ς₅ς₆ς₁₇)] inbiti Nac (-uiti Npc).

Book 4: 4. 2 priuata] -bata Nac, 6. 4–5 boues (*bis*)] uobes (*bis*) Nac, 11. 5 deprauat] -bat Nac, 14. 3 nouis] -bis Nac, 18. 1 iuuamur] iuba- Nac, 30. 1 nouis (Npc*)] nob· Nac, 30. 1 iuuat] -bat Nac, 31. 2 priuati] -bati Nac.

Book 5: 5. 12. 2 nouit] -bit Nac, 13. 4 uenificus] bene- Nac, 15. 5 ciuibus] cibi- Nac, 22. 2 renouabo] -babo Nac.

Book 6: 7. 3 alueo] -beo Nac, 13. 3 liberauero] -bero Nac, 31. 7 uis] bis Nac, 34. 3 haue (*Eras.*)] habe N.

Book 7: 2. 2 uilium] bi- Nac, 6. 1 Liuius ρ] Libius N, 14. 6 lassauit (Hacς₆ς₁₆ssς₁₇)] -bit N, 31. 3 ignauos] -bos Nac.

Dittography (cf. 'Anticipation', 'Perseveration')

doubling of consonants[10]

Book 1: 1. 8 defluant] deff- Nac, 3. 2 proprietas] propri|tetas Nac, 12. 3 solstitio] solis|stitio Nac, 12. 3 ubique] ubiq;|que Nac, 1. 13 reperiendi] reppe- N, 3. 1 pectore] peccatore Nac, 11. 3 tyrannicae] tirra- Nac?, 11. 5 utilius] utillius Nac.

Book 2: 3. 3 referam] reff- Nac, 15. 3 possumus] -summus Nac, 16. 2 deficit] deffic& Nac, 17. 6 referri] ref|ferri Nac, 18. 6 tyrannus (tirannus R)] tirrannus N, 18. 8 tyran- (*bis*)] tirran- (*bis*) Nac, 21. 3 defensurus] deffe- Nac, 21. 5 tyranno] tirra- Nac, 24. 1 referre] refferre Nac, 24. 4 referre] refferre Nac, 25. 2 sumus] summus Nac, 28. 2 facile] facc- Nac, 29. 2 sumus] sum|mus Nac, 35. 3 referre] reff- Nac.

Book 3: 3. 2 sumus (*bis*)] summus (*bis*) Nac, 7. 2 referre] reff- Nac, 9. 2 defendisse] deff- Nac, 12. 4 rettulerim] rettullerim Nac, 12. 4 deficiet] dif|ficiet Nac, 15. 1 colens] collens Nac, 15. 4 demus] demmus Nac, 19. 3 tyranni] tyrr- Nac, 20. 2 possumus R] -summus N, 23. 1 referam] reff- Nac, 30. 4 noli tibi] nollittibi Nac, 35. 4 referre] reff- Nac, 35. 4 referri] reff- Nac, 36. 3 sumite] summite Nac, 37. 4 patri] pattri Nac (*ut vid.*), 37. 4 remissurum] rem missurum Nac.

Book 4: 6. 2 moles] moll- Nac, 6. 5 paucas] pacucas Nac, 6. 5 pascua] pasccua Nac, 12. 2 defendo] deff- Nac, 17. 3 agi sibi] agissibi Nac?, 17. 4 reperies] repp- N, 18. 2 animali-bus R] anni- N, 22. 4 comitata] commi- Nac, 30. 2 Persicum] -siccum Nac.

Book 5: 1. 5 repetant] reppetant Nac, 7. 6 potest] p potest Nac, 12. 6 stomachus] stomm- Nac, 14. 5 colite] collite Nac, 17. 2 Catilinam…Catilina] catilli- (*bis*) Nac, 17. 4 supremum (CQOVK)] supp- N, 17. 7 grati simus] gratissimus Nac, 20. 4 solemni] soll- Nac, 23. 1 uelis] uellis Nac.

Book 6: 5. 2 aureos (au#|reos)] aur|reos Nac?, 9. 3 imitabor] immi- Nac, 15. 2 emis a] emissa Nac, 40. 1 si tibi] sit tibi Nac.

Book 7: 2. 3 intolerabilis] intolle- Nac, 27. 3 intolerabile] intoll- N, 28. 1 rettuleris] retulleris Nac.

---

[10] The doubling of vowels is much less common: e.g., 2. 2. 2 quin] qui in Nac, 4. 5. 2 naturae] natu-urae Nac, 28. 2 ferunt] fuerunt Nac, 5. 7. 5 imperat] -raat Nac, 7. 17. 2 quin] qui|in Nac.

doubling of syllables or words

Book 2: 7. 1 sit] sit||sit N (sit 1° *eras.*, sit 2° *cancel.* ; sit R)

Book 3: 38. 2 siue (2°)] siue siue Nac

Book 4: 11. 3 reuersurus] reuersus|rus Nac, 21. 1 bono (bono##)] *fort.* bonono Nac, 22. 3 tutior] tutitior Nac, 34. 5 lubricam (lu##b-)] ludibricam Nac?

Book 5: 7. 2 Stoicos] stocicos Nac (*ut vid.*), 9. 1 oportet (R)] orpor- N, 11. 3 beneficium (4°)] beneneficium Nac, 12. 6 mutat] mutatat Nac, 16. 2 sentiet] sententiet Nac, 16. 5 solebat] sole|solebat Nac

Book 6: 18. 1 exegisset] exegisset & Nac, 18. 1 sedulitate] sed utilitatem Nac, 25. 3 locum] loco cum Nac (*post* officio), 35. 5 infitiationem] infini|tiationem Nac, 40. 2 subsidere] subdesidere Nac

Book 7: 4. 8 sic uetant] sicut &ant Nac, 14. 4 sedulitatis] sed utilitatis Nac.

Haplography

Book 1: 2. 4 aut occasio] autcasio Nac, 3. 1 perdidisse] perdisse Nac, 3. 1 tuis] tus Nac, 3. 3 alii (1°)] ali Nac,[11] 3. 10 suum] sum Nac, 8. 2 diuitiis] -tis Nac, 13. 1 tolleret] -re Nac (*ante* cor-), 13. 1 Corinthii] -thi Nac, 13. 3 summum] sumum Nac, 15. 5 Claudii] claudi Nac, 15. 6 oportet] opt& Nac.

Book 2: 8. 1 certas] -ta Nac (*ante* summas), 9. 2 ignominiae (*fort. pr. man.*)] -nomiae Nac, 11. 3 committendum] -mitendum Nac, 12. 1 prorsus] prosus Nac,[12] 12. 2 ingessisset] ingesi- Nac (*corr. pr. man.*), 14. 3 inflammabat] inflama- Nac, 18. 2 difficilis] -le Nac (*ante* est), 18. 2 suaserit] suar& Nac, 22 laetitiae est] laetitiaest Nac, 24. 2 statim] statm Nac, 27. 3 flammae] flamae Nac, 30. 1 loqueremur] loquemur Nac, 30. 2 nullius] -lus Nac, 31. 4 reddidi] reddi Nac, 32. 1 consummauit] -sumauit Nac, 34. 3 repellendorum] replendorum Nac, 35. 2 abhorrent] -ren Nac (*ante* deinde).

Book 3: 1. 2 quae recentia] quaerentia Nac, 13. 1 infitiatores] infitiares Nac, 15. 2 parariis] -ris Nac, 18. 1 filii] fili Nac, 19. 2 ut ille] utile Nac, 20. 1 sui iuris] suiuris Nac, 31. 2 consummatam] -sumatam Nac, 37. 2 transcurrerent] transcurrent Nac.

Book 4: 3. 2 facillime] facili me Nac, 6. 4 tener (te *ss. pr. man, ut vid.*)] ner Nac, 6. 6 ad (1°) (d *add. pr. man., ut vid.*)] a Nac, 8. 2 suum (u *ss. fort. pr. man.*)] sum Nac, 8. 3 dixisses] -se Nac (*ante* siue), 8. 3 nomina (in *ss. fort. pr. man.*)] noma Nac, 11. 3 auctore] acture Nac, 12. 2 accusatoribus] acu- Nac, 12. 3 salubritatis] -britis Nac, 12. 4 eadem] edem Nac, 13. 1 tenerrimisque (Npc2, ri *ss.*)] tenermisque Nac, tenerisque Npc1 (m *expunct.*), 18. 1 dissociat] diso- Nac, 18. 1 subitas] sub|tas Nac, 18. 2 sanguis] -gus Nac, 18. 2 hominem] -ne Nac (*ante* in-), 19. 1 metuendus] metuens Nac, 21. 1 propositi] propiti Nac, 21. 4 consummatae (BMψ)] -sumatae N, 21. 6 suppliciis] -cis

---

[11] Some instances of -*i* for -*ii* and -*is* for -*iis* in the endings of second decl. nouns and adjs in -*ius* / -*ium* could reflect variations in spelling used by S. (see also the next n.). Since I will normalize spelling in my edition (-*ii*, -*iis*), I put the variations on record here: they are not numerous (four instances in Book 1, two in Book 3, one each in Books 4 and 5, none in Books 2, 6, 7). A form in -*is* produces a preferable clausular cadence at 3. 15. 2 (-*tis pararis facit* = double cretic vs. -*tis parariis facit* = cretic + double iamb), where I have decided to admit it.

[12] **N**'s scribe wrote *prosus* here and at 7. 2. 6, *prorsus* at 3. 30. 4; the former is widely attested (*TLL* 10. 2154. 59–63), and it is conceivably what Seneca wrote. In both places the change to *prorsus* in **N** is certainly early (**R** has only that form) and probably scribal (I would say certainly scribal at 2. 12. 1); to judge from the apparatus in Reynolds's editions of *Dial.* (*Ira* 1. 20. 8) and *EM* (12. 3, 47. 18, 54. 1, 70. 2, 87. 23), the manuscripts of those works offer only *prorsus* (the adverb does not occur in **NQ**). From among similar adverbs, *rursus* (nine times), *introrsus*, and *quorsus* (once each) are spelled only thus in **N** (*retrorsus/m*, *deorsus/m*, and *sursus/m* do not occur).

Nac, 25. 2 moliantur] molantur Nac, 25. 2 molliant] moli- Nac, 27. 2 proditor] protor Nac, 28. 1 statos] -to Nac (*ante* flatu), 28. 6 quod de] quo de Nac, 29. 3 iudicem] dicem Nac (*post* eum), 31. 4 mihi (Npc*, chi *add. ss.*)] mi Nac, 32. 2 uinci] unci Nac, 35. 2 promittente] promitte Nac, 36. 2 ait] at Nac, 37. 1 Philippus] Philipus Nac, 37. 3 Philippus R] Philipus N, 38. 1 praeclusurus] p̄clus‖us Nac, 39. 2 appellare] ape- N.

Book 5: 1. 3 tam] am Nac (*post* uidi: *ex* VIDITAM?), 3. 2 summittit] -mitit Nac, 4. 4 ceteris] teris Nac, 5. 1 aduersus] adsus Nac, 6. 1 beneficiis] -cis Nac, 6. 7 uolentem] -te Nac (*ante* nihil), 7. 5 commodare] como- Nac, 10. 2 quod datur] quo datur Nac, 11. 2 et ut] ut Nac, 11. 5 inducit] ducit Nac (*post* spem), 12. 1 difficultates] difi- Nac, 12. 7 profuturaque] proturaque Nac, 13. 4 accipit R] acipit N, 14. 2 antequam manus (ma *ss. pr. man.*)] antequamanus Nac, 15. 4 uenenis] uenis Nac, 16. 4 reddidit] reddid Nac (*ante* ut), 17. 1 currere] curre‖ Nac, 17. 1 coepero (Npc2, ce- Npc1)] ‖pero Nac, 17. 2 pernegauit] pernauit Nac, 18 quousque] quosque Nac, 19. 1 mei] ei Nac (*post* dicam), 20. 5 nec non] nec Nac, 20. 5 nullum in] nullum Nac, 22. 4 admonitione] admotione Nac, 23. 1 in iniuriam] iniuriam Nac, 24. 1 in Hispania] inspania Nac, 24. 2 a cognitione] agnitione Nac, 25. 4 religiose] reliose Nac.

Book 6: 5. 2 reddidi] reddi Nac, *ut vid.*, 7. 4 lanceae] lancae Nac, 8. 1 sic quidam] siquidam Nac, 13. 2 incommodo] incomo- Nac, 14. 4 emissem] -se Nac (*ante* in), 15. 2 occupationis] -ni Nac (*ante* suae), 15. 3 pluris] pluri Nac (*ante* est), 15. 7 solitudine] soltudine Nac, 16. 6 admonitionibus] admonibus Nac, 19. 1 mea] me Nac (*ante* ad), 26. 2 sanandus] sandus Nac, 27. 1 sollicitudinem] soli- Nac, 28. 2 nullius] nullus Nac, 28. 3 potestate (*pr. man., ut vid.*)] potate Nac, 30. 2 referre] -fere Nac, 30. 6 summum] sumum Nac, 31. 8 quod] quo Nac (*ante* dicitur), 31. 8 toto te] tote Nac, 31. 11 demaratus (-rathus Npc)] dematus Nac, 31. 11 Demarato (-ratho Npc)] demato Nac, 32. 2 difficile] difi- Nac, 37. 3 difficultatibis] difi- Nac, 38. 5 pectoris sui] pectorisui Nac, 40. 2 quo modo] quo mo Nac, 41. 1 cupiditatem] cupitatem Nac, 43. 1 quam dantur] quantur Nac, 43. 3 qui nimis] quimis Nac.

Book 7: 1. 5 fata diuersa] fat aduersa Nac, 1. 6 difficilis] diffilis Nac, 2. 1 meditatione] meditaone Nac, 2. 4 in incerta] incerta Nac, 2. 6 prorus] prosus Nac, 4. 1 sapientis] -ti Nac (*ante* sunt), 4. 2 dicimur (ci *ss. pr. man., ut vid.*)] dimur Nac, 4. 6 deorum] dorum Nac, 6. 1 Ciceronis] cironis Nac, 7. 1 tollit] tolit Nac, 7. 2 effringi] fringi Nac, 7. 3 sed non] sed Nac, 7. 5 decerneretur] decernetur Nac, 8. 2 prout] pro Nac, 9. 5 etiam ad] etiamd Nac, 11. 1 summam] sumam Nac, 12. 6 tuum] tum Nac, 13 amantes] -te Nac (*ante* solent), 15. 1 creditoris] -dioris Nac, 15. 3 uult] uul Nac, 15. 4 succedit] suce- Nac (*fort. corr. pr. man.*), 16. 1 reddidisse (ρ.)] rededisset Nac (rededisse Npc R), 16. 4 redderes] rede- Nac, 18. 2 uti] ut Nac (*ante* illo), 19. 8 auiditate] auitate Nac, 19. 8 reddere] redere Nac, 20. 3 regum] regnum Nac, 22. 1 honestissimae] honesti‖simae Nac, 26. 2 infelicitas] felicas Nac, 26. 4 quid leuitatem] qui le- Nac, 26. 5 familiarissimorum] falia- Nac, 27. 3 dissociet] diso- Nac, 27. 3 dissupet] disu- Nac, 28. 1 iuuenem] iue- Nac, 31. 4 distribuunt (*fort. pr. man.*)] -bunt Nac, 31. 5 deterruit] deteru- Nac.

Anticipation

Book 1: 1. 13 antecedit] diante- Nac (*ante* dicam), 1. 13 quod] quo Nac (*ante* sentio), 10. 5 tribuemusque] tribuemus‖quem Nac (*ante* non), 11. 5 factura] -ri Nac, *ut vid.* (*ante* in), 12. 3 ne cui] nec cui Nac; cf. 9. 3 prostare] prostrare Nac.

Book 2: 5. 2 tanti] -to Nac (*ante* malo), 6. 1 quomodo] quodmodo Nac, 13. 3 tumultuosius] -tiosius Nac, 19. 2 posui] posuit Nac (*ante* tyrannum), 27. 2 sua] suo Nac (*ante* diuo Augusto).

Book 3: 4. 2 aliquis incidere] -quid incedere Nac, 8. 3 quae] quem Nac (*ante* non rem), 19. 2 ipsa (*corr. pr. man.*)] ipse Nac (*ante* lege), 23. 2 satiatus] -tum Nac (*ante* miles), 24 dederim] -rit Nac (*ante* uixit), 26. 2 anulum] ex anulum Nac (*ante* extraxit), 27. 4 manu] manum Nac (*ante* missum), 35. 1 ita] itam (i.e., -ā) Nac (*ante* dicam), 35. 2 liberatus] -to Nac (*ante* periculo), 35. 4 gratia] -tiam Nac (*ante* in maius), 37. 2 recedente] -tem Nac (*ante* limitem).

Book 4: 5. 3 uis] uisa Nac (*ante* aestiui), 6. 6 aetatum (Npc*)] -tium Nac (*et post et ante* omnium), 16. 2 probationes] -ne Nac (*ante* nostrę), 17. 3 quos] quod Nac (*ante* ad-), 17. 3 pudorique] -risque Nac (*ante* est), 18. 4 qua] quia Nac, *ut vid.* (*ante* uita), 21. 1 qui (1°)] quia Nac (*ante* ali-), 21. 4 qui (3°)] Iqui Nac (*ante* in), 22. 1 rebus] remus Nac (*ante* humanis), 23. 2 mundus (*fort. pr. man.*)] musdus Nac, 27. 3 natura] -ram Nac (*ante* ad auaritiam), 39. 2 illud (1°)] illi Nac (*ante* mali).

Book 5: 1. 3 neminem] memi- Nac, 3. 1 suos magno] suos certaminibus magno Nac (*expunx. pr. man.*), 4. 1 potes] potest Nac (*ante* et), 6. 4 transcursu] -sus Nac (*ante* strinxit), 6. 4 media] -dias Nac (*ante* successit), 7. 4 et (2°)] ut Nac (*ante* ut ita), 9. 3 dedi] dedit Nac (*ante* iterum), 9. 3 periculo] -lum Nac (*ante* beneficium), 10. 3 exemplis] -pli Nac (*ante* prosequi), 11. 4 aliquis ut] aliquisui Nac (*ante* alteri), 11. 4 sibi dat] sibitdat Nac, 11. 5 dabit et] et dabit Nac, 12. 2 nodo operose] nodoso|perose Nac, *ut vid.*, 17. 2 diruti] diruiti Nac, 19. 4 si] sic Nac (*ante* hic), 19. 6 peruenit ad] perueniat Nac, 19. 9 adfinibus] adinfibus Nac, 22. 1 ingrati] -tis Nac (*ante* segnes), 24. 1 spargente] -tem Nac (*ante* cum).

Book 6: 5. 4 illi] illi & Nac (*post* et beneficium, *ante* debeam et), 14. 4 non] ha- Nac (*librarius* habuissem, *quod sequitur, scribere coepit, dein* ha eras.), 23. 4 seruare] rer- Nac, 23. 4 ultima] -mam Nac (*ante* habitam), 27. 2 quanto satius] quantusatius Nac, 30. 5 ignorauere] -ueres Nac (*ante* uires suas), 31. 12 in qua] inquam Nac (*post* quam, *ante* nemo), 33. 3 creditur abundare] creditu|ra ab- Nac, 33. 4 qui (2°)] quia Nac, 38. 1 morte] -tem Nac (*ante* non), 38. 1 tamen] to Nac (*ante* solet).

Book 7: 1. 7 otii] ostii Nac (*ante* sunt), 9. 1 pretia] -tias Nac (*ante* sanguinis), 11. 2 me] meo Nac (*ante* constituerat toto), 12. 1 liberi] liberis Nac (*ante* sunt), 12. 2 sciat se] sciasse Nac, 19. 7 Phalarim] -rit Nac, *ut vid.* (*ante* et), 21. 1 qui scis] quis scis Nac, 22. 1 quaere] quaerei Nac (*ante* cui), 26. 2 iniuria] -riam Nac (*ante* impellat), 27. 1 si] sit Nac (*ante* tibi), 27. 3 concordiam] -dia Nac, *ut vid.* (*ante* qua), 30. 2 exacerbare] exarcer- Nac.

Perseveration

Book 1: 3. 6 interpretationem] -num Nac (*post* Horum nominum), 11. 1 quo] quod Nac (*post* quod…quod…), 13. 3 simile] -lem Nac (*post* enim).

Book 2: 1. 4 facienda] -dam Nac (*post* palam), 5. 3 uenturi] -tura Nac (*post* maxima), 11. 5 uis] suis Nac (*post* gratos), 18. 6 dignus] -num Nac (*post* parum), 20. 2 urbis] turbis (*post* aut) Nac.

Book 3: 2. 2 uirtute] -tem Nac (*post* gratiam N, gratia *Gertz*), 3. 4 conlata] -tam Nac (*post* -tiam -tram), 37. 2 insulae] -lame Nac (*post* magnam).

Book 4: 6. 6 aetatum (Npc*)] -tium Nac (*et post et ante* omnium), 11. 2 ei nulla (#ei nulla)] se inulla Nac (*post* spes), 11. 6 intestatis] -ti Nac (*post* recepturi), 12. 2 gratia] -tiam Nac (*post* reum, *ante* laborantem), 14. 3 sine gloria] sine|ingloria Nac, 17. 1 ingrato] -tos Nac (*post* nullus), 18. 1 tuti] tuto Nac (*post* alio), 18. 1 quam quod] nam quod Nac (*post* nam quo), 21. 4 quid] qui Nac (*post* si), 24. 2 uolebam] -bat Nac (*post* cogitat), 33. 3 cessura] censura Nac (*post* bene), 34. 3 et (2°)] set Nac (*post* negas).

Book 5: 6. 2 gratias] grates gratias Nac (*post* Sogrates), 8. 4 primum] sum|mum Nac (*post* nihil summum), 9. 1 a qua ad] a quo a Nac, 9. 2 clementia] -tia est Nac (*post* liberalitas est), 10. 3 diutius] diutius est Nac (*post* partium est), 11. 4 alteri dedit] alteri dedit alteri Nac, 11. 5 dare] sibi dare Nac (*post* sibi dat), 12. 1 bona] bonam Nac (*post* operam), 15. 6 omni] -nis Nac (*post* bellis), 20. 4 accessit] -si Nac (*post* commodi), 20. 7 quam] aquam Nac (*post* ista), 25. 6 ad] aut Nac (*post* aut altero uerbo).

Book 6: 3. 2 ignari] signari Nac (*post* urbes), 4. 6 paenitentia] penitentiam Nac (*post* dantem), 7. 1 aliquid qui] aliquid quid Nac, 12. 2 boues] suo bes Nac (*post* op(t)imos), 27. 4 post] potest Nac (*post* est), 30. 3 ipsaque consuetudine] ipsamque -nem Nac (*post* stupentem), 31. 12 in qua] inquam Nac (*post* quam), 34. 1 propius] proprius Nac (*post* proprium).

Book 7: 2. 1 eoque] eo quo Nac, 2. 2 ministerio] -ium Nac (*post* uilium), 2. 4 suo] suum Nac (*post* dubium), 10. 3 quaesita] -tam Nac (*post* naturam), 16. 3 fidem] fides Nac (*post* homines), 19. 5 natura] -ram Nac (*post* tantam), 20. 2 id quo] id quod Nac, 28. 3 publico] in publico Nac (*post* inique), 28. 3 conuiciantis] conuin|ciantis Nac, 31. 4 auctore] -rem Nac (*post* beneficiorum).

Aspiration error

h added

Book 1: 2. 5 ora] hora Nac, 3. 1 onerat] hon- Nac, 4. 6 ac] hac Nac, 9. 3 ac] hac Nac, 11. 4 ac] hac Nac, 11. 5 abundanti] ha- Nac, 12. 3 abundat] ha- Nac, 13. 2 ac] hac Nac, 14. 1 ac] hac Nac.

Book 2: 2. 1 oneroso] hon- Nac, 14. 3 ac] hac Nac, 21. 5 ab eo] habeo Nac.

Book 3: 6. 2 Macedonum] mache- Nac, 13. 2 erimus] herimus Nac, 18. 1 an] han Nac?, 28. 2 ac] hac Nac, 28. 5 ostium] hos- Nac, >*1515*, 28. 5 ostiarii] hostiari Nac, 36. 2 ac] hac, 36. 2 an] han Nac.

Book 4: 1. 3 abunde] hab- Nac, 11. 3 abituris] ha- Nac, 27. 3 aciem] haciem Nac, 30. 4 inertes] in|hertes Nac, 37. 2 is] his Nac.

Book 5: 1. 4 abes] habes Nac, 6. 1 Thraciae] trachiae Nac, 6. 4 animum] ha- Nac, 6. 7 is] his Nac, 8. 6 nihilo minus] nihil ho- Nac, 12. 2 nihilo minus] nihil ho- Nac.

Book 6: 11. 2 inertem] inher- Nac, 23. 4 is (1°)] his Nac, 34. 1 ostio] hos- Nac.

Book 7: 8. 2 Socraten] -then Nac, 10. 2 aut (2°)] haut Nac.

h omitted

Book 1: 3. 4 pulcherrimus] pulcer- Nac, 15. 2 adhortatio] ador- Nac.

Book 2: 3. 3 hodie] odiae Nac, 9. 1 pulchrius] pulcrius Nac, 19. 1 amphitheatro] ampi- N (R), 35. 3 exhortatio] exor- Nac.

Book 3: 13. 2 pulchritudine R] pulcridu- N, 37. 1 hostium] os- N.

Book 4: 13. 2 extrahant (*corr. pr. man.?*)] -traant Nac, 15. 1 hortantia] or- Nac, 20. 3 hamum] amum Nac, 21. 1 hominis] ominis Nac, 22. 4 pulcherrima] pulcer- Nac, 22. 4 trahunt] traunt Nac, 23. 2 detrahas] -traas Nac, 28. 1 haustus] ausitus Nac, 29. 3 nihil] nil Nac, 33. 2 hac] ac Nac.

Book 5: 6. 1 Thraciae] trachiae Nac, 6. 2 Archelaus] arce- Nac.

Book 6: 6. 5. 4 schola] scola Nac.

Book 7: 3. 1 hauritur] auri- Nac.

Misreadings of *scriptura continua* (a selection)

Book 1: 1. 2 ingrati animi. id euenire] ingra|tia nimii deuenire Nac, 1. 11 mallent esse patitur] mallen| tes sepatitur Nac, 3. 5 quales solent qui dant] qualis solentes sequidant Nac (-lis Pré.), 3. 8 ita ut] it aut Nac, 4. 1 tenue retunditur] tenuere tunditur Nac, 4. 5 aures oblectare] auresublec- Nac,, 11. 1 exornat aut] exornata ut Nac, 11. 6 feminae aut] feminea ut Nac (*cauda* added to second *e* by the hand that separated *e* and *a*), 11. 6 dedito retia (rae- Npc)] deditur aetia Nac, 14. 1 stabularii aut] stabularia|ut Nac, 15. 4 exitura descendunt (d 2° *in ras.*)] exitur adesce[#?][#?]unt Nac.

Book 2: 12. 1 aiunt socculum] aiuncto culum Nac, 20. 1 disputari de M.] disputa idem Nac, 21. 2 illi pecuniam (*fort. pr. man.*)] illunecunia Nac, 29. 5 esse te malles] essit emalles Nac, 35. 5 maria emetienda] mariae mentienda Nac.

Book 3: 8. 4 inibit aetimationem] -bita | aestimationem Nac, 12. 2 ille ornamenta] illeor menta Nac, 14. 2 materiam litium] materia militium Nac, 33. 1 hostes equum] hostae secum Nac (hostes ecum *Hos.*), 34 prima elementa] primæ lementa Nac.

Book 4: 2. 2 stare; tu illam] star& uillam Nac, 4. 1 maxima Epicuro] maximepicuro Nac, 6. 1 negas esse] negasse se Nac, 6. 1 flumina emisit] flumine misit Nac, 6. 1 ac latentium] adate tium Nac, 8. 3 accepisses. Annaeo] -se san- Nac, 15. 3 quem e] que me Nac, 19. 4 cuius te] cum|iuste Nac, 20. 3 qui aegro] quia ęgo Nac, 30. 3 ablatas #e] ablata[#?]|se Nac, 34. 2 obrepsit at] orepsitat Nac.

Book 5: 3. 1 Laecedaemonii (*bis*)] lacae demonii (*bis*) N (clemonii 1°), 6. 4 timentem e] timente|me Nac, 6. 4 ista solis] stas olis Nac, 6. 4 obiectu sui abscondit] obiectus uia ab- Nac, 9. 1 nocitura uitandi] nocitur|auitadi Nac, 12. 2 quod erepant] quo derepant Nac, 17. 7 plus sed] pluss|ed Nac, 19. 8 altercatione seposita] -nes epo- Nac? (-e se- in ras.).

Book 6: 1 erit aut peragi] erita uper agi Nac, 3. 1 praeter ius] praeterius Nac, 3. 2 in depositi causa (cau|sa Npc)] inde positi ca|usa Nac, 15. 2 rem inaestimabilem] remina|estimabilem Nac, 17. 1 opera enixior] operæ nixior Nac, 27. 2 quanto satius] quantusatius Nac, 31. 4 qua sibi] quas|ibi Nac, 31. 12 capite tiaram] capit|etiaram Nac, 32. 3 tota uita] totauit Nac, 35. 1 nihilo minus] nichil ominus Nac (nih- Npc R).

Book 7: 1. 5 fata diuersa] fat aduersa Nac, 3. 1 prisci stemma] priscis|temma Nac, 4. 8 sic uetant] sicut &ant Nac, 5. 1 nihilo minus] nihil ominus N (*sic fere semper*), 7. 3 conspectu siderum] conspectus|derum Nac, 15. 1 litora emensum] litore men-sum Nac, 15. 2 Hercules Atheniensium] -le sath- Nac, 15. 2 operis enituit (*pr. man.?*)] operi sentuit Nac, 19. 6 siluas eruperunt] silua se ruperunt Nac, 20. 2 subministrabo ψ (summ- CQUJV)] sum mi- N, 20. 2 marmora et uestes] marmorae tu|estes Nac, 21. 2 redit (*perf.*) ad eandem R] reddi ita deandem Nac (redi it adeandem Npc), 28. 1 nostro paulatim] nos propaulatim Nac, 31. 4 sortiti spargunt] sortitis parcunt Nac.

Miscellaneous confusions, omissions, additions, and substitutions that fall into none of the preceding categories:

Book 1: 1. 2 effetum] effectum Nac (*ut vid.*), 2. 5 inpune] in|pugne Nac, 33. 2 soluta ac] solutaque hac Nac, 3. 6 illis] illius Nac, 4. 3 sunt] sum, 5. 4 eripuit] pipuit Nac, 8. 1 reliquisse] relin- Nac, 9. 3 admissis] amis- Nac, 10. 4 admissum] amis- Nac, 10. 5 quae-dam] quae Nac, 11. 2 quaedam (1°)] quandam Nac, 12. 4 fastidium] -dio Nac, 13. 1 animos] -mo Nac, 13. 2 honorem] -re Nac (-ē *sec. cur.*, *ut vid.*), 15. 2 aperire] ac perire Nac, 15. 3 honesta] -tam Nac, 15. 6 puto] peto Nac (*ut vid.*), 15. 6 malam] mala Nac (*ut vid.*)

Book 2: 1. 2 gratiam] -tia Nac, 3. 3 ad me] a me Nac, 4. 2 minimum] animum Nac (*ut vid.*), 4. 2 rogandus (*corr. pr. man.*)] rogatus Nac, 10. 1 fallendus] fauellendus Nac, 10. 1 inutiliter] inute iliter Nac, 10. 4 admoneam (*corr. pr. man.*)] amoneam Nac, 11. 1 sinis] sine Nac, 15. 3 fastidiat] fastiz- Nac, 17. 1 talentum] talenpum Nac, 17. 3 exibit] exhibuit Nac, 17. 4 exercitato] -tio Nac, 18. 7 excipio] -pit Nac, 18. 7 an (2°)] ac Nac, 19. 2 quia] qui Nac, 21. 1 redemptore] -torem Nac, 21. 3 aliquis dignus] aliquidignis Nac, 29. 4 negatum] -tus Nac, 29. 5 indulgentia] -tiam Nac, 35. 1 refugiat] -gat Nac, 35. 2 quos] quod Nac.

Book 3: 1. 1 quosdam] quodam Nac, 1. 4 debent] -b& Nac, 2. 3 ad quod] aquod Nac, 8. 3 arentibus] arien- Nac, 9. 2 momentis] -ti Nac, 18. 2 repentina] -nam Nac, 21. 2 erudiuntur] eruuntur Nac, 22. 1 altius] alius Nac, 23. 5 misi] misit Nac, 27. 1 Caesarem] caesar Nac, 28. 5 inquam] -quan Nac, 29. 8 ipsum] ipsud Nac, 32. 2 gentes] -te Nac, 32. 2 suos] suo Nac, 32. 3 Xenophontem] xenph- Nac, 32. 5 filio] -lium Nac, 32. 5 quantam] -to Nac?, 33. 3 nobili (-li##)] -lium Nac *ut vid.*, 33. 4 patrum] -truum Nac, 33. 5 etiam] &am Nac, 34 beneficium] -cioum Nac, 34 mei] ne Nac, 35. 2 beneficium] -cioum Nac, 35. 4 uinci] uincit uinci Nac, 35. 5 perituram] -tura Nac, 36. 1 illis] illi Nac, 36. 2 ipsos] ipso Nac, 36. 3 optantes] -tates Nac, 37. 4 stringit] strmgit Nac, 37. 4 potestate] -tem Nac, 38. 2 uerborum] ueborum Nac, 38. 2 ingenii] -genti Nac, 38. 2 quantum] -tus Nac, 38. 2 hominum] homineum Nac, 38. 3 fortunatius (-ti#us Npc2)] -tious Nac, -tiuus Npc1.

Book 4: 1. 2 ulla…parsimonia] ullam…parsimoniam Nac, 2. 2 ordine] -nem Nac, 2. 3 sequor] secor Nac, 3. 1 Nunc (n *ss. pr. man.*)] Nuc Nac, 3. 3 fenus] -num Nac, 4. 3 expertes] exp&rtes Nac, 5. 2 ciborum (ci#b-)] cimb- Nac (*ut vid.*), 5. 3 uasto] uato Nac, 5. 3 quid in ipsis] qui inpissis Nac, 6. 3 quem] quae Nac, 6. 3 unde (4°) (n *ss. pr. man.*, *ut vid.*)] ude Nac, 6. 4 es] est Nac, 6. 5 calamo] -mos Nac, 7. 1 post] pos Nac, 7. 2 eundem (n *ss. pr. man.*, *ut vid.*)] eud- Nac, 8. 1 Mercurium] -rius Nac, 9. 1 sine] si In Nac (*corr. man. post.*), 10. 2 quemadmodum] -modo Nac, 11. 3 ut scias] uscias Nac, 11. 3 conscientia] -tiam Nac, 11. 5 ad] an Nac, 12. 2 obligaturus] -gatum us Nac, 12. 2 ipse] inse Nac, 12. 5 ergo] ego Nac, 14. 2 ergo] ego Nac, 14. 4 ipso] -sos Nac, 15. 1 uitanda] -dam Nac, 16. 2 inutilem] -tile Nac, 17. 2 opinionem] -ne Nac, 18. 2 facillimus] facillissimus Nac, 18. 2 unguium uis] -gium ius Nac, 18. 2 terribilem] -le Nac, 19. 2 contactu] contractu Nac, 19. 3 grato ut] gato & Nac, 19. 4 esse? huius] essemus Nac, 20. 3 qui (1°)] Inui Nac *ut vid.*, 20. 3 qui (2°)] quid Nac, 21. 5 ipsam] ipsa Nac, 21. 6 quid ####mihi] quid di[#?][#?]mihi Nac, 22. 2 ipso] ipsos Nac, 22. 2 animos] -mus Nac, 23. 4 seducti] -ducit Nac, 24. 2 est] es Nac, 25. 2 commodo (quo *expunct.*, commo *ss.*)] quodo Nac, 25. 3 beneficium] been- Nac, 27. 1 dicitur] -mur Nac, 27. 5 damnato] -napo Nac, 28. 2 frumentum (*corrr. pr. man.*, *ut vid.*)] -tus Nac, 30. 4 qualiscumque] quali|cumque Nac (*ut vid.*), 31. 4 uerbo] uebo Nac, 31. 5 fasces] faces Nac, 32. 2 potest (t *ss.*)] po est Nac, 33. 3 conperta (com- Npc)] coperta Nac, 34. 3 quod] quoi Nac (*ut vid.*), 36. 1 dignus] dignu Nac, 37. 1 habebat] -ba Nac, 37. 1 transtulit] trant- Nac, 37. 3 stigmata] stima- Nac, 37. 4 inscriberentur] -retur Nac, 37. 4 litus] litu Nac, 37. 5 misericors] -cos Nac, 38. 1 a cognito] adcognito Nac, 38. 2 naufragio (*fort. pr. man.*)] naf- Nac.

Book 5: 1. 1 quo (2°)] quod Nac, 1. 3 natura] -ram Nac, 1. 4 usque eo (usque##eo)] usque adeo Nac (*fort.*), 1. 5 mora] moram Nac, 2. 4 enim] e Nac, 2. 4 morietur] orietur Nac, 4. 1 fortuna] fot- Nac, 4. 2 uincitur] -cimur Nac, 4. 3 fortuna (*corr. pr. man.*)] fot- Nac, 6. 1 rex] lex Nac, 6. 3 ac] a Nac, 6. 6 Archelao] ache- Nac, 7. 1 hanc (*corr. pr. man.*)] hac Nac, 7. 5 agit] agi Nac, 7. 6 damno] damn Nac (o *add. ss.*), 9. 3 gratiam (2°)] gratia Nac, 9. 4 nos] non Nac, 10. 4 secundam] secud- Nac, 10. 4 pulcherrima] pulchrerima

Nac, 11. 2 abutimur] -tur Nac, 12. 3 honesta et] honesta ut Nac, 12. 6 miseriae] miseri Nac, 13. 2 uiro] a uiro Nac, 14. 2 atque] aque Nac, 14. 3 ratione (ratio *ss. pr. man.*)] ne Nac, 15. 4 potentia] -iam Nac, 15. 5 senatus] sena Nac, 19. 6 profueris] fueris Nac, 22. 1 referre] -ret Nac, 22. 1 hos] hoc Nac.

Book 6: 4. 4 recepit] receperat Nac (*ut vid.*), 4. 4 ne] nec Nac, 5. 5 ego cum] ego sum Nac, 6. 3 superueniens] -ies Nac, 7. 1 colligit] -gi Nac, 7. 3 equi] &qui Nac, 7. 4 quid (2º)] qui Nac, 11. 1 loca] locum Nac (*ut vid.*), 12. 1 profuit] -fui Nac, 12. 1 inquis] iniquis Nac, 13. 1 sum tam] su&am Nac, 15. 2 ualetudinem] -ne Nac (*ut vid.*), 15. 3 empta] epta Nac, 15. 7 fultura] futura Nac, 16. 1 ex medico et] ex medico Nac, 16. 4 suspecta] -tam Nac, 19. 5 quis] qis Nac, 20. 2 prosit] possit Nac, 23. 1 umquam] um Nac, 23. 4 accepturos] accepituros Nac, 23. 6 fine] finem Nac, 25. 3 ad N] a Nac, 25. 4 succurrat] -ant Nac, 27. 1 tui] tu Nac, 27. 5 uis] suis Nac, 27. 5 succurri] -rit Nac, 29. 1 numquam (*corr. pr. man., ut vid.*)] num Nac, 30. 2 summa] -mam Nac, 30. 2 uaria materia] -iam -iam Nac, 30. 5 rupere] upere Nac, 31. 4 multitudinem] -ne Nac (*ut vid.*), 31. 4 numquam] un- Nac, 31. 11 obstiterat] obsiste- Nac, 32. 2 pressisset] res- Nac, 35. 5 inprecaris] imprecars Nac, 37. 1 expulerat] -ra Nac, 38. 1 fortasse] -ses Nac, 38. 2 empto] epto Nac.

Book 7: 1. 4 sic] si Nac, 1. 7 contempsit] contep- Nac, 2. 2 uentri] uetri Nac, 4. 8 pecunia] -niam Nac (*ut vid.*), 6. 1 rettuli] ret|tulit Nac, 7. 4 inscriptus est] in- et Nac, 7. 5 gestam (R)] -ta N, 8. 2 rettuli] retulit Nac, 10. 1 rettuli] -lit Nac, 10. 5 delectat] -tant Nac, 13 amorem] -re Nac, 14. 4 huic] hic Nac, 14. 6 negares] -re Nac, 16. 3 aliquam] -qua Nac, 16. 4 nam quem] namq̄; Nac, 16. 4 eo] eum Nac, 17. 1 distinguendum R] distingendum N, 21. 1 hic] huic Nac, 21. 2 at] a Nac, 25. 1 unguento] ungento N, 26. 4 transilientem] -lentem Nac, 27. 1 in qua] iniqua Nac, 28. 2 sequens] -ques Nac, 28. 2 ulla] ullam Nac, 28. 3 ignosce] icnoce Nac, 31. 3 proicit] prodicit Nac.

A Supplement to Mazzoli 1982

To the list of manuscripts of *De beneficiis* in Mazzoli 1982, supplemented by Malaspina 2001a, 50–1, the following can be added: except for those preceded by an asterisk, which are complete (or at least continuous) texts, most items are very slight excerpts of the fourteenth and fifteenth centuries.

COLOGNY, Fondation Martin Bodmer Cod. Bodmer 186, s. XV, Italy: *De beneficiis* 5. 14. 4 excerpted on f. 117^v (https://www.e-codices.unifr.ch/en/searchresult/list/one/fmb/cb-0186).

DARMSTADT, Universitäts- und Landesbibliothek Darmstadt Hs 784, an. 1533: excerpts of *Ben.*, *Clem.*, other Senecan and pseudo-Senecan texts on f. 156^{r}a–158^{r}a (http://www.manuscripta-mediaevalia.de/dokumente/html/obj31908825).

* FABRIANO, Biblioteca Multimediale (già comunale) 'R. Sassi' MS 173, s. XIV: *De beneficiis* on f. 200^r–225^r (https://manus.iccu.sbn.it/opac_SchedaScheda.php?ID=249136).

FABRIANO, Biblioteca Multimediale (già comunale) 'R. Sassi' MS 197, s. XV: excerpts of *De beneficiis* on f. 2^r–3^r (https://manus.iccu.sbn.it/opac_SchedaScheda.php?ID=263497).

LONDON, British Library Add. M 30935, s. XV: 'Auctoritates illustres Senecae' and 'Excerpta Senecae de Beneficiis' on f. 36–48 (http://searcharchives.bl.uk/, search term 'Add. M 30935').

* LUCCA, Biblioteca statale 1439, s. XIV$^{4/4}$: *De beneficiis* on f. 60^r–96^r (acephalous).

MELK, Benediktinerstift Cod. 1414, s. XIII, Italy?: excerpts of *De beneficiis* on f. 115^{v}a–119^v (https://manuscripta.at/?ID=9150).

NEW HAVEN, Yale University Library Marston 87, s. XV$^{med.}$, northern Italy: excerpts of *De beneficiis* on f. 103^r–104^r (https://pre1600ms.beinecke.library.yale.edu/docs/pre1600.mars087.htm).

* OXFORD, Bodleian Library Canon. Class. lat. 308, s. XIV: *De beneficiis* on f. 8^r–40^v (*Clem.* on f. 1^r–6^v, excerpts also on f. 41^r–42^r: https://medieval.bodleian.ox.ac.uk/catalog/manuscript_2339).

OXFORD, Bodleian Library Laud. Misc. 280, s. XII$^{ex.}$, Germany: excerpts of *De beneficiis* on f. 101^{r}a–114^{v}b, with a quotation (6. 11. 3 *quod consummat et res et animus*…13. 3 *te mihi profuisse dicas quam me tibi*) on f. 117^{r}a–b (excerpts of *Clem.* on f. 114^{v}b–116^{r}a: https://medieval.bodleian.ox.ac.uk/catalog/manuscript_7094).[1]

* OXFORD, Merton College Library 300, *c.*1300, France (Toul: Gerard Iohannes): *De beneficiis* on f. 134^v–156^r (*Clem.* on f. 132^r–134^v, *Apoc.* on f. 205^v–207^r: https://medieval.bodleian.ox.ac.uk/catalog/manuscript_10398).

PARIS, Bibliothèque de l'Arsenal 711, s. XII/XIII: excerpts of *De beneficiis* on f. 232^r–234^v (excerpts of *Clem.* on f. 234^v–235^v: https://archivesetmanuscrits.bnf.fr/ark:/12148/cc799280).

---

[1] See Munk Olsen 1989, 124, where, however, reference is made only to an '*extrait*' from *Ben.* on f. 117: I am very grateful to Andrew Dunning of the Bodleian Library for kindly tracking the quotation down once he had regained access to the Library during the pandemic.

* PARMA, Biblioteca Palatina MS Pal. 82, *c.*1430–50: *De beneficiis* (56 folia, the sole contents of the manuscript: https://manus.iccu.sbn.it//opac_SchedaScheda.php?ID= 115098).

ROME, Biblioteca Casanatense MS 904, s. XV: excerpts of *De beneficiis* on f. 200ᵛ–205ᵛ (excerpts of *Clem.* on f. 199ʳ–200ᵛ: https://manus.iccu.sbn.it//opac_SchedaScheda. php?ID =16013).

* ROME, Biblioteca dell'Accademia nazionale dei Lincei e Corsiniana Cors. 1849 (43 G 15), *c.*1400: *De clementia* and *De beneficiis* f. 2ʳ–91ᵛ: https://manus.iccu.sbn.it/opac_ SchedaScheda.php?ID=150785).

* SALZBURG, Stiftsbibliothek Sankt Peter Codex b. VI. 8 (R. 259), s. XV: *De beneficiis* 1–4 on f. 1ʳ–43ʳ (additamenta on f. 43ʳ–47ʳ: http://18.235.151.129/detail. php?msid=10791).

VATICAN, Barb. lat. 27, s. XVI, Italy: excerpts of *De beneficiis* on f. 2ʳ–9ᵛ (excerpts of *Clem.* on 15ʳ–17ʳ; Buonocore 2000, 56–7).

VATICAN, Barb. lat. 148s. XIV, Italy: excerpt of *De beneficiis* on f. 1ᵛ (Buonocore 2000, 57, https://digi.vatlib.it/view/MSS_Barb.lat.148).

VATICAN, Barb. lat. 1777, s. XVII, Italy: excerpts of *De beneficiis* on f. 177ʳ–183ʳ (Buonocore 2000, 57).

VATICAN, Borgh. 188, s. XIII, southern France (?): excerpts of *De beneficiis* on f. 76ᵛ–77ʳ (Buonocore 2000, 58, https://digi.vatlib.it/view/MSS_Borgh.188).

VATICAN, Reg. lat. 535, s. XIII^1, France: excerpts of *De beneficiis* on pp. 411, 418, 440, 446, 455, 467, 468, 481 in the *Chronicon* of Helinand de Froidmont (Buonocore 2000, 72, https://digi.vatlib.it/view/MSS_Reg.lat.535).

VATICAN, Reg. lat. 1875, s. XIVᵉˣ· (f. 13–41) + an. 1473–4 (f. 1–12, 42–178): excerpts of *De beneficiis* on f. 75ᵛ–76ʳ, of Clem. on f. 75ᵛ, among the *Flores philosophorum* (f. 74ᵛff.; Buonocore 2000, 75, https://digi.vatlib.it/view/MSS_Reg.lat.1875).

VATICAN, Vat. lat. 1622, s. XIVᵉˣ·, Italy: *De beneficiis* 4. 10. on f. 94ᵛ (added s. XIV/XV; Buonocore 2000, 80).

VATICAN, Vat. lat. 4256, s. XV^1, Italy: excerpts of *De beneficiis* on f. 36ᵛ–37ʳ (Buonocore 2000, 87–8: 'ff. 31–59ᵛ *flores seu auctoritates excerptae ex Aristotele, Platone, Boethio, Seneca*').

VATICAN, Vat. lat. 5114, s. XIV/XV, northern Italy: *flores* from *De beneficiis* 3–6 on f. 59ᵛ–61ᵛ (Buonocore 2000, 88, https://digi.vatlib.it/view/MSS_Vat.lat.5114).

VATICAN, Vat. lat. 5994, s. XIV/XV, Italy: excerpts of *De beneficiis* 1. 1. 2–2. 25. 3 on f. 77ᵛ (Buonocore 2000, 89: 'ff. 75–83ᵛ, *sententiae morales ex auctoribus profanis*'; https:// digi.vatlib.it/view/MSS_Vat.lat.5994).

VIENNA, Österreichische Nationalbibliothek Cod. 322, s. XIVⁱⁿ·, Bologna(?): excerpts of *De beneficiis* and *De clementia* on f. 4ʳ–7ᵛ (http://data.onb.ac.at/rec/AC13957799; https://manuscripta.at/?ID=9720).

Note also:

BRUXELLES, Bibliothèque royale 20030–20032, s. XIII$^{2/4}$: the chief witness to the second version of the *Flores paradisi*, which comprised excerpts from eleven works of Seneca, including *De beneficiis* and *Clem.*: Munk Olsen 2000, 170–1.

PARIS, Bibliothèque Nationale lat. 15982, s. XIII: the chief witness to the third version of the *Flores paradisi*, in which excerpts of S. (including *Ben.* and *Clem.*) and Cicero alone of classical authors are preserved (Munk Olsen 2000, 170–1; https://gallica.bnf.fr/ark:/12148/btv1b9078048j.r=15982?rk=21459;2).

TROYES, Bibliothèque municipale 186, s. XIII[1], Clairvaux: excerpts from *De beneficiis* constitute the last entry, and only secular text, included in the *Liber exceptionum ex libris viginti trium auctorum* compiled by William of Montague (d. 1246) from books at Clairvaux:[2] see Rouse and Rouse 1979, 139–45 (listing seven other copies of the *Liber*),[3] Munk Olsen 2000, 170.

VATICAN, Pal. lat. 957, ss. XII (f. 1–96, Italy) + XIV (f. 97–184, France): Excerpts of *De beneficiis* 1–2 on f. 147^v–151^v; f. 97–184 = *Florilegium Angelicum*, on which see Rouse and Rouse 1976 (Pal. lat. 957 described on pp. 111–12), Rouse 1979, 133–4, Munk Olsen 2000, 167.

---

[2] Excerpts of *De beneficiis* in earlier manuscripts from Clairvaux are preserved in Troyes Bibliothèque municipale 215 (s. XII$^{ex.}$) and 1915 (s. XII/XIII), representatives of the *Florilegium Duacense* that is also transmitted in Douai, Bibliothèque municipale 285 (s. XII[2]) and 533 (s. XII/XIII or XIII[1]), and Saint-Omer, Bibliothèque municipale 8 (s. XII$^{ex.}$): see Munk Olsen 1979, 84–9, 1985, 450, 848, 867–8, 870–1.

[3] Klosterneuburg, Stiftsbibliothek 331, s. XV; London, British Library Royal 7 B XIII, s. XIII$^{ex.}$; Oxford, Trinity College Library MS 41, s. XIII; Paris, Bibliothèque Nationale lat. 2115, s. XIII/XIV, and lat. 15983, s. XIII; Tortosa, Biblioteca de la cathedral 139, s. XIII; Worcester, Cathedral Library F. 51, s. XIV.

Bibliography

Abel, K. 1987. *Senecas* lex vitae. Pöner Stoische Studien. Marburg.

Albertini, E. 1923. *La composition dans les ouvrages philosophique de Sénèque.* Paris.

Albrecht, M. von. 2008. 'Seneca's Language and Style. I'. *Hyperboreus* 14:68–90.

Alexander, W. H. 1934. 'Notes on the *De Beneficiis* of Seneca'. *Classical Quarterly* 28:54–5.

Alexander, W. H. 1937. 'Further Notes on the Text of Seneca's *De Beneficiis*'. *Classical Quarterly* 31:55–60.

Alexander, W. H. 1950–2. 'Lucius Annaeus Seneca *De beneficiis libri VII*: The Text Emended and Explained'. *University of California Publications in Classical Philology* 14:1–45.

Axelson, B. 1933. *Senecastudien: Kritische Bemerkungen zu Senecas Naturales quaestiones.* Lund.

Axelson, B. 1939. *Neue Senecastudien: Textkritische Beiträge zu Senecas Epistulae morales.* Leipzig.

Badstübner, E. 1888. 'Coniectanea Annaeana'. In *Genethliacon Gottingense: Miscellanea philologica in honorem Seminarii Regii Philologici Gottingensis.* Halle. 80–3.

Badstübner, E. 1901. *Beiträge zur Erklärung und Kritik der philosophische Schriften Senecas.* Hamburg.

Baehrens, W. A. 1912. *Beiträge zur lateinischen Syntax.* Leipzig.

Birt, T. 1928. 'Marginalien zu lateinischen Prosaikern'. *Philologus* 83:31–54.

Bischoff, B. 1975. 'Paläographie und frühmittelalterliche Klassikerüberlieferung'. *La cultura antica nell'Occidente latino dal VII all'XI secolo*: 18–24 aprile 1974. Centro italiano di studi sull' alto Medioevo. Spoleto. 1:59–86.

Bourgery, A. 1913. 'Notes critiques sur le texte de Sénèque'. *Revue de Philologie* 37:95–109.

Bourgery, A. 1922. *Sénèque prosateur: Études littéraires et grammaticales sur la prose de Sénèque le philosophe.* Paris.

Brakman, C. 1909. *Ammianea et Annaeana.* Leiden.

Brakman, C. 1928. 'Annaeana'. *Mnemosyne* 56:139–58.

Brugnoli, G. 1998. 'Percorsi della tradizione manoscritta di *Seneca*'. In *Seneca nel bimillenario della nascità,* ed. S. Audano. Pisa. 77–101.

Buck, J. 1908. *Seneca De beneficiis und De clementia in der Überlieferung.* Tübingen.

Buonocore, M. 2000. 'Per un *iter* tra i codici di Seneca alla Biblioteca Apostolica Vaticana: Primi traguardi'. *Giornale italiano di filologia* 52:17–100.

Busche, K. 1917–18. 'Zu Senecas Büchern De beneficiis und De clementia'. *Rheinisches Museum* 72:464–72.

Busonero, P. 2000. 'Un caso esemplare di antigrafo e apografo nella tradizione di Seneca: il Pal. Lat. 1547 e il Reg. Lat. 1529'. *Seneca e il suo tempotti del Convegno internazionale di Roma–Cassino: 11–14 novembre 1998.* Biblioteca di Filologia e critica 6. Rome. 295–337.

Castiglioni, L. 1920. 'Note critiche ai libri "De Beneficiis" di L. Anneo Seneca'. *Miscellanea di studi critici in onore di Ettore Stampini.* Turin and Geneva.

Cooper, J. M., and J. F. Procopé (trans.). 1995. *Seneca: Moral and Political Essays.* Cambridge.

Cornelissen, J. J. 1870. *Coniectanea latina.* Deventer.

Courtney, E. 1974. 'Conjectures in Seneca's Prose Works'. *Bulletin of the Institute of Classical Studies* 21:100–6.

Feldman, J. 1887. *Observationes ad L. A. Senecam criticae*. Ostrowo.

Festa, N. 1900. 'In L. A. Senecae de beneficiis libros animadversiones criticae'. *Studi italiani di filolgica classica* 8:429–38.

Gemoll, W. 1890. *Kritische Bemerkungen zu lateinischen Schriftstellern*. Liegnitz.

Georgii, H. 1929. 'Textkritische Beiträge zu Seneca'. *Philologus* 84:110–15.

Gertz, M. C. 1874. *Studia critica in L. Annaei Senecae Dialogos*. Copenhagen.

Gertz, M. C. 1876. *L. Annaei Senecae Libri De beneficiis et De clementia*. Berlin.

Goodyear, F. R. D. (ed.). 1972. *The 'Annals' of Tacitus*. Vol. 1. Cambridge.

Graver, M., and A. A. Long (trans.). 2015. *Seneca. Letters on Ethics: To Lucilius*. Chicago.

Griffin, M. T. 2013. *Seneca on Society: A Guide to 'De Beneficiis'*. Oxford.

Gronovius, J. F. 1639. *Iohannis Frederici Gronovii observationum libri III*. Leiden.

Haase, F. (ed.). 1878. *L. Annaei Senecae opera quae supersunt*. Vol. 3. Leipzig.

Häberlin, C. 1890. 'Quaestiones criticae in L. A. Senecae de beneficiis libri'. *Rheinisches Museum* 45:21–49.

Haupt, M. 1875-6. *Opuscula*. 3 vols. Leipzig.

Havet, L. 1898. 'Pararius substantif'. *Archiv für lateinische Lexikographie und Grammatik mit Einschluss des alteren Mittellateins*. 10:523–7.

Hedicke, E. 1899. *Studia Bentleiana, II: Seneca Bentleianus*. Freienwald.

Hermes, E. 1874. *Quaestiones criticae in L. Annaei Senecae epistularum moralium, part. II*. Meurs.

Holmes, N. 2004. '*Ferimus*'. *Classical Quarterly* 54:296–7.

Kaster, R. A. 2005. *Emotion, Restraint, and Community in Ancient Rome*. New York.

Kaster, R. A. 2016a. 'Making Sense of Suetonius in the Twelfth Century'. In *Canonical Texts and Scholarly Practices: A Global Comparative Approach*, ed. A. T. Grafton and G. W. Most. Cambridge. 110–35.

Kaster, R. A. (ed.). 2016b. *C. Suetoni Tranquilli De uita Caesarum libri VIII et De grammaticis et rhetoribus liber*. Oxford.

Kaster, R. A. 2016c. *Studies on the Text of Suetonius' 'De uita Caesarum'*. Oxford.

Kaster, R. A. 2020. 'Notes on Seneca De beneficiis 7. 19. 5–31. 2'. *Rationes Rerum* 16:223–41.

Kaster, R. A. 2021. 'The Vulgate Text of Seneca's De beneficiis, 1475–1650'. In *Classics and Classicists: Essays on the History of Scholarship in Honour of Christopher Stray*, ed. S. Harrison and C. Pelling. Berlin. 59–80.

Kiekebusch, W. 1912. *De Pinciani in Senecae philosophi De beneficiis et De clementia libros castigationibus*. Greifswald.

Kienzle, L. 1906. *Die Kopulativpartikeln et, que, atque, bei Tacitus, Plinius, Seneka*. Tübingen.

Klammer, H. 1878. *Animadversiones Annaeanae grammaticae*. Bonn.

Koch, H. A. 1874. *Observationes criticae in L. Annaeum Senecam*. Nuremburg.

Kronenberg, A. J. 1907. 'Ad Senecae Libros De Beneficiis et De Clementia'. *Classical Quarterly* 1:284–9.

Kronenberg, A. J. 1923. 'Ad Senecam'. *Classical Quarterly* 17:42–9.

Kruczkiewicz, B. 1877. Review of Gertz. *Zeitschrift für die österreichischen Gymnasien* 28:427–40.

Lejay, P. 1901. Review of Badstübner 1901. *Revue critique d'histoire et de littérature*. 52:128–30.

Leo, F. 1895. *Plautinische Forschungen: Zur Kritik und Geschichte der Komödie*. Berlin.

Lindsay, W. M. 1915. *Notae Latinae: An Account of Abbreviation in Latin MSS of the Early Minuscule Period (c. 700–850)*. Cambridge.

Lipsius, I. 1585. *Iusti Lipsi Electorum liber secundus*. Antwerp.

Madvig, J. N. 1871-84. *Adversaria critica*. 3 vols. Copenhagen.

Malaspina, E. (ed.). 2001a. *L. Annaei Seencae De clementia libri duo*. Culture antiche. Studi e testi, 13. Alessandria.

Malaspina, E. 2001b. 'La "preistoria" delle tradizione recenziore del "De clementia" (a proposito di Paris. Bibl. nat., Lat. 15085 e Leipzig, Stadtbibl., Rep. I, 4, 47)'. *Revue d'Histoire des Textes* 31:147–65.

Malaspina, E. (ed.). 2016. *L. Annaeus Seneca: De clementia libri duo*. Biblioteca Teubneriana. Berlin.

Matthias, T. 1888. 'Emendationes ad L. Annaei Senecae Opera'. *Commentationes philologicae quibus Ottoni Ribbeckio...congratulantur discipuli Lipsienses*. Leipzig. 175–85.

Mayor, J. E. B. 1907. 'Corruption of the Text of Seneca'. *Journal of Philology* 30:208–10.

Mazzoli, G. 1974. 'Restauri testuali nel *De beneficiis* di Seneca'. *Bollettino del comitato per l'edizione nazionale dei classici greci e latini* 22:53–98.

Mazzoli, G. 1977. 'Altri restauri testuali al *De beneficiis* e al *De clementia* di Seneca'. *Bollettino del comitato per l'edizione nazionale dei classici greci e latini* 25:70–88.

Mazzoli, G. 1978. 'Ricerche sulla tradizione medioevale del *De Beneficiis* e del *De Clementia*'. *Bollettino del comitato per l'edizione nazionale dei classici greci e latini* 26:85–110.

Mazzoli, G. 1982. 'Ricerche sulla tradizione medievale del *De beneficiis* e del *De clementia* di Seneca, III: Storia della tradizione manoscrita'. *Bollettino dei Classici. Academia nazionale dei Lincei* 3:165–223.

Modius, F. 1584. *Nouantiquae lectiones tributae in epistolas centum*. Frankfurt.

Mostert, M. 1989. *The Library of Fleury: A Provisional List of Manuscripts*. Hilversum.

Mück, H. 1890. *Observationes criticae grammaticae in L. Annaei Senecae scripta philosophica*. Marburg.

Müller, H. J. 1881. *Symbolae ad emendandos scriptores Latinos, Pt. 2*. Jahresbericht über das Luisenstädtische Gymnasium. Berlin.

Müller, J. 1892. *Kritische Studien zu Seneca De beneficiis und De clementia*. Sitzungsberichte der kaiserliche Akademie der Wissenschaften in Wien, Philosophisch–Historische Classe, Band 127. Vienna.

Munk Olsen, B. 1979. 'Les classiques latines dans les florilèges médiévaux antérieures au XIIe siècle'. *Revue d'histoire des textes* 9:47–121.

Munk Olsen, B. 1985. *L'étude dels auteurs classiques latins aux XIe et XIIe siècles*. Vol. 2. Paris.

Munk Olsen, B. 1989. *L'étude dels auteurs classiques latins aux XIe et XIIe siècles*. Vol. 3.2. Paris.

Munk Olsen, B. 2000. 'Les florilèges et les abrégés de Sénèque au Moyen Age'. *Giornale italiano di filologia* 52 (2000) 163–83.

Muretus, M. A. 1580. *M. Antonii Mureti variarum lectionum libri XV*. Antwerp.

Niemeyer, K. 1899. 'Zu Seneca'. *Philologus* 58:437–50.

Ouellette, H. T. (ed.). 1982. *William of Malmesbury 'Polyhistor': A Critical Edition*. Medieval and Renaissance Texts and Studies, 10. Binghamton, NY.

Pasoli, E. 1953. 'De quibusdam Senecae locis corruptis aut difficilioribus'. *Latinitas* 1:269–73.

Pellegrin, E. 1978. *Les manuscrits classiques latins de la Bibliothèque vaticane*. Vol. 2. 1: *Fonds Patetta et Fonds de la Reine*. Paris.

Pinkster, H. 2015. *The Oxford Latin Syntax*. Vol. 1: *The Simple Clause*. Oxford.

Préchac, F. (ed.). 1921. *Sénèque: De la clémence*. Paris.

Radermacher, L. 1891. *Observationes in Euripidem miscellae*. Bonn.

Reinecke, G. 1890. *De coniunctionum usu apud Senecam philosophum*. Münster.

Reynolds, L. D. 1983. 'The Younger Seneca [*Apocolocyntosis, De beneficiis* and *De clementia, Dialogues, Letters*]'. In *Texts and Transmission: A Survey of the Latin Classics*, ed. L. D. Reynolds. Oxford. 357–75.

Rossbach, O. 1888. *De Senecae philosophi librorum recensione et emendatione*. Breslau.

Rossbach, O. 1907. Review of Hos. 1. *Berliner philologische Wochenschrift* 47:1478–90.

Rouse, R. H. 1979. ' "*Florilegia*" and Latin Classical Authors in Twelfth- and Thirteenth-Century Orléans'. *Viator* 10:131–60.

Rouse, R. H., and M. A. Rouse. 1976. 'The *Florilegium Angelicum*: Its Origin, Content, and Influence'. In *Medieval Learning and Literature: Essays Presented to Richard William Hunt*, ed. J. J. G. Alexander and M. T. Gibson. Oxford. 66–114.

Rouse, R. H., and M. A. Rouse. 1979. *Preachers, Florilegia and Sermons: Studies on the 'Maniplus florum' of Thomas of Ireland*. Studies and Texts, 47. Toronto.

Schmeling, G. 2011. *A Commentary on the 'Satyrica' of Petronius*. With the collaboration of Aldo Setaioli. Oxford.

Schultess, F. 1878. Review of Klammer 1878. *Jenaer Literaturzeitung* 5:511–12.

Shackleton Bailey, D. R. 1970. 'Emendations of Seneca'. *Classical Quarterly* 20:350–63.

Sjögren, H. 1919–20. 'Kleine textkritische Beiträge'. *Eranos* 19:163–72.

Sonntag, M. 1913. *L. Annaei Senecae De beneficiis libri explanantur*. Leipzig.

Stangl, T. 1909. *Pseudoasconiana. Textgestaltung und Sprache der anonymen Scholien zu Ciceros vier ersten Verrinen*. Paderborn.

Stangl, T. 1910. Review of Brakman 1909. *Berliner Philologische Wochenschrift* 34:1068–71.

Stephanus, H. 1586a. *Ad Senecae lectionem proodopoeia*. [Paris].

Stephanus, H. 1586b. *Epistolae ad Jacobum Dalechampium*. [Paris].

Thomas, E. 1893. 'Miscellae quaestiones in L. Annaeum Senecam philosophum'. *Hermes* 28:277–311.

Thomas, E. 1900. *Schedae criticae novae in Senecam rhetorem*. Philologus Supplementband, 8. Leipzig.

Thurot, C. 1874. Review of Madvig 1871–84, vol. 2 (1873). *Revue critique d'histoire et de littérature* 25:49–54.

Timpanaro, S. 1970. '*Positivus pro comparativo* in Latino'. *Studia Florentina Alexandro Ronconi sexagenario oblata*. Rome. 455–81.

Valmaggi, L. 1905–6. 'Seneca, *De beneficiis* I, 3, 5: *Bollettino di filologia classica* 12:160.

Walter, F. 1927. 'Zu Curtius, Seneca, Tacitus'. *Philologische Wochenschrift* 47:1565–8.

Walter, F. 1930. 'Zu Curtius, Seneca, Tacitus'. *Bayerische Blätter für das Gymnasial-Schulwesen* 66:254–7.

Walter, F. 1943–4. 'Zu Cicero, Livius, Seneca, Festus u. a.'. *Rheinisches Museum* 92:191–2.

Watt, W. S. 1994. 'Notes on Seneca, *De Beneficiis*, *De Clementia*, and *Dialogi*'. *Harvard Studies in Classical Philology* 96:225–39.

Watt, W. S. 2001. 'Notes on Seneca's Philosophical Works'. *Rheinisches Museum* 144:231–3.

Weidner, A. 1864. *Criticarum scriptionum specimen*. Cologne.

Weise, O. 1882. 'Zu Seneca'. *Neue Jahrbücher für Philologie und Paedagogik* 125:640.

Werth. 1891. 'De Ciceronis et Senecae locis aliquot'. In *Schedae philologae Hermanno Usener a sodalibus Seminarii Regii Bonnensis oblatae*. Bonn. 35–46.

Weyman, C. 1900. Review of Hos. 1. *Literarisches Centralblatt für Deutschland*. 51:1209–12.

Index of Manuscripts

This index includes the manuscripts mentioned in the text and footnotes of the Introduction and Chapters 1-7 and Appendix 1, and the *sigla* of the hyparchetypes of the medieval manuscript tradition. It does not include manuscripts that are merely listed in citations of variant readings, in the *apparatus critici* of Chapters 1-7, or in Appendixes 2 (on the archetype's characteristic blunders) and 3 (a list of previously unreported manuscripts of *De beneficiis*).

Admont, Stiftsbibliothek 221 (**U**) 4

Basel, Öffentliche Bibliothek der Universität F.IV.14 59 n. 34

Cambridge, Trinity College O.3.31 (**V**) 4, 99
Cherbourg, Bibliothèque municipale 21 (**H**) 3, 109 n. 20, 131, 160, 172

Florence, Biblioteca Medicea Laurenziana Plut. 76.36 (**F**) 4
Florence, Biblioteca Medicea Laurenziana Plut. 45.25 (**T**) 3, 79 n. 24
Florence, Biblioteca Medicea Laurenziana San Marco 286 (**I**) 4

Leipzig, Universitätsbibliothek 1607 3 n. 7
Leipzig, Universitätsbibliothek Rep. I 47–I (**Q**) 5, 42, 91, 181–5
London, Lambeth Palace Library MS 232 (**D**) 3

Munich, Bayerische Staatsbibliothek Clm 2544 (**M**) 5, 36, 42 n. 7, 91, 181–5

Oxford, Balliol College Library 129 (ς_{10}) 6, 18

Paris, Bibliothèque nationale lat. 6331 (**B**) 5, 91 n. 36
Paris, Bibliothèque nationale lat. 6382 (**P**) 3
Paris, Bibliothèque nationale lat. 6383 (**E**) 3
Paris, Bibliothèque nationale lat. 6389 (ς_{11}) 6
Paris, Bibliothèque nationale lat. 6626 (**O**) 3, 172
Paris, Bibliothèque nationale, lat. 6630 (**J**) 4, 99
Paris, Bibliothèque nationale lat. 7698 (ς_{7}) 6
Paris, Bibliothèque nationale lat. 8542 + lat. fonds Baluze 270 (**K**) 4, 20
Paris, Bibliothèque nationale lat. 8544 (ς_{12}) 6, 131 n. 11
Paris, Bibliothèque nationale lat. 8546 (ς_{13}) 6
Paris, Bibliothèque nationale lat. 8717 (ς_{14}) 7, 24

Paris, Bibliothèque nationale lat. 11855 (ς_{15}) 7
Paris, Bibliothèque nationale lat. 15085 (**C**) 3, 23, 42, 91, 183 n. 6
Paris, Bibliothèque nationale lat. 15425 (**W**) 4
Paris, Bibliothèque nationale lat. 16592 (**S**) 5, 23

Vatican, Archivio Capitulare di San Pietro C.121 (ς_{2}) 6, 7, 23 n. 6, 49 n. 16, 144, 166 n. 6
Vatican, Palatinus lat. 1538 (ς_{21}) 7
Vatican, Palatinus lat. 1539 (ς_{20}) 7
Vatican, Palatinus lat. 1540 (ς_{19}) 7
Vatican, Palatinus lat. 1547 (**N**) 1, 3, 5, 7, 9–11, 15, 17, 20–3, 26–30, 35–6, 38–9, 42–6, 49–52, 54–8, 59 n. 34, 61, 63–5, 67–71, 73, 75–9, 81–2, 84–5, 87, 89–91, 93–7, 99, 101–6, 109 nn. 19, 22, 110–14, 118–20, 124–5, 127, 129–32, 134–5, 138, 140 n. 18, 141, 144, 149, 153, 155, 157, 161–4, 166 n. 6, 167–74, 176–7, 179, 181–5
Vatican, Reginensis lat. 1529 (**R**) 1–4, 17, 20, 22–3, 26, 29, 36, 38, 42–5, 51 n. 21, 55, 58, 60 n. 35, 70, 73, 77, 79 n. 22, 84 n. 28, 85, 91, 93 n. 40, 102, 109, 110 n. 24, 112, 113, 116, 118–19, 124–5, 131 n. 12, 140, 153, 155, 162, 169, 173 n. 19, 181–5
Vatican, Vaticanus lat. 1769 (ς_{8}) 6, 23 n. 6
Vatican, Vaticanus lat. 2212 (ς_{3}) 6, 22 n. 6, 49, 166 n. 6
Vatican, Vaticanus lat. 2213 (ς_{9}) 6
Vatican, Vaticanus lat. 2214 (ς_{16}) 7
Vatican, Vaticanus lat. 2215 (ς_{17}) 7
Vatican, Vaticanus lat. 2216 (ς_{4}) 6, 23, 49, 166 n. 6
Vatican, Vaticanus lat. 2220 (ς_{18}) 7

WolfenbütteL, Herzog-August Bibliothek 274 Gud. Lat. (**G**) 4, 59, 92–4, 109 n. 20, 110, 120, 163
Wrocław, Biblioteka Uniwersytecka IV.F.39 (ς_{5}) 6, 29, 49, 94, 163, 166 n. 6

ρ (proximate source of the medieval tradition's
  two main branches, φ and ψ) 2
φ 2–3, 5, 6, 38
ψ (source of the two sub-families, π and γ) 2–3,
  61, 63, 89, 91, 102, 183 n. 6

π 2–3, 6, 42, 137, 172
γ 4–6, 19, 26 n. 12, 42, 137, 142
σ1 (excerpts comprising a blend of
  φ and γ) 5
σ2 (excerpts derived primarily from φ) 5

Index of Passages

This index primarily catalogues the passages of *De beneficiis* discussed in Chapters 1–7 and passages from the works of Seneca and other authors that are cited in the text and footnotes of those discussions. The index does not include passages cited in excerpts of other scholars' writings and in the lists of variant readings and the archetype's characteristic blunders in Appendix 1 and 2.

Année épigraphique 1979 no. 434 88
Apuleius, Lucius
  Metamorphoses
    4. 25 27
    9. 36 27
Asconius Pedianus, Quintus
  Pro Milone 35. 6C. 87
Augustinus, Aurelius
  De ciuitate Dei 15. 27. 3 48

Caesar, Gaius Iulius
  Bellum ciuile
    1. 51. 4 85
    3. 82 92 n. 37
  De bello Gallico
    1. 43. 8 81
    5. 43. 3 92 n. 37
Cicero, Marcus Tullius
  Aratea 12 85
  Brutus
    109 47
    257 57
  *De amici*tia 41 177 n. 24
  De finibus
    4. 65 133
    5. 4 177 n. 24
  De inuentione 2. 171 177 n. 24
  De lege agraria 2. 94 177 n. 24
  De natura deorum 1. 108 119
  De officiis
    1. 35 92 n. 37
    1. 36 71
    3. 47 47
    3. 95 103
  De oratore 2. 33 177 n. 24
  De republica
    1. 29. 2 100
    1. 39 30
  De senectute
    71 177 n. 24
    83 99 n. 7

Diuinatio in Caecilium
  16 57
  45 177 n. 24
Epistulae ad Atticum
  1. 5. 4 57
  6. 4. 1 82
  7. 1. 2 177 n. 24
  9. 9. 4 104
  10. 9a. 1 (Caelius) 92 n. 37
  15. 3. 1 27
Epistulae ad Familiares
  4. 4. 3 177 n. 24
  6. 10b. 2 34
  9. 15. 2 177 n. 24
  9. 16. 2 (Caesar) 57
  11. 12. 2 57
  12. 13. 1 57
In Catilinam
  1. 12 90
  2. 29 90
  3. 2 90
  3. 22 90
  4. 11 177 n. 24
In Verrem
  2. 1. 10 86 n. 30
  2. 2. 95 87
Lucullus 10 57
Orator 119 96 n. 4
Philippicae
  9. 9 53 n. 28
  14. 1 92 n. 37
Pro Cluentio
  21 87
  62 141
Pro Flacco 3 96 n. 3
Pro Plancio 13 57
Pro Roscio Amerino 10 57
Corpus Inscriptionum Latinarum
  2. 2242 47
  3. 2609 88
  5. 7108 47

Corpus Inscriptionum Latinarum (cont.)
  5. 7797 47
  9. 2220 64
  10. 3969 88
  10. 5809 88
  11. 1828 88
Columella, Lucius Junius Moderatus
  8. 10. 1 64
Curtius Rufus, Quintus
  8. 7. 4 106

Digesta
  2. 4. 11. pr. 93
  12. 2. 34. 9 147
  17. 1. 12. 1 93
  34. 3. 7. 6 93
  34. 3. 9. pr. 93

Festus, Sextus Pompeius
  178. 30–31 L. 66 n. 4
  362. 35 L. 47
Fronto, Marcus Cornelius
  Epistulae ad amicos 1. 13. 1 57
  Epistuale ad Marcum 3. 14. 5 57
Frontinus, Sex. Iulius
  Strategemata 1. 11. 2 92

Gellius, Aulus
  4. 2. 11 66 n. 5
  9. 2. 2 71
  15. 31. 1 62

Isidorus
  Origines 19. 19. 7 48
Iuvenalis, Decimus Iunius
  8. 189 39

Jeremiah 17:1 119

Lex Irnitana 88
Livius, Titus
  3. 38. 2 64
  3. 68. 5 81
  3. 71. 1 92
  4. 2. 4 81
  5. 18. 12 90
  6. 3. 7 127
  7. 34. 13 92
  7. 36. 12 127
  25. 35. 6 127
  25. 38. 10 96 n. 4
  26. 7. 8 64
  26. 41. 22 127
  29. 11. 12 47
  29. 16. 4 180 n. 33

  29. 25. 3 57
  30. 14. 7 92
  30. 40. 5 47
  31. 18. 2 141
  31. 22. 5 64
  39. 16. 3 53 n. 28
  40. 13. 5 133
  42. 3. 7 90
Lucanus, Marcus Annaeus
  6. 749 146
Lucretius Carus, Titus
  3. 15–16, 18 107

Ovidius Naso, Publius
  Fasti 2. 672 90
  Metamorphoses 8. 685 73 n. 14

Palladius, Rutilius Taurus Aemilianus
  12. 7. 15 48
Petronius
  15. 9 92
  47. 2 133
  119. 1 (24) 133
Phaedrus
  1. 22 95
Plautus, Titus Maccius 95
  Aulularia 526 71
  Bacchides 490 57
  Cistellaria 737, 739 117
  Menaechmi 831–32 53 n. 28
  Rudens
    328 53 n. 28
    650 27
Plinius Secundus, Gaius
  Naturalis Historia
    5. 90 97–8
    8. 10 115
    18. 32 62
    37. 152 127
Plinius Caecilius Secundus, Gaius
  Epistulae
    6. 29. 6 39
    8. 17. 1 141
Publilius Syrus
  C. 20 66

Quintilianus, Marcus Fabius
  Declamationes minores
    257. 12 30
    275. 6 95
    297. 6 96 n. 4
    344. 10 95
  Institutio Oratoria
    1. 10. 29 133
    8. 3. 66 177 n. 24

8. 3. 68 90
11. 3. 165 177 n. 24
[Quintilianus]
   Declamationes maiores 15. 7 95

Sallustius Crispus, Gaius
   Bellum Catilinae
      12. 2 27
      52. 9 27
   Historiae 1 *Oratio Lepidi* §5 133
   Iugurtha 82. 3 92 n. 37
Senatus Consultus de Cn. Pisone patre 88
Seneca, Lucius Annaeus
   Agamemnon 457 130
   Apococolocyntosis 7. 4 36 n. 31
   Consolatio ad Heluiam
      6. 4 130
      6. 8 119
      10. 7 90
      10. 10 119
      11. 5 130
      12. 2 156
      13. 7 23
      16. 6 179
   Consolatio ad Marciam
      1. 2 23
      2. 2 155
      3. 4 102
      12. 2 122
      19. 6 43
      22. 1 115
      22. 6 71
      23. 5 43
      26. 6 34
   Consolatio ad Polybium
      1. 1 43
      2. 1 37 n. 34, 131
      6. 1 122
      16. 3 96 n. 4
      18. 6 170
   De beneficiis 1, 6
      1. 1. 1 15–16
      1. 1. 2 16, 38
      1. 1. 3 103 n. 12
      1. 1. 5–6 163
      1. 1. 6 16–17
      1. 1. 8 17–18, 132
      1. 1. 9 18, 107, 168
      1. 1. 10 84
      1. 1. 13 84
      1. 2. 1 18–19
      1. 2. 2 122, 175
      1. 2. 3 19–20, 122, 175
      1. 2. 5 20–1
      1. 3. 3 21–2

1. 3. 4 22 n. 6
1. 3. 4–5 22–3
1. 3. 8 23–4
1. 3. 9 24
1. 4. 1 132
1. 4. 5 168
1. 5–7 167
1. 5. 1 24–6
1. 5. 2 26–7, 33–4
1. 7. 1 27–8
1. 7. 3 139
1. 8. 1 28
1. 9. 1–2 28–9
1. 9. 2 93 n. 40
1. 9. 3 29–30
1. 9. 4 30–1
1. 9. 5 31–2
1. 10. 4 32–3
1. 11. 1 33
1. 12. 1 33–4
1. 12. 3 34–5, 150 n. 6
1. 14. 1 35–6
1. 14. 2 36–7
1. 14. 3 46, 123, 164
1. 15. 4 29
2. 1. 1 38, 68
2. 1. 2 38–9
2. 2. 1 39
2. 3. 3 20 n. 5
2. 4. 1 39–40
2. 5. 2 40–1
2. 5. 3 41–4
2. 10. 2 45–6
2. 11. 1 43 n. 9, 46
2. 11. 2 46, 123
2. 11. 5 46–7
2. 12. 1 45, 47–8
2. 12. 2 47–48
2. 13. 1 48–9
2. 13. 2 49–50, 125 n. 3,
   173 n. 18
2. 14. 1 50
2. 14. 2 50
2. 14. 5 16, 51–2
2. 16. 2 53
2. 17. 3 53
2. 17. 4 53–4
2. 18. 3 54–5
2. 18. 7 55–6
2. 18. 8 77
2. 19. 1 55 n. 30
2. 20. 2 168
2. 23 124
2. 23. 1 121
2. 23. 2 56, 103 n. 12

Seneca, Lucius Annaeus (*cont.*)

2. 24. 2 65 n. 1, 168
2. 24. 2–3 56–7, 163
2. 26. 2 57–8, 168
2. 27. 1 58–9
2. 29. 1 59–60
2. 29. 6 43
2. 30. 1 113
2. 31. 1 60
2. 31. 2–3 60
2. 31. 5 55 n. 30
2. 33. 2 61
2. 34. 3 61–2
2. 34. 4 59, 62
2. 35. 2 63
2. 35. 3 63–4, 103 n. 12
2. 35. 4 64
3. 1. 1 84
3. 1. 2 65
3. 1. 4 19
3. 1. 5 66
3. 2. 1 70
3. 2. 1–2 66–7
3. 2. 3 67
3. 3. 1–2 67–9
3. 5. 1 69–70
3. 5. 2 70–1, 158
3. 6–17 82
3. 6. 1 82–3, 168
3. 6. 2 71
3. 7. 3 71–2, 75
3. 7. 6 72–3
3. 8. 3 116 n. 32
3. 9. 3 73–4
3. 10. 3 74
3. 11. 1 72, 75
3. 11. 2 75–6
3. 12. 2 76–7
3. 12. 3 77–8
3. 13. 1 103 n. 12
3. 14. 1 110
3. 14. 3 78–9
3. 15. 3 79
3. 16 81
3. 16. 1–2 80
3. 16. 3 79–81
3. 16. 4 81
3. 17. 1 110
3. 17. 1–2 81–2
3. 17. 4 23
3. 18–28 82
3. 18. 1–3 82–3
3. 18. 4 83–4
3. 20. 1 36 n. 33

3. 22. 3–4 84–5
3. 22. 4 85
3. 23. 2 85
3. 23. 4 86
3. 26. 1–2 86–8, 100
3. 27. 4 88
3. 28. 1 55 n. 30, 88
3. 28. 2 88
3. 28. 3 88–9
3. 29–38 82
3. 29. 1 82
3. 29. 2 83
3. 29. 5 89–90
3. 30. 1 110
3. 31. 1–2 90
3. 31. 5 90–1
3. 32. 5 49 n. 18
3. 32. 6 55 n. 30
3. 33. 1 24 n. 9, 161 n. 1
3. 33. 4 87
3. 35. 1–2 91
3. 35. 4 110
3. 36. 2 168
3. 36. 3 92
3. 37. 4 92–3
3. 38. 2 43 n. 9
4. 1. 1 16
4. 1. 2 16, 84
4. 2 103 n. 12
4. 2. 1–2 94
4. 3. 1 24 n. 8, 94–6
4. 4. 2 170 n. 16
4. 5. 1 97, 110
4. 5. 3 97–8, 170 n. 16
4. 6. 1 19, 98–9
4. 6. 3 70
4. 6. 5 97 n. 5
4. 7. 1 97
4. 7. 2 88 n. 33
4. 8. 1 88 n. 33, 99–100
4. 9. 3 102
4. 9. 1 101
4. 9. 2–3 101–2
4. 10. 1 103
4. 10. 5 95
4. 11. 3 103
4. 12. 3–4 104–5
4. 13. 1 105
4. 13. 2 45
4. 13. 3 101
4. 14. 2–3 163
4. 15 84
4. 15. 4 84
4. 17. 2 72, 84

4. 18. 2 105–7, 157
4. 19. 1–2 107–8
4. 20. 3 65. n. 3
4. 21. 4 108
4. 21. 6 108–9
4. 22. 2–3 109–11
4. 23. 1 55 n. 30
4. 25. 2 97
4. 27. 1 93 n. 40
4. 27. 1–3 111–12
4. 27. 5 112
4. 28. 1 113, 180
4. 28. 1ff. 18
4. 28. 5–6 112–13
4. 31. 5 113
4. 32. 1–2 113–14
4. 32. 3 114
4. 32. 3–4 114–15
4. 33. 2 68
4. 33. 3 77 n. 20
4. 34. 3 19, 115
4. 34. 5 115–16
4. 35. 1 116–17
4. 35. 2 45 n. 11
4. 35. 3 115
4. 36. 2 9 n. 17
4. 37. 1 88 n. 33
4. 37. 2 117
4. 37. 3 38
4. 37. 3–4 119
4. 37. 4 117–18
4. 37. 5 118
4. 38. 2 118–19
4. 39. 2 16
4. 39. 3 153 n. 10
4. 40. 2 119–20
5. 1. 1 121
5. 1. 4 121–2
5. 1. 5 122, 175
5. 3. 1 122–3
5. 4. 2–3 123–4, 153, 156
5. 5. 2 124, 152
5. 5. 4 124–5, 173 n. 18
5. 6. 5 77
5. 6. 6 125, 184 n. 10
5. 7 126
5. 7. 2 139
5. 7. 4 161 n. 1
5. 7. 6–8. 1 125 n. 2
5. 8. 2 126
5. 8. 5 19
5. 10. 1 45 n. 11, 126–7
5. 10. 2 128
5. 10. 3–4 127–8

5. 11 126
5. 11. 1 118
5. 11. 3–4 128–9
5. 11. 4 43 n. 9
5. 12. 2 129–30
5. 12. 3 130–2
5. 12. 4 132–3
5. 12. 6 133
5. 13. 1–2 133–4
5. 13. 2 135
5. 14. 1–3 134–6
5. 14. 3 130 n. 11
5. 14. 5 136–7
5. 15. 1 133
5. 15. 3 179
5. 15. 4–5 163
5. 15. 4–6 137
5. 16. 4 60, 66 n. 6, 137–8
5. 18 138–9
5. 19. 1 139
5. 19. 4–5 139–40,
5. 19. 5 19
5. 19. 9 108
5. 20. 2 183 n. 6
5. 20. 6 140
5. 21. 1 140–1
5. 21. 2 141
5. 22. 1 141–2
5. 22. 4–23. 2 140 n. 18
5. 23. 1 156
5. 23. 2 140 n. 18
5. 24. 1 130
5. 24. 1–2 142
5. 25. 1 184–5
5. 25. 5 142–3
5. 35. 5 156–7
6. 1 43 n. 9, 144
6. 2. 1–2 144–5
6. 4. 5 179
6. 5. 5 19
6. 6. 3 126
6. 7. 1 87
6. 8. 1 87, 145–6
6. 8. 2 146–7
6. 8. 4 147
6. 9. 1 46, 55 n. 30, 123
6. 9. 3 147–8
6. 13. 1–2 148
6. 13. 3–4 148–9
6. 13. 5 172
6. 14. 3 87
6. 15. 1 149
6. 16. 1–2 149–50
6. 16. 4 150

Seneca, Lucius Annaeus (*cont.*)
  6. 16. 4–5 163
  6. 16. 6–7 163
  6. 19. 2, 4 150
  6. 19. 5 150
  6. 21. 2–3 163
  6. 22. 1 34
  6. 23. 1 150–1, 157
  6. 23. 2 151
  6. 23. 6 151–2
  6. 24. 2 152–3
  6. 25. 4 153
  6. 27. 3 103 n. 12
  6. 28. 1–2 153–4
  6. 29. 1 162
  6. 30. 2 144, 150
  6. 33. 2 70
  6. 33. 3 154–5
  6. 34. 1 155
  6. 34. 4 17
  6. 35. 4 155–6
  6. 35. 5 119, 143 n. 21
  6. 37. 1 45
  6. 37. 3 156–7
  6. 38. 3 157–8
  6. 39. 1 158
  6. 40. 1 60
  6. 40. 2 158–9
  6. 41. 1 159
  6. 41. 2 159
  6. 42. 2 159–60
  6. 43. 3 68, 87
  7. 1. 1 161
  7. 2. 2 106
  7. 2. 4 161–2
  7. 2. 5–6 162–3
  7. 4. 3 163–4
  7. 5. 7 63 n. 39
  7. 6. 1 164
  7. 6. 3 164–5
  7. 7. 3 164
  7. 8. 1 165
  7. 8. 2–3 165–6
  7. 12 167
  7. 12. 4 140
  7. 12. 5–13 166–7
  7. 14. 1 166
  7. 14. 1–3 167–8
  7. 14. 4 150 n. 6
  7. 14. 6 132
  7. 15. 1 168
  7. 15. 3 169–70
  7. 16. 1 170
  7. 18. 1 132

  7. 19. 2 170
  7. 19. 3 156
  7. 19. 4 170–1
  7. 19. 5, 7 171–2
  7. 19. 8 125 n. 3, 162, 172–3
  7. 19. 9 173–4
  7. 20. 1 71
  7. 20. 3 150 n. 6
  7. 20. 4–5 174–5
  7. 21. 1 179
  7. 24. 1 55 n. 30, 65. n. 3
  7. 24. 2 122, 175
  7. 26. 1 175
  7. 26. 4 175–6
  7. 27. 1 159 n. 16, 161, 176–7
  7. 27. 2 183 n. 8
  7. 27. 3 107, 155
  7. 28. 3 39 n. 2, 177–8, 183 n. 9
  7. 29. 1 178
  7. 30. 1 177 n. 25, 178
  7. 30. 2 178–80
  7. 31. 2 175, 180
  7. 31. 3 108
De breuitate uitae
  2. 4 58, 144
  3. 1 70
  7. 3 156
  8. 2 122
  10. 3 88
  10. 14 43
  11. 1 106
  12. 8 119
  14. 1 105–6
  20. 3 139
  27. 6 144
De clementia 1, 5, 181
  1. 1. 3 106
  1. 12. 3 93 n. 40
  1. 18. 2 85
  1. 24. 2 43
  2. 1. 1 179
  2. 1. 3 79
  2. 2. 2 87
  2. 3. 1 161 n. 1
  2. 7. 1 87 n. 32
De constantia sapientis
  5. 4 34
  5. 6 157
  6. 2–3 179
  19. 4 92
De ira
  1. 7. 5 71
  1. 11. 3 179
  1. 11. 5 145

1. 18. 4 147
1. 19. 8 116 n. 32
1. 33. 2 179
2. 2. 6 45
2. 5. 1 172
2. 5. 4 45
2. 7. 2 102
2. 10. 5 45
2. 13. 1 130
2. 17. 2 163
2. 21. 1-2 152
2. 25. 2 45
2. 33. 1 23
2. 33. 6 147
2. 34. 1 122
3. 1. 1 95
3. 11. 2 45
3. 21. 1 34
3. 22. 2 143
3. 22. 3 87 n. 32
3. 24. 4 68
3. 26. 4 164
3. 28. 4 145
3. 35. 5 130
3. 42. 1 102
3. 42. 3 106
3. 43. 1 144

De otio
1. 4 144
2. 1 95
3. 3 53

De prouidentia
2. 1 97
3. 3 179

De tranquillitate animi
3. 5 173
6. 2 39
7. 5 96
9. 3 157
8. 3 153
11. 10 34, 47

De uita beata
9. 1 173
19. 1 21
22. 5 52 n. 27
23. 2 87
24. 4 68

Dialogi 17, 45
Epistulae Morales 45
5. 7 43
9. 5 126
10. 1 45
11. 3 39 n. 2
12. 6 172

13. 6 179
14. 11 86
17. 8 115
19. 11 46 n. 12
19. 12 29
22. 3 68
22. 8 46 n. 12
23. 10 161
24. 5 109
25. 1 76
26. 3 102
28. 2 157
28. 4 165
30. 12 143
30. 17 102
37. 1 163
37. 5 34
40. 2 153
40. 10 153
48. 9 178
49. 3 46 n. 12, 172
51. 9 156
52. 20 170
53. 12 106
56. 2 153
58. 3 178
58. 20 68
59. 6 106
66. 13 17
66. 23 46 n. 12
66. 44 130
66. 51 109
67. 11 23
68. 4 46 n. 12
71. 14 46 n. 12
71. 24 46 n. 12
71. 35 122
71. 36 46 n. 12
74. 6 108
75. 15 21
76. 25 152
77. 7 46 n. 12
78. 3 157
79. 12 99
81. 1 147
81. 2 38
81. 6 29, 58
81. 9 66
82. 19 21, 46 n. 12
82. 23 106
83. 7 64
84. 6 165
84. 7 46 n. 12
87. 5 179

Seneca, Lucius Annaeus (*cont.*)
85. 34 46 n. 12
88. 12 86
88. 17 101
88. 37 119
89. 19–20 179
91. 6 107
92. 25 107
93. 12 158
94. 8 179
95. 29 108
95. 33 72
101. 9 108
102. 6–7 179
102. 18 172
106. 1 156
108. 4 68
109. 8 36 n. 31
113. 27 107
114. 1 157
114. 13 27 n. 14
114. 21 153
116. 5 107, 136
118. 6 87 n. 32
118. 12 68
124. 7 86
124. 21 172
Hercules Furens 1288 90
Medea 604 38
Naturales Quaestiones 46
1. pr. 7 173
1. 1. 5 165
1. 2. 8 52 n. 27
1. 2. 9 165
1. 16. 3 119
1. 17. 2 153
2. 5. 2 157
2. 8. 1 52 n. 27
2. 11. 2 77
2. 19. 1 165
2. 23. 1 143
2. 24. 3 152
2. 28. 2 130
2. 38. 3 173
2. 53. 2 173
2. 57. 3 99
3. pr. 5 119
3. 4. 1 179
3. 15. 8 143
3. 25. 5 116 n. 32
3. 25. 10 97
3. 27. 3 157

3. 27. 12 132
3. 29. 7 109
4a. 2. 3 127, 130
4a. 2. 28 46 n. 13
4b. 13. 5 173
5. 1. 1 77
5. 16. 4 172
6. 1. 11 115
6. 5. 3 173
6. 8. 2 128
6. 24. 2 131
6. 32. 4 175
7. 1. 2 165
7. 1. 4 68
7. 1. 7 96 n. 4
7. 4. 3 139
7. 5. 1 153
7. 8. 1 127
Phoenissae 589 147
Troades 612 147
Seneca, Marcus Annaeus
Controuersiae
2. 3. 7 115
2. 6. 2 115
3. pr. 13 133
9. pr. 4 99 n. 7
Servius
In Aeneidem 1. 92 64
Silius Italicus, Tiberius Catius Asconius
Punica 6. 397–98
73 n. 14
Suetonius Tranquillus,
Gaius 2
Augustus
24. 1 95
40. 1 24 n. 9
Claudius 20. 1 79 n. 24
Nero 54 92 n. 37

Tacitus, Cornelius 2
Annales
1. 4. 4 32
1. 76. 3 106
2. 40 156
14. 36. 5 92 n. 37
Germania 30. 2 92
Historiae
1. 57. 2 92 n. 37
4. 44 93
Terentius Afer, Publius
Andria 526 27
Eunuchus 1071 95

Valerius Flaccus, Gaius
  Argonautica 4. 378 73 n. 14
Valerius Maximus
  2. 7. 2 92
  8. 8. 2 24 n. 9
Varro, Marcus Terrentius
  De lingua Latina
    6. 71 64
    6. 82 85
  Res Rusticae
    1. 17. 1 84
    3. 5. 6 64
    3. 16. 5 64
Velleius Paterculus, Gaius
  2. 52. 3(4) 53 n. 28
Vergilius Maro, Publius
  Aeneid 2, 61

  1. 632 90
  6. 507–8 73 n. 14
  Georgics 3. 552 85
Vincent of Beauvais
  Speculum Doctrinale
    4. 49 131
    4. 50 44
  Speculum Historiale
    5. 28 63
    5. 29 131

William of Malmesbury
  Polyhistor (ed. Ouellette)
    p. 141. 43 93
    p. 142. 19 117
    p. 142. 29 142

Index of Names

This index includes only personal names (including names of deities) and excludes names that appear only in extracts quoted for analysis, not in the analysis itself. The names are listed in the form used in this book (thus 'Pompey', not 'Pompeius Magnus, Cn.'); Seneca, referred to as 'S.' throughout Chapters 1–7, is here 'Seneca';[1] other ancient authors can be traced via the Index of Passages. When a name appears in both the text and a footnote on the same page, only the text is cited.

Agricola, R. 8, 36, 55, 94, 80
Albertini, E. 29
Albrecht, M. von 97 n. 5
Alexander, W. H. 15, 23, 34 n. 28, 36, 43, 49, 54, 56, 62, 70, 72 n. 13, 75, 77–80, 83, 87, 89, 108, 110, 119, 130, 135, 139, 154, 158, 166, 168–9, 174, 179
Alexander the Great 162
Apollodorus of Cassandreia 172
Archelaus of Macedon 125
Axelson, B. 54 n. 28, 84, 97, 103, 127, 130, 152, 156, 158

Badstübner, E. 74, 151
Baehrens, W. A. 53, 60, 121
Basore, J. W. 30, 69 n. 12, 88, 100, 105, 109, 115 n. 29, 125, 137–9
Bentley, R. 23, 148 n. 14
Birt, T. 89
Bischoff, B. 2 n. 3
Bourgery, A. 53, 60, 89
Brugnoli, G. 2 n. 3
Bücheler, F. 36 n. 31
Buck, J. 1 n. 3, 15, 18, 28, 30 n. 21, 32–3, 35–6, 38, 42, 54, 57, 59, 61 n. 36, 62, 69–76, 81 n. 25, 84 n. 28, 89–90, 101, 110, 112, 116, 126, 128, 131–3, 135, 146–7, 149, 151, 153, 157, 159, 162, 165, 174, 177 n. 26, 179
Busche, K. 21, 100
Busonero, P. 1 n. 3

Caesar (cos. 59) 138
Caligula 47–8
Castiglioni, L. 72, 108, 168, 174
Chrysippus 24, 53
Cleanthes 135
Connan, F. 24 n. 9

Cooper, J. M. 83 n. 27
Cornelissen, J. J. 158 n. 14
Crassus (cos. 70 and 55) 138
Cujas, J. 24 n. 9
Curio, C. S. 10, 36, 36, 62, 69, 110, 160, 163, 169

Diodorus (Epicurean) 21
Diogenes 124
Duhn, F. de 145 n. 1

Epicurus, Epicureans 94, 107
Erasmus, D. 8–10, 17–20, 22, 24 n. 9, 33, 38, 40, 51, 53, 55, 59, 62, 64–5, 77–9, 81, 90, 92–3, 97, 102, 106, 109 n. 21, 110–11, 117, 119, 121, 131–2, 143, 149–50, 160, 163, 166 n. 6, 167, 169–71, 177, 180, 183–4
Eurynome 24

Feldman, L. 16, 21, 57, 135, 177
Fickert, K. R. 11, 17–18, 22, 34, 38, 49 nn. 17, 19, 51 n. 22, 74 n. 18, 78, 83, 92–3, 114, 117, 129, 141, 144, 146, 149–50, 166 n. 6, 173, 179, 180 n. 33
Fraenkel, E. 108

Gemoll, W. 125
Gertz, M. C. 1 nn. 1, 3, 11, 16–17, 19, 21–6, 29–36, 38–9, 41–3, 45–7, 49–50, 52–4, 57–8, 62–4, 66–8, 71–3, 74 n. 18, 75, 77–8, 85–6, 89, 91, 93–5, 99–102, 104, 107, 110 n. 23, 111–14, 117–19, 121–2, 124–5, 127, 129 n. 8, 131–5, 137, 139–41, 144–6, 150–7, 159–60, 162, 167–9, 171, 173–6, 180
Goodyear, F. R. D. 42
Gothofredus, D. 7 n. 15
Graces (*Gratiae*) 21–4

---

[1] The whole book concerns Seneca, of course: the list in this index comprises passages which refer expressly to his authorial habits and the like.

Graver, M. 21
Griffin, M. T. 16 n. 2, 31, 33, 35, 38 n. 1, 50, 53,
    57, 69, 72, 74, 80, 83 n. 27, 84–5, 88, 96 n. 2,
    102 n. 11, 103 n. 13, 104–5, 109, 113 n. 26,
    115 n. 29, 130 n. 9, 138–9, 141, 147, 151,
    166–7, 179
Gronovius, J. F. 10, 18, 22, 26, 29, 48, 52 n. 24,
    65, 86, 102 n. 10, 114, 127, 130, 143, 146, 150,
    179, 184
Gruter, J. 3 n. 6, 7, 10–11, 16, 24 n. 9, 26, 32,
    45 n. 11, 49, 52, 65–6, 68, 73, 78, 87, 89,
    93 n. 40, 96 n. 2, 100, 102, 106–7, 108 n. 17,
    114, 116, 121–2, 127–8, 138, 140, 154, 157,
    158 n. 14, 159, 165, 167 n. 10, 168, 173, 184
Gundermann, G. 40 n. 4, 42, 49, 74, 86,
    116, 126

Haase, F. 11, 17, 22, 24 n. 9, 33–4, 36, 38, 49, 58,
    64, 73, 77, 79, 81, 92, 99–100, 110 n. 22, 111,
    114, 121, 126, 131, 135, 137, 141, 144, 165,
    173, 180
Häberlin, C. 21
Haupt, M. 11, 29, 50, 128, 135, 151, 177
Hellegouarc'h, J. 53 n. 28
Hermes, E. 151
Hine, H. 132, 152 n. 8, 161 n. 1
Holmes, N. 96
Hosius, C. 11, 15, 20, 24 n. 9, 25–7, 29–33, 34
    n. 38, 36, 38, 42, 46, 49, 52–5, 57–9, 64, 68,
    72–3, 75, 77, 81, 86–7, 89, 91, 93, 96 n. 2, 99,
    102, 104–5, 113, 116–18, 121, 127, 133, 135,
    137, 141, 144, 145 n. 1, 146, 149, 151–2, 155,
    170–1, 173 n. 20, 179–80

Inwood, B. 16 n. 2, 31, 33, 35, 38 n. 1, 50, 53, 57,
    69, 72, 74, 80, 84, 88, 96 n. 2, 102 n. 11, 104–5,
    109, 113 n. 26, 115 n. 29, 130 n. 9, 138–9, 141,
    151, 179
Iunius Pennus, M. (pr. 201) 47
Iunius Pennus, M. (cos. 167) 47
Iunius Pennus, M. (tr. pl. 126) 47

Jerome, St. 9

Kaster, R. A. 7 n. 15, 39 n. 2, 79 n. 24
Kekulé, R. 1 n. 1, 11, 52 n. 25, 67 n. 7, 93 n. 40,
    110 n. 24, 113, 145 n. 1, 153, 182 n. 3
Kiekebusch, W. 10 n. 18
Kienzle, L. 30
Klammer, H. 105
Koch, H. A. 72, 75, 152, 177
Kronenberg, A. J. 52, 89, 97, 152, 175
Kruczkiewicz, B. 49

Lejay, P. 151, 154
Lentulus, Cn. 58–9
Leo, F. 41
Liber (deus) 100
Lindsay, W. M. 28 n. 16, 40 n. 4
Lipsius, J. 8, 10, 16 n. 2, 18, 23 n. 6, 24 n. 9,
    26 n. 10, 29, 41, 47, 64–5, 72, 82, 86, 88, 99,
    114–15, 127, 130, 132, 140, 144, 146, 150, 166,
    167, 183 n. 8
Long, A. A. 21

Madvig, J. N. 23–5, 49, 52, 54, 59, 62, 68, 72–3,
    76, 100, 108, 119, 124–6, 135, 143, 147–8, 151,
    155, 157, 165, 174–5, 178–9
Malaspina, E. 2 nn. 3–5, 5, 181, 186 n. 2, 204
Manlius Capitolinus Imperiosus,
    T. (dict. 363) 93
Manlius Imperiosus Torquatus, T. (cos. 347) 93
Matthias, T. 74 n. 18
Mayor, J. E. B. 29
Mazzoli, G. 1 n. 3, 2, 5–6, 16, 20 n. 5, 29, 36, 39,
    42, 44, 49, 52, 70, 76, 89, 94, 110, 129–30,
    131 n. 11, 169, 171, 174, 181–3, 204
Mostert, M. 2 n. 3
Mucius Scaevola 109
Müller, H. J. 135
Müller, J. 35, 139, 179 n. 31
Munk Olsen, B. 2 n. 4, 3 n. 8
Muretus, M. A. 10, 16, 31 n. 23, 47, 55, 59, 63,
    66, 71–2, 79, 82–3, 96, 102, 106–7, 114, 117,
    120, 122, 127–8, 137, 140, 172

Nazarius, St. 1
Nesen, W. 9
Núñez de Toledo y Guzmán, Hernan.
    See Pincianus

Oltramare, P. 132 n. 14

Panaetius 136
Pasoli, E. 43
Pellegrin, E. 2 n. 3
Phalaris 172
Phidias 61
Philip of Macedon 117
Pincianus 10, 29 n. 18, 32, 35 n. 30, 44, 52 n. 24,
    59, 62, 69, 91, 94, 105, 111, 128, 130, 142 n. 20,
    144, 150, 161, 169–70, 180 n. 33
Pinkster, H. 19 n. 4, 23 n. 7, 100 n. 8
Pompeius Pennus 47–8
Pompey 138
Pomponius, M. (tr. pl. 363) 93–4
Porsenna 109

Préchac, F. 1 n. 3, 11, 16, 23, 26–7, 30, 36, 39,
  43–4, 46, 49–50, 52, 55, 58, 64, 67, 69 n. 11,
  75–6, 78 n. 22, 82, 87, 89, 91, 93–4, 96 n. 2,
  101, 104, 108, 119, 127, 129, 131 n. 11, 142,
  145–6, 150, 155, 158, 165–6, 171, 174, 176–7,
  178 n. 29
Procopé, J. F. 83 n. 27

Quinctius Pennus Capitolinus Crispinus,
  T. (cos. 354) 47
Quinctius Pennus Cincinnatus, T. (cos. 431) 47

Reinecke, G. 64
Reynolds, L. D. 36 n. 31, 45, 46 n. 12, 181,
  197 n. 12
Rhenanus, B. 9
Ribbeck, O. 41
Rossbach, O. 27 n. 13, 89, 145 n. 1, 172, 179
Rubenius, A. 143
Ruhkopf, F. R. 8, 11, 65, 133 n. 15, 147

Scaliger, J. J. 48
Schmeling, G. 133
Schultingh, J. 152 n. 8
Schweighäuser, J. 36 n. 31
Seneca (S., Senecan) 1–2, 6, 16–19, 20 n. 5,
  21–40, 42–6, 53–6, 58, 60, 64–73, 75,
  77–8, 81–8, 90–1, 93–102, 104–8, 110–12,
  114–20, 122–30, 133–46, 148, 150–4,
  156–61, 163, 166–68, 172, 174–7,
  179–80
Shackleton Bailey, D. R. 33, 42, 43 n. 8, 104, 139,
  142, 168
Siesbye, O. 23, 39, 95, 146
Sjögren, H. 35–6, 50, 99
Socrates 124–5
Sonntag, M. 83
Stangl, T. 121
Stephanus, H. 59 n. 33, 102
Stoics, Stoic 20 n. 5, 21, 33, 52, 60, 63, 111,
  129, 134

Thomas, E. 89–90, 157
Timpanaro, S. 32 nn. 25, 26

Vincent of Beauvais 44–5, 63, 131
Vogel, E. F. 11, 38, 146

Wackernagel, J. 159, 176
Walsh, P. G. 53 n. 28
Walter, F. 74
Watt, W. S. 58, 88–9, 103, 105, 154, 159, 162
Weidner, A. 55
Weise, O. 48
Wesenberg, A. S. 72–3, 122, 157
William of Malmesbury 93, 117, 142